ELITE STUDENT EDITION

5 STEPS TO A

5™

AP Microeconomics
2023

Eric R. Dodge, PhD

McGraw Hill

New York Chicago San Francisco Athens London Madrid Mexico City
Milan New Delhi Singapore Sydney Toronto

1 2 3 4 5 6 7 8 9   LHS   27 26 25 24 23 22 (Cross-Platform Prep Course only)
1 2 3 4 5 6 7 8 9   LHS   27 26 25 24 23 22 (Elite Student Edition)

ISBN   978-1-264-54734-0 (Cross-Platform Prep Course only)
MHID   1-264-54734-X

e-ISBN   978-1-264-54808-8 (e-book Cross-Platform Prep Course only)
e-MHID   1-264-54808-7

ISBN   978-1-264-54835-4 (Elite Student Edition)
MHID   1-264-54835-4

e-ISBN   978-1-264-54884-2 (e-book Elite Student Edition)
e-MHID   1-264-54884-2

McGraw Hill, the McGraw Hill logo, *5 Steps to a 5,* and related trade dress are trademarks or registered trademarks of McGraw Hill and/or its affiliates in the United States and other countries and may not be used without written permission. All other trademarks are the property of their respective owners. McGraw Hill is not associated with any product or vendor mentioned in this book.

AP, Advanced Placement Program, and *College Board* are registered trademarks of the College Board, which was not involved in the production of, and does not endorse, this product.

The series editor was Grace Freedson, design by Jane Tenenbaum.

McGraw Hill products are available at special quantity discounts to use as premiums and sales or for use in corporate training programs. To contact a representative, please visit the Contact Us pages at www.mhprofessional.com.

McGraw Hill is committed to making our products accessible to all learners. To learn more about the available support and accommodations we offer, please contact us at accessibility@mheducation.com. We also participate in the Access Text Network (www.accesstext.org), and ATN members may submit requests through ATN.

CONTENTS

So, you've decided to bite the bullet and invest in a book designed to help you earn a 5 on your AP Microeconomics exam. Congratulations! You have taken the first of many small steps toward this goal. An important question remains: Why this book?

Priority number one, both for your AP course and for this book, is to prepare you to do well enough on the AP Microeconomics exam to earn college credit. I firmly believe that this book has a comparative advantage over your other options. First, I have written this text with a certain conversational approach, rather than a flurry of formulas and diagrams that you must remember. Sure, some memorization is required for any standardized test, but a memorizer of formulas is in deep trouble when asked to analyze the relative success of several possible economic policies or to draw fine distinctions between competing economic theories. Using this book to supplement and reinforce your understanding of the theories and relationships in economics allows you to apply your analytical skills to the exam, and this gives you a significant advantage over the formula-memorizing exam taker. If you spend less time memorizing formulas and take the extra time to understand the basics, you will get along just fine with this book, and you will do extremely well on the AP Economics exams.

Second, as a college professor who has taught economics to thousands of students, I have a strong understanding of where the learning happens and where the mistakes are made.

Third, as a reader and writer of AP exams, I can tell you where points are lost and where a 5 is made on the free-response questions. Most important, I am a realist. You want to know what it takes to earn a 5 and not necessarily the finer points of the Federal Reserve System, the Sherman Antitrust Act, or the NAFTA.

Take the time to read the first four chapters of this book, which are designed to help you understand the challenge that lies ahead and to provide you with tips for success on the exam.

Take the diagnostic exam to see where you stand before beginning your review. The bulk of this book is a comprehensive review of microeconomics with practice questions at the end of each chapter. These questions are designed to quickly test your understanding of the material presented in each chapter, not necessarily to mirror the AP exam. For exam questions that are more typical of what you will experience in May, I have provided you with two practice exams in microeconomics. These are practice exams, complete with essay questions, sample responses, and scoring guidelines.

There have been several important updates since the first edition. The second edition included expanded coverage of game theory, reflecting the growing use of game theory in the AP Microeconomics curriculum. In that edition, I included a free-response question involving game theory because the people who develop the AP exam had been urging high school AP teachers to devote more time to game theory. Such urgings are usually a strong hint of a future free-response question, and indeed in 2007, the Microeconomics exam included, for the first time, a free-response game-theory question.

In the 2018 edition of this book, I included details of the impact that trade barriers, such as tariffs and quotas, have on competitive markets. While the topic of trade barriers has been present in the AP Microeconomics course outline for several years, it was not tested extensively in the free-response section until 2012. That edition also added coverage of the market for capital in the factor markets chapter to reflect a growing emphasis in both teaching and testing more than simply labor markets. I also brought some of the coverage of externalities more in line with recent AP exams and the rubrics that were used to grade them.

To reflect more recent points of emphasis in the AP exam, the 2019 edition expanded the explanation of how certain costs can be identified and computed in a graph. I also provided additional graphing tips and modified some questions in the practice exams.

The 2021 edition reflects some changes that the College Board has made to the AP Microeconomics curriculum. For the most part, the content is quite similar to what has been taught, and tested, for the last decade or more. While the changes are not fundamentally changing the Microeconomics course, it is important that this book keeps pace with those changes. More specific details about the changes to the Microeconomics course are given in Chapter 1. This current edition adds more complexity to coverage of game theory and monopsony to address recent FRQs and to anticipate future ways of testing this material. As with every edition, I adjust free-response questions and rubrics to better reflect how those questions are being scored at the annual Reading.

I do not see any reason to continue talking about the book when we could just dive in. I hope that you enjoy this book and that you find it a useful resource. Good luck!

ACKNOWLEDGMENTS

A special "thank you" must go out to Amanda Stiglbauer for her excellent work on the teacher's materials for this edition of the book. "Stigs" is an outstanding high school teacher, friend, and colleague. As always, this book is dedicated to my wife, Dr. Melanie Fox, and our three sons, Eli, Max, and Theo. You guys are amazing and inspiring. Thank you.

ABOUT THE AUTHOR

Eric R. Dodge was born in Portland, Oregon, and attended high school in Tigard, Oregon. He received a bachelor's degree in business administration from the University of Puget Sound in Tacoma, Washington, before attending the University of Oregon for his master's and doctoral degrees in economics. While at the University of Oregon, he received two graduate student awards for teaching and became a die-hard fan of the Ducks. Since 1995, he has been teaching economics at Hanover College in Hanover, Indiana, the oldest private college in the state. The author teaches principles of microeconomics and macroeconomics, intermediate microeconomic theory, labor economics, environmental economics, industrial organization, statistics, econometrics, and the economics of dams.

Since 2000, Eric Dodge has served as a faculty consultant for the AP economics program and has been a reader and writer of free-response questions, table leader, and question leader at the annual AP Economics Reading. With coauthor Melanie Fox, he has also written three recently published books: *Economics Demystified, 500 Microeconomics Questions: Ace Your College Exams,* and *500 Macroeconomics Questions: Ace Your College Exams.* He lives in historic Madison, Indiana, with his wife, Melanie; sons Eli, Max, and Theo; and a neurotic, rain-fearing dog.

INTRODUCTION: THE FIVE-STEP PROGRAM

The Basics

Not too long ago, you agreed to enroll in AP Microeconomics. Maybe you saw a flyer and the allure of economic knowledge was just too much to resist, or maybe a respected teacher encouraged you to challenge yourself and you took the bait. Either way, you find yourself here, flipping through a book that promises to help you culminate this life-changing experience with the highest of honors, a 5 in AP Microeconomics. Can it be done without this book? Sure, there are many excellent teachers of AP Microeconomics out there who teach, coax, and cajole their students into a 5 every year. But for the majority of students in your shoes, the marginal benefits of buying this book far outweigh the marginal costs.

Introducing the Five-Step Preparation Program

This book is organized as a five-step program to prepare you for success on the exam. These steps are designed to provide you with the skills and strategies vital to the exam and the practice that can lead you to that perfect 5. Each of the five steps will provide you with the opportunity to get closer and closer to that prize trophy 5.

Following are the five steps:

Step 1: Set Up Your Study Program

In this step, you'll read a brief overview of the AP Microeconomics exam, including an outline of topics and the approximate percentage of the exam that will test knowledge of each topic. You will also follow a process to help determine which of the following preparation programs is right for you:

- Full school year: September through May
- One semester: January through May
- Six weeks: Basic training for the exam

Step 2: Determine Your Test Readiness

In this step, you'll take a diagnostic exam in microeconomics. This pretest should give you an idea of how prepared you are to take the real exam before beginning to study for it.

- Go through the diagnostic exam step by step and question by question to build your confidence level.
- Review the correct answers and explanations so that you see what you do and do not yet fully understand.

Step 3: Develop Strategies for Success

In this step, you'll learn strategies to help you do your best on the exam. These strategies cover both the multiple-choice and free-response sections of the exam. Some of these tips are based on my understanding of how the questions are designed, and others have been gleaned from my years of experience reading (grading) the AP Economics exams.

- Learn to read multiple-choice questions.
- Learn how to answer multiple-choice questions, including whether or not to guess.
- Learn how to plan and write the free-response questions.

Step 4: Review the Knowledge You Need to Score High

In this step, you'll review the material you need to know for the test. This review section takes up the bulk of this book. It contains a comprehensive review of microeconomics.

There is a lot of material here, enough to summarize a yearlong experience in AP Microeconomics and highlight the, well, highlights. Some AP courses will have covered more material than yours; some will have covered less. The bottom line is that if you thoroughly review this material, you will have studied all that is tested on the exam, and you will significantly increase your chances of scoring well. This edition gives new emphasis to some areas of microeconomics to bring your review more in line with recent exams. For example, recent editions included more discussion of tariffs and game theory, and more graphing tips in the microeconomics review. This edition goes even further with game theory to anticipate future FRQs on the AP Micro exam.

Step 5: Build Your Test-Taking Confidence

In this step, you'll complete your preparation by testing yourself on practice exams. This section contains two complete exams in microeconomics, solutions, and, sometimes more important, advice on how to avoid the common mistakes. Once again, recent editions of this book have updated the free-response exams to more accurately reflect the content tested on recent AP exams. Be aware that these practice exams are *not* reproduced questions from actual AP Microeconomics exams, but they mirror both the material tested by AP and the way in which it is tested.

Lastly, at the back of this book you'll find additional resources to aid your preparation. These include the following:

- A brief bibliography
- A list of websites related to AP Microeconomics
- A glossary of terms related to the AP Microeconomics exam
- A summary of formulas related to the AP Microeconomics exam

Introduction to the Graphics Used in This Book

To emphasize particular skills and strategies, several icons appear in the margins, alerting you to pay particular attention to the accompanying text. We use these three icons:

This icon indicates a very important concept or fact that you should not pass over.

This icon calls your attention to a strategy that you might want to try.

This icon alerts you to a tip that you might find useful.

Boldfaced words indicate terms that are included in the glossary. Throughout the book you will also find marginal notes, boxes, and starred areas. Pay close attention to these areas because they can provide tips, hints, strategies, and further explanations to help you reach your full potential.

Set Up Your Study Program

CHAPTER 1

What You Need to Know About the AP Microeconomics Exam

IN THIS CHAPTER

Summary: Learn what topics are tested, how the test is scored, and basic test-taking information.

Key Ideas

✪ Most colleges will award credit for a score of 4 or 5; some will award credit for a score of 3.
✪ Multiple-choice questions account for two-thirds of your final score.
✪ Free-response questions account for one-third of your final score.
✪ Your composite score on the two test sections is converted to a score on the 1-to-5 scale.

Background Information

The AP Economics exams that you are taking were first offered by the College Board in 1989. Since then, the number of students taking the tests has grown rapidly. In 1989, 3,198 students took the Microeconomics exam, and by 2021 that number had increased to 80,199.

Some Frequently Asked Questions About the AP Economics Exams

Why Take the AP Economics Exams?

Although there might be some altruistic motivators, let's face it: most of you take the AP Economics exams because you are seeking college credit. The majority of colleges and universities will accept a 4 or 5 as acceptable credit for their Principles of Microeconomics or Macroeconomics courses. A number of schools will even accept a 3 on an exam. This means you are one or two courses closer to graduation before you even begin working on the "freshman 15." Even if you do not score high enough to earn college credit, the fact that you elected to enroll in AP courses tells admission committees that you are a high achiever and serious about your education. In recent years, close to two-thirds of students have scored a 3 or higher on their AP Microeconomics exam.

What Is the Format of the Exams?

Table 1.1 Summarizes the format of the AP Macro and Micro exams

AP MACROECONOMICS		
Section	*Number of Questions*	*Time Limit*
I. Multiple-Choice Questions	60	1 hour and 10 minutes
II. Free-Response Questions	3	Planning time: 10 minutes Writing time: 50 minutes

AP MICROECONOMICS		
Section	*Number of Questions*	*Time Limit*
I. Multiple-Choice Questions	60	1 hour and 10 minutes
II. Free-Response Questions	3	Planning time: 10 minutes Writing time: 50 minutes

Who Writes the AP Economics Exams?

Development of each AP exam is a multiyear effort that involves many education and testing professionals and students. At the heart of the effort is the AP Economics Development Committee, a group of college and high school economics teachers who are typically asked to serve for three years. The committee and other college professors create a large pool of multiple-choice questions. With the help of the testing experts at Educational Testing Service (ETS), these questions are then pretested with college students enrolled in Principles of Microeconomics and Macroeconomics for accuracy, appropriateness, clarity, and assurance that there is only one possible answer. The results of this pretesting allow each question to be categorized by degree of difficulty. Several more months of development and refinement later, Section I of the exam is ready to be administered.

The free-response essay questions that make up Section II go through a similar process of creation, modification, pretesting, and final refinement so that the questions cover the necessary areas of material and are at an appropriate level of difficulty and clarity.

The committee also makes a great effort to construct a free-response exam that allows for clear and equitable grading by the AP readers.

At the conclusion of each AP reading and scoring of exams, the exam itself and the results are thoroughly evaluated by the committee and by ETS. In this way, the College Board can use the results to make suggestions for course development in high schools and to plan future exams.

What Topics Appear on the Exams?

The College Board, after consulting with teachers of economics, develops a curriculum that covers material that college professors expect to cover in their first-year classes. This curriculum has recently undergone a revision and the new outline for the Microeconomics course is provided below. Based upon this outline of topics, the multiple-choice exams are written such that those topics are covered in proportion to their importance to the expected economics understanding of the student. If you find this confusing, think of it this way: Suppose that faculty consultants agree that market failure and the role of government topics are important to the microeconomics curriculum, maybe to the tune of 8 to 13 percent. So if about 10 percent of the curriculum in your AP Microeconomics course is devoted to these topics, you can expect roughly 10 percent of the multiple-choice exam to address these topics. Remember, this is just a guide, and each year the exam differs slightly in the percentages.

Microeconomics

Unit 1: Basic Economic Concepts

This unit covers the foundations of microeconomic thinking, decision-making under constraints, and rational choice.

Topics:
  Scarcity
  Resource allocation and economic systems
  Production possibilities curve
  Comparative advantage and gains from trade
  Cost-benefit analysis
  Marginal analysis and consumer choice

Exam Coverage
  12%–15%

Unit 2: Supply and Demand

This unit provides the basics for understanding how markets work, with an introduction to the supply and demand model.

Topics:
  Demand
  Supply
  Elasticity
  Market equilibrium, disequilibrium, and changes in equilibrium
  The effects of government intervention in markets
  International trade and public policy

Exam Coverage
  20%–25%

Unit 3: Production, Cost, and the Perfect Competition Model

This unit describes the factors that drive the behavior of companies and the model of perfect competition.

Topics:

The production function

Short- and long-run production costs

Types of profit

Profit maximization

Perfect competition

Exam Coverage

22%–25%

Unit 4: Imperfect Competition

This unit explores how imperfectly competitive markets work and how game theory is used to predict behavior in oligopolies.

Topics:

Monopoly

Price discrimination

Monopolistic competition

Oligopoly and game theory

Exam Coverage

15%–22%

Unit 5: Factor Markets

This unit demonstrates how markets and marginal decision-making are used to describe the workings of factor markets.

Topics:

Introduction to factor markets

Changes in factor demand and factor supply

Profit-maximizing behavior in perfectly competitive factor markets

Monopsonistic markets

Exam Coverage

10%–13%

Unit 6: Market Failure and the Role of Government

This unit looks at the conditions under which markets may fail and the effects of government intervention in markets.

Topics:

Socially efficient and inefficient market outcomes

Externalities

Public and private goods

The effects of government intervention in different market structures

Income and wealth inequality

Exam Coverage

8%–13%

My Teacher (and the Syllabus) Keeps Talking About "Big Ideas" and "Skill Categories." What Are These?

Most of the new curricular revision was a big-picture way of describing, and teaching, the key concepts in the AP Microeconomics course. While these are critical to your teacher's preparation, and fundamentally guide the way in which your teacher structures the course, as a student preparing for the exam you probably don't need to have a deep understanding of what is happening behind the scenes. In other words, your course will be new and improved because of these revisions, but your fantastic teacher is doing the heavy lifting on making sure these are woven throughout the course.

But in case you're still curious, there are four skill categories that identify important skills that an AP Micro student should master throughout the course. The table below provides a brief summary.

	Title	An example
Category 1	Principles of Models: Define economic principles and models.	Can you describe the similarities and differences between the model of perfect competition and monopolistic competition in the long run?
Category 2	Interpretation: Explain given economic outcomes.	If production of a good is creating external costs on third parties, can you prescribe a policy for addressing these external costs?
Category 3	Manipulation: Determine outcomes of specific economic situations.	If the price elasticity of demand for a good is 2.5, and the price falls by 10%, can you calculate the estimated change in total spending on this good?
Category 4	Graphing and Visuals: Model economic situations using graphs or visual representations.	Can you draw an accurately labeled graph that shows a profit-maximizing monopolist earning positive economic profit?

There are also four Big Ideas that will appear throughout your course. These are intended to reinforce common concepts that are key to a deep understanding of microeconomics. The four Big Ideas are:

1. Scarcity and Markets
2. Costs, Benefits, and Marginal Analysis
3. Production Choices and Behavior
4. Market Inefficiency and Public Policy

Much more detail on these Big Ideas and the Skill Categories can be found in the "AP Microeconomics Course and Exam Description" that is found at https://apcentral .collegeboard.org/pdf/ap-microeconomics-course-and-exam-description.pdf?course= ap-microeconomics.

Who Grades My AP Economics Exam?

From confidential sources, I can tell you that nearly 100,000 free-response essay booklets are dropped from a three-story building, and those that fall into a small cardboard box are given a 5, those that fall into a slightly larger box are given a 4, and so on until those that fall into a dumpster receive a 1. It's really quite scientific!

Okay, that's not really how it's done. Instead, every June a group of economics teachers gather for a week to assign grades to your hard work. Each of these "Faculty Consultants," or "Readers," spends a day or so getting trained on one question and one question only. Because each reader becomes an expert on that question, and because each exam book is anonymous, this process provides a very consistent and unbiased scoring of that question. During a typical day of grading, a random sample of each reader's scores is selected and cross-checked by other experienced "Table Leaders" to ensure that the consistency is maintained throughout the day and the week. Each reader's scores on a given question are also statistically analyzed to make sure that they are not giving scores that are significantly higher or lower than the mean scores given by other readers of that question. All measures are taken to maintain consistency and fairness for your benefit.

Will My Exam Remain Anonymous?

Absolutely. Even if your high school teacher happens to randomly read your booklet, there is virtually no way they will know it is you. To the reader, each student is a number and to the computer, each student is a bar code.

What About That Permission Box on the Back?

The College Board uses some exams to help train high school teachers so that they can help the next generation of economics students to avoid common mistakes. If you check this box, you simply give permission to use your exam in this way. Even if you give permission, your anonymity is still maintained.

How Is My Multiple-Choice Exam Scored?

The multiple-choice section of each Economics exam is 60 questions and is worth two-thirds of your final score. Your answer sheet is run through the computer, which adds up your correct responses. The total scores on the multiple-choice sections are based on the number of questions answered correctly. The "guessing penalty" has been eliminated, and points are no longer deducted for incorrect answers. As always, no points are awarded for unanswered questions. The formula looks something like this:

$$\text{Section I Raw Score} = N_{\text{right}}$$

How Is My Free-Response Exam Scored?

Your performance on the free-response section is worth one-third of your final score and consists of three questions. Another change to the exam is that the first question will always be scored out of 10 points, and the second and third questions will each be scored out of 5 points. Because the first question is longer than the other two, and therefore scored on a higher scale, it is given a different weight in the raw score. If you use the following sample formula as a rough guide, you'll be able to gauge your approximate score on the practice questions.

$$\text{Section II Raw Score} = (1.50 \times \text{Score 1}) + (1.50 \times \text{Score 2}) + (1.50 \times \text{Score 3})$$

So How Is My Final Grade Determined and What Does It Mean?

With a total composite score of 90 points, and 60 being determined on Section I, the remaining 30 must be divided among the three essay questions in Section II. The total composite score is then a weighted sum of the multiple-choice and the free-response sections. In the end, when all of the numbers have been crunched, the Chief Faculty Consultant converts the range of composite scores to the 5-point scale of the AP grades.

Table 1.2 gives you a very rough example of a conversion, and as you complete the practice exam, you may use this to give yourself a hypothetical grade, keeping in mind that every year the conversion changes slightly to adjust for the difficulty of the questions from year to year. You should receive your grade in early July.

Table 1.2 Sample Score Conversion

MICROECONOMICS		
Composite Score Range	AP Grade	Interpretation
73–90	5	Extremely well qualified for college credit
58–72	4	Well qualified
45–57	3	Qualified
33–44	2	Possibly qualified
0–32	1	No recommendation

Example:

In Section I, you receive 50 correct and 10 incorrect responses on the microeconomics practice exam. In Section II, your scores are 7/10, 5/5, and 5/5.

$$\text{Weighted Section I} = 50$$

$$\text{Weighted Section II} = (1.50 \times 7) = (1.50 \times 5) = (1.50 \times 5)$$
$$= 10.50 + 7.5 + 7.5 = 25.5$$

Composite Score $= 50 + 25.5 = 75.5$, which would be assigned a 5.

How Do I Register and How Much Does It Cost?

If you are enrolled in AP Microeconomics in your high school, your teacher is going to provide all of these details, but a quick summary wouldn't hurt. After all, you do not have to enroll in the AP course to register for and complete the AP exam. When in doubt, the best source of information is the College Board's website: www.college-board.com.

In 2021–2022 the fee for taking an exam was $96 for each exam. Students who demonstrate financial need may receive a partial refund to help offset the cost of testing. There are also several *optional* fees that *can* be paid if you want your scores rushed to you or if you wish to receive multiple grade reports.

The coordinator of the AP program at your school will inform you where and when you will take the exam. If you live in a small community, your exam might not be administered at your school, so be sure to get this information.

What If My School Only Offered AP Macroeconomics and Not AP Microeconomics, or Vice Versa?

Because of budget and personnel constraints, some high schools cannot offer both Microeconomics and Macroeconomics. The majority of these schools choose the macro side of the AP program, but some choose the micro side. This puts students at a significant disadvantage when they sit down for the Microeconomics exam without having taken the course. Likewise, Macroeconomics test takers have a rough time when they have not taken the Macroeconomics course. If you are in this situation, and you put in the necessary effort, I assure you that buying this book will give you more than a fighting chance on either exam even if your school did not offer that course.

What Should I Bring to the Exam?

On exam day, I suggest bringing the following items:

- Two sharpened number 2 pencils and an eraser that doesn't leave smudges.
- Two black or blue-colored pens for the free-response section. Some students like to use two colors to make their graphs stand out for the reader.
- A watch so that you can monitor your time. You never know whether the exam room will have a clock on the wall. You cannot have a watch that accesses the Internet, and make sure you turn off any beep that goes off on the hour.
- Your school code.
- Your photo identification and social security number.
- Tissues.
- Your quiet confidence that you are prepared!

What Should I *Not* Bring to the Exam?

It's probably a good idea to leave the following items at home:

- A calculator. It is not allowed for the Microeconomics or Macroeconomics exam. However, this does not mean that math will not be required. Questions involving simple computations have recently appeared on the exams, and later in the book I point out a few places where knowing a little math can earn you some points.
- A cell phone, smart watch, camera, tablet, laptop computer, or walkie-talkie.
- Books, a dictionary, study notes, flash cards, highlighting pens, correction fluid, a ruler, or any other office supplies.
- Portable music of any kind.
- Clothing with any economics on it.
- Panic or fear. It's natural to be nervous, but you can comfort yourself that you have used this book well and that there is no room for fear on your exam.

How to Plan Your Time

IN THIS CHAPTER

Summary: The right preparation plan for you depends on your study habits and the amount of time you have before the test.

Key Idea

✪ Choose the study plan that's right for you.

Three Approaches to Preparing for AP Exams

What kind of preparation program for the AP exam should you use? Should you carefully follow every step, or are there perhaps some steps you can bypass? That depends not only on how much time you have but also on what kind of student you are. No one knows your study habits, likes, and dislikes better than you do. So you are the only one who can decide which approach to use. This chapter presents three possible study plans, labeled A, B, and C. Look at the brief profiles that follow. These will help you determine which plan is right for you. Table 2.1 summarizes each study plan, with a suggested timetable for each.

You're a **full-school-year prep student** if:

1. You are the kind of person who likes to plan for everything very far in advance.
2. You buy your best friend a gift two months before their birthday because you know exactly what to choose, where you will buy it, and how much you will pay for it.
3. You like detailed planning and everything in its place.
4. You feel that you must be thoroughly prepared.
5. You hate surprises.

If you fit this profile, consider **Plan A**.

You're a **one-semester prep student** if:

1. You buy your best friend a gift one week before their birthday because it sort of snuck up on you, yet you have a clear idea of exactly what you will be purchasing.
2. You are willing to plan ahead to feel comfortable in stressful situations but are okay with skipping some details.
3. You feel more comfortable when you know what to expect, but a surprise or two is cool.
4. You're always on time for appointments.

If you fit this profile, consider **Plan B**.

You're a **six-week prep student** if:

1. You buy your best friend a gift for their birthday, but you need to include a belated card because you missed it by a couple of days.
2. You work best under pressure and tight deadlines.
3. You feel very confident with the skills and background you've learned in your AP Economics classes.
4. You decided late in the year to take the exam.
5. You like surprises.
6. You feel okay if you arrive 10 to 15 minutes late for an appointment.

If you fit this profile, consider **Plan C**.

Table 2.1 Three Different Study Schedules

MONTH	PLAN A: FULL SCHOOL YEAR	PLAN B: ONE SEMESTER	PLAN C: SIX WEEKS
September to October	Introduction; Chapters 1 to 4	—	—
November	Chapters 5 to 6	—	—
December	Chapter 7	—	—
January	Chapter 8	Chapters 1 to 4	—
February	Chapter 9; Micro Practice Exam 1	Chapters 5 to 7; Micro Practice Exam 1	—
March	Chapter 10	Chapters 8 to 9	—
April	Chapter 11	Chapters 10 to 11	Skim Chapters 1 to 9; all rapid reviews; Micro Practice Exam 1
May	Review everything; Micro Practice Exam 2	Review everything; Micro Practice Exam 2	Skim Chapters 10 to 11; Micro Practice Exam 2

Calendar for Each Plan

Plan A: You Have a Full School Year to Prepare

Use this plan to organize your study during the coming school year.

SEPTEMBER–OCTOBER (Check off the activities as you complete them.)

_____ Determine the student mode (A, B, or C) that applies to you.

_____ Carefully read Chapters 1 to 4 of this book.

_____ Take the diagnostic exam.

_____ Pay close attention to your walk-through of the diagnostic exam.

_____ Get on the web and take a look at the AP website(s).

_____ Skim the review chapters in Step 4 of this book. (Reviewing the topics covered in this section will be part of your yearlong preparation.)

_____ Buy a few color highlighters.

_____ Flip through the entire book. Break the book in. Write in it. Toss it around a little bit . . . highlight it.

_____ Get a clear picture of your own school's AP Economics curriculum.

_____ Begin to use this book as a resource to supplement the classroom learning.

NOVEMBER (the first 10 weeks have elapsed)

_____ Read and study Chapter 5, "Fundamentals of Economic Analysis."

_____ Read and study Chapter 6, "Demand, Supply, Market Equilibrium, and Welfare Analysis."

DECEMBER

_____ Read and study Chapter 7, "Elasticity, Microeconomic Policy, and Consumer Theory."

_____ Review Chapters 5 to 6.

JANUARY (20 weeks have elapsed)

_____ Read and study Chapter 8, "The Firm, Profit, and the Costs of Production."

_____ Review Chapters 5 to 7.

FEBRUARY

_____ Take Microeconomics Practice Exam 1 in the first week of February.

_____ Evaluate your Micro strengths and weaknesses.

_____ Study appropriate chapters to correct your Micro weaknesses.

_____ Read and study Chapter 9, "Market Structures, Perfect Competition, Monopoly, and Things Between."

_____ Review Chapters 5 to 8.

MARCH (30 weeks have now elapsed)

_____ Read and study Chapter 10, "Factor Markets."

_____ Review Chapters 5 to 9.

APRIL

_____ Read and study Chapter 11, "Public Goods, Externalities, and the Role of Government."

_____ Review Chapters 5 to 10.

MAY (first two weeks) (THIS IS IT!)

_____ Review Chapters 5 to 11—all the material!

_____ Take Practice Exam 2.

_____ Score yourself.

_____ Get a good night's sleep before the exam. Fall asleep knowing that you are well prepared.

GOOD LUCK ON THE TEST!

Plan B: You Have One Semester to Prepare

If you have already completed one semester of economic studies, the following plan will help you use those skills you've been practicing to prepare for the May exam.

JANUARY–FEBRUARY

_____ Carefully read Chapters 1 to 4 of this book.

_____ Take the diagnostic exam.

_____ Pay close attention to your walk-through of the diagnostic exam.

_____ Read and study Chapter 5, "Fundamentals of Economic Analysis."

_____ Read and study Chapter 6, "Demand, Supply, Market Equilibrium, and Welfare Analysis."

_____ Read and study Chapter 7, "Elasticity, Microeconomic Policy, and Consumer Theory."

_____ Take Microeconomics Practice Exam 1 in the last week of February.

_____ Evaluate your Micro strengths and weaknesses.

_____ Study appropriate chapters to correct your Micro weaknesses.

MARCH (10 weeks to go)

_____ Read and study Chapter 8, "The Firm, Profit, and the Costs of Production."

_____ Read and study Chapter 9, "Market Structures, Perfect Competition, Monopoly, and Things Between."

_____ Review Chapters 5 to 7.

APRIL

_____ Read and study Chapter 10, "Factor Markets."

_____ Read and study Chapter 11, "Public Goods, Externalities, and the Role of Government."

_____ Review Chapters 5 to 9.

MAY (first two weeks) (THIS IS IT!)

_____ Review Chapters 5 to 11—all the material!

_____ Take Microeconomics Practice Exam 2.

_____ Score yourself.

_____ Get a good night's sleep before the exam. Fall asleep knowing that you are well prepared.

GOOD LUCK ON THE TEST!

Plan C: You Have Six Weeks to Prepare

Use this plan if you have been studying economics for six months or more and intend to use this book primarily as a specific guide to the AP Microeconomics exam. If you have only six weeks to prepare, now is not the time to try to learn everything. Focus instead on the essential points you need to know for the test.

APRIL 1–15

_____ Skim Chapters 1 to 4 of this book.

_____ Skim Chapters 5 to 6.

_____ Carefully go over the Rapid Review sections of Chapters 5 to 8.

_____ Complete the Microeconomics Practice Exam 1.

_____ Score yourself and analyze your errors.

_____ Skim and highlight the Glossary at the end of the book.

APRIL 15–MAY 1

_____ Skim Chapters 9 to 11.

_____ Carefully go over the Rapid Review sections of Chapters 9 to 11.

_____ Continue to skim and highlight the Glossary at the end of the book.

MAY (first two weeks) (THIS IS IT!)

_____ Carefully go over the Rapid Review sections of Chapters 5 to 11.

_____ Take Microeconomics Practice Exam 2.

_____ Score yourself and analyze your errors.

_____ Get a good night's sleep before the exam. Fall asleep knowing that you are well prepared.

GOOD LUCK ON THE TEST!

STEP **2**

Determine Your Test Readiness

CHAPTER **3**   Take the Diagnostic Exam

CHAPTER 3

Take the Diagnostic Exam

IN THIS CHAPTER

Summary: This chapter includes a diagnostic exam for microeconomics. It is intended to give you an idea of where you stand with your preparation. The questions have been written to approximate the coverage of material that you will see on the AP exam and are similar to the review questions at the end of each chapter in this book. Once you are done with the exam, check your work against the given answers, which also indicate where you can find the corresponding material in this book. Also provided is a way to convert your score to a rough AP score.

Key Ideas

✪ Practice the kind of multiple-choice and free-response questions you will be asked on the real exam.
✪ Answer questions that approximate the coverage of topics on the real exam.
✪ Check your work against the given answers.
✪ Determine your areas of strength and weakness.
✪ Earmark the pages that you must give special attention.

Diagnostic Exam

MICROECONOMICS—SECTION I

ANSWER SHEET
Record your responses to the exam questions in the spaces below.

1 Ⓐ Ⓑ Ⓒ Ⓓ Ⓔ	21 Ⓐ Ⓑ Ⓒ Ⓓ Ⓔ	41 Ⓐ Ⓑ Ⓒ Ⓓ Ⓔ
2 Ⓐ Ⓑ Ⓒ Ⓓ Ⓔ	22 Ⓐ Ⓑ Ⓒ Ⓓ Ⓔ	42 Ⓐ Ⓑ Ⓒ Ⓓ Ⓔ
3 Ⓐ Ⓑ Ⓒ Ⓓ Ⓔ	23 Ⓐ Ⓑ Ⓒ Ⓓ Ⓔ	43 Ⓐ Ⓑ Ⓒ Ⓓ Ⓔ
4 Ⓐ Ⓑ Ⓒ Ⓓ Ⓔ	24 Ⓐ Ⓑ Ⓒ Ⓓ Ⓔ	44 Ⓐ Ⓑ Ⓒ Ⓓ Ⓔ
5 Ⓐ Ⓑ Ⓒ Ⓓ Ⓔ	25 Ⓐ Ⓑ Ⓒ Ⓓ Ⓔ	45 Ⓐ Ⓑ Ⓒ Ⓓ Ⓔ
6 Ⓐ Ⓑ Ⓒ Ⓓ Ⓔ	26 Ⓐ Ⓑ Ⓒ Ⓓ Ⓔ	46 Ⓐ Ⓑ Ⓒ Ⓓ Ⓔ
7 Ⓐ Ⓑ Ⓒ Ⓓ Ⓔ	27 Ⓐ Ⓑ Ⓒ Ⓓ Ⓔ	47 Ⓐ Ⓑ Ⓒ Ⓓ Ⓔ
8 Ⓐ Ⓑ Ⓒ Ⓓ Ⓔ	28 Ⓐ Ⓑ Ⓒ Ⓓ Ⓔ	48 Ⓐ Ⓑ Ⓒ Ⓓ Ⓔ
9 Ⓐ Ⓑ Ⓒ Ⓓ Ⓔ	29 Ⓐ Ⓑ Ⓒ Ⓓ Ⓔ	49 Ⓐ Ⓑ Ⓒ Ⓓ Ⓔ
10 Ⓐ Ⓑ Ⓒ Ⓓ Ⓔ	30 Ⓐ Ⓑ Ⓒ Ⓓ Ⓔ	50 Ⓐ Ⓑ Ⓒ Ⓓ Ⓔ
11 Ⓐ Ⓑ Ⓒ Ⓓ Ⓔ	31 Ⓐ Ⓑ Ⓒ Ⓓ Ⓔ	51 Ⓐ Ⓑ Ⓒ Ⓓ Ⓔ
12 Ⓐ Ⓑ Ⓒ Ⓓ Ⓔ	32 Ⓐ Ⓑ Ⓒ Ⓓ Ⓔ	52 Ⓐ Ⓑ Ⓒ Ⓓ Ⓔ
13 Ⓐ Ⓑ Ⓒ Ⓓ Ⓔ	33 Ⓐ Ⓑ Ⓒ Ⓓ Ⓔ	53 Ⓐ Ⓑ Ⓒ Ⓓ Ⓔ
14 Ⓐ Ⓑ Ⓒ Ⓓ Ⓔ	34 Ⓐ Ⓑ Ⓒ Ⓓ Ⓔ	54 Ⓐ Ⓑ Ⓒ Ⓓ Ⓔ
15 Ⓐ Ⓑ Ⓒ Ⓓ Ⓔ	35 Ⓐ Ⓑ Ⓒ Ⓓ Ⓔ	55 Ⓐ Ⓑ Ⓒ Ⓓ Ⓔ
16 Ⓐ Ⓑ Ⓒ Ⓓ Ⓔ	36 Ⓐ Ⓑ Ⓒ Ⓓ Ⓔ	56 Ⓐ Ⓑ Ⓒ Ⓓ Ⓔ
17 Ⓐ Ⓑ Ⓒ Ⓓ Ⓔ	37 Ⓐ Ⓑ Ⓒ Ⓓ Ⓔ	57 Ⓐ Ⓑ Ⓒ Ⓓ Ⓔ
18 Ⓐ Ⓑ Ⓒ Ⓓ Ⓔ	38 Ⓐ Ⓑ Ⓒ Ⓓ Ⓔ	58 Ⓐ Ⓑ Ⓒ Ⓓ Ⓔ
19 Ⓐ Ⓑ Ⓒ Ⓓ Ⓔ	39 Ⓐ Ⓑ Ⓒ Ⓓ Ⓔ	59 Ⓐ Ⓑ Ⓒ Ⓓ Ⓔ
20 Ⓐ Ⓑ Ⓒ Ⓓ Ⓔ	40 Ⓐ Ⓑ Ⓒ Ⓓ Ⓔ	60 Ⓐ Ⓑ Ⓒ Ⓓ Ⓔ

Diagnostic Exam: AP Microeconomics

SECTION I
Time—70 Minutes
60 Questions

For the following multiple-choice questions, select the best answer choice and record your choice on the answer sheet provided.

1. Scarcity is best defined as

   (A) the difference between limited wants and limited economic resources.
   (B) the difference between the total benefit of an action and the total cost of that action.
   (C) the difference between unlimited wants and limited economic resources.
   (D) the opportunity cost of pursuing a given course of action.
   (E) the difference between the marginal benefit and marginal cost of an action.

2. Which of the following statements is most consistent with a capitalist market economy?

   (A) Economic resources are allocated according to the decisions of the central bank.
   (B) Private property is fundamental to innovation, growth, and trade.
   (C) A central government plans the production and distribution of goods.
   (D) Most wages and prices are legally controlled.
   (E) Most economic resources are owned by the government and leased to the citizens in exchange for lower taxes.

3. The graph in Figure D.1 shows a nation's production possibilities curve (PPC) for the production of bread and butter. Which of the following is true?

   (A) The opportunity cost of producing more butter is a decreasing amount of bread.
   (B) Point X represents unemployed economic resources.
   (C) The opportunity cost of producing more butter is a constant amount of bread.
   (D) Point X represents a labor force that has become less productive.
   (E) The opportunity cost of producing more butter is an increasing amount of bread.

4. The graph in Figure D.1 shows a nation's production possibilities curve (PPC) to produce bread and butter. Suppose that production technology in butter production improves. All else being equal, how will this affect the PPC and the opportunity cost of producing bread?

   (A) The vertical intercept of the PPC increases; the opportunity cost of bread decreases.
   (B) The vertical intercept of the PPC decreases; the opportunity cost of bread decreases.
   (C) The horizontal intercept of the PPC increases; the opportunity cost of bread increases.
   (D) The vertical intercept of the PPC increases; the opportunity cost of bread increases.
   (E) The horizontal intercept of the PPC decreases; the opportunity cost of bread decreases.

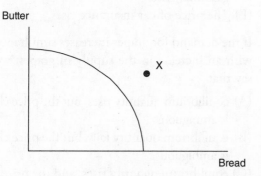

Figure D.1

5. Jess likes to purchase $1 tacos from the taco truck near her school. If Jess uses marginal analysis, how many tacos will she consume on a given day?

   (A) Jess will stop consuming tacos when the marginal benefit of the next taco is equal to zero.
   (B) Jess will stop consuming tacos when the marginal benefit of the next taco is less than zero.
   (C) Jess will stop consuming tacos when the marginal benefit of the next taco is equal to $1.
   (D) Jess will stop consuming tacos when the marginal cost of the next taco is equal to $1.
   (E) Jess will stop consuming tacos when the marginal cost of the next taco is equal to zero.

6. A small bakery has been so busy that they have hired two part-time employees. This is an example of a business changing its _____ resource.

   (A) capital
   (B) profit
   (C) land
   (D) entrepreneurial
   (E) labor

7. Felipe wants to go see a concert next month. He knows that the concert, including his drive to and from the arena, will take five hours. Which of the following is the best example of an implicit cost that Felipe should consider before deciding whether to attend the concert?

   (A) The price of the concert ticket
   (B) The highest wage he could earn if he worked five hours
   (C) The cost of gasoline needed to drive to the concert
   (D) The price of snacks and drinks he would buy at the arena
   (E) His estimate of how much he will enjoy the concert

8. Theo and Eliza can both paint the fence and wax the car after school. For every hour of waxing the car, Theo can paint eight sections of fence and Eliza can paint two sections of fence. Based on this information, the most efficient division of labor would be

   (A) Theo should paint the fence because he has a comparative advantage in painting.
   (B) Eliza should wax the car because she has an absolute advantage in waxing.
   (C) Theo should wax the car because he has a comparative advantage in painting.
   (D) Eliza should paint the fence because she has an absolute advantage in painting.
   (E) Theo should paint the fence because he has an absolute advantage in waxing.

9. Which of the following is true of equilibrium in a perfectly competitive market for good X?

   (A) A shortage of good X exists.
   (B) The quantity demanded equals the quantity supplied of good X.
   (C) A surplus of good X exists.
   (D) The government regulates the quantity of good X produced at the market price.
   (E) Deadweight loss exists.

10. The competitive market for gasoline, a normal good, is currently in a state of equilibrium. Which of the following would most likely increase the price of gasoline?

    (A) Household income falls.
    (B) Technology used to produce gasoline improves.
    (C) The price of subway tickets and other public transportation falls.
    (D) The price of crude oil, a raw material for gasoline, rises.
    (E) The price of car insurance rises.

11. If the demand for grapes increases simultaneously with an increase in the supply of grapes, we can say that

    (A) equilibrium quantity rises, but the price change is ambiguous.
    (B) equilibrium quantity falls, but the price change is ambiguous.
    (C) equilibrium quantity rises, and the price rises.
    (D) equilibrium quantity falls, and the price falls.
    (E) the quantity change is ambiguous, but the equilibrium price rises.

12. In the competitive market for cherry pie, we observe the equilibrium price has risen and the equilibrium quantity has fallen. Which of the following could explain this?

    (A) Income has increased, and cherry pie is a normal good.
    (B) The price of raw cherries has increased.
    (C) The technology used to produce cherry pies has increased.
    (D) The price of apple pies has decreased.
    (E) The number of cherry pie producers has increased.

13. In Figure D.2, identify the area that corresponds to total dollars spent on this product.

    (A) 0ACB
    (B) 0FCB
    (C) AFC
    (D) ACE
    (E) FCE

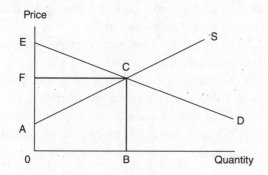

Price

Figure D.2

14. In Figure D.2, identify the area of consumer surplus.

    (A) 0ACB
    (B) 0FCB
    (C) AFC
    (D) ACE
    (E) FCE

15. Suppose the price of beef rises by 10 percent and the quantity of beef demanded falls by 20 percent. We can conclude that

    (A) demand for beef is price elastic and consumer spending on beef is falling.
    (B) demand for beef is price elastic and consumer spending on beef is rising.
    (C) demand for beef is price inelastic and consumer spending on beef is falling.
    (D) demand for beef is price inelastic and consumer spending on beef is rising.
    (E) demand for beef is unit elastic and consumer spending on beef is constant.

16. If the price of firm A's cell phone service rises by 5 percent and the quantity demanded for firm B's cell phone service increases by 10 percent, we can say that

    (A) demand for firm B is price elastic.
    (B) supply for firm B is price elastic.
    (C) firms A and B are substitutes because the cross-price elasticity is greater than zero.
    (D) firms A and B are complements because the cross-price elasticity is less than zero.
    (E) firms A and B are complements because the cross-price elasticity is greater than zero.

17. A binding price floor is imposed in a competitive market. How will this change consumer surplus and producer surplus, and will there be a shortage or surplus of the product exchanged?

	CONSUMER SURPLUS	PRODUCER SURPLUS	SHORTAGE OR SURPLUS?
(A)	Decreases	Increases	Surplus
(B)	Decreases	Increases	Shortage
(C)	Increases	Decreases	Shortage
(D)	Increases	Decreases	Surplus
(E)	Decreases	Decreases	Surplus

18. An excise tax of $T is imposed on the sellers of a product exchanged in a competitive market. Which of the following statements accurately describes the outcome?

    (A) If the supply curve is less elastic than the demand curve, consumers pay a higher share of the tax and there is deadweight loss.
    (B) If the supply curve is more elastic than the demand curve, consumers pay a lower share of the tax and there is deadweight loss.
    (C) If the demand curve is perfectly elastic, producers pay the entire burden of the tax and there is zero deadweight loss.
    (D) If the supply curve is perfectly elastic, consumers pay the entire burden of the tax and there is zero deadweight loss.
    (E) If the demand curve is perfectly inelastic, consumers pay the entire burden of the tax and there is zero deadweight loss.

19. Professor Peach spends her entire budget on tea and biscuits to maximize her utility. The price of tea is $2 per cup and the price of each biscuit is $3. At her current consumption levels, the marginal utility of tea is 22 utils and the marginal utility of biscuits is 33 utils, and she has used her entire budget. What should Professor Peach do to maximize her utility?

    (A) She should increase tea consumption and decrease biscuit consumption.
    (B) She should decrease both tea consumption and biscuit consumption.
    (C) She should decrease tea consumption and increase biscuit consumption.
    (D) She should increase both tea consumption and biscuit consumption.
    (E) She should change nothing.

20. Which of the following describes the theory behind the demand curve?

    (A) Decreasing marginal utility as consumption rises
    (B) Increasing marginal cost as consumption rises
    (C) Decreasing marginal cost as consumption rises
    (D) Increasing total utility at an increasing rate as consumption rises
    (E) The substitution effect of a price decrease is larger than the income effect.

21. If a consumer is not required to pay a monetary price for each cookie she consumes, the consumer will stop eating cookies when

    (A) the total utility from eating cookies is equal to zero.
    (B) the substitution effect outweighs the income effect from eating cookies.
    (C) the ratio of marginal utility divided by total utility is equal to one.
    (D) the marginal utility from eating the last cookie is zero.
    (E) the marginal utility from eating the next cookie is increasing at a decreasing rate.

22. In the short run, a firm employs labor and capital to produce gadgets. If the annual price of capital increases, what will happen to the short-run cost curves?

    (A) The marginal cost and average variable cost curves will shift upward.
    (B) The average fixed cost and average total cost curves will shift upward.
    (C) The marginal cost and average fixed cost curves will shift upward.
    (D) The marginal cost, average fixed cost, average variable cost, and average total cost curves will all shift upward.
    (E) Only the average fixed cost curve will shift upward.

23. A pizza restaurant is operating in the short run and looking at expenses for next month. Which of the following is a variable cost for the owners of the restaurant?

    (A) Rent on the building
    (B) Cost of Wi-Fi in the building
    (C) Cost of deliveries of cheese and pepperoni
    (D) Insurance payments on pizza delivery cars
    (E) Payments to keep the website updated

Questions 24 and 25 are based on the production data in the following table.

QUANTITY OF LABOR EMPLOYED (L)	TOTAL PRODUCT OF LABOR (Q)
0	0
1	10
2	18
3	24
4	28
5	30
6	31
7	30

24. What is the marginal product of labor for the third unit of labor?

(A) 24
(B) 6
(C) 8
(D) 3
(E) 12

25. What is the average product of labor for the fifth unit of labor?

(A) 5
(B) 30
(C) 6
(D) 2
(E) 25

Questions 26 to 28 are based on the table of costs below for a perfectly competitive firm.

OUTPUT	AVERAGE FIXED COST	AVERAGE VARIABLE COST	MARGINAL COST
0			
1	$10	$5	$5
2	$5	$3.50	$2
3	$3.33	$4.33	$6
4	$2.50	$5	$7
5	$2	$5.60	$8

26. The total fixed cost of producing a quantity of 4 is

(A) $5.
(B) $7.50.
(C) $7.
(D) $2.50.
(E) $10.

27. The first unit of output to exhibit diminishing marginal productivity is the _____ unit.

(A) 1st
(B) 2nd
(C) 3rd
(D) 4th
(E) 5th

28. At a quantity of 4, what is the total cost of production?

(A) $7.50
(B) $2.50
(C) $15
(D) $30
(E) $14.50

Questions 29 to 30 are based on Figure D.3, which illustrates the short-run cost curves of a perfectly competitive firm.

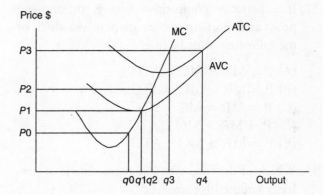

Figure D.3

29. The shutdown point is seen at:

(A) $P0, q0$
(B) $P1, q1$
(C) $P2, q2$
(D) $P3, q3$
(E) $P3, q4$

30. If the market price of the output increases from *P*1 to *P*3, the profit-maximizing firm will

    (A) increase output from *q*1 to *q*4 and earn positive economic profits.
    (B) increase output from *q*1 to *q*4 and earn a normal profit.
    (C) increase output from *q*1 to *q*3 and earn positive economic profits.
    (D) increase output from *q*1 to *q*3 and earn a normal profit.
    (E) increase output from *q*1 to *q*2 and earn economic losses.

31. If the perfectly competitive price is currently below minimum average total cost, we can expect which of the following events in the long run?

    (A) The price will rise and each firm's output will fall as firms exit the industry.
    (B) Market equilibrium quantity will increase as firms exit the industry.
    (C) Nothing. The industry is currently in long-run equilibrium.
    (D) Profits will fall as the market price increases.
    (E) The price will rise to the breakeven point as firms exit the industry.

32. If a perfectly competitive firm is maximizing profit and short-run profits are positive, which of the following must be true?

    (A) $P = MR = MC = ATC$
    (B) $P > MR = MC = ATC$
    (C) $P = MR = MC > ATC$
    (D) $P = MR = MC < ATC$
    (E) $P = MR > MC = ATC$

33. Which of the following is a characteristic of perfectly competitive markets?

    (A) Product differentiation
    (B) Barriers to entry
    (C) Strategic behavior
    (D) Very few producers
    (E) Price-taking behavior

34. When a perfectly competitive market has come to long-run equilibrium, we know that

    (A) economic profit is zero and accounting profit is greater than zero.
    (B) economic profit and accounting profit are both zero.
    (C) price is greater than average total cost.
    (D) price is equal to average variable cost.
    (E) accounting profit is zero and economic profit is greater than zero.

35. Perfectly competitive markets are said to be allocatively efficient because output is where

    (A) $P = ATC$.
    (B) $P = MC$.
    (C) $P = AVC$.
    (D) economic profit is zero.
    (E) $P = MR$.

36. When a monopolist has maximized profit,

    (A) price is set equal to marginal cost, creating zero economic profit.
    (B) output is set where price is equal to average total cost.
    (C) price is set above marginal cost, creating allocative inefficiency.
    (D) any short-run profit will be eliminated through the long-run entry of new firms.
    (E) output is set where price is equal to marginal cost, eliminating any deadweight loss.

37. Assuming positive profits are possible, when a monopolist sets output to maximize profit, we know that

    (A) $P = MR = MC = ATC$.
    (B) $P = MR = MC > ATC$.
    (C) $P > MR > MC = ATC$.
    (D) $P > MR > MC > ATC$.
    (E) $P > ATC > MR = MC$.

Questions 38–40 are based on Figure D.4, which illustrates a profit-maximizing monopolist.

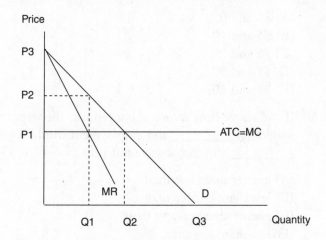

Figure D.4

38. When the monopolist maximizes profit, output will be set at ____ and price will be set at ____.

 (A) Q2; P1
 (B) Q1; P1
 (C) Q1; P2
 (D) Q3; P3
 (E) Q2; P2

39. At the monopoly outcome, consumer surplus is equal to the following area:

 (A) (P2 − P1) × Q1
 (B) 1/2 × (P3 − P1) × Q2
 (C) 1/2 × (P2 − P1) × (Q2 − Q1)
 (D) 1/2 × P3 × Q3
 (E) 1/2 × (P3 − P2) × Q1

40. If this monopolist were regulated to produce a break-even level of output, output will be set at ____ and price will be set at ____.

 (A) Q2; P1
 (B) Q1; P1
 (C) Q1; P2
 (D) Q3; P3
 (E) Q2; P2

41. Which of the following is necessarily a characteristic of oligopoly?

 (A) Free entry into and exit from the market
 (B) A few large producers
 (C) One producer of a good with no close substitutes
 (D) A homogenous product
 (E) No opportunities for collusion between firms

42. The market structures of perfect competition and monopolistic competition share which of the following characteristics?

 (A) Ease of entry and exit in the long run
 (B) Homogenous products
 (C) Perfectly elastic demand for the firm's product
 (D) Long-run positive profits
 (E) Product differentiation

43. Monopolistic competition is often characterized by

 (A) strong barriers to entry.
 (B) a long-run price that exceeds average total cost.
 (C) a price that exceeds average variable cost, causing excess capacity.
 (D) a homogenous product.
 (E) many resources devoted to advertising.

44. If the government wishes to regulate a natural monopoly so that it produces an allocatively efficient level of output, it would be at an output

 (A) where price is equal to average total cost.
 (B) where marginal revenue equals marginal cost.
 (C) where normal profits are made.
 (D) where price is equal to average variable cost.
 (E) where price is equal to marginal cost.

Use the following payoff matrix to answer Questions 45 and 46.

		FIRM Z	
		Ph	Pl
FIRM Y	Ph	Y: $15,000 Z: $13,000	Y: $20,000 Z: $12,000
	Pl	Y: $14,000 Z: $22,000	Y: $16,000 Z: $15,000

45. Two oligopolists must simultaneously decide on a pricing strategy, either set a high price (Ph) or a low price (Pl). Once the price is set, it cannot be changed. If the firms do not collude, the outcome of the game will be

 (A) both firms set a low price.
 (B) Firm Y sets a high price and Firm Z alternates between the high price and low price.
 (C) both firms set a high price.
 (D) Firm Y sets the high price and Firm Z sets the low price.
 (E) Firm Y sets the low price and Firm Z sets the high price.

46. Two oligopolists must simultaneously decide on a pricing strategy, either set a high price (Ph) or a low price (Pl). Once the price is set, it cannot be changed. If the firms can successfully collude, the outcome of the game will be:

    (A) both firms set a low price.
    (B) both Firm Y and Firm Z alternate between the high price and low price.
    (C) both firms set a high price.
    (D) Firm Y sets the high price and Firm Z sets the low price.
    (E) Firm Y sets the low price and Firm Z sets the high price.

47. Which of the following is most likely to decrease the demand for kindergarten teachers?

    (A) An increase in funding for education
    (B) Increased immigration of foreign citizens and their families
    (C) A decrease in the average number of children per household
    (D) Subsidies given to college students who major in elementary education
    (E) A decrease in the number of classes the state requires for a teaching certificate

48. Which of the following statements is true about the demand for labor?

    (A) It rises if the price of a substitute resource falls and the output effect is greater than the substitution effect.
    (B) It falls if the price of the output produced rises.
    (C) It falls if the price of a complementary resource falls.
    (D) It falls if the demand for the output produced by labor increases.
    (E) It falls if the labor becomes more productive.

Questions 49 and 50 are based on the table of employment data below.

WAGE (W)	QUANTITY OF LABOR SUPPLIED	MARGINAL REVENUE PRODUCT OF LABOR (MRP$_L$)
$4	0	
$5	10	$7
$6	20	$6
$7	30	$5
$8	40	$4

49. If a firm is hiring labor in the perfectly competitive labor market, the wage and employment will be

    (A) $4 and 0.
    (B) $5 and 10.
    (C) $6 and 20.
    (D) $7 and 30.
    (E) $8 and 40.

50. If the above firm were a monopsonist, the wage would be _____ and employment would be _____ the competitive outcome.

    (A) greater than; less than
    (B) less than; greater than
    (C) greater than; greater than
    (D) less than; less than
    (E) less than; the same as

51. Interstate trucking companies hire three factors of production in shipping goods from point A to point B: labor (drivers), capital (trucks and trailers), and diesel fuel. Which of the following would cause the demand for capital to increase?

    (A) A recession decreases the demand for goods.
    (B) Wages paid to drivers are increasing in the labor market.
    (C) Diesel fuel prices are decreasing in the fuel market.
    (D) Interest rates on borrowing are increasing in credit markets.
    (E) The price of capital is decreasing.

Questions 52 and 53 are based on Figure D.5, which illustrates a profit-maximizing employer.

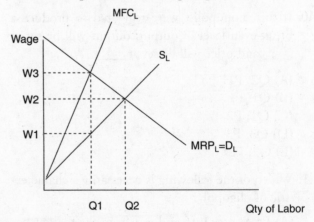

Figure D.5

52. If this firm is the sole employer in the labor market, how much labor would be employed and what is the wage that would be paid?

   (A) Q1; W3
   (B) Q1; W1
   (C) Q2; W2
   (D) Q1; W2
   (E) Q2; W1

53. If this firm hires the efficient quantity of labor in this market, employment would be _____ and the wage would be _____.

   (A) Q1; W3
   (B) Q1; W1
   (C) Q2; W2
   (D) Q1; W2
   (E) Q2; W1

54. A firm hires labor and capital in competitive-factor markets. The price of labor is $6, and the price of capital is $12. Currently the marginal product of labor is 24 units, and the marginal product of capital is 36 units. Can the firm adjust the hiring of labor and capital to produce the same output at a lower cost?

   (A) No, the firm is hiring the least-cost combination of labor and capital.
   (B) Yes, the firm should hire more of both labor and capital.
   (C) Yes, the firm should hire less of both labor and capital.
   (D) Yes, the firm should hire more labor and less capital.
   (E) Yes, the firm should hire less labor and more capital.

55. Which of the following is the best example of a public good?

   (A) A visit to the orthodontist
   (B) A session at the tanning salon
   (C) A large pizza
   (D) A cup of coffee
   (E) The International Space Station

56. A negative externality in the market for a good exists when

   (A) the market overallocates resources to the production of this good.
   (B) spillover benefits are received by society.
   (C) the marginal social benefit equals the marginal social cost.
   (D) total welfare is maximized.
   (E) the marginal private cost exceeds the marginal social cost.

57. Which of the following tax systems is designed to redistribute income from the wealthy to the poor?

   (A) A progressive tax system
   (B) A regressive tax system
   (C) A proportional tax system
   (D) An excise tax system
   (E) A tariff system

58. The two characteristics of a private good are

   (A) excludable and rival.
   (B) open-access and rival.
   (C) nonexcludable and nonrival.
   (D) excludable and nonrival.
   (E) nonexcludable and rival.

59. Suppose we observe a nation's Gini ratio has fallen from .75 to .45 over 20 years. What might explain this change?

   (A) The nation's level of human capital has fallen.
   (B) The nation has used more regressive taxes.
   (C) The nation's markets have become less competitive.
   (D) The nation has used more progressive taxes.
   (E) The nation's degree of social and economic discrimination has worsened.

60. Consumers of gadgets generate spillover benefits to their communities, and the gadget market does not account for these social benefits. Which of the following would be an appropriate government response to improve efficiency in the gadget market?

   (A) Impose a tax on each gadget produced.
   (B) Ban the consumption of gadgets.
   (C) Impose a tax on each gadget consumed.
   (D) Set a price ceiling in the gadget market.
   (E) Provide a subsidy for each gadget consumed.

› Answers and Explanations

This diagnostic exam was designed to test you on topics that you will see on the AP Microeconomics exam in the approximate proportions that you will see them. Chronologically they appear in the approximate order of their review in Step 4 of this book, but this is not the case on the AP exam. Topics on the practice exams are shuffled.

Questions from Chapter 5

1. **C**—This is the definition of scarcity.

2. **B**—In a capitalistic market economy, the central government has minimal roles in the production and distribution of goods. Resources are allocated based on relative, not absolute, prices, and prices are determined in markets. The role of private property is central to capitalism.

3. **E**—A concave, or bowed out, PPC illustrates the principle of increasing opportunity costs. It is more and more difficult (costly) to produce increasing amounts of a good.

4. **D**—When technology improves for butter production, it means that the same number of resources can produce more butter; this shifts the vertical intercept upward. The opportunity cost of bread rises because every additional unit of bread now comes at a larger sacrifice of butter production.

5. **C**—The marginal cost of the next taco is always $1, so a rational consumer will stop when the marginal benefit falls to equal marginal cost.

6. **E**—Employees are the labor resource for a firm.

7. **B**—If Felipe could work for five hours instead of attending the concert, those forgone wages are an implicit cost of the concert. An explicit cost is something he directly pays out of his pocket.

8. **A**—If Theo waxes the car, he gives up eight sections of painted fence, while Eliza would only give up two sections of fence. Because the opportunity cost of waxing is higher for Theo, he has a comparative advantage in painting and Eliza has a comparative advantage in waxing. Theo should paint the fence and Eliza should wax the car.

Questions from Chapter 6

9. **B**—In a market free of price controls or other distortions, equilibrium occurs at a price where $Q_d = Q_s$. Graphically this is where the demand curve intersects the supply curve. Here, social welfare is maximized, allocative efficiency is attained, and there exists no deadweight loss.

10. **D**—If the price of a production input (or resource) increases, the supply curve shifts leftward and the price of gasoline rises. Hint: Having a strong grasp of what shifts supply and demand curves will really pay off. Draw these shifting curves in the margin of the exam book!

11. **A**—Increased demand, by itself, increases equilibrium quantity and increases the price of grapes. Increased supply, by itself, increases equilibrium quantity and decreases the price of grapes. So quantity definitely increases, but the price change is unknown because it depends on how far the curves shift in relation to each other. Quickly draw these in the exam book.

12. **B**—If the price has risen and quantity has fallen, look for something that would cause the supply curve to decrease, or shift leftward. The higher price of raw cherries, a key input in the production of cherry pie, would decrease the supply of cherry pies.

13. **B**—Total spending is the price multiplied by the quantity demanded, or the area of the rectangle with height to point F and width of point B.

14. **E**—Consumer surplus is the area above the price and below the demand curve. It is the difference between the price consumers would have paid and the price they did pay.

Questions from Chapter 7

15. **A**—If the percentage change in Q_d is greater than the percentage change in price, the good is elastic. In this situation of rising prices, total spending on beef will fall because the upward effect of prices is outweighed by the downward effect of quantity.

16. **C**—The cross-price elasticity measures how sensitive the Q_d of good X is to a change in the price of good Y. If this elasticity is greater than zero, the two goods are substitutes; if it is negative, the two goods are complements.

17. **A**—A binding price floor is designed to help producers, so it is set above the equilibrium price. At this price floor, $Q_s > Q_d$, so a surplus of the product exists. The higher price and decreased quantity cause consumer surplus to fall and producer surplus to rise.

18. **E**—A vertical demand curve will put the entire burden of the tax on consumers because the price will rise by exactly $T. There is no deadweight loss because the equilibrium quantity doesn't change. It's important to remember that the group, buyers or sellers, that pays the higher burden of the tax is the group that has the lowest price elasticity. And any time a tax decreases the market equilibrium quantity, deadweight loss will emerge.

19. **E**—A consumer has maximized her utility when the marginal utility per dollar is equal for both products. When we divide marginal utility by the price, we see that $MU_{tea}/P_{tea} = MU_{biscuits}/P_{biscuits} = 11$ utils per dollar.

20. **A**—One of the foundations of the law of demand is falling marginal utility as more of a good is consumed. You can eliminate any choices that refer to marginal cost, and a downward-sloping demand curve would not be the result of total utility that increases at an increasing rate.

21. **D**—A consumer stops eating cookies when total utility is maximized, which corresponds to when $MU = 0$. Because marginal utility falls with consumption, the very next cookie will give the consumer disutility ($MU < 0$), so she stops.

Questions from Chapter 8

22. **B**—An increase in the price of capital is an increase in total fixed costs. This increases AFC. Since $ATC = AFC + AVC$, it also increases ATC. Because fixed costs do not change with output, marginal cost and variable cost remain the same.

23. **C**—A variable cost is something that increases and decreases with output. If the restaurant is busy, they will need more cheese and pepperoni next month. All other options would remain constant, or fixed, no matter if the restaurant was busy or slow next month.

24. **B**—Marginal product of labor is the change in output when the next unit of labor is employed. When the third unit of labor is hired, output rises from 18 to 24 units, so marginal product is 6 additional units of output.

25. **C**—Average product of labor is the total output divided by the units of labor hired to produce that output. In other words, it is output per unit of labor. At the fifth unit of labor, total output is 30, so average product is equal to 30 divided by 5, or 6 units per worker.

26. **E**—TFC are constant, so if AFC = $10 at $q = 1$ and AFC = TFC/q, then TFC must be $10 at *any* quantity. Know the way in which all total and average costs are related.

27. **C**—This question tests whether you know the relationships between production and cost. Marginal cost and marginal product are inverses of each other. Because the MC of producing the third unit is rising, the MP must be falling.

28. **D**—At a quantity of 4, TFC = $10 and TVC = AVC × q = $5 × 4 = $20. Since TC = TFC + TVC, TC = $30.

Questions from Chapter 9

29. **B**—The shutdown point is at minimum AVC. If the price falls below this point, the firm finds it rational to produce nothing in the short run and incur losses equal to TFC.

30. **C**—When the price rises, the perfectly competitive firm finds a higher level of output where $P = MR = MC$. Since this price lies above the ATC curve, positive economic profits are possible.

31. **E**—The question describes a situation where short-run losses are being incurred. In the long run, firms exit, shifting market supply leftward, increasing market price until the firms earn normal, or breakeven, profits.

32. **C**—In perfect competition, price and marginal revenue are identical, and the firm maximizes profit by producing where price and marginal revenue are equal to marginal cost. If positive

profits are being made, it must be the case that price is greater than average total cost.

33. **E**—Perfect competition is described by many firms producing identical products in a market with no barriers to entry. These characteristics imply that firms cannot affect the price; they're price takers. Strategic behavior, like advertising, is impossible under these conditions.

34. **A**—In the long run, perfectly competitive firms earn zero economic profit. Unlike economic profit, accounting profit does not include the implicit costs of operating the business, so accounting profit will always be greater than economic profit.

35. **B**—Allocative efficiency is achieved when the marginal benefit to society is equal to the marginal cost to society. In perfectly competitive markets, this occurs because price equals marginal cost for the last unit produced and consumed. This is true even if profits are positive, zero, or negative.

36. **C**—One of the important results of monopoly is that while output is set where MR = MC, price is set from the demand curve, so $P >$ MC. This creates inefficient resource allocation and deadweight loss that is not eliminated in the long run.

37. **E**—For a monopolist, price is always greater than marginal revenue, and profit is maximized when marginal revenue equals marginal cost, so you can eliminate any choices where these conditions are not met. If profit is positive, price must also be greater than average total cost.

38. **C**—A monopolist sets output where MR = MC, and this happens at Q1. But price comes from the demand curve, so from Q1 go up to demand, and the price is set at P2.

39. **E**—Consumer surplus is the area above the price and below the demand curve at the monopoly output. This area forms a triangle with a width of Q1 units and a height of (P3 − P2) units. The area of a triangle is 1/2 × (width) × (height).

40. **A**—The breakeven point would occur at the output where price equals average total cost.

41. **B**—Oligopolies are industries dominated by a few large firms but can have either homogenous or differentiated products. All other choices describe other market structures in the chapter.

42. **A**—These two market structures are fairly similar, and free entry and exit is one of the characteristics that they share. They also share the characteristic of normal profits in the long run but do not share homogenous products or efficiency.

43. **E**—Monopolistic competition is characterized by product differentiation. One way that firms differentiate their products and protect market share is through extensive advertising.

44. **E**—In perfect competition, $P =$ MR = MC and resources are allocated efficiently. Since a monopoly will not have the situation where $P =$ MR, regulators might try to force the firm to produce where $P =$ MC. This point may or may not ensure a long-run profit for the firm.

45. **C**—Both firms have dominant strategies to always choose the high price. This means that no matter what the other firm does, each firm sees that Ph is always more profitable than Pl.

46. **A**—When firms cannot collude, they will pursue their individual dominant strategies and price high. However, if they can successfully collude, they can both increase profits by agreeing to set the low price.

Questions from Chapter 10

47. **C**—Demand for any type of labor is derived from the demand for the good or service that the labor produces. With fewer children in the household, there will be less demand for kindergarten classes and teachers.

48. **A**—When the price of a substitute resource (like capital) falls, two effects move the demand for labor in opposite directions. The firm wants to substitute for more capital and less labor, but lower costs prompt more output to be produced, and this can require more labor. If the output effect outweighs the substitution effect, demand for labor may increase even if capital is less expensive. Labor demand will increase if the labor becomes more productive or if the price of the output produced rises.

49. **C**—Competitive labor markets are characterized by hiring where $W = \text{MRPL}$. This is another example of decision making where marginal costs (wage paid) equal marginal benefits (MR × MPL).

50. **D**—A monopsonist is like a monopolist on the hiring side of the firm. Monopsonists hire where $\text{MFC} = \text{MRPL}$, and because MFC lies above the labor supply curve, this means that they will hire fewer workers and pay lower wages than the competitive outcome.

51. **D**—Diesel fuel is a complementary input for the capital trucks and trailers, so a lower price of this input would increase demand for capital. The lower price of capital would increase the quantity of capital hired, but wouldn't shift the entire demand curve.

52. **B**—The monopsonist hires to the point where marginal factor cost is equal to the marginal revenue product of labor, and this happens at Q1 units of labor. The wage comes from the labor supply curve, so the wage paid is W1.

53. **D**—The efficient quantity of employment is where the demand curve intersects the supply curve. This would correspond to the outcome for a perfectly competitive labor market.

54. **D**—The least-cost combination of labor and capital is employed when the marginal product per dollar is equal for both inputs. Currently the marginal product per dollar is 4 units per dollar (24/$6) compared to 3 units per dollar (36/$12) for capital. Since each dollar paid to labor produces more output, the firm should increase labor hiring and decrease capital hiring until $\text{MP}_L/w = \text{MP}_K/r$.

Questions from Chapter 11

55. **E**—Public goods cannot be divided among consumers. If one consumes a public good, the next person is not denied consumption of it. All other choices are goods and services that are both rival and excludable.

56. **A**—When individuals and firms exchange a good that imposes costs on third parties, they have created a negative externality. The market produces "too much" because these spillover costs are not reflected in the private (or market) supply curve.

Resources are overallocated to the production of this good.

57. **A**—A progressive tax system means that higher levels of income pay higher proportions of their income to the tax collector. This system is designed to redistribute income from higher tax brackets to lower tax brackets.

58. **A**—A private good, like a hamburger, is excludable because sellers can exclude nonpayers from consuming the good. Private goods are also rival because one person's consumption of a unit means another person cannot also consume that same unit of the good.

59. **D**—When a Gini ratio has fallen, it means that the income distribution has become more equal in a nation. Progressive taxes are those that tax a higher percentage of income as income rises. This is one way that government can redistribute income from the wealthiest to the poorest segments of society.

60. **E**—Positive externalities should be encouraged, but markets ignore the spillover benefits to the rest of society. Subsidies would promote more transactions and move the market outcome closer to the socially efficient outcome.

AP Microeconomics Diagnostic Exam

SECTION II

Free-Response Questions
Planning Time—10 minutes
Writing Time—50 minutes

At the conclusion of the planning time, you have 50 minutes to respond to the following three questions. Approximately half of your time should be given to the first question, and the second half should be divided evenly between the remaining two questions. Be careful to clearly explain your reasoning and to provide clear labels to all graph axes and curves.

1. The following graph shows a typical seller of burritos in a monopolistically competitive market for burritos.

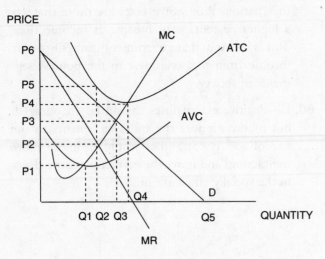

(A) Using the labels in the graph, identify the following:

   i. The profit-maximizing quantity
   ii. The price of a burrito when the firm has maximized profit
   iii. The allocatively efficient output

(B) Using the labels in the graph, identify the following:

   i. The area of short-run economic profit or loss
   ii. The area of consumer surplus

(C) In the long run, do you expect there to be the same number of firms, more firms, or fewer firms in this market? Explain.

(D) Given your response in (C), will the long-run price of burritos be higher, lower, or the same as the short-run price of burritos?

(E) In the long-run equilibrium, will deadweight loss exist? Explain.

2. The market for apples is perfectly competitive and in long-run equilibrium. Due to consumer unrest about the price of apples, the government is considering a price ceiling.

(A) In a correctly labeled graph, draw the market for apples. In the graph, identify

   i. The equilibrium price and quantity in the market, labeled P_M and Q_M respectively.
   ii. An effective price ceiling, labeled P_C.
   iii. The quantity of apples exchanged at the price floor, labeled Q^*.

(B) If the price ceiling is effective, is there a shortage of apples, a surplus of apples, or neither? Explain.

(C) In your graph from (A), shade the area of deadweight loss due to the effective price ceiling.

3. Sissy is an employer of labor in a competitive labor market at a wage of $12. Sissy's firm produces cat toys in a competitive output market at a price of $2. The table below shows how output changes in the short run with different levels of employment. Labor is Sissy's only variable input, and the firm has fixed costs equal to $8.

UNITS OF LABOR (L)	CAT TOYS PRODUCED (Q)
0	0
1	8
2	15
3	21
4	26
5	30
6	33
7	35
8	31

(A) Using marginal analysis, how many units of labor should Sissy employ to maximize her short-run profits? Explain.

(B) Based on your answer to (A),

   i. Identify the number of cat toys that will be produced.
   ii. Calculate Sissy's short-run economic profit. Show your work.

(C) Based on your answer to (B) (ii), should Sissy shut down in the short run? Explain.

Free-Response Grading Rubric

Question 1 (10 points)

Part (A): 3 points
i. One point is earned for identifying Q2 as the profit-maximizing output.
ii. One point is earned for identifying P4 as the price.
iii. One point is earned for identifying Q3 as the allocatively efficient output (where P = MC).

Part (B): 2 points
i. One point is earned for identifying the area (P5 – P4) × Q2 as the area of economic losses. Alternatively, the point could be earned by stating the area of (P4 – P5) × Q2 is the economic profit (a negative value).
ii. One point is earned by identifying the area 1/2 × (P6 – P4) × Q2 as the area of consumer surplus.

Part (C): 2 points
• One point is earned for stating there will be fewer firms in the long run.
• One point is earned for explaining that the short-run losses will prompt exit of some firms in the long run.

Part (D): 1 point
One point is earned for stating that the price of burritos will be higher in the long run.

Part (E): 2 points
• One point is earned for stating that deadweight loss will exist in the long run.
• One point is earned for explaining that in the long run the price will still be greater than marginal cost.

Question 2 (5 points)

Part (A): 3 points
These are graphing points.
i. One point is earned for drawing a correctly labeled graph of the apple market with P_M and Q_M. The market demand curve must be downward sloping, and the market supply curve must be upward sloping.
ii. One point is earned for drawing a horizontal P_c that lies below P_M.
iii. One point is earned by identifying Q^* from the intersection of P_c and the supply curve.

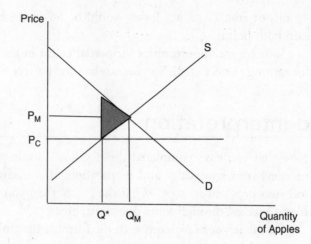

Part (B): 2 points

- One point is earned for stating that there is a shortage of apples.
- One point is earned by explaining that at P_c the quantity demanded exceeds the quantity supplied.

Part (C): 1 point

One point is earned for correctly shading the area of deadweight loss in the graph.

Question 3 (5 points)

Part (A): 1 point

- One point is earned for stating that the firm should employ 3 units of labor and for explaining that at 3 units of labor, the marginal revenue product of labor (MRP_L) is equal to the wage (W), but at the fourth unit of labor, $MRP_L < W$.

Part (B): 2 points

i. One point is earned for stating that Sissy will produce 21 cat toys.
ii. One point is earned for calculating profit and showing the work.
    Profit = $2 \times 21 - \$12 \times 3 - \$8 = -\$2$.

Part (C): 2 points

- One point is earned for stating that Sissy should not shut down in the short run.
- One point is earned for explaining that her total revenue exceeds total variable cost. If she shut down, she would lose $8 rather than $2.

Are there ever any opportunities for partial credit in FRQs?

Yes, these are often called "consistency points," and these allow you to earn points on subsequent sections of an FRQ, so long as your responses are consistent with earlier incorrect responses.

For example, let's look at Problem 1. In part (B)(i) you should have found an area of economic losses, but suppose you state that you have found positive economic profits. You are not going to earn the point in (B)(i). However, in part (C) you state that there will be more firms because the profit attracts entry. You would most likely earn the two points in (C) because you were consistently correct. You could even earn the point in (D) for stating that the price of burritos would fall.

In Problem 3, maybe you stated in (A) that Sissy will hire 4 units of labor. Wrong, no point there. However in part (B)(i) you state that her output is 26 cat toys (consistent with

4 units of labor) and her losses would be $4 (consistent with 26 cat toys), so you could earn both points.

So there are opportunities for partial credit in the FRQs, but you really want to shoot for earning perfect credit so you can bag the perfect 5.

Scoring and Interpretation

Now that you have completed the diagnostic exam and checked your answers, it is time to assess your knowledge and preparation. If you saw some questions that caused you to roll your eyes and mutter "What the . . . ?" then you can focus your study on those areas. If you breezed through some questions, great!

Calculate your raw score with the formula that follows. If you left any multiple-choice questions blank, there is no penalty. Take this raw score on the diagnostic exam and compare it to the table that follows to estimate where you might score at this point.

Calculate Your Score:

Multiple-Choice Questions:

$$\frac{}{(\# \ right)} = \frac{}{MC \ raw \ score}$$

Free-Response Questions:

Free-Response Raw Score = $(1.50 \times Score\ 1) + (1.50 \times Score\ 2) + (1.50 \times Score\ 3)$
= _____

Add the raw scores from the multiple-choice and free-response sections to obtain your total raw score for the diagnostic exam. Use the following table to determine your grade, remembering these are rough estimates using questions that are not actually from AP exams, so do not read too much into this conversion from raw score to AP score.

MICROECONOMICS	
Raw Diagnostic Score	AP Grade
73–90	5
58–72	4
45–57	3
33–44	2
0–32	1

No matter how you scored on the diagnostic exam, it is time to begin to review for your AP Microeconomics exam.

STEP 3

Develop Strategies for Success

CHAPTER 4 How to Approach Each Question Type

CHAPTER 4

How to Approach Each Question Type

IN THIS CHAPTER

Summary: Use these question-answering strategies to raise your AP score.

Key Ideas

Multiple-Choice Questions

✪ Read the question carefully.

✪ Try to answer the question yourself before reading the answer choices.

✪ Guess if you can eliminate one or more answer choices.

✪ Remember that drawing a picture can help.

✪ Don't spend too much time on any one question.

Free-Response Questions

✪ Write clearly and legibly.

✪ Be consistent from one part of your answer to another.

✪ Draw a graph if one is required.

✪ If the question can be answered with one word or number, don't write more.

✪ Pay attention to the prompts.

Section I: Multiple-Choice Questions

Because you are a seasoned student accustomed to the educational testing machine, you have surely participated in more standardized tests than you care to count. You probably know some students who always seem to ace the multiple-choice questions and some students who would rather set themselves on fire than sit for another round of "bubble trouble." I hope that with a little background and a few tips, you might improve your scores in this important component of the AP Microeconomics exam.

First, the background. Every multiple-choice question has three important parts:

1. The **stem** is the basis for the actual question. Sometimes this comes in the form of a fill-in-the-blank statement, rather than a question.

   Example
   Average fixed cost is computed by dividing total fixed cost by:

   Example
   If a negative externality exists in the production of a good, what must be true of the market for this product?

2. **The correct answer option.** Obviously, this is the one selection that best completes the statement, or responds to the question in the stem. Because you have purchased this book, you will select this option many, many times.

3. **Distractor options.** Just as it sounds, these are the incorrect answers intended to distract the person who decided not to purchase this book. You can locate this person in the exam room by searching for the individual who is repeatedly smacking their forehead on the desktop.

Students who do well on multiple-choice exams are so well prepared that they can easily find the correct answer, but other students do well because they are savvy enough to identify and avoid the distractors. Much research has been done on how to best study for, and complete, multiple-choice questions. You can find some of this research by using your favorite Internet search engine, but here are a few tips that many economics students find useful.

1. *Let's be careful out there.* You must carefully read the question. This sounds pretty obvious, but you would be surprised how tricky those test developers can be. For example, rushing past and failing to see the use of a negative can throw a student.

   Example
   Which of the following is *not* true of firms in perfect competition?

   A. Firms produce a homogenous good.
   B. Firms engage in price discrimination.
   C. Firms earn a normal profit in the long run.
   D. Firms have no ability to influence the market price.
   E. Firms produce the output where price is equal to marginal cost.

   A student who is going too fast and ignores the negative *not* might select option (A) because it is true of perfectly competitive firms, and it was the first option that the student saw.

2. *See the answer, be the answer.* Many people find success when they carefully read the question and, before looking at the alternatives, visualize the correct answer. This allows the person to narrow the search for the correct option and identify the distractors. Of course this visualization tip is most useful for students who have used this book to thoroughly review the economic content.

Example

The profit-maximizing monopolist sets output where:

> Before you even look at the options, you should know that the answer is "MR = MC." Find that option, and then quickly confirm to yourself that the others are indeed wrong.

3. *Never say never.* Words like "never" and "always" are called absolute qualifiers. If these words are used in one of the choices, it is rarely the correct choice.

Example

Which of the following is true about production in the short run?

A. MP is always greater than AP.
B. MP is never increasing.

> If you can think of any situation where the statements in (A) and (B) are untrue, then you have discovered distractors and can eliminate these as valid choices.

4. *Easy is as easy does.* It's exam day and you're all geared up to set this very difficult test on its ear. The first question looks like a no-brainer. Of course! The answer is 7, choice C. But rather than smiling at the satisfaction that you knew the answer, you doubt yourself. Could it be that easy? Sometimes they are just that easy.

5. *Sometimes a blind squirrel finds an acorn.* Should you guess? If you have no clue which choice is correct, guessing is a no-lose strategy. Even with a wild guess, you have a 20 percent chance of getting it right. If you leave it blank, you have no chance. I am sure that you can do the math.

6. *Draw it, nail it.* Many questions can be easily answered if you do a quick sketch in the margins of your test book. Hey, you paid for that test book; you might as well use it.

Example

In the market for new automobiles, a normal good, a decrease in consumer income will cause output and the price to change in which of the following ways?

	OUTPUT	PRICE
(A)	No change	Increase
(B)	Decrease	Decrease
(C)	Increase	No change
(D)	No change	No change
(E)	No change	Decrease

These types of questions are particularly difficult because the answer requires two ingredients. First, it requires a very thorough understanding of the demand and supply model, and here is where your graph comes in. Second, you must be able to determine how an event like lower consumer income affects the market for a normal good. The first thing you should do is quickly draw the situation given to you in the question: the market for automobiles. Show a downward-sloping demand curve shifting to the left and you can see that option (B) is correct. The graph speaks for itself.

7. *Come back, come back!* There are 60 questions and none of these is worth more than the other. If you are struggling with a particular question, circle it in your exam book and move on. Another question deeper into the exam might jog a memory of a theory you studied or something you learned from a practice exam in this book. You can then go back and quickly slay the beast. But if you spend a ridiculous amount of time on one question, you will feel your confidence and your time slipping away. This leads to my last tip.

8. *Timing is everything, kid.* You have about 70 seconds of time for each of the 60 questions. Keep an eye on your watch as you pass the halfway point. If you are running out of time and you have a few questions left, skim them for the easy (and quick) ones so that the rest of your scarce time can be devoted to those that need a little extra reading or thought.

Other things to keep in mind:

- Take the extra half of a second required to clearly fill in the bubbles.
- Don't smudge anything with sloppy erasures. If your eraser is smudgy, ask the proctor for another.
- Absolutely, positively check that you are bubbling the same line on the answer sheet as the question you are answering. I suggest that every time you turn the page you double-check that you are still lined up correctly.

Section II: Free-Response Questions

Your score on the FRQs amounts to one-third of your grade, and as a longtime reader of essays, I assure you there is no other way to score highly than to know your stuff. While you can guess on a multiple-choice question and have a one-in-five chance of getting the correct answer, there is no room for guessing in this section. There are, however, some tips that you can use to enhance your FRQ scores.

1. *Easy to read = easy to grade.* Organize your responses around the separate parts of the question and clearly label each part of your response. In other words, do not hide your answer; make it easy to find and easy to read. It helps you, and it helps the reader see where you're going. *Trust me, helping the reader can never hurt.* This leads to a related tip: Write in English, not Sanskrit. Even the most levelheaded and unbiased reader has trouble keeping their patience while struggling to read sloppy handwriting. I have seen three readers spend almost 10 minutes using the Rosetta stone to decipher a paragraph of text that was obviously written by a time-traveling student from the Byzantine Empire.

2. *Consistently wrong can be good.* The free-response questions are written in several parts, each building upon the first. If you are looking at an eight-part question, it can be scary. However, these questions are graded so that you can salvage several points even if you do not correctly answer the first part. The key thing for you to know is that you must be consistent, even if it is consistently wrong. For example, you might be asked to draw a graph showing a monopolist who has chosen the profit-maximizing level of output. Following sections might ask you to label the price, economic profit, consumer surplus, and deadweight loss—each being determined by the choice of output. So let's say you draw your diagram, but you label an incorrect level of output. Obviously you

are not going to receive that point. But if you proceed by labeling price, economic profit, consumer surplus, and deadweight loss correctly at your *incorrect* quantity, you would be surprised how forgiving the grading rubric can be.

3. *Have the last laugh with a well-drawn graph.* There are some points that require an explanation (i.e., "Describe how . . ."). Not all free-response questions require a graph, but a garbled paragraph of explanation can be saved with a perfect graph that tells the reader you know the answer to the question. This does not work in reverse.

4. *If I say draw, you better draw, Tex.* There are what readers call "graphing points," and these cannot be earned with a well-written paragraph. For example, if you are asked to draw the monopoly scenario described above, certain points will be awarded for the graph and only the graph. A delightfully written and entirely accurate paragraph of text will not earn the graphing points. You also need to clearly label graphs. You might think that downward-sloping line is obviously a demand curve, but some of those graphing points will not be awarded if lines and points are not clearly, and accurately, identified. And please, *please*, draw your graph larger than a postage stamp. If the reader cannot clearly see the important aspects of the graph, you will not earn those points.

5. *Give the answer, not a dissertation.* There are some parts of a question where you are asked to simply "identify" something. For example, "Identify the price if this firm were a monopolist" or "Identify the area that corresponds to deadweight loss." This type of question requires a quick piece of analysis that can literally be answered in one word or number. That point will be given if you provide that one word or number whether it is the only word you write or the fortieth that you write. For example, you might be given a table that shows how a firm's output changes as it hires more workers. One part of the question asks you to identify the optimal number of workers that the firm should hire. Suppose the correct answer is 4. The point is given if you say "4," "four," and maybe even "iv." If you write a 500-word Magna Carta concluding with the word "four," you will get the point but will have wasted precious time. This brings me to . . .

6. *Welcome to the magical kingdom.* If you surround the right answer to a question with a paragraph of economic wrongness, you will usually get the point, so long as you say the magic word. The only exception is a direct contradiction to the right answer. For example, suppose that when asked to *identify* the optimal number of workers, you spend a paragraph describing how the workers are unionized and therefore are subject to a price ceiling and that the exchange rate between those workers and the production possibility frontier means the answer is four. You will get the point! You said they should hire four, and "four" were the magic words. However, if you say that the answer is four, but that it is also five and on Mondays it is seven, you have contradicted yourself and the point will not be given.

7. *Marginally speaking.* This point is made throughout the microeconomics review contained in this book, but it bears repeating here as a valuable test-taking strategy. In economics, anything that is optimal or efficient or rational or cost minimizing or profit maximizing can be answered by telling the reader that the marginal benefits must equal the marginal costs. Depending on the situation, you might have to clarify that "marginal benefit" to the firm is "marginal revenue" or to the employer "marginal revenue product." If the question asks you *why* the answer is four, there is always a very short phrase that readers look for so that they may award the point. This answer often includes the appropriate marginal comparison.

8. *Identify, Illustrate, Define, Indicate, and Explain.* Each part of a free-response question includes a prompt that tells you what the reader will be looking for so that the points can be awarded. If the question asks you to "identify" something, you may need only one word or a short phrase to receive all the points. Writing a paragraph here will only waste your time. As mentioned, any reference to "illustrate" will require you to draw, or redraw, a graph to receive points. If the question asks you to "define" a concept, you will need to devote more time to providing your best definition of that concept. If you are prompted to "indicate" something, you must simply state what is expected to happen. For example, suppose you are told that a price floor has been installed in the market for soybeans and you are asked to indicate what will happen to deadweight loss. All you need to do to earn the point is indicate that deadweight loss will increase. You may also get the point if you clearly indicate, preferably with an arrow, in a graph of the soybean market that there is now an area of deadweight loss. The most time-intensive prompt is usually one that involves "explain." Suppose you are told that the government has eliminated the minimum wage. Then you are asked to explain how this will affect wages and employment in these labor markets. To give yourself the best chance at receiving all the points, your response must provide two parts. First, give a clear statement of what exactly will happen; second, explain why it is going to happen.

Here are some other things to keep in mind:

- The free-response section begins with a 10-minute reading period. Use this time well to jot down some quick notes to yourself so that when you actually begin to respond, you will have a nice start.
- The first parts of the free-response questions are the easiest parts. Spend just enough time to get these points before moving on to the more difficult sections.
- The questions are written in logical order. If you find yourself explaining Part C before responding to Part B, back up and work through the logical progression of topics.
- Abbreviations are your friends. You can save time by using commonly accepted abbreviations for economic variables and graphical curves, and you will get more adept at their use as your mastery improves. For example, in macroeconomics you can save some time by using "OMO" rather than "open market operation," and in microeconomics you can use "MRP" rather than "marginal revenue product."
- Show your work. In recent years, the exam has included more mathematical components that allow you to demonstrate that you know a particular economic concept by computing something. Virtually all these problems include the prompt "show your work," and you will *not* earn points if you have not set up the mathematical problem correctly and shown your work clearly. For example, suppose that price is $5 and 10 units are sold at this price; you are asked to compute total revenue and show your work. You know that total revenue (P × Q) is obviously $50, but if you simply state that total revenue is $50, you will not earn the point, because you did not show your work. The simple fix for this is to write: $TR = P \times Q = \$5 \times 10 = \$50$. Point earned!

STEP 4

Review the Knowledge You Need to Score High

CHAPTER 5

Fundamentals of Economic Analysis

IN THIS CHAPTER

Summary: If there are two concepts that you should have down pat, they are (1) scarce resources require decision makers to make decisions that involve costs and benefits and (2) these decisions are best made when the additional benefits of the action are exactly offset by the additional costs of the action. This chapter presents material that, at least on the surface, appears to be "Econ-lite." Some readers might make the mistake of simply glossing over it on the way to meatier topics. I urge you to take the time to reinforce these early concepts, for they should, like a bad earworm, stick in your subconscious throughout your preparation for the AP exam.

Key Ideas
- ✪ Scarcity
- ✪ Opportunity Cost
- ✪ Marginal Analysis
- ✪ Cost-Benefit Analysis
- ✪ Production Possibilities
- ✪ Functions of Economic Systems

5.1 Scarce Resources

Main Topics: *Economic Resources, Scarcity, Trade-Offs, Opportunity Cost, Cost-Benefit Analysis, Marginal Analysis*

Economic Resources

Economics is the study of how people, firms, and societies use their scarce productive resources to best satisfy their unlimited material wants.

Resources, or factors of production, are commonly separated into four groups:

- *Labor.* Human effort and talent, physical and mental. This can be augmented by education and training (human capital).
- *Land* or *natural resources.* Any resource created by nature. This may be arable land, mineral deposits, oil and gas reserves, or water.
- *Physical capital.* Human-made equipment like machinery as well as buildings, roads, vehicles, and computers.
- *Entrepreneurial ability.* The effort and know-how to put the other resources together in a productive venture.

Scarcity

All of the above resources are scarce, or in limited supply. Since productive resources are scarce, it makes sense that the production of goods and services must be scarce.

Example:

Sometimes it is easier to see this if you look at the production of something familiar, like the production of a term paper:

- *Labor.* Your hours of research, writing, and rewriting. As we all know, these hours are scarce, or limited to the number of waking hours in the day.
- *Land/natural resources.* Paper (trees) and electricity (rivers, coal, natural gas, wind, solar). Not only are these in scarce supply, but your ability to acquire these resources is also limited by your income, which is a result of using some of your scarce labor hours to work for a wage.
- *Capital.* Your computer, printer, desk, pens and pencils, and the library and sources within it.
- *Entrepreneurial ability.* The skill it takes to compile the research into a coherent, thoughtful, and articulate piece of academic work.

Trade-Offs

The fact that we are faced with scarce resources implies that individuals, firms, and governments are constantly faced with trade-offs.

Individuals

Consumers choose between housing arrangements (Do I rent an apartment or buy a home?), transportation options, grocery store items, and many other daily purchases. Workers and students must choose from a wide range of employment opportunities. (Do I pick up an extra shift? Do I pursue my MBA or PhD?)

Firms

For the firm, decisions are often centered on which good or service can be provided, how much should be produced, and how to go about producing those goods and services.

A local restaurant considers whether or not to stay open later on Saturday night. A steel company must decide whether to open a steel plant in Indiana or Indonesia.

Governments

Every society, in one form or another, places many tough decisions in the hands of government, both local and national. Not surprisingly, local government is faced with issues that are likely to have an immediate impact on the lives of local citizens. (Should we use tax revenues to pave potholes in the streets or buy a new city bus?) At the national level, not all citizens would feel the impact immediately, but the stakes are likely much higher. (Should we open protected wilderness areas to oil and gas exploration? Should we impose a tariff on imported rice?)

Regardless of the decision maker—individual, firm, or government—the reality of scarce resources creates a trade-off between the opportunity that is taken and the opportunity that was not taken and thus forgone. The value of what was given up is called the **opportunity cost**.

Opportunity Cost

At the most basic level, the opportunity cost of doing something is all that you sacrifice to do it. In other words, if you use a scarce resource to pursue activity X, the opportunity cost of activity X is activity Y, the next best use of that resource. In the next section of this chapter, we will discuss costs in a little more detail.

> **Example:**
> You have one scarce hour to spend between studying for an exam or working at a coffee shop for $8 per hour. If you study, the opportunity cost of studying is $8.

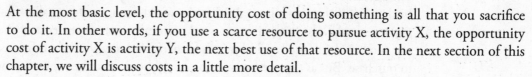

> **Example:**
> You have one scarce hour to spend between studying for an exam or working at a coffee shop for $8 per hour or mowing your uncle's lawn for $10 per hour. If you choose to study, what is the opportunity cost of studying?

Be careful! A common mistake is to add up the value of *all* your other options ($18), but this misses an important point. In this scenario, and in many others, you have one hour to allocate to one activity, thus giving up the others. By choosing to study, you really only gave up one thing: mowing the lawn *or* serving cappuccinos, not both.

The opportunity cost of using your resource to do activity X is the value the resource would have in its *next best alternative use*. Therefore, the opportunity cost of studying is $10, the better of your two alternatives.

At this point, you might be wondering, "Does everything have a dollar figure attached to it? Can't we just enjoy something without slapping a price tag on it?"

This is an excellent question, and the concept can often be a difficult point to explain. If you have one scarce hour and you could either work at the coffee shop for $8 or take a restful nap, the opportunity cost of working is the nap, which certainly has value. How can we place a dollar value on the nap? Maybe you are giving serious thought to taking the nap, but your employer at the coffee shop really needs you to work. Maybe your employer offers you $10 to forgo the nap and come to work. After some consideration, you still choose the nap. Surely there is a price (the wage) that would be high enough to entice you to come to work at the coffee shop. If your employer offered you just enough to compensate you for the nap you gave up, you have found the value that you placed on the nap.

Cost-Benefit Analysis

Many people, even those who aren't studying economics (gasp!), make decisions by weighing the costs of an action against the benefits of that action. This process is called **cost-benefit analysis**. For example, Melanie is thinking about buying a ticket to an outdoor music festival. There are many questions that she must answer before making a decision to buy, or not to buy, the ticket. Can she afford the cost of the ticket? If she takes some time off from her job, how much in earnings will she give up? Will the musical performers live up to expectations? Will the weather be nice, or is it likely to be stormy and ruin the experience? These questions address the costs and the benefits of attending the festival. Let's explore the costs first.

Total Cost

The total cost of doing something is the value of all things given up to do that thing. These costs can come in two categories: explicit and implicit.

Explicit Costs

The explicit costs of a decision are the direct out-of-pocket expenses of making that decision. In the case of the music festival, Melanie would need to add up all of the money she would pay to attend. These explicit costs would typically include the cost of the ticket, gas for her car, food or drink she would buy while there, and any shirts or other souvenirs she expects to purchase. But as the previous section of the book describes, there are other costs involved.

Implicit Costs

The implicit costs of making a decision is the value of the next best thing you could have done. For example, if Melanie is taking Friday off from her job so that she can go to the festival, any lost wages would be an implicit cost of the decision to attend. We will talk more about explicit and implicit costs in Chapter 8 when we discuss firms that incur costs in producing their goods and services.

When we add up all of the explicit and implicit costs of a decision, like attending the music festival, we have the total cost of that decision.

Total Benefit

The total benefit of a decision really depends on the person making the decision and their personal evaluation of how much enjoyment they expect to receive. One way to conduct this evaluation is to ask yourself, "What is the absolute most money I would pay to take this action?" In the case of the music festival, Melanie would look at the performers, the venue, and maybe the weather forecast, and determine the highest dollar value she would ever consider paying to attend. Economists also describe this maximum price as a person's **willingness to pay**.

The Decision

So, should Melanie attend the music festival? If she is making this decision using cost-benefit analysis, she will carefully add up all of the costs of attending, and then evaluate her willingness to pay for attending and compare it to the total costs. She will choose to attend if her total benefit (willingness to pay) is greater than or equal to her total cost. If it is not, then she will not make the decision to attend.

- When making a decision, a person will choose something—let's call it Z—if the total benefit of Z is greater than or equal to the total cost of Z.

- If the total cost of Z is greater than the total benefit of Z, a person will not choose Z.

Marginal Analysis

Another way of making decisions is to weigh the costs and benefits of doing, or consuming, "the next one." You have one cup of coffee and are deciding whether to have another (the next one). You have studied five hours for an economics exam and need to decide if it is in your best interest to study another hour (the next one).

These decisions are said to be made at the margin. The next cup of coffee brings with it *additional* benefits to the consumer, but comes at *additional* costs. The rational consumer weighs the additional benefits against the additional costs.

Marginal: "the next one," or "additional," or "incremental."

This concept is seen throughout economics and we cover it throughout this book, but let's briefly look at **marginal analysis** from a consumer's point of view.

Marginal cost (MC): The additional cost incurred from the consumption of the next unit of a good or service.

Marginal benefit (MB): The additional benefit received from the consumption of the next unit of a good or service. Another way of measuring marginal benefit is to ask yourself, "How much would I pay for the next unit of this good?"

Example:

The soda machine down the hall charges me $1 for every can of pop. The decision to buy another soda is another example of marginal analysis. If I expect to receive at least $1 in additional benefit, or if I am willing to pay $1 or more to have it, buying another soda is a rational decision. This decision can be seen in Figure 5.1.

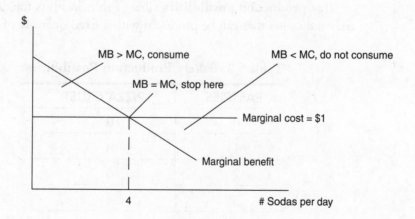

Figure 5.1

So how many sodas will I consume in a typical day? For each of the first three sodas, my MB > $1, the marginal cost of the next soda. The fourth soda provides me with exactly $1 in marginal benefit, so I find it exactly worth my while to buy it. The fifth soda is not bought because the MC > MB. Notice that my MB declines as I consume more sodas. This is a fairly predictable relationship, since I am likely to enjoy my first soda of the day more than my fifth.

Rule:

Do something if the marginal benefits ≥ marginal costs of doing it.

Stop doing something when the marginal benefits = marginal costs of doing it.

Never do something when the marginal benefits < marginal costs of doing it.

You will find this to be true in consumption, production, hiring, and many other economic decisions.

5.2 Production Possibilities

Main Topics: *Production Possibilities Curve, Resource Substitutability, Law of Increasing Costs, Comparative Advantage and Specialization, Efficiency, Growth*

Production Possibilities Curve

To examine production and opportunity cost, economists find it useful to create a simplified model of an individual, or a nation, that can choose to allocate its scarce resources between the production of two goods or services. For now we assume that those resources are being fully employed and used efficiently.

Example:

The owner of a small bakery can allocate a fixed amount of labor (the chef and her helpers), capital (mixers, pans, and ovens), natural resources (raw materials), and her entrepreneurial talent toward the production of pastries and pizza crusts.

The **production possibilities** table (Table 5.1) lists the different combinations of pastries and crusts that can be produced with a fixed quantity of scarce resources.

Table 5.1 Bakery Production Possibilities

PASTRIES	PIZZA CRUST
0	10
1	8
2	6
3	4
4	2
5	0

If the chef wishes to produce one more pastry, she must give up two pizza crusts. If she wishes one more crust, she must give up one-half of a pastry.

In other words:

The opportunity cost of a pastry is two crusts.
The opportunity cost of a pizza crust is one-half of a pastry.

We can graphically depict Table 5.1 in a **production possibility curve**. Each point on the curve represents some maximum output combination of the two products. Some refer to this curve as a **production possibility frontier** because it reflects the outer limit of production. Any point outside the frontier (e.g., 4, 8) is currently unattainable and any point inside the frontier (e.g., 1, 2) fails to use all the bakery's available resources in an efficient way. We talk more about efficiency at the end of this section.

So here you might wonder, "Why is there a limit to the production of these goods? In other words, why doesn't the frontier just expand to allow an unlimited amount of either?"

Over the course of time, the frontier is believed to expand. But at any given point in time, we must confront the scarcity problem again. The resources used to produce these goods are scarce, and thus, the production frontier is going to act as a binding constraint. The concept of economic growth is introduced in this chapter and also discussed in the macroeconomics course, but for the time being, the frontier looks like Figure 5.2.

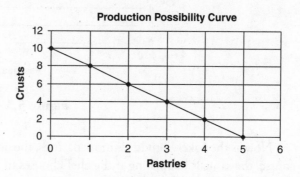

Figure 5.2

The opportunity cost of each good is also apparent in the slope of the production possibility curve itself. We ignore the fact that the curve slopes downward and simply focus on its magnitude, or absolute value.

- The slope of the curve, 2 in our case, measures the opportunity cost of the good on the *x*-axis.
- The inverse of the slope, ½ in our case, measures the opportunity cost of the good on the *y*-axis.

Notice that with a straight line, the opportunity cost of producing more of each good is always a constant. Is this realistic?

Resource Substitutability

Suppose our bakery chef is currently producing 10 pizza crusts and zero pastries. But today she decides that she should produce one pastry and eight crusts. In Figure 5.2, this decision appears fairly straightforward.

What we often forget is that resources must be reallocated from pizza crust production to pastry production. Labor, capital, and natural resources must be removed from crust production and moved into pastry production.

Perhaps some of the capital (i.e., pans) in the bakery are better suited to pizza crust production than pastry production. Certainly raw materials like chocolate and frosting are not very useful for pizza crust production but are extremely valuable to pastry production.

The same could be said for individual laborers. Maybe the entrepreneur herself was trained as a French pastry chef and can make pizza crusts but not as well as she can make éclairs. The fact that these resources are better suited to the production of one good, and less easily adaptable to the production of the other good, gives us the concept of . . .

Law of Increasing Costs

The **law of increasing costs** tells us that the more of a good that is produced, the greater its opportunity cost. This reality gives us a production possibility curve that is concave, or *bowed outward*, as seen in Figure 5.3.

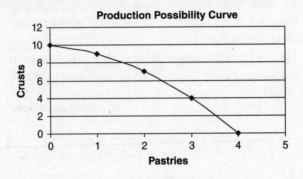

Figure 5.3

Now as the bakery produces more pastries, the opportunity cost (slope) begins to rise. Of course, the same is happening if the chef chooses to produce more crusts. Because resources are not perfectly adaptable to alternative uses, our production possibility curve is unlikely to be linear and will probably become steeper as production moves downward along the curve.

Comparative Advantage and Specialization

I went to the dentist's office the other day. For 30 minutes the dental hygienist took an x-ray, and then cleaned and flossed my teeth. When she was done, the dentist popped in, peeked at her handiwork, studied my x-ray, and sent me on my way with a new toothbrush. Why did my dentist let the hygienist do all the cleaning and flossing, when she is perfectly capable of doing the task? Because the dentist's scarce time resource is better used performing tasks like oral surgery. The opportunity cost of the dentist flossing my teeth is the revenue earned from a procedure that only she is qualified to perform. Forgoing the revenue from the oral surgery is avoided by assigning the cleaning tasks to the hygienist, whose specialty is oral hygiene but not oral surgery.

The law of increasing costs tells us that it becomes more costly to produce a good as you produce more of it. This reality prompts us to find other, less expensive ways to get our hands on additional units. The concepts of **specialization** and **comparative advantage** describe the way that individuals, nations, and societies can acquire more goods at lower cost.

Example:

Suppose our bakery, which can produce both pizza crust and pastries, shares the local market with a pizza parlor. The pizza parlor can also produce pastries, but it might rather produce pizza crusts. Each firm would like to produce more goods at lower cost. Table 5.2 shows the production possibilities of these two firms and the opportunity costs of producing more of each good. To make things simpler, we assume that both businesses have access to the same economic resources.

Table 5.2 Production Possibilities and Opportunity Costs

BAKERY		PIZZA PARLOR	
Pastries	Crusts	Pastries	Crusts
10	0	5	0
0	5	0	10
OPPORTUNITY COSTS		OPPORTUNITY COSTS	
1 pastry costs	1 crust costs	1 pastry costs	1 crust costs
½ crust	2 pastries	2 crusts	½ pastry

Because the bakery can produce more pastries than the pizza parlor, the bakery has **absolute advantage** in pastry production. The pizza parlor has absolute advantage in crust production. Simply being able to produce more of a good does not mean that the firm produces that good at a lower opportunity cost.

Both producers could produce pastries, but the bakery can produce pastries at lower opportunity cost (0.5 crusts versus 2 crusts). The bakery is said to have **comparative advantage** in the production of pastries. Likewise, the table illustrates that the pizza parlor has the comparative advantage in pizza crusts (0.5 pastries versus 2 pastries). These producers can, and indeed should, **specialize** by producing only pastries at the bakery and only crusts at the pizza parlor. Because these firms are specializing and producing at lower cost, not only do they benefit by earning more profit, but consumers across town also benefit from purchasing goods at lower prices.

In microeconomics, the principle of comparative advantage explains why the pediatrician delivers the babies while the electrician wires the house and not the other way around. In macroeconomics, this principle is the basis for showing how nations can gain from free trade. To see the microeconomics gains from specialization, we do a game called "before and after."

Before. Each firm devotes half of its resources to pastry production and half to crust production.

Total citywide pastry production =   5 + 2.5 = 7.5
Total citywide crust production = 2.5 + 5   = 7.5

After. Each firm specializes in the production of the good for which it has comparative advantage.

Total citywide pastry production = 10 +   0 = 10
Total citywide crust production =   0 + 10 = 10

Figure 5.4 shows both production possibility frontiers and how a combination of 10 crusts and 10 pastries (specialization) was previously unattainable and is superior to when each firm produced at the midpoint (50/50) of their individual frontiers.

Another Way of Determining Comparative Advantage

The previous example showed how a comparison of the opportunity cost of producing two outputs (pizza crusts and pastries) can determine which firm, or nation, has the comparative advantage in production of those goods. Another way of figuring out comparative advantage is to compare how many *inputs* must be sacrificed to produce different outputs.

Let's shift gears and talk about two nations that can produce both chocolate and kazoos. The table below Figure 5.4 shows how many hours of work (inputs) must be used to produce one pound of chocolate and one box of kazoos.

> "Know the different ways of showing comparative advantage. This is a potential free-response question."
> —AP Teacher

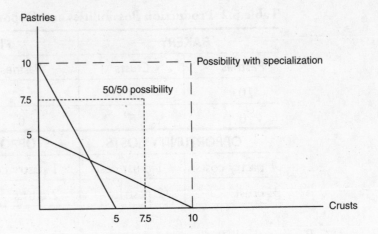

Figure 5.4

	HOURS TO PRODUCE 1 POUND OF CHOCOLATE	**HOURS TO PRODUCE 1 BOX OF KAZOOS**
Taiwan	5	1
Brazil	2	4

If Taiwan were to produce one pound of chocolate, it would take five hours, so the opportunity cost of chocolate is the five boxes of kazoos that could have been produced with those five hours of labor. On the other hand, if Brazil were to produce one pound of chocolate, it would take two hours of work, making the opportunity cost of chocolate one-half of a box of kazoos that would have taken four hours of work to complete. Since it only costs Brazil one-half of a box of kazoos to make one pound of chocolate, Brazil has comparative advantage in making chocolate.

We can quickly see that Taiwan has the comparative advantage in making kazoos. If Taiwan were to produce one box of kazoos, it would cost one-fifth of a box of chocolate. Alternatively, if Brazil produced a box of kazoos, it would cost the nation two pounds of chocolate.

If these nations were to trade based on comparative advantage, Brazil would export chocolate to Taiwan, and Taiwan would export kazoos to Brazil.

- If firms and individuals produce goods based on their comparative advantage, society gains more production at lower cost.

Efficiency

If not all available resources are being used to their fullest, the economy is operating at some point inside the production possibility frontier. This is clearly inefficient. But even if the economy is operating at some point on the frontier, who is to say that it is the point that is most desired by the citizens? If it does not happen to be the point that society most wants, we are also facing an inefficient situation.

In this production possibility model, there are two types of efficiency:

Productive efficiency. The economy is producing the maximum output for a given level of technology and resources. All points on the production possibilities frontier are productively efficient.

Allocative efficiency. The economy is producing the optimal mix of goods and services. By optimal, we mean that it is the combination of goods and services that provides the most net benefit to society. If society is allocatively efficient, it is operating at the best point on the frontier.

How do we determine which point is the best point? Remember how I determined the optimal number of sodas to consume every day? Suppose we could measure, society-wide, the marginal social benefit (MSB) received from the consumption of pizza crusts. Like my MB for sodas, the MSB for crusts is falling as more crusts are consumed. We already know that the marginal social cost (MSC) of producing pizza crusts increases. The marginal social cost of producing and marginal social benefit of consuming more pizza crusts are illustrated in Figure 5.5.

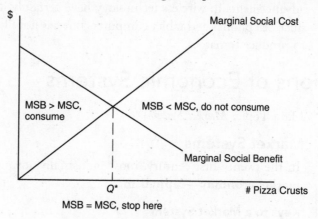

Figure 5.5

The allocatively efficient amount of pizza crusts is Q^*, the quantity where the MSB of the next crust is exactly equal to the MSC of producing it. If we produce anything beyond this point, we have created a situation where the MSC of producing it exceeds our MSB of consuming it. Clearly we should devote those resources to other goods that we desire to a greater degree and that are produced at a lower marginal social cost. Later in this book, we will see other examples of market outcomes that do not produce the allocatively efficient quantity of a good or service. When this happens, we call it a **market failure**.

Growth

At a given point in time, the bakery (or a nation's economy) cannot operate beyond the production frontier. However, as time passes, it is likely that firms and nations experience economic growth. This results in a production possibilities frontier that moves outward, expanding the set of production and consumption.

Economic growth, the ability to produce a larger total output over time, can occur if one or all of the following occur:

- An increase in the quantity of resources. For example, the bakery acquires another oven.
- An increase in the quality of existing resources. For example, the chef acquires the best assistants in the city.
- Technological advancements in production. For example, electric mixers versus hand mixers.

Figure 5.6 illustrates economic growth for the bakery.

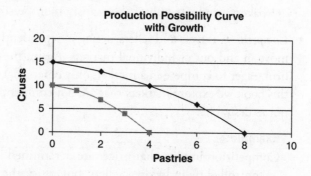

Figure 5.6

Notice that the frontier has not increased proportionally. The maximum number of crusts that could possibly be produced has increased by 50 percent, while the maximum number of pastries has increased by 100 percent.

Economic growth almost always occurs in this way. For example, technological advancements in wireless technology have certainly increased the nation's capacity to produce cell phones and tablet computers but has not likely measurably increased our capacity to produce tomatoes.

5.3 Functions of Economic Systems

Main Topic: *Market Systems*

Market Systems

In the twenty-first century, most industrially advanced nations have gravitated toward a **market economy—capitalism.**

Keys to a Market System

> "This concept, although an easy one, is a definite MC question. Don't miss it."
> —Adam, AP Student

- *Private Property.* Individuals, not government, own most economic resources. This private ownership encourages innovation, investment, growth, and trade.

  #### Example:
  If the state owned the bakery's ovens, mixers, and even the building itself, how much of an incentive would our entrepreneur have to maintain the equipment, the inventory, or even the quality of the product? Knowing that the state could take these resources with very little notice, our chef might just do the bare minimum, and if this situation happened all over town, the local economy would languish.

- *Freedom.* Individuals are free to acquire resources to produce goods and services and free to choose which of their resources to sell to others so that they may buy their own goods and services.

  #### Example:
  The bakery can freely use its resources to produce rolls, pastries, croissants, and anything else it believes leads to profitability. Of course, this freedom is limited by legal constraints. The bakery cannot sell illegal drugs from the back door, and the chef is not free to offer open-heart surgery with her bagels.

- *Self-Interest and Incentives.* Individuals are motivated by self-interest in their use of resources. Entrepreneurs seek to maximize profit while consumers seek to maximize happiness. With these incentives, goods are sold and bought.

  #### Example:
  Our bakery owner, motivated by profit, seeks to offer products that appeal to her customers. Customers, seeking to maximize their happiness, consume these bakery products only if they satisfy their personal tastes and wants.

- *Competition.* Buyers and sellers, acting independently, and motivated by self-interest, freely move in and out of individual markets. Again, the issue of incentives is powerful. A new firm, eager to compete in a market, only enters that market if profits are available. Later in this book we explore markets that are not competitive and discover that the outcomes are not as desirable.

  #### Example:
  Competition implies that prices are determined in the marketplace and not controlled by individual sellers, buyers, or the government. Our bakery owner employs labor at the going market wage, which is determined in the

competitive local labor market. She offers baked products at the going price, which is determined in the competitive local market for those goods.

- *Prices.* Prices send signals to buyers and sellers, and resource allocation decisions are made based on this information. Prices also serve to ration goods to those consumers who are most willing and able to pay those prices. Prices coordinate the decentralized economic activity of millions of individuals and firms in a way that no one central economic figure can hope to achieve. Prices, not just for goods and services but also for labor and other resources, are the delivery mechanism for the previous incentives—profit for the firm and happiness for the consumer.

Example:

As the price of labor, relative to capital, changes, the bakery chef might be motivated to readjust her employment of assistants. Changes in the relative price of her products might prompt consumers to readjust their purchasing decisions.

› Review Questions

1. Economics is best described as

   (A) the study of how scarce material wants are allocated between unlimited resources.
   (B) the study of how scarce labor can be replaced by unlimited capital.
   (C) the study of how decision makers choose the best way to satisfy their unlimited material wants with a scarce supply of resources.
   (D) the study of how unlimited material wants can best be satisfied by allocating limitless amounts of productive resources.
   (E) the study of how capitalism is superior to any other economic system.

2. A student decides that, having already spent three hours studying for an exam, she should spend one more hour studying for the same exam. Which of the following is most likely true?

   (A) The marginal benefit of the fourth hour is certainly less than the marginal cost of the fourth hour.
   (B) The marginal benefit of the fourth hour is at least as great as the marginal cost of the fourth hour.
   (C) Without knowing the student's opportunity cost of studying, we have no way of knowing whether or not her marginal benefits outweigh her marginal costs.
   (D) The marginal cost of the third hour was likely greater than the marginal cost of the fourth hour.
   (E) The marginal benefit of the third hour was less than the marginal cost of the third hour.

The island nation of Beckham uses economic resources to produce tea and crumpets. Use the following production possibilities frontier for questions 3 and 4.

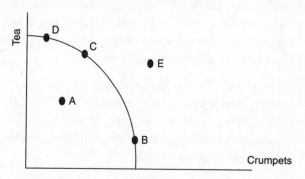

3. Economic growth is best represented by a movement from

   (A) A to B.
   (B) B to C.
   (C) C to D.
   (D) D to E.
   (E) E to A.

4. The shape of this PPF tells us that

   (A) economic resources are perfectly substitutable from production of tea to production of crumpets.
   (B) citizens prefer that an equal amount of tea and crumpets be produced.
   (C) the opportunity cost of producing crumpets rises as more crumpets are produced.
   (D) the opportunity cost of producing crumpets is constant along the curve.
   (E) the opportunity cost of producing tea falls as you produce more tea.

5. Ray and Dorothy can both cook and can both pull weeds in the garden on a Saturday afternoon. For every hour of cooking, Ray can pull 50 weeds and Dorothy can pull 100 weeds. Based on this information, how should they allocate their time?

(A) Ray pulls weeds, since he has absolute advantage in cooking.

(B) Dorothy pulls weeds, since she has absolute advantage in cooking.

(C) Dorothy cooks, since she has comparative advantage in cooking.

(D) Ray cooks, since he has comparative advantage in cooking.

(E) Dorothy pulls weeds, since she has comparative advantage in cooking.

> Answers and Explanations

1. **C**—It is important to remember that society has a limitless desire for material wants, but satisfaction of these wants is limited by scarce economic resources. Economics studies how to solve this problem in the best possible way.

2. **B**—If we observe her studying for the fourth hour, then it must be the case that the MB ≥ MC of studying for that next hour. If we observe her putting her books away and doing something else, the opposite must be true.

3. **D**—Economic growth is an outward expansion of the entire PPF. A movement from the interior to the frontier (A to B) is not growth; it just tells us that some unemployed resources (A) are now being used to their full potential (B).

4. **C**—When the PPF is concave (or bowed outward) it is an indicator of the law of increasing costs. This is a result of economic resources not being perfectly substitutable between tea and crumpets. A baking sheet used to bake crumpets might be quite useless in producing tea leaves.

5. **D**—For Ray, the opportunity cost of cooking is 50 weeds, while Dorothy's opportunity cost of cooking is 100 unpulled weeds. Ray does not pull weeds because he has comparative advantage in cooking. Dorothy does not cook because she has comparative advantage in weed pulling.

> Rapid Review

Economics: The study of how people, firms, and societies use their scarce productive resources to best satisfy their unlimited material wants.

Resources: Called factors of production, these are commonly grouped into the four categories of labor, physical capital, land or natural resources, and entrepreneurial ability.

Scarcity: The imbalance between limited productive resources and unlimited human wants. Because economic resources are scarce, the goods and services a society can produce are also scarce.

Trade-offs: Scarce resources imply that individuals, firms, and governments are constantly faced with difficult choices that involve benefits and costs.

Opportunity cost: The value of the sacrifice made to pursue a course of action.

Cost-benefit analysis: The process of weighing all of the costs of an action against all of the benefits of that action.

Total cost: The sum of the explicit and implicit costs of an action, or decision, being considered.

Explicit cost: The out-of-pocket costs of an action being considered.

Implicit cost: The cost of an action being considered, measured by the value of the next-best forgone alternative.

Total benefit: The sum of all expected enjoyment, as measured by willingness to pay, of an action being considered.

Marginal: The next unit or increment of an action.

Marginal social benefit: The additional benefit that society receives from the consumption of the next unit of a good or service.

Marginal social cost: The additional cost that society incurs from the production of the next unit of a good or service.

Marginal analysis: Making decisions based on weighing the marginal benefits and costs of that action. The rational decision maker chooses an action if the $MB \geq MC$.

Production possibilities: Different quantities of goods that an economy can produce with a given amount of scarce resources. Graphically, the trade-off between the production of two goods is portrayed as a production possibility curve or frontier (PPC or PPF).

Production possibility curve or frontier (PPC or PPF): A graphical illustration that shows the maximum quantity of one good that can be produced, given the quantity of the other good being produced.

Law of increasing costs: The more of a good that is produced, the greater the opportunity cost of producing the next unit of that good.

Absolute advantage: This exists if a producer can produce more of a good with the same quantity of resources, or the same quantity of goods with fewer resources, than all other producers.

Comparative advantage: A producer has comparative advantage if it can produce a good at lower opportunity cost than all other producers.

Specialization: When firms focus their resources on production of goods for which they have comparative advantage, they are said to be specializing.

Productive efficiency: Production of maximum output for a given level of technology and resources. All points on the PPF are productively efficient.

Market failure: A market outcome for which the quantity produced is not allocatively efficient ($MSB \neq MSC$) and either too many or too few units are produced.

Allocative efficiency: Production of the combination of goods and services that provides the most net benefit to society. The optimal quantity of a good is achieved when the MSB = MSC of the next unit. This only occurs at one point on the PPF.

Economic growth: This occurs when an economy's production possibilities increase. It can be a result of more resources, better resources, or improvements in technology.

Market economy (capitalism): An economic system based on the fundamentals of private property, freedom, self-interest, and prices.

CHAPTER 6

Demand, Supply, Market Equilibrium, and Welfare Analysis

IN THIS CHAPTER

Summary: A thorough understanding of the way in which the market system determines price and quantity pays dividends both in microeconomics and macroeconomics. In the absence of government intervention and/or externalities, the competitive market also provides the most efficient outcome for society.

Key Ideas

✪ Demand
✪ Supply
✪ Equilibrium
✪ Consumer and Producer Surplus

6.1 Demand

Main Topics: *Law of Demand, Income and Substitution Effects, The Demand Curve, Quantity Demanded Versus Demand, Determinants of Demand*

For many years now, you have understood the concept of demand. On the surface, the concept is rather simple: people tend to purchase fewer items when the price is high than they do when the price is low. This is such an intuitively appealing concept that your typical consumer cares little about the rationale and still manages to live a happy life. As someone knee-deep in reviewing to take the AP Microeconomics exam, you need to go "behind the scenes" of demand. Intuition will take you only so far; you need to know the underlying theory of what is perhaps the most widely understood, and sometimes misunderstood, economic concept.

Law of Demand

Let's get this part out of the way. The **law of demand** is commonly described as follows: *Holding all else equal* (ceteris paribus), *when the price of a good rises, consumers decrease their quantity demanded for that good.* In other words, there is an inverse, or negative, relationship between the price and the quantity demanded of a good.

"*Holding all else equal*"? Economic models—demand is just one of many such models— are simplified versions of real behavior. In addition to the price, there are many factors that influence how many units of a good consumers purchase. In order to predict how consumers respond to changes in one variable (price), we must assume that all other relevant factors are held constant. Say we observed that last month the price of orange juice fell, consumer incomes rose, the price of apple juice increased, and consumers bought more orange juice. Was this increased orange juice consumption because the price fell, because incomes rose, or perhaps because apple juice became more expensive? Maybe it increased for all these reasons. Maybe for none of these reasons. It is impossible to isolate and measure the effect of one variable (i.e., orange juice prices) on the consumption of orange juice if we do not control (hold constant) these other external factors. At the heart of the law of demand is a consumer's willingness and ability to pay the going price. If the consumer becomes more willing, or more able, to consume a good, then either the price has fallen or one of these external factors has changed. We spend more time on these demand "determinants" a little later in this chapter.

Income and Substitution Effects

One of the important factors behind the scenes of the law of demand is the economic mantra "*only relative prices matter.*" I'm sure you have heard the stories from your parents or grandparents about how the price of a cup of coffee back in the good old days was just a nickel. Today you might get the same coffee for $1.75. These prices are simply **money** (or **absolute**, or **nominal**) **prices**, and when it comes to a demand decision, a money price alone is near useless. However, if you think about the money price in terms of (1) what other goods $1.75 could buy or (2) how much of your income is absorbed by $1.75, then you're talking **relative** (or **real**) **prices**. These are what matter. The number of units of any other good Y that must be sacrificed to acquire the first good X measures the relative price of good X.

Example:

Let's keep things simple and say that you divide your $10 daily income between apple fritters at today's prices of $1 each and chocolate chip bagels at $2 each. These are the money prices of your labor and of these two yummy snacks.

Table 6.1 Money vs. Relative Prices

	MONEY PRICE		RELATIVE PRICE		SHARE OF INCOME	
	Today	Tomorrow	Today	Tomorrow	Today	Tomorrow
Fritter	$1	$2	1/2 bagel	1 bagel	1/10	1/5
Bagel	$2	$2	2 fritters	1 fritter	1/5	1/5

Today at the price of $1, the relative cost of a fritter is one-half of a bagel (see Table 6.1). Relative to your income, it amounts to one-tenth of your budget.

Tomorrow, when the price doubles to $2 per fritter, two things happen to help explain, and lay the foundation for, the law of demand:

1. The relative price of a fritter has risen to one bagel, and the relative price of a bagel has fallen from two fritters to one fritter. Since fritters are now *relatively more expensive*, we would expect you to consume more bagels and fewer fritters. This is known as the ***substitution effect***.

2. Relative to your income, the price of a fritter has increased from one-tenth to one-fifth of your budget. In other words, if you were to buy only fritters, today you can purchase 10 but tomorrow the same income would only buy you 5. This lost purchasing power is known as the ***income effect***.

- ***Substitution effect.*** The change in quantity demanded resulting from a change in the price of one good relative to the price of other goods.
- ***Income effect.*** The change in quantity demanded resulting from a change in the consumer's purchasing power (or real income).

When the price of fritters increased, both of these effects caused our consumer (you) to decrease the quantity demanded, thus predicting a response consistent with the law of demand.

So at this point you might ask, "*How would a consumer react if the prices of fritters and bagels and daily income had all doubled?*"

Since the price of fritters, relative to the price of bagels, and relative to daily income, has not changed, the consumer is unlikely to alter behavior. This is why we say that only relative prices matter.

The Demand Curve

The residents of a small midwestern town love to quench their summer thirsts with lemonade. Table 6.2 summarizes the townsfolk's daily consumption of cups of lemonade at several prices, holding constant all other factors that might influence the overall demand for lemonade. This table is sometimes referred to as a **demand schedule**.

Table 6.2 Demand Schedule for Lemonade

PRICE PER CUP ($)	QUANTITY DEMANDED (CUPS PER DAY)
.25	120
.50	100
.75	80
1.00	60
1.25	40

The values in Table 6.2 reflect the law of demand: *Holding all else equal, when the price of a cup of lemonade rises, consumers decrease their quantity demanded for lemonade.* It is often quite useful to convert a demand schedule like the one above into a graphical representation, the **demand curve** (Figure 6.1).

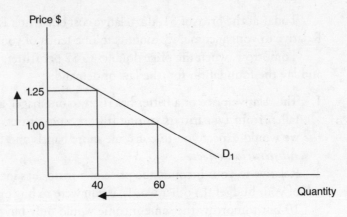

Figure 6.1

Quantity Demanded Versus Demand

The law of demand predicts a downward- (or negative-) sloping demand curve (Figure 6.1). If the price moves from $1 to $1.25 and all other factors are held constant, we observe a decrease in the *quantity demanded* from 60 to 40 cups. It is important to place special emphasis on "quantity demanded." If the price of the good changes and all other factors remain constant, the demand curve is held constant, and we simply observe the consumer moving along the fixed demand curve. If one of the external factors change, the entire demand curve shifts to the left or right. These external factors are referred to as determinants, or shifters, of demand.

Determinants of Demand

So, what are all of these factors that we insist on holding constant? These **determinants of demand** influence both the willingness and ability of the consumer to purchase units of the good or service. In addition to the price of the product itself, there are a number of variables that account for the total demand of a good like lemonade:

- Consumer income.
- The price of a substitute good such as iced tea.
- The price of a complementary good such as a Popsicle.
- Consumer tastes and preferences for lemonade.
- Consumer expectations about future prices of lemonade.
- Number of buyers in the market for lemonade.

- *Consumer Income*

Demand represents the consumer's willingness and ability to pay for a good. Income is a major factor in that "ability" to pay component. For most goods, when income increases, demand for the good increases. Thus, for these **normal goods**, increased income results in a graphical rightward shift in the entire demand curve. There are other **inferior goods**, fewer in number, where higher levels of income produce a decrease in the demand curve.

Example:
When looking to furnish a first college apartment, many students increase their demand for used furniture at yard sales. Upon graduation and employment in their first real job, new graduates increase their demand for new furniture and decrease their demand for used furniture. For them, new furniture is a normal good, while used furniture is an inferior good.

- An *increase in demand* is viewed as a *rightward shift* in the demand curve. There are two ways to think about this shift:

  a. At all prices, the consumer is willing and able to buy more units of the good. In Figure 6.2 you can see that at the constant price of $1, the quantity demanded has risen from two to three.

  b. At all quantities, the consumer is willing and able to pay higher prices for the good.

- Of course, the opposite is true of a *decrease in demand*, or *leftward shift* of the demand curve. In Figure 6.2 you can see that at the constant price of $1, the quantity demanded has fallen from two to one.

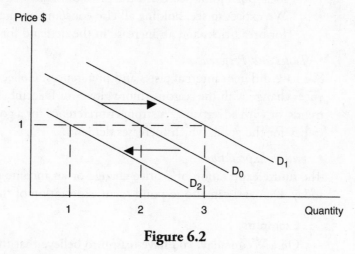

Figure 6.2

- *Price of Substitute Goods*

Two goods are substitutes if the consumer can use either one to satisfy the same essential function, therefore experiencing the same degree of happiness (utility). If the two goods are substitutes, and the price of one good X falls, the consumer demand for the substitute good Y decreases.

Example:

Mammoth State University (MSU) and Ivy Vine College (IVC) are considered substitute institutions of higher learning in the same geographical region. Ivy Vine College, shamelessly seeking to increase its reputation as an "elite" institution, increases tuition, while Mammoth State's tuition remains the same. We expect to see, holding all else constant, a decrease in quantity demanded for IVC degrees and an increase in the overall demand for MSU degrees. (See Figures 6.3 and 6.4.)

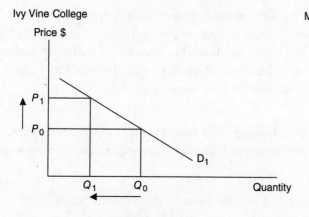

Figure 6.3

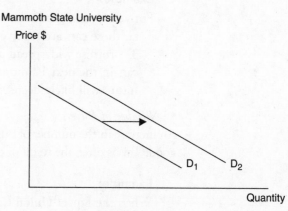

Figure 6.4

- *Price of Complementary Goods*

Two goods are complements if the consumer receives more utility from consuming them together than she would receive consuming each separately. I enjoy consuming tortilla chips by themselves, but my utility increases if I combine those chips with a complementary good like salsa or nacho cheese dip. If any two goods are complements, and the price of one good X falls, the consumer demand for the complement good Y increases.

Example:

College students love to order late-night pizza delivered to their dorm rooms. The local pizza joint decreased the price of breadsticks, a complement to the pizzas. We expect to see, holding all else constant, an increase in quantity demanded for breadsticks and an increase in the demand for pizzas.

- *Tastes and Preferences*

We have different internal tastes and preferences. Collectively, consumer tastes and preferences change with the seasons (more gloves in December, fewer lawn chairs), with fashion trends, or with advertising. A stronger preference for a good is an increase in the willingness to pay for the good, which increases demand.

- *Future Expectations*

The future expectation of a price change or an income change can cause demand to shift today. Demand can also respond to an expectation of the future availability of a good.

Example:

On a Wednesday, you have reason to believe that the price of gasoline is going to rise $.05 per gallon by the weekend. What do you do? Many consumers, armed with this expectation, increase their demand for gasoline today. We might predict the opposite behavior, a decrease in demand today, if consumers expect the price of gasoline to fall a few days from now.

Demand can also be influenced by future expectations of an income change.

Example:

One month prior to your college graduation day, you land your first full-time job. You have signed an employment contract that guarantees a specific salary, but you will not receive your first paycheck until the end of your first month on the job. This future expectation of a sizable increase in income often prompts consumers to increase their demand for normal goods now. Maybe you would start shopping for a car, a larger apartment, or several business suits.

Example:

For years, auto producers have been promising more alternative-fuel cars, but so far these cars are relatively difficult to find on dealership lots. Suppose the "Big 3" promise widespread availability of affordable electric and hydrogen fuel cell cars in the next 12 months. This expectation of increased availability in the future will likely decrease the demand for these cars today.

- *Number of Buyers*

An increase in the number of buyers, holding other factors constant, increases the demand for a good. This is often the result of demographic changes or increased availability in more markets.

Example:

When the Soviet Union fractured and the Russian government began allowing more foreign investment, corporations such as Coca-Cola, Apple, and

McDonald's found millions of new buyers for their products. Globally, the demand for colas, iPads, and burgers increased.

Example

As the average age of Americans has gradually increased, there are now more people above the age of 70 years old. This demographic change has caused an increase in the demand for prescription drugs, hip replacements, and other medical services.

6.2 Supply

Main Topics: *Law of Supply, Increasing Marginal Costs, The Supply Curve, Quantity Supplied Versus Supply, Determinants of Supply*

If there are three words that you need to have in your arsenal for the AP exams, they are "Demand and Supply," or "Supply and Demand" if you are the rebellious type. The previous section covered the demand half of this duo, and so it stands to reason that we should spend a little time studying the other side. Unlike demand, few of us have ever had up-close-and-personal experience as suppliers. Because you likely lack such personal experience with supply, it is helpful to put yourself in the shoes of someone who wishes to profit from the production and sale of a product. If something happens that would increase your chances of earning more profit, you increase your supply of the product. If something happens that will hurt your profit opportunities, you decrease your supply of the product.

Law of Supply

Drumroll, please. The **law of supply** is commonly described as follows: "*Holding all else equal (ceteris paribus), when the price of a good rises, suppliers increase their quantity supplied for that good.*" In other words, there is a direct, or positive, relationship between the price and the quantity supplied of a good.

Again, we insist on qualifying our law with the phrase "*holding all else equal.*" Similar to the *demand model,* the *supply model* is a simplified version of real behavior. In addition to the price, there are several factors that influence how many units of a good producers supply. In order to predict how producers respond to fluctuations in one variable (price), we must assume that all other relevant factors are held constant. Before we talk about these external supply determinants, let's examine what is happening behind the scenes of the law of supply.

Increasing Marginal Costs

The more you do something (e.g., a physical activity), the more difficult it becomes to do the next unit of that activity. Anyone who has run laps around a track, lifted weights, or raked leaves in the yard understands this. If you were asked to rake leaves, as more hours of raking are supplied, it becomes physically more and more difficult to rake the next hour. We also include the opportunity cost of the time involved in the raking, and you surely know that time is precious to a student. If you have a paper to write or an exam to cram for, raking leaves for an hour comes at a dear cost. In terms of forgone opportunities, the marginal cost of raking leaves rises as you postpone that paper or study session.

When we discussed production possibilities in Chapter 5, we addressed a key economic concept: as more of a good is produced, the greater is its marginal cost.

- As suppliers increase the quantity supplied of a good, they face rising marginal costs.
- As a result, they only increase the quantity supplied of that good if the price received is high enough to at least cover the higher marginal cost.

The Supply Curve

A small town has a thriving summer sidewalk lemonade stand industry. Table 6.3 summarizes the daily quantity of cups of lemonade offered for sale at several prices, holding constant all other factors that might influence the overall supply of lemonade. This table is sometimes referred to as a **supply schedule**.

Table 6.3 Supply Schedule for Lemonade

PRICE PER CUP ($)	QUANTITY SUPPLIED (CUPS PER DAY)
.25	40
.50	60
.75	80
1.00	100
1.25	120

> "Make sure on the AP test to include all labels, especially arrows." —Adam, AP Student

The values in this table reflect the law of supply: *"Holding all else equal, when the price of a cup of lemonade rises, suppliers increase their quantity supplied for lemonade."* Remember those profit opportunities? If kids can sell more cups of lemonade at a higher price, they will do so. It is often quite useful to convert a supply schedule like the one in Table 6.3 into a graphical representation, the **supply curve** (Figure 6.5).

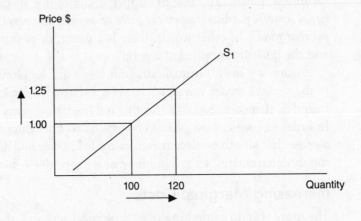

Figure 6.5

Quantity Supplied Versus Supply

> "This is an important distinction to make." —AP Teacher

The law of supply predicts an upward- (or positive-) sloping supply curve (Figure 6.5). When the price moves from $1 to $1.25, and all other factors are held constant, we observe an increase in the *quantity supplied* from 100 cups to 120 cups. Just as with demand, it is important to place special emphasis on "quantity supplied." When the price of the good changes, and all other factors are held constant, the supply curve is held constant; we simply observe the producer moving along the fixed supply curve. If one of the external factors changes, the entire supply curve shifts to the left or right. These external factors are referred to as determinants, or shifters, of supply.

Determinants of Supply

Lemonade producers are willing and able to supply more lemonade if something happens that promises to increase their profit opportunities. In addition to the price of the product itself, there are a number of variables, or **determinants of supply**, that account for the total supply of a good like lemonade:

- The cost of an input (e.g., sugar) to the production of lemonade
- Technology and productivity used to produce lemonade
- Taxes or subsidies on lemonade
- Producer expectations about future prices
- The price of other goods that could be produced
- The number of lemonade stands in the industry

- *Cost of Inputs*

If the cost of sugar, a key ingredient in lemonade, unexpectedly falls, it has now become less costly to produce lemonade, and so we should expect producers all over town, seeing the profit opportunity, to increase the supply of lemonade at all prices. This results in a graphical rightward shift in the entire supply curve.

- An *increase in supply* is viewed as a *rightward shift* in the supply curve. There are two ways to think about this shift:

    1. At all prices, the producer is willing and able to supply more units of the good. In Figure 6.6 you can see that at the constant price of $1, the quantity supplied has risen from two to three.

    2. At all quantities, the marginal cost of production is lower, so producers are willing and able to accept lower prices for the good.

- Of course, the opposite is true of a *decrease in supply*, or *leftward shift* of the supply curve. In Figure 6.6 you can see that at the constant price of $1, the quantity supplied has fallen from two to one.

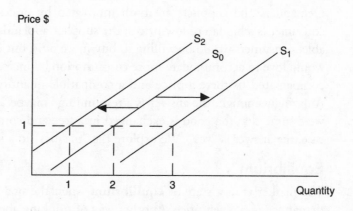

Figure 6.6

- *Technology or Productivity*

A technological improvement usually decreases the marginal cost of producing a good, thus allowing the producer to supply more units, and is reflected by a rightward shift in the supply curve. If kids all over town began using electric lemon squeezers rather than their sticky bare hands, the supply of lemonade would increase.

- *Taxes and Subsidies*

A per-unit tax is treated by the firm as an additional cost of production and would therefore decrease the supply curve, or shift it leftward. Mayor McScrooge might impose a 25-cent tax on every cup of lemonade, decreasing the entire supply curve. A subsidy is essentially the anti-tax, or a per-unit gift from the government because it lowers the per-unit cost of production. In the next chapter we will look more closely at how taxes and subsidies affect markets.

- *Price Expectations*

A producer's willingness to supply today might be affected by an expectation of tomorrow's price. If it were the 2nd of July and lemonade producers expected a heat wave and a 4th of July parade in two days, they might hold back some of their supply today and hope to sell it at an inflated price on the holiday. Thus, today's quantity supplied at all prices would decrease.

- *Price of Other Outputs*

Firms can use the same resources to produce different goods. If the price of a milkshake were rising and profit opportunities were improving for milkshake producers, the supply of lemonade in a small town would decrease and the quantity of supplied milkshakes would increase.

- *Number of Suppliers*

When more suppliers enter a market, we expect the supply curve to shift to the right. If several of our lemonade entrepreneurs are forced by their parents to attend summer camp, we would expect the entire supply curve to move leftward. Fewer cups of lemonade would be supplied at each and every price.

6.3 Market Equilibrium

Main Topics: *Equilibrium, Shortage, Surplus, Changes in Demand, Changes in Supply, Simultaneous Changes in Demand and Supply*

Demanders and suppliers are both motivated by prices, but from opposite camps. The consumer is a big fan of low prices; the supplier applauds high prices. If a good were available, consumers would be willing to buy more of it, but only if the price is right. Suppliers would love to accommodate more consumption by increasing production but only if justly compensated. Is there a price and a compatible quantity where both groups are content? Amazingly enough, the answer is a resounding "maybe." Discouraged? Don't be. For now we assume that the good is exchanged in a free and competitive market, and if this is the case, the answer is "yes." We explore the "maybes" in a later chapter.

Equilibrium

The market is in a state of **equilibrium** when the quantity supplied equals the quantity demanded at a given price. Another way of thinking about equilibrium is that it occurs at the quantity where the price expected by consumers is equal to the price required by suppliers. So if suppliers and demanders are, for a given quantity, content with the price, the market is in a state of equilibrium. If there is pressure on the price to change, the market has not yet reached equilibrium. Let's combine our lemonade tables from the earlier sections in Table 6.4.

Table 6.4 Combining Demand and Supply Schedules

PRICE PER CUP ($)	QUANTITY DEMANDED (CUPS PER DAY)	QUANTITY SUPPLIED (CUPS PER DAY)	$Q_d - Q_s$	SITUATION	PRICE SHOULD
.25	120	40	80	Shortage	Rise
.50	100	60	40	Shortage	Rise
.75	80	80	0	Equilibrium	Be Stable
1.00	60	100	−40	Surplus	Fall
1.25	40	120	−80	Surplus	Fall

At a price of 75 cents, the daily quantity demanded and quantity supplied are both equal to 80 cups of lemonade. The equilibrium (or market clearing) price is therefore 75 cents per cup. In Figure 6.7 the equilibrium price and quantity are located where the demand curve intersects the supply curve. Holding all other demand and supply variables constant, there exists no other price where $Q_d = Q_s$.

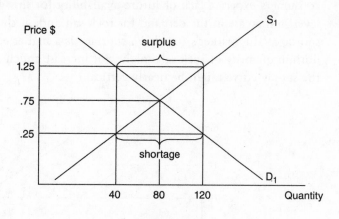

Figure 6.7

Shortage

A **shortage** exists at a market price when the quantity demanded exceeds the quantity supplied. This is why a shortage is also known as **excess demand**. At prices of 25 cents and 50 cents per cup, you can see the shortage in Figure 6.7. Remember that consumers love low prices so the quantity demanded is going to be high. However, suppliers are not thrilled to see low prices and therefore decrease their quantity supplied. At prices below 75 cents per cup, lemonade buyers and sellers are in a state of **disequilibrium**. The disparity between what the buyers want at 50 cents per cup and what the suppliers want at that price should remedy itself. Thirsty demanders offer lemonade stand owners prices slightly higher than 50 cents and, receiving higher prices, suppliers accommodate them by squeezing lemons. With competition, the shortage is eliminated at a price of 75 cents per cup.

Surplus

A **surplus** exists at a market price when the quantity supplied exceeds the quantity demanded. This is why a surplus is also known as **excess supply**. At prices of $1 and $1.25 per cup, you can see the surplus in Figure 6.7. Consumers are reluctant to purchase as much lemonade as suppliers are willing to supply and, once again, the market is in disequilibrium. To entice more consumers to buy lemonade, lemonade stand owners offer slightly discounted cups of lemonade and buyers respond by increasing their quantity demanded. Again, with competition, the surplus would be eliminated at a price of 75 cents per cup.

• Shortages and surpluses are relatively short-lived in a competitive market as prices rise or fall until the quantity demanded again equals the quantity supplied.

Changes in Demand

While our discussion of market equilibrium implies a certain kind of stability in both the price and quantity of a good, changing market forces disrupt equilibrium, either by shifting demand, shifting supply, or shifting both demand and supply.

"Explain your logic every time you shift a curve, no matter what!"
—Jake, AP Student

Increase in Demand

About once a winter a freak blizzard hits southern states like Georgia and the Carolinas. You can bet that the national media show video of panicked southerners scrambling for bags of rock salt and bottled water. Inevitably a reporter tells us that the price of rock salt has skyrocketed to $17 per bag. What is happening here? In Figure 6.8, the market for rock salt is initially in equilibrium at a price of $2.79 per bag. With a forecast of a blizzard, consumers expect a lack of future availability for this good. This expectation results in a feverish increase in the demand for rock salt and, at the original price of $2.79, there is a shortage. The market's cure for a shortage is a higher equilibrium price. (Note: The equilibrium quantity of rock salt might not increase much, since blizzards are short-lived and the supply curve might be nearly vertical.)

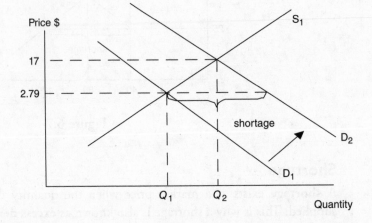

Figure 6.8

Decrease in Demand

The most recent recession was damaging to the automobile industry. When average household incomes fell in the United States, the demand for cars, a normal good, decreased. Manufacturers began offering deeply discounted sticker prices, zero-interest financing, and other incentives to reluctant consumers so that they might purchase a new car. In Figure 6.9 you can see that the original price of a new car was at P_1. Once the demand for new cars fell, there was a surplus of cars on dealer lots at the original price. The market cure for a surplus is a lower equilibrium price; ultimately, fewer new cars were bought and sold.

• When demand increases, equilibrium price and quantity both increase.
• When demand decreases, equilibrium price and quantity both decrease.

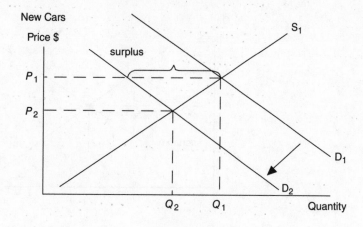

Figure 6.9

Changes in Supply

Increase in Supply

Advancements in computer technology and production methods have been felt in many markets. Figure 6.10 illustrates how, because of better technology, the supply of laptop computers has increased. At the original equilibrium price of P_1, there is now a surplus of laptops. To eliminate the surplus, the market price must fall to P_2 and the equilibrium quantity must rise to Q_2.

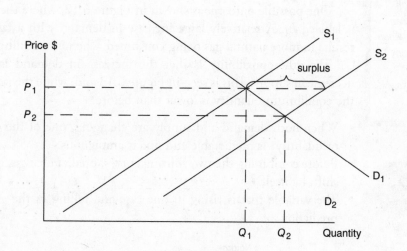

Figure 6.10

Decrease in Supply

Geopolitical conflict in the Middle East usually slows the production of crude oil. This decrease in the global supply of oil can be seen in Figure 6.11. At the original equilibrium price of P_1 per barrel, there is now a shortage of crude oil on the global market. The market eliminates this shortage through higher prices and, at least temporarily, the equilibrium quantity of crude oil falls.

- When supply increases, equilibrium price decreases and quantity increases.
- When supply decreases, equilibrium price increases and quantity decreases.

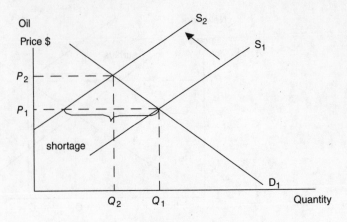

Figure 6.11

Simultaneous Changes in Demand and Supply

When both demand and supply change at the same time, predicting changes in price and quantity becomes a little more complicated. An example should illustrate how you need to be careful.

An extremely cold winter results in a higher demand for energy such as natural gas. At the same time, environmental safeguards and restrictions on drilling in protected wilderness areas have limited the supply of natural gas. An increase in demand, by itself, creates an increase in both price and quantity. However, a decrease in supply, by itself, creates an increase in price and a decrease in quantity. When these forces are combined, we see a double whammy on higher prices. But when trying to predict the change in equilibrium quantity, the outcome is uncertain and depends on which of the two effects is larger.

One possible outcome is shown in Figure 6.12, where the initial equilibrium outcome is labeled E_1. A relatively large increase in demand with a fairly small decrease in supply results in more natural gas being consumed. The new equilibrium outcome is labeled E_2.

The other possibility is that the increase in demand is relatively smaller than the decrease in supply. This is seen in Figure 6.13 and, while the price is going to increase again, the equilibrium quantity is lower than before.

> "Use different colored pens when drawing multiple curves on a single graph. This helps keep things clear when you shift many curves at a time." —Jake, AP Student

- When both demand and supply are changing, one of the equilibrium outcomes (price or quantity) is predictable and one is ambiguous.
- Before combining the two shifting curves, predict changes in price and quantity for each shift, by itself.
- The variable that is rising in one case and falling in the other case is your ambiguous prediction.

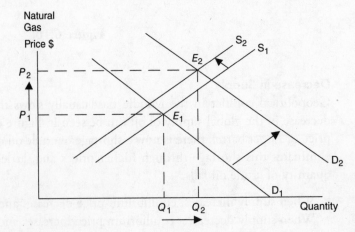

Figure 6.12

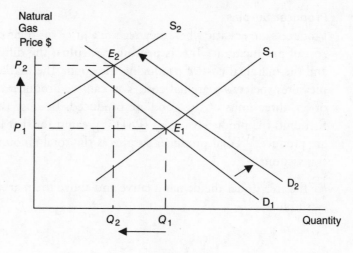

Figure 6.13

6.4 Welfare Analysis

Main Topics: *Total Welfare, Consumer Surplus, Producer Surplus*

Total Welfare

The competitive market, free of government and externalities, produces an equilibrium outcome that provides the maximum amount of total welfare for society. Society consists of all consumers and all producers and, in the marketplace, each party seeks the other so that they can make an acceptable transaction at the going market price. Each party expects to gain in these transactions. **Total welfare** is the sum of two measures of these gains: consumer surplus and producer surplus. Some textbooks, perhaps even the one you have used, refer to this sum of consumer and producer surplus as "total surplus."

Consumer Surplus

You know that great feeling you get when you pay a price that is lower than you expected, or is lower than you were willing to pay? That's **consumer surplus**, the difference between your highest willingness to pay and the price you actually pay. The market demand curve, at each quantity, measures society's marginal benefit, or willingness to pay (the price). You can see consumer surplus in Figure 6.14. At a price of $5, three units of the good are purchased. Because the highest willingness to pay is for the first unit, the area of consumer surplus (CS1) is greatest for that unit and diminishes as more units are consumed. Total consumer surplus is the total amount earned by these three consumer transactions.

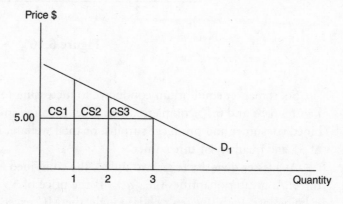

Figure 6.14

Producer Surplus

Producers are ecstatic when they receive a price for their product that is above the marginal cost of producing it. This is **producer surplus**, the difference between the price received and the marginal cost of producing the good. The market supply curve, at each quantity, measures society's marginal cost. You can see producer surplus in Figure 6.15. At a price of $5, three units of the good are produced. Because the marginal cost is lowest for the first unit, the producer surplus (PS1) is greatest for that unit and diminishes as more units are produced. Total producer surplus is the total amount earned by these three producer transactions.

- The area under the demand curve and above the market price is equal to total consumer surplus.

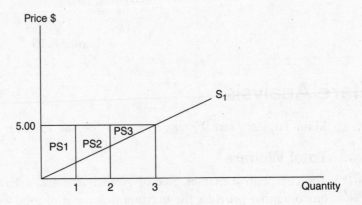

Figure 6.15

- The area above the supply curve and below the market price is equal to total producer surplus.

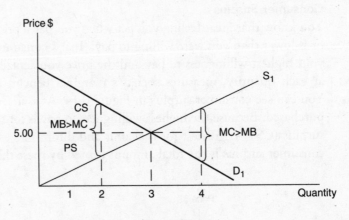

Figure 6.16

So, is market equilibrium conducive to increasing total welfare for society? Combining Figures 6.14 and 6.15 completes the market pictured in Figure 6.16. We see that the combined consumer and producer surplus, or total welfare, is greatest at the equilibrium price of $5 and quantity of three units.

At a lesser quantity (e.g., two units), the combined area is smaller than at a quantity of three. At greater quantities (i.e., $q = 4$) the price of $5 exceeds MB, so consumer surplus is being lost. If this weren't bad enough, the MC exceeds the price at $q = 4$, so producer surplus is being lost. Thus, if total welfare is falling at quantities less than three and at quantities greater than three, total welfare must be maximized at the market equilibrium quantity of three and price of $5.

A little bit of math can be a big help! Although the AP Microeconomics exam does not allow you to use a calculator, there are times when you will be required to do mathematical computations to earn points. In recent years, free-response questions have asked students to compute the area of consumer or producer surplus. It's really as simple as computing the area of a triangle: ½ × base × height. Typical exam questions will provide enough information for you to see the dimensions of the triangle (base and height) and then perform the multiplication. Let's see how this is done in the following graph.

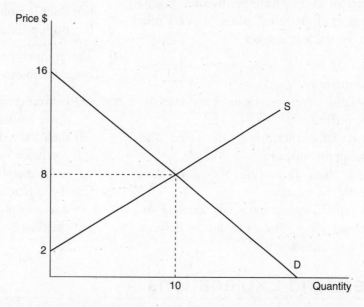

Suppose you were given this graph on a free-response question. Could you identify and compute the areas of consumer and producer surplus? It's important to remember that the consumer surplus is the area of the triangle below the demand curve and above the market price, whereas producer surplus is the area of the triangle above the supply curve and below the market price. Of course, both of these areas also depend on the equilibrium quantity, which will be the same for both triangles. Using the numbers from the graph, we compute as follows:

Consumer surplus = ½ × (10 units wide) × ($8 high) = $40

Producer surplus = ½ × (10 units wide) × ($6 high) = $30

You can now handle any similar questions on your exam.

› Review Questions

1. When the price of pears increases, we expect the following:

(A) Quantity demanded of pears rises.
(B) Quantity supplied of pears falls.
(C) Quantity demanded of pears falls.
(D) Demand for pears falls.
(E) Supply of pears rises.

2. If average household income rises and we observe that the demand for pork chops increases, pork chops must be

(A) an inferior good.
(B) a normal good.
(C) a surplus good.
(D) a public good.
(E) a shortage good.

3. Suppose that aluminum is a key production input in the production of bicycles. If the price of aluminum falls, and all other variables are held constant, we expect

   (A) the demand for aluminum to rise.
   (B) the supply of bicycles to rise.
   (C) the supply of bicycles to fall.
   (D) the demand for bicycles to rise.
   (E) the demand for bicycles to fall.

4. The market for denim jeans is in equilibrium, and the price of polyester pants, a substitute good, rises. In the jean market

   (A) supply falls, increasing the price and decreasing the quantity.
   (B) supply falls, increasing the price and increasing the quantity.
   (C) demand falls, increasing the price and decreasing the quantity.
   (D) demand rises, increasing the price and increasing the quantity.
   (E) supply and demand both fall, causing an ambiguous change in price but a definite decrease in quantity.

5. The apple market is in equilibrium. Suppose we observe that apple growers are using more pesticides to increase apple production. At the same time, we hear that the price of pears, a substitute for apples, is rising. Which of the following is a reasonable prediction for the new price and quantity of apples?

   (A) Price rises, but quantity is ambiguous.
   (B) Price falls, but quantity is ambiguous.
   (C) Price is ambiguous, but quantity rises.
   (D) Price is ambiguous, but quantity falls.
   (E) Both price and quantity are ambiguous.

6. The competitive market provides the best outcome for society because

   (A) consumer surplus is minimized, while producer surplus is maximized.
   (B) the total welfare is maximized.
   (C) producer surplus is minimized, while consumer surplus is maximized.
   (D) the difference between consumer and producer surplus is maximized.
   (E) the total cost to society is maximized.

› Answers and Explanations

1. **C**—If the price of pears rises, either quantity demanded falls or quantity supplied rises. Entire demand or supply curves for pears can shift but only if an external factor, not the price of pears, changes.

2. **B**—When income increases and demand increases, the good is a normal good. Had the demand for pork chops decreased, they would be an inferior good.

3. **B**—This is a determinant of supply. If the raw material becomes less costly to acquire, the marginal cost of producing bicycles falls. Producers increase the supply of bicycles. Recognizing this as a supply determinant allows you to quickly eliminate any reference to a demand shift.

4. **D**—When a substitute good becomes more expensive, the demand for jeans rises, increasing price and quantity.

5. **C**—Increased use of pesticides increases the supply of apples. If the price of a substitute increases, the demand for apples increases. Combining these two factors predicts an increase in the quantity of apples but an ambiguous change in price. *To help you see this, draw these situations in the margin of the exam.*

6. **B**—When competitive markets reach equilibrium, no other quantity can increase total welfare (consumer + producer surplus). Total welfare is maximized at that point.

› Rapid Review

Law of demand: Holding all else equal, when the price of a good rises, consumers decrease their quantity demanded for that good.

All else equal: To predict how a change in one variable affects a second, we hold all other variables constant. This is also referred to as the "ceteris paribus" assumption.

Absolute (or money) prices: The price of a good measured in units of currency.

Relative prices: The number of units of any other good Y that must be sacrificed to acquire the first good X. Only relative prices matter.

Substitution effect: The change in quantity demanded resulting from a change in the price of one good relative to the price of other goods.

Income effect: The change in quantity demanded that results from a change in the consumer's purchasing power (or real income).

Demand schedule: A table showing quantity demanded for a good at various prices.

Demand curve: A graphical depiction of the demand schedule. The demand curve is downward sloping, reflecting the law of demand.

Determinants of demand: The external factors that shift demand to the left or right.

Normal goods: A good for which higher income increases demand.

Inferior goods: A good for which higher income decreases demand.

Substitute goods: Two goods are consumer substitutes if they provide essentially the same utility to the consumer. A Honda Accord and a Toyota Camry might be substitutes for many consumers.

Complementary goods: Two goods are consumer complements if they provide more utility when consumed together than when consumed separately. Cars and gasoline are complementary goods.

Law of supply: Holding all else equal, when the price of a good rises, suppliers increase their quantity supplied for that good.

Supply schedule: A table showing quantity supplied for a good at various prices.

Supply curve: A graphical depiction of the supply schedule. The supply curve is upward sloping, reflecting the law of supply.

Determinants of supply: One of the external factors that influences supply. When these variables change, the entire supply curve shifts to the left or right.

Market equilibrium: Exists at the only price where the quantity supplied equals the quantity demanded. Or, it is the only quantity where the highest price consumers are willing to pay is exactly the lowest price producers are willing to accept.

Shortage: Also known as *excess demand,* a shortage exists at a market price when the quantity demanded exceeds the quantity supplied. The price rises to eliminate a shortage.

Disequilibrium: Any price where quantity demanded is not equal to quantity supplied.

Surplus: Also known as *excess supply,* a surplus exists at a market price when the quantity supplied exceeds the quantity demanded. The price falls to eliminate a surplus.

Total welfare: The sum of consumer surplus and producer surplus. The free market equilibrium provides maximum combined gain to society. This is also called total surplus.

Consumer surplus: The difference between your willingness to pay and the price you actually pay. It is the area below the demand curve and above the price.

Producer surplus: The difference between the price received and the marginal cost of producing the good. It is the area above the supply curve and under the price.

CHAPTER 7

Elasticity, Microeconomic Policy, and Consumer Theory

IN THIS CHAPTER

Summary: It is critical to remember that behind the faceless supply and demand curves are individuals making decisions. These decisions are made with the rational decision maker's best interests at the top of the agenda but are influenced by many variables. This chapter begins by focusing on how sensitive consumer decisions are to external forces and how policies might affect the market and influence those choices. It concludes by analyzing the theory behind how consumers make choices to maximize their happiness.

Key Ideas

✪ Price Elasticity of Demand
✪ Income Elasticity
✪ Cross-Price Elasticity
✪ Price Elasticity of Supply
✪ The Impact of Taxes and Subsidies
✪ The Impact of Price Controls
✪ Tariffs and Quotas
✪ Utility Maximization

7.1 Elasticity

Main Topics: *Price Elasticity of Demand, Determinants of Elasticity, Total Revenue and Elasticity, Income Elasticity, Cross-Price Elasticity of Demand, Price Elasticity of Supply*

Studying the economic concept of elasticity is much like a corporate executive workshop, the topic of which is "Sensitivity Training." When we observe a consumer's purchase decision, say for good X, change in response to a change in some external variable (the price of good X or her income), **elasticity** helps us measure the sensitivity of her consumption to that external change. We also examine the sensitivity of suppliers of good X to a change in the price of good X. We use basic mathematical relationships to measure elasticity, but it is useful to remember that all elasticity formulas measure sensitivity to a change.

Price Elasticity of Demand

The law of demand tells us that: "*All else equal, when the price of a particular good falls, the quantity demanded for that good rises.*" But what it fails to answer for us is "by how much"? Will it be a relatively large increase in quantity demanded or will it be almost negligible? In other words, we would like to measure how sensitive consumers are to a change in the price of this good.

Price Elasticity of Demand Formula

$$E_d = (\%\Delta \text{ in quantity demanded of good X})/(\%\Delta \text{ in the price of good X})$$

Note: The law of demand ensures that E_d is negative, but for ease of interpretation, economists usually ignore the fact that price elasticity of demand is negative and simply use the absolute value. The greater this ratio, the more sensitive, or responsive, consumers are to a change in the price of good X.

Range of Price Elasticity

Economists like to classify things. It's a sickness, but it is usually done for a reason. (You do need to know these for the exam.) For example, we classify price elasticities based on how sizable the reaction of consumers is to a change in the price. Rather than describing consumers as "really responsive" or "really, really responsive" or "super-duper responsive," we classify consumer responses as elastic or inelastic. The examples that follow should clarify things.

> **Example:**
>
> The price of a laptop computer increases by 10 percent, and we observe a 20-percent decrease in quantity demanded. Using the above formula:
>
> $$E_d = (-20\%)/(+10\%) = -2, \text{ or simply } E_d = 2$$

- If $E_d > 1$, demand is said to be "**price elastic**" for good X. The responsiveness of the consumer exceeded, in percentage terms, the initial change in the price.

> **Example:**
>
> The price of a package of chewing gum increases by 10 percent, and we observe a 5-percent decrease in quantity demanded. Using the above formula:
>
> $$E_d = (5\%)/(10\%) = .5$$

- If $E_d < 1$, demand is said to be "**price inelastic**" for good X. The initial change in the price exceeded, in percentage terms, the responsiveness of the consumer.

> **Example:**
>
> The price of oranges increases by 5 percent, and the quantity demanded decreases by 5 percent. Using our elasticity formula:
>
> $$E_d = (5\%)/(5\%) = 1$$

- If $E_d = 1$, demand is said to be "**unit elastic**" for good X. The initial change in the price is exactly equal to, in percentage terms, the responsiveness of the consumer.

When describing or calculating elasticity measures, you *must* use percentage changes.

Elasticity on the Demand Curve

Take a very simple demand curve for cheeseburgers: $P = 6 - Q_d$, and plot this demand curve in Figure 7.1.

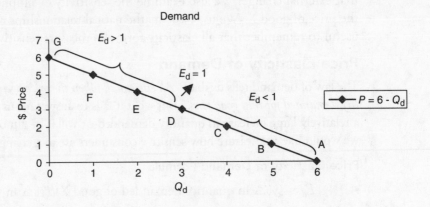

Figure 7.1

Table 7.1 summarizes changes in price, quantity demanded, and price elasticity at each point on the demand curve.*

As you can see in Figure 7.1, the price elasticity of demand is not constant at points A through G on the demand curve. Specifically, as the price rises, E_d rises, telling us that consumers are more price sensitive at higher prices than they are at lower prices. This makes good intuitive sense. When the price is relatively low (e.g., point B), a 10-percent increase in price might be almost negligible to consumers. But if the original price is quite high (point F), then a 10-percent increase in the price is pretty drastic. In fact, if we divide the demand curve in half, you can see that above the midpoint (point D), demand is price elastic and below the midpoint, demand is price inelastic. At the midpoint, demand is unit elastic.

Table 7.1 Price Elasticity at Points Along Demand

POINT	PRICE PER CHEESEBURGER	QUANTITY DEMANDED OF CHEESEBURGERS	PRICE ELASTICITY (E_d)
A	0	6	= 0
B	1	5	= .2
C	2	4	= .5
D	3	3	= 1
E	4	2	= 2
F	5	1	= 5
G	6	0	= ∞

*Note: To calculate the elasticity at each point on the demand curve in Figure 7.1, I used an equivalent way of calculating percentage change. Your AP test may or may not include similar calculations, but you do need to know how elasticity changes along a demand curve.

The Midpoint Formula

Calculating the percentage change between two prices or quantities on a demand curve is not always easy; after all, the percentage change between two values depends on which of them is the initial value. For example, if a price increases from $100 to $125, this is a 25-percent increase. If the price falls from $125 to $100, this is a 20-percent decrease. The two prices on the demand curve are the same, but the percentage change between them depends on where we begin.

To avoid some of the difficulties of calculating these types of changes, we can use what is known as the midpoint formula. Let's use P_1 and Q_1 to represent the first point on the demand curve and P_2 and Q_2 to represent the second point. The midpoint formula calculates the price elasticity of demand between those two points by using the average price (P_{avg}) and average quantity (Q_{avg}) between them. The midpoint formula is therefore

$$E_d = \left(\frac{\Delta Q_d}{\Delta P}\right) \times \left(\frac{P_{avg}}{Q_{avg}}\right)$$

Let's say that the initial price of a hypothetical product is $16, and 20 units are demanded. When the price rises to $20, quantity demanded falls to 10 units. The average price between these two points is $18, and the average quantity is 15 units. When we use the midpoint formula, we compute

$$E_d = \left(\frac{\Delta Q_d}{\Delta P}\right) \times \left(\frac{P_{avg}}{Q_{avg}}\right) = \left(\frac{10}{\$4}\right) \times \left(\frac{\$18}{15}\right) = 3.$$

Some recent AP Microeconomics exams have required the use of the midpoint formula, so it is important to be able to perform such calculations to maximize your free-response points.

Special Cases

If it is true that any increase in the price results in no decrease in the quantity demanded, then we are describing the special case where demand for the good is **perfectly inelastic.** Figure 7.2 shows the demand (D_0) for a life-saving pharmaceutical, for which there is no substitute, and without which the patient dies. The vertical demand curve tells us that no matter what percentage increase, or decrease, in price, the quantity demanded remains the same. Mathematically speaking, $E_d = 0$.

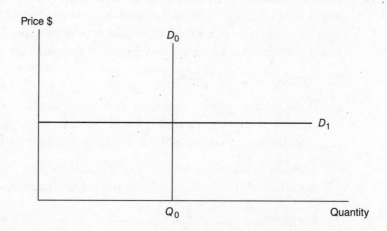

Figure 7.2

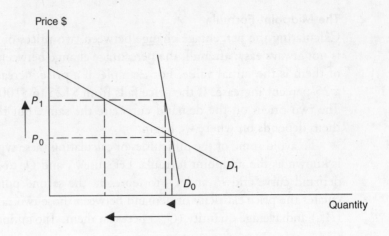

Figure 7.3

In the case where a decrease in the price causes the quantity demanded to increase without limits, then we have the special case where demand is **perfectly elastic** for that good. Figure 7.2 shows demand for a good (D_1), maybe one farmer's grain, which has many substitutes. A horizontal demand curve tells us that even the smallest percentage change in price causes an infinite change in quantity demanded. Mathematically speaking, $E_d = \infty$.

Comparing the vertical (perfectly inelastic) demand curve to the horizontal (perfectly elastic) demand curve allows us to draw an important generalization. As a demand curve becomes more vertical, the price elasticity falls and consumers become more price inelastic. The opposite generalization can be made as the demand curve becomes more horizontal. Figure 7.3 illustrates some general points about slope and elasticity. Notice that for the same price increase, the decrease in quantity demanded is much larger for the demand curve (D_1) that is closer to horizontal. This demand curve is more elastic relative to the nearly vertical (D_0) demand curve.

- In general, the more vertical a good's demand curve (D_0), the more inelastic the demand for that good.
- The more horizontal a good's demand curve (D_1), the more elastic the demand for that good.
- Despite this generalization, be careful; elasticity and slope are *not* equivalent measures.

Determinants of Elasticity

Perfectly elastic and perfectly inelastic demand curves are usually reserved for the hypothetical example, but they illustrate that E_d differs across consumer goods. Your intuition is that consumers respond to a price change in different ways. A 10-percent increase in the price of a car might have a drastically different consumer response from what we observe from a 10-percent increase in the price of a college education, a package of mechanical pencils, or a hotel stay in Fort Lauderdale. Let's look at some general explanations for why elasticity differs.

1. Number of Good Substitutes

   If the price of good X increases, and many substitutes exist, the decrease in quantity demanded can be quite elastic. For this reason, we expect E_d of orange juice to be high, since there are many substitutes available to drinkers of fruit juice.

   Corollary. Oftentimes you hear of a good that is a "necessity" or a "frivolity." These adjectives are reiterating a relative lack of or a relative wealth of good substitutes.

   Example:
   The more narrowly the product is defined, the more elastic it becomes. If we narrow our focus from orange juice down to one brand of orange juice (e.g., Minute Maid),

the number of substitutes grows and we predict that so too does the price elasticity of demand for Minute Maid brand orange juice. Likewise, the demand for blue Chevrolet SUVs is more elastic than the demand for Chevrolet SUVs, which, in turn, is more elastic than the demand for all SUVs.

2. Proportion of Income

If the price of a good increases, the consumer loses purchasing power. If that good takes up a large proportion of the consumer's income, he greatly feels the pinch of the income effect, and his responsiveness might be significant. If the price of toothpicks increased by 10 percent, the typical household probably would not feel the lost purchasing power and E_d would be low. The opposite would be true if the price of food items increased by 10 percent.

Example:

A young full-time college student is purchasing her education by the credit-hour and supporting herself with a part-time job on the weekends and evenings. Since the student is living on a relatively small monthly income, if the price of a credit-hour increases, the response might be very elastic. The student might drop down to part-time status or drop out of college all together so that she can save enough money to return next quarter.

3. Time

Consumers faced by a rising price are usually fairly resourceful in their ability to find a way of decreasing the quantity demanded of a good. The difficulty faced by consumers is that they might not have time, at least not initially, to find a substitute for the more expensive good. We expect price elasticity to increase as more time passes after the initial increase in the price.

Example:

If the price of gasoline rises, consumers driving large SUVs do not immediately switch to small cars and the E_d is low for gasoline. But given enough time, if the gas price remains high, the E_d for gasoline increases.

Total Revenue and Elasticity

Discussing price elasticity and making simple calculations is not just a delightful academic exercise for students. Knowing how sensitive consumers are to changes in price is important to those who benefit from selling goods to those consumers—the sellers. Sellers compute total revenues collected from selling goods. It is also important to note that the dollars spent by consumers is equal to the dollars received as revenue by sellers.

$$\text{Total revenue} = \text{Price} \times \text{Quantity demanded} = \text{Total spending}$$

A seller might think, "If I continue to raise the price, my total revenues must continue to rise." A student of microeconomics knows that this is flawed logic, because quantity demanded falls when the price rises, making the impact on total revenue uncertain.

$$\text{Here's what's happening: (Price}\uparrow) \times (\text{Quantity demanded}\downarrow)$$
$$= \text{Total revenue} \updownarrow$$

With price going up and quantity demanded going down, it's like a tug-of-war between two teams, with total revenue being pulled in the direction of the strongest team.

Whether or not the total revenue increases with a price increase depends on whether or not the gain from the higher price offsets the loss from lower quantity demanded. Price elasticity is an excellent way to predict how total revenue changes with a price change. This is sometimes called the total revenue test. Table 7.2 extends our earlier table by adding a column for total revenue at points A through G.

Table 7.2 Total Revenue and Price Elasticity

POINT	PRICE PER CHEESEBURGER	QUANTITY DEMANDED OF CHEESEBURGERS	TOTAL = REVENUE $P \times Q_d$ = TOTAL SPENDING	PRICE ELASTICITY (E_d)
A	$0	6	$0	0
B	1	5	5	0.2
C	2	4	8	0.5
D	3	3	9	1
E	4	2	8	2
F	5	1	5	5
G	6	0	0	∞

As you can see, if the price rises in the inelastic range of the demand curve, total revenues rise. However, if the price continues to rise into the elastic range, total revenues begin to fall. Why? Maybe a reminder of what it means for demand to be elastic helps to predict which team wins the tug-of-war.

- Inelastic demand $E_d < 1$: % $\Delta Q_d <$ % ΔP, so total revenue increases with a price increase.
- Elastic demand $E_d > 1$: % $\Delta Q_d >$ % ΔP, so total revenue decreases with a price increase.
- Unit elastic demand $E_d = 1$: % $\Delta Q_d =$ % ΔP, so total revenue remains the same.

In Figures 7.4 and 7.5, we can graphically illustrate the connection between the demand curve, elasticity, and total revenue.

If we start at the top of the demand curve and begin to lower the price, Figure 7.5 clearly shows that total revenue rises until quantity demanded equals three, and then falls until we reach a quantity of six units demanded. If the price is falling and total revenue is rising, it must be the case that the quantity demanded is rising by a larger percentage than the percentage by which price is falling: an elastic response. And if the price continues to fall and total revenue is falling, it must be the case that the percentage increase in quantity demanded is smaller than the percentage by which the price is falling: an inelastic response. The quantity of three in Figure 7.4 represents the midpoint of this particular demand curve and allows us to divide the demand curve into the elastic half (above the midpoint price of $3) and the inelastic half (below $3). This will always be true of any linear demand curve.

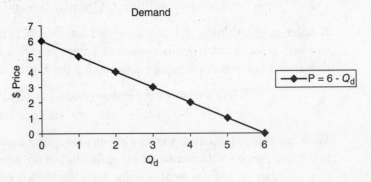

Figure 7.4

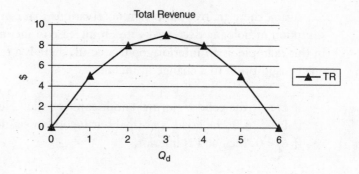

Figure 7.5

- At prices above the midpoint of a linear demand curve, consumers have an elastic response to a small change in price.
- At prices below the midpoint of a linear demand curve, consumers have an inelastic response to a small change in price.

Income Elasticity of Demand

In the case of the **income elasticity**, it is a measure of how sensitive consumption of good X is to a change in a consumer's income.

$$E_I = (\% \Delta Q_d \text{ good X})/(\% \Delta \text{ income})$$

Example:

Jason's income rises 5 percent, and we see his consumption of fast-food meals rises 10 percent.

$$E_I = (10\%)/(5\%) = 2$$

So what do we make of this? First, because E_I is greater than zero, we can determine that fast-food meals are a **normal** good for Jason. Second, at least in this example, the consumption of fast-food meals is quite income elastic. A relatively small percentage increase in income causes a large—in fact, twofold—percentage increase in fast-food meals. Some refer to these goods as **luxuries**.

Example:

Jen's income rises 5 percent, and we observe her consumption of bread rises 1 percent.

$$E_I = (1\%)/(5\%) = .2$$

Once again, this measure would indicate that bread is a **normal** good, as more income prompts more bread consumption. However, the relatively small increase in consumption compared to the increase in income tells us that bread demand is relatively income inelastic. This makes sense; after all, how much more bread does one really wish to consume as one's income rises? If Jen's income doubled, would she double, or more than double, her consumption of bread? These goods are often referred to as **necessities**.

Example:

Consumer income increases by 5 percent, and we observe consumption of packaged bologna decreases by 2 percent.

$$E_I = (-2\%)/(5\%) = -.4$$

Again, there are two important observations that can be made here. First, because consumption of bologna decreased with an increase in income, we can conclude that bologna, in this example, is an **inferior** good. Second, there is a relatively inelastic response in bologna consumption to a change in income.

- If $E_I > 1$, the good is normal and income elastic (a luxury).
- If $1 > E_I > 0$, the good is normal but income inelastic (a necessity).
- If $E_I < 0$, the good is inferior.

Cross-Price Elasticity of Demand

Consumers also change their consumption of good X when the price of a related good, good Y, changes. The sensitivity of consumption of good X to a change in the price of good Y is called the **cross-price elasticity of demand**.

$$E_{x,y} = (\%\Delta\ Q_d\ \text{good X})/(\%\Delta\ \text{Price good Y})$$

Example:
The price of eggs increases by 1 percent, and the consumption of bacon falls 2 percent. The fact that bacon consumption fell when eggs became more expensive tells us that these goods are complementary goods.

$$E_{x,y} = (\%\Delta\ Q_d\ \text{bacon})/(\%\Delta\ \text{Price eggs}) = -2\%/1\% = -2$$

Example:
The price of Honda cars increases by 2 percent and consumption of Ford cars increases by 4 percent. Because Ford cars saw increased consumption when Honda cars got more expensive, the two goods are substitutes.

$$E_{x,y} = (\%\Delta\ Q_d\ \text{Ford})/(\%\Delta\ \text{Price Honda}) = 2\%/1\% = +2$$

- A cross-price elasticity of demand less than zero identifies complementary goods.
- A cross-price elasticity of demand greater than zero identifies substitute goods.

Price Elasticity of Supply

Now that we have addressed the sensitivity of consumer consumption of good X, let us discuss elasticity from the supplier's perspective. When the price of good X changes, we expect quantity supplied to change. The law of supply predicts that as the price of good X increases, so too does quantity supplied. But what we do not know is, "by how much?" The price elasticity of supply helps to measure this response.

Price Elasticity of Supply Formula

$$E_s = (\%\Delta\ \text{in quantity supplied of good X})/(\%\Delta\ \text{in the price of good X})$$

Note: The law of supply ensures that E_s is positive. The greater this ratio, the more sensitive, or responsive, suppliers are to a change in the price of good X.

The Element of Time
Perhaps the most important determinant of how price elastic suppliers are in a particular industry is the time that it takes suppliers to change the quantity supplied once the price of the good itself has changed. This flexibility, of course, is different for different types of producers.

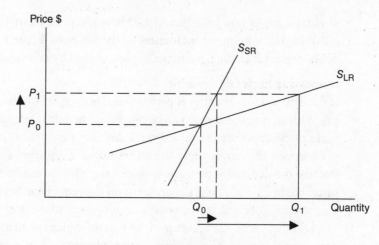

Figure 7.6

Example:

A local attorney produces hours of legal service in a small midwestern town from her small office. At the current market price, for an hour of legal advice, she works a 40-hour workweek with the help of one clerical employee. If the price of an hour of legal assistance rises by 10 percent in the local market, initially our attorney responds by working a few additional minutes each weekday evening and on Saturday, but the constraints of the calendar allow for only an increase of 5 percent in the hours that she supplies.

$$\text{Short-term } E_s = (5\%)/(10\%) = .5$$

If this higher price is maintained for a month or two, the attorney might ask her employee to work additional hours, thus allowing the small office to increase the quantity of hours supplied by 10 percent. And if the price continues to stay at the higher rate, she might expand the office and employ a junior associate and thus increase the hours supplied by 20 percent.

$$\text{Long-term } E_s = (20\%)/(10\%) = 2$$

Because suppliers, once the price of the good has changed, usually cannot quickly change the quantity supplied, economists predict that the price elasticity of supply increases as time passes. Figure 7.6 illustrates the short-term (S_{SR}) and long-term (S_{LR}) supply curves for our attorney. In general, the less steep the supply curve, the more elastic suppliers are in response to a change in the price.

7.2 Microeconomic Policy and Applications of Elasticity

Main Topics: *Excise Taxes, The Role the Supply Curve Plays in the Impact of an Excise Tax, Subsidies, Price Floors, Price Ceilings*

Excise Taxes

Government occasionally imposes an **excise tax** on the production of a good or service. Because it is a per-unit tax on production, the firm responds as if the marginal cost of producing each unit has risen by the amount of the tax. Graphically this results in a vertical shift in the supply curve by the amount of the tax. The reasons for this tax are usually twofold: (1) to increase revenue collected by the government and/or (2) to decrease consumption of a good that might be harmful to some members of society. For these reasons, tobacco is a good example of an excise tax. Can an excise tax on tobacco raise money for government? Can it deter people from smoking? Let's use our two extreme demand curves to see where these goals might, or might not, be achieved and how the price elasticity of demand plays a critical role on where the burden, or **incidence**, of the tax rests. Economists commonly express the incidence of the tax as the percentage of the tax paid by consumers, in the form of a higher price.

Demand Is Perfectly Inelastic

If the demand for cigarettes is perfectly inelastic ($E_d = 0$), then the demand curve (D_0) is vertical. With an untaxed supply (S_0) of cigarettes, the initial price of a pack of cigarettes is P_0 and Q_0 packs of cigarettes are consumed every day. If a per-unit tax of T is imposed on the producers of cigarettes, the supply curve shifts upward by T. *Be careful! This is not an "increase in supply"!* Because the demand is perfectly inelastic, the equilibrium quantity remains at Q_0, but the new price rises to $P_0 + T$. Total dollars spent on cigarettes increases from $P_0 \times Q_0$ to $(P_0 + T) \times Q_0$. The revenue collected by the government is equal to the area of the rectangle $T \times Q_0$.

Did our excise tax accomplish our goals? Since quantity remained constant, the tax did nothing to decrease the harmful effects of smoking in society and only increased tax revenues for the government. In fact, because the quantity demanded did not fall, this scenario creates the largest revenue rectangle collected by the government. Who paid the burden of the tax? In Figure 7.7, you can see that the entire tax was paid by consumers in the form of a new price exactly equal to the old price plus the tax.

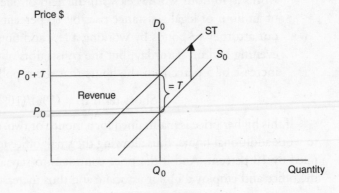

Figure 7.7

Demand Is Perfectly Elastic

Figure 7.8 shows that if the demand for cigarettes is perfectly elastic ($E_d = \infty$), then the demand curve (D_0) is horizontal. With an untaxed supply (S_0) of cigarettes, the initial price of a pack of cigarettes is P_0 and Q_0 packs of cigarettes are consumed daily. The per-unit tax of T shifts the supply curve upward by T, but with a perfectly elastic demand curve, the equilibrium price of cigarettes does not change, while equilibrium quantity demanded falls to Q_1. Total spending by consumers falls to the area $P_0 \times Q_1$. Tax revenue for the government is a much smaller rectangle $T \times Q_1$.

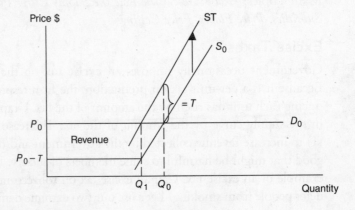

Figure 7.8

Who paid for the tax in this case? Because the price of a pack of cigarettes did not increase after the tax, it was not the consumers. Each producer receives a price of P_0 but must then pay T to the government, so the net price received from each pack of cigarettes is $(P_0 - T)$. So the producer pays the entire share of the tax when demand is perfectly elastic. Compared to the perfectly inelastic scenario, the government collected much fewer tax revenue dollars, but the maximum decrease in harmful cigarette consumption is a definite plus.

With these two extreme cases as benchmarks, we can conclude that as demand is more inelastic, consumers pay a higher share of an excise tax. Government revenues from the excise tax increase with inelastic demand, but the goal of decreasing consumption sees only minimal success. Table 7.3 summarizes the effects of a higher excise tax and how these depend on the price elasticity of demand.

Table 7.3 Price Elasticity of Demand and Tax Incidence

PRICE ELASTICITY OF DEMAND	GOVERNMENT REVENUE	DECREASE IN CONSUMPTION	INCIDENCE OF TAX PAID BY CONSUMERS	INCIDENCE OF TAX PAID BY SUPPLIERS
$E_d = \infty$	The least	The most	0%	100%
$E_d > 1$	Falling	Sizeable	Less than 50%	More than 50%
$E_d < 1$	Rising	Minimal	More than 50%	Less than 50%
$E_d = 0$	The most	Zero	100%	0%

Since cigarette demand is usually inelastic, significant improvements in the health of consumers is probably not the primary outcome of higher excise taxes, although they would seem to be effective revenue-generating devices. Ironically, although the tax is actually imposed on suppliers of cigarettes, most of the burden of the tax falls upon consumers. Figure 7.9 illustrates an inelastic demand for cigarettes, before and after an excise tax.

The Role the Supply Curve Plays in the Impact of an Excise Tax

We have seen that the greater the price elasticity of demand, the smaller the portion of the tax paid by consumers. It is also true that the price elasticity of supply plays a role in determining how much a tax will cause the price to increase and therefore helps to determine which group, consumers or producers, pays a higher burden of a tax.

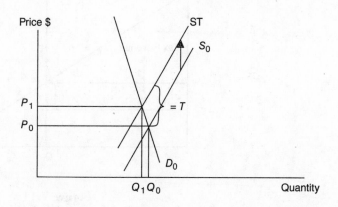

Figure 7.9

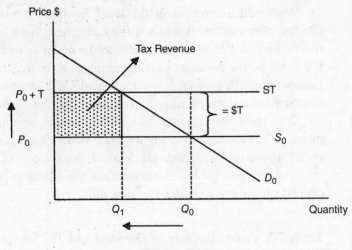

Figure 7.10

It again helps to see if we look at two extremes: a perfectly elastic supply curve and a perfectly inelastic supply curve.

A perfectly elastic, or horizontal, supply curve tells us that even a very small change in the price will cause an infinitely large change in the quantity supplied. A per-unit tax T imposed on suppliers causes this horizontal supply curve to shift upward by the amount of the tax. In Figure 7.10, you can see that the new equilibrium price is exactly T higher than the old price P_0, so consumers pay the entire burden of the tax. The equilibrium quantity decreases from Q_0 to Q_1, and the government collects tax revenue equal to $T \times Q_1$.

A perfectly inelastic, or vertical, supply curve illustrates the special case where any change in the price creates absolutely no change in quantity supplied. Figure 7.11 shows that in this case, the supply curve cannot vertically shift. At the equilibrium quantity Q_0, suppliers would like to charge a higher price than P_0, but any price above P_0 creates a surplus, and this surplus will clear only at the equilibrium price P_0. Therefore the firms must pay T to the government for each of the Q_0 units that are sold and consumers continue to pay the original price of P_0. In this special case, producers pay the entire burden of the tax because, after paying the tax, they receive only $(P_0 - T)$ on each unit. The government collects total revenue equal to $T \times Q_0$.

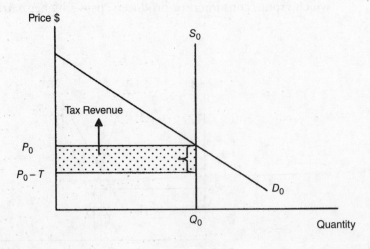

Figure 7.11

Table 7.4 summarizes the effects of a higher excise tax and how these depend on the price elasticity of supply.

Table 7.4 Price Elasticity of Supply and Tax Incidence

PRICE ELASTICITY OF SUPPLY	GOVERNMENT REVENUE	DECREASE IN CONSUMPTION	INCIDENCE OF TAX PAID BY CONSUMERS	INCIDENCE OF TAX PAID BY PRODUCERS
$E_s = \infty$	The least	The most	100%	0%
$E_s > 1$	Falling	Sizeable	More than 50%	Less than 50%
$E_s < 1$	Rising	Minimal	Less than 50%	More than 50%
$E_s = 0$	The most	Zero	0%	100%

By now you are probably wondering, "How can I keep all of this straight?" If we consider the extreme cases of perfectly elastic and perfectly inelastic demand and supply curves, we can draw some general conclusions.

- As the price elasticity of demand falls, and the price elasticity of supply rises, the greater the consumer's share of a per-unit excise tax. Why? Because this describes a situation where the consumer response to a higher price is negligible and the producer's response is sizable. The group that has the best ability to respond to the higher post-tax price is going to make out better.
- Conversely, as the price elasticity of demand rises and the price elasticity of supply falls, the producer's share of a per-unit excise tax rises.

Loss to Society

KEY IDEA

There is also a cost to society when an excise tax is imposed on a competitive market. In the hypothetical soda market depicted in Figure 7.12, the equilibrium quantity is 100 and the equilibrium price is $1. At this point, the marginal benefit to society exactly equals the marginal cost and net benefit; total welfare (combined consumer and producer surplus) is the greatest. When a $1 excise tax is imposed, the price of sodas paid by consumers increases to $1.80, and the number (amount) of sodas consumed decreases to 80. After sellers pay the excise tax, the price they receive falls to $0.80. The government collects $80 = 1×80 in tax revenue. With the tax, consumers and producers demand and supply 20 fewer units than

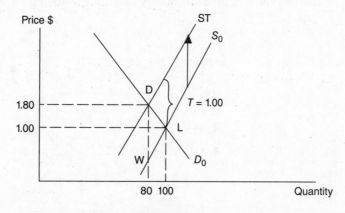

Figure 7.12

without the tax. For these 20 units that go unproduced, the marginal benefit to consumers exceeds the marginal costs to producers. The fact that these 20 units go unproduced and unconsumed results in an inefficient outcome. The triangle labeled DWL used to be earned by society in the form of consumer and producer surplus. With the excise tax, society loses this area; it goes to no one. Economists call this area **deadweight loss** (DWL), or the net benefit sacrificed by society when such a per-unit tax is imposed. In fact, with the numbers given, we can calculate the deadweight loss as the area of the triangle that is 20 units wide and $1 tall. Since the key to deadweight loss is a large decrease in quantity below the untaxed outcome, the area of deadweight loss to society increases as the demand or supply curves get more elastic.

Note: Taxes such as these are not the only sources of distortions away from market efficiency. For example, production often generates pollution (a negative externality), which creates a situation where harmful spillover costs are incurred by third parties. Left unregulated, these costs are not captured by the market price and the market will not produce the "correct" amount of a good. These sources of inefficiency, or market failures, are addressed in Chapter 11.

- Taxes create lost efficiency by moving away from the equilibrium market quantity where MB = MC to society.
- The area of deadweight loss (triangle DWL) increases as the quantity moves further from the competitive market equilibrium quantity.

Subsidies

A per-unit **subsidy** on good X has the opposite effect of an excise tax, because firms respond as if the subsidy has lowered the marginal cost of production, therefore resulting in a downward vertical shift in the supply curve for good X. *Be careful here! This is not a "decrease in supply"!* Since subsidies come from the government, they are certainly not designed as revenue-generating devices. Ideally, their primary goal is to support producers of a good or service that has significant benefit to society so that it can be produced in greater quantities and at lower prices to consumers. This form of positive externality is also explored in Chapter 11. Public university education is a common example of this type of subsidy.

Figure 7.13 illustrates the market for public university education where the demand (D_0) and unsubsidized supply (S_0) curves produce an equilibrium price P_0 (tuition) and quantity Q_0 (degrees earned). If government decides that provision of bachelor's degrees is a beneficial service to society, a per-student subsidy U is given to the public university system. The subsidy decreases tuition to P_1 and increases the number of undergraduate degrees received. Notice that the producers receive, after the subsidy, ($P_1 + U$) for each student at the new quantity of Q_1. Like an excise tax, a subsidy distorts the market and creates deadweight loss. By creating an incentive for producers to increase production beyond the market quantity, producers end up producing "too many" units of the good. In the

"Taxes and subsidies are usually tested in both the multiple-choice section and as part of a free-response question."
—AP Teacher

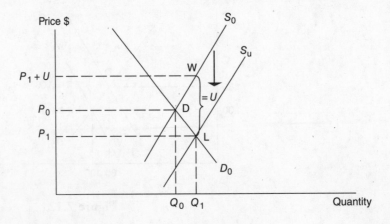

Figure 7.13

hypothetical example depicted in Figure 7.13, the deadweight loss is the area of the triangle labeled "DWL." Once again, as we will see in Chapter 11, subsidies like this can actually improve efficiency in the market and correct a market failure.

How does the price elasticity of demand factor into this outcome? If the demand for public university education is elastic, then a relatively small percentage decrease in the price of tuition creates a sizable percentage increase in the number of degrees earned by members of society. If demand is price inelastic, it takes a much larger percentage decrease in the price to achieve the same percentage increase in degrees earned.

Price Floors

In some cases, the market-determined equilibrium price P_0 is deemed "too low" by some members of society. Typically, suppliers who feel that the market price is not high enough to cover production costs and earn a decent living make this argument. If the government agrees with this argument, a **price floor** may be installed at some level above the equilibrium price. A price floor is a legal minimum price below which the product cannot be sold. Another example is a minimum wage in a market for labor. An effective price floor in the market for milk is seen in Figure 7.14. An ineffective price floor would be a price set below the equilibrium price. After all, a price floor sets a minimum legal price so if a price floor is set *below* equilibrium, the market would simply revert to the higher equilibrium price and the price floor would have no impact.

The resulting surplus of milk is not eliminated through the market, and the government usually agrees, as part of the price floor arrangement, to purchase the surplus milk. For consumers, the result of the policy is a higher price of milk (and other dairy products) at grocery stores, a decrease in milk consumption, and an increase in taxpayer-supported government spending. The amount of government spending to purchase the surplus is equal to $(P_F) \times$ surplus. If the price elasticities of demand or supply are large, the surplus, and resulting government spending, rises.

By providing an incentive for producers to produce beyond where MB = MC, the price floor policy causes efficiency to be lost. For gallons of milk above Q_0, MC > MB; there is an overallocation of resources to milk production. Quite simply, the policy produces a situation where "too much" milk is produced, and this is inefficient.

- A price floor is installed when producers feel the market equilibrium price is "too low."
- A price floor creates a permanent surplus at a price above equilibrium.
- If the government purchases the surplus, taxpayers eventually pay the bill.
- The more price elastic the demand and supply curves, the greater the surplus and the greater the government spending to purchase the surplus.
- The price floor reduces net benefit by overallocating resources to the production of the good.

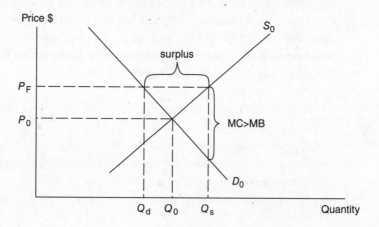

Figure 7.14

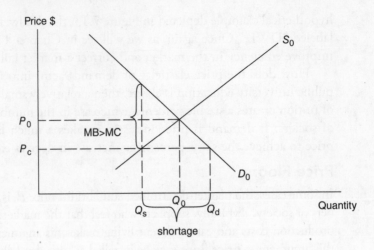

Figure 7.15

Price Ceilings

For some goods and services, the market equilibrium price is judged to be "too high." Consumers who feel that the price is so high that it prevents a significant fraction of citizens from being able to consume a good, usually express this sentiment. If the government agrees with this argument, a **price ceiling** may be installed at a level below the equilibrium price. A price ceiling is a legal maximum price above which the product cannot be bought and sold. An effective price ceiling in the market for rental apartments (rent control) is seen in Figure 7.15. An effective price ceiling must be set below the equilibrium price. Because the price ceiling sets a legal maximum price, a ceiling set *above* the equilibrium price would quickly revert back to the market equilibrium outcome and have no impact.

The resulting shortage of rent-controlled apartments is not eliminated through the market, and this creates a sticky situation for low-income households, the group for which the policy was intended. Many suppliers completely remove their rental units from the market, converting them into office space or condominiums. Others attempt to increase profits by lowering levels of health and safety maintenance, or by charging exorbitant fees for a key to the apartment. For families lucky enough to find rent-controlled space, the result of this policy is certainly lower rents, but the shortage also tends to create an underground or "black" market for apartments where a vacant apartment might go to the highest bidder, regardless of financial need. If the price elasticities of demand or supply are large, the shortage, and the negative consequences of it, increase.

Again, this form of price control results in lost efficiency for society. When suppliers reduce their quantity supplied below the competitive equilibrium quantity, there is a situation where MB > MC, and we see an underallocation of resources in the rental apartment market. This policy, intended to help low-income families, creates a situation where "too little" of the good is produced.

"Always remember on the graphs that floors are HIGH and ceilings are LOW."
—Kristy, AP Student

- A price ceiling is installed when consumers feel the market equilibrium price is "too high."
- A price ceiling creates a permanent shortage at a price below equilibrium.
- The more price elastic the demand and supply curves, the greater the shortage.
- The price ceiling reduces net benefit by underallocating resources to the production of the good.

7.3 Trade Barriers

Main Topics: *Tariffs, Quotas*

The issue of free trade is hotly politicized. Proponents usually argue that free trade raises the standard of living in **both nations**, and most economists agree. Detractors argue that free trade, especially with nations that pay lower wages than those paid to domestic workers, costs domestic jobs in higher-wage nations. The evidence shows that in some industries, job losses have certainly occurred as free trade has become more prevalent. To protect domestic jobs, nations can impose trade barriers. Tariffs and quotas are among the most common of barriers.

Tariffs

In general, there are two types of tariffs. A **revenue tariff** is an excise tax levied on goods that are not produced in the domestic market. For example, the United States does not produce bananas. If a revenue tariff were levied on bananas, it would not be a serious impediment to trade, and it would raise a little revenue for the government. A **protective tariff** is an excise tax levied on a good that is produced in the domestic market. Though this tariff also raises revenue, the purpose of this tariff, as the name suggests, is to protect the domestic industry from global competition by increasing the price of foreign products.

Example:

The hypothetical domestic supply and demand for steel is pictured in Figure 7.16.
  The domestic price is $100 per ton and the equilibrium quantity of domestic steel is 10 million tons. Maybe other nations can produce steel at lower cost. As a result, in the competitive world market, the price is $80 per ton. At that price, the United States would demand 12 million tons but only produce 8 million tons, and so 4 million tons are **imported**. It is important to see that in the competitive (free-trade) world market, consumer surplus is maximized and no deadweight loss exists. You can see the consumer surplus as the triangle below the demand curve and above the $80 world price.
If the steel industry is successful in getting a protective tariff passed through Congress, the world price rises by $10, increasing the quantity of domestic steel supplied and reducing the amount of steel imported from 4 million to 2 million tons. A higher price and lower consumption reduces the area of consumer surplus and creates deadweight loss.

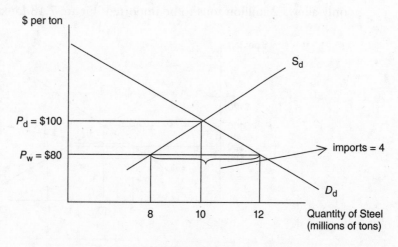

Figure 7.16

Figure 7.17

Economic Effects of the Tariff

- *Consumers pay higher prices and consume less steel.* If you are building airplanes or door hinges, you have seen an increase in your costs.
- *Consumer surplus has been lost.*
- *Domestic producers increase output.* Domestic steel firms are not subject to the tariff, so they can sell more steel at the price of $90 than they could at $80.
- *Declining imports.* Fewer tons of imported steel arrive in the United States.
- *Tariff revenue.* The government collects $10 × 2 million = $20 million in tariff revenue as seen in the shaded box in Figure 7.17. This is a transfer from consumers of steel to the government, not an increase in the total well-being of the nation.
- *Inefficiency.* There was a reason the world price was lower than the domestic price. It was more efficient to produce steel abroad and export it to the United States. By taxing this efficiency, the United States promotes the less efficient domestic industry and stunts the efficient foreign sector. As a result, resources are diverted from the efficient to the inefficient sector.
- *Deadweight loss now exists.*

Quotas

Quotas work in much the same way as a tariff. An **import quota** is a maximum amount of a good that can be imported into the domestic market. With a quota, the government only allows 2 million tons to be imported. Figure 7.18 looks much like Figure 7.17, only

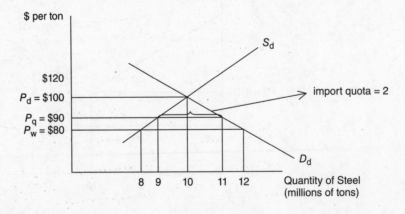

Figure 7.18

"It is important to know the differences between tariffs and quotas."
—Lucas, AP Student

without revenue collected by government. So the impact of the quota, with the exception of the revenue, is the same: higher consumer prices and inefficient resource allocation.

Tariffs and quotas share many of the same economic effects.

- Both hurt consumers with artificially high prices and lower consumer surplus.
- Both protect less efficient domestic producers at the expense of efficient foreign firms, creating deadweight loss.
- Both reallocate economic resources toward less efficient producers.
- Tariffs collect revenue for the government, while quotas do not.

7.4 Consumer Choice

Main Topics: *Utility; Unconstrained Consumer Choice; Diminishing Marginal Utility; Constrained Utility Maximization; Constrained Utility Maximization, Two Goods*

Utility

If you pull back the curtain on the law of demand to study how consumers behave, much insight can be gained. It's important to remember that people demand things because *those things make those people happy*. We choose to consume mundane items like electricity or crackers, or luxury items like trans-Atlantic flights and tickets to an NFL game, because they provide us with happiness. In economics, we call this happiness (or benefit, or satisfaction, or enjoyment) **utility**.

While in the course of a week, consumption of more and more pints of Cherry Garcia ice cream is likely to increase our **total utility**, it is probably safe to say that the first pint in a week provides more **marginal utility** than the second, third, or fourth pint. If you recall from Chapter 5, analysis of marginal changes is extremely important in modeling how individuals make decisions.

- Total utility (TU) is the total amount of happiness received from the consumption of a certain amount of a good.
- Marginal utility (MU) is the additional utility received (or sometimes lost) from the consumption of the *next* unit of a good.
- Mathematically speaking: $MU = \Delta TU/\Delta Q$ (this ΔQ is likely to equal 1 if you are consuming one additional unit at a time).

Example:

Table 7.5 summarizes the utility gained from consumption of successive cups of coffee in a typical morning at work. Some choose to measure utility in hypothetical "**utils**," but I like to think about these as "happy points."

As our coffee drinker (Joe) goes from zero to one cup of coffee, his total happiness from coffee drinking increases from zero to 20 happy points. The incremental, or marginal, change is also 20 points. The marginal utility is simply calculated as the difference between the totals as Joe consumes consecutive cups of coffee.

Unconstrained Consumer Choice

So how much coffee should our desk jockey consume in a typical morning? Assuming that he does not have to pay for each cup and can freely use the coffee machine, one might assume that Joe consumes unlimited amounts of coffee. Using Table 7.5 or Figure 7.19, you can easily see that total utility initially rises, peaks, and then begins to fall as more coffee is consumed. If Joe is a consumer who seeks to maximize happiness, and this seems

Table 7.5 Total and Marginal Utility

# CUPS (Q)	TOTAL UTILITY (TU) ("HAPPY POINTS")	MARGINAL UTILITY (MU)
0	0	—
1	20	20
2	35	15
3	45	10
4	50	5
5	45	−5
6	35	−10

a reasonable aim, he would not consume more than four cups of coffee, even if he were not asked to pay for each cup.

- Even if the monetary price of good X is zero, the rational consumer stops consuming good X at the point where total utility is maximized.

Diminishing Marginal Utility

In Figure 7.19 you can see a relationship between total utility and coffee consumption. There is the obvious rise, peak, and fall of total utility as the number of cups increases. But closer inspection reveals that, as more coffee is consumed, total utility rises at a slower and slower rate. Since marginal utility is the rate at which total utility changes, marginal utility must be falling.

The **law of diminishing marginal utility** says that in a given time period, the marginal utility from consumption of one more of that item falls. A graphical depiction of marginal utility, also the slope of total utility, is seen in Figure 7.20.

Constrained Utility Maximization

Now we require Joe to pay a price P_c for additional cups of coffee. With a fixed daily income and a price that must be paid, this individual is now a **constrained utility maximizer**. Joe must ask himself: "Does the next cup of coffee provide at least $\$P_c$ worth of additional happiness?" If Joe answers "yes" to this question for the first three cups of coffee, he maximizes his utility by stopping at three cups. If his answer is "no" to the fourth cup, he does not consume it.

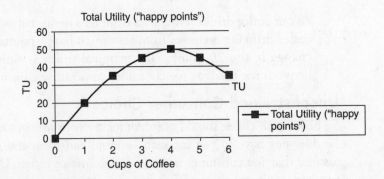

Figure 7.19

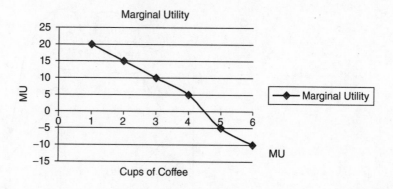

Figure 7.20

Does this sound familiar? It should, as it is another example of how a consumer never does something if the marginal benefit (in this case, utility) gained is exceeded by the marginal cost incurred.

- When required to pay a price, the utility-maximizing consumer stops consuming when $MB = P$.

- This MB also represents the highest price, or "willingness to pay," our consumer would be willing to pay for the next cup.

Demand Curve Revisited

Using the logic outlined above as an example, what would happen if the price of coffee fell? If Joe was facing a new lower price, you should expect that Joe would rationally increase his daily consumption of cups of coffee. Have you heard this behavior described before? Sure! It's the law of demand, and it has a tight connection to the law of diminishing marginal utility.

Imagine you are a consumer who has already paid for and consumed the first pint of ice cream this week. Would your willingness to pay for the second pint of ice cream be the same as your willingness to pay for the first pint? Doubtful, because the second pint does not provide the same marginal utility as the first. In order to entice you to purchase and consume additional pints of Cherry Garcia ice cream, the price must fall to compensate you for your falling marginal utility.

This law of diminishing marginal utility is the backbone of the law of demand. To convert the relationship between marginal utility and quantity consumed at any price, we might ask you how much you are willing to pay to consume successive pints of ice cream. Because of diminishing marginal utility, you offer to pay less for additional units. Thus, we can then construct your monthly demand curve for ice cream. Figure 7.21 illustrates how diminishing marginal utility from consumption of a good can be converted to a demand curve for that good.

Constrained Utility Maximization, Two Goods

Economists see a consumer, constrained by income and prices, as living within a budget constraint. In a simple case where one good is consumed, the consumer maximizes utility by buying units of good X up to the point where the marginal utility of the last unit of good X is equal to the price. Most consumers allocate limited income between many goods and services, each with a price that must be paid. To see how a consumer maximizes utility in this situation, we consider a two-good case where, in addition to daily cups of coffee, Joe also purchases scones. We start with a "rule" and then proceed to solve a couple of problems.

"Learn the definitions first. This will make the logic much more obvious."
—David,
AP Student

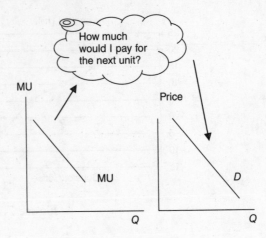

Figure 7.21

Utility Maximizing Rule

Given limited income, consumers maximize utility when they buy amounts of goods X and Y so that the marginal utility per dollar spent is equal for both goods. Another way to think about it is that they seek the most "bang for their bucks." Mathematically, this **utility maximizing rule** is expressed:

$$MU_x/P_x = MU_y/P_y \text{ or } MU_x/MU_y = P_x/P_y$$

If the consumer has used all income and the above ratios are equal, they are said to be in equilibrium. Under this condition, no other combination of X and Y provides more total utility.

Example:

Joe has daily income of $20, each cup of coffee costs $P_c = \$2$, and each scone costs $P_s = \$4$. Table 7.6 provides us with Joe's marginal utility received in the consumption of each good.

Table 7.6 Marginal Utility for Two Goods

CUPS OF COFFEE	MU OF COFFEE	# OF SCONES	MU OF SCONES
1	10	1	30
2	8	2	24
3	6	3	20
4	4	4	16
5	2	5	14
6	1	6	8

- It is very important to remember that consuming more of one good causes the *marginal utility* to fall, but the *total utility* to rise.

In order to maximize Joe's utility, he seeks a combination of coffee and scones so that $MU_c/\$2 = MU_s/\$4$ and spends exactly his income of $20. Another way to solve this problem is to rearrange these ratios so that:

$$MU_c/MU_s = \$2/\$4 = .5$$

There are several combinations of coffee and scones in Table 7.6 where the ratio of marginal utilities is one-half. For example, Joe could consume one cup of coffee (MU = 10) and three scones (MU = 20) for a total utility of 84 (10 + 30 + 24 + 20). But this combination would only spend a total of $14, and surely Joe would be happier if he used all of his income.

- To find the total utility of consuming cups of coffee, sum up the marginal utility of each cup consumed. Do the same for scones to calculate total utility.

Another possibility is to consume two cups of coffee (MU = 8) with four scones (MU = 16). This does indeed spend exactly $20. The total utility of 108 confirms that Joe is happier with this combination of coffee and scones. There exists one other combination of goods that satisfies our rule: four cups of coffee (MU = 4) with six scones (MU = 8) expends too much money ($32) for Joe's income.

So according to our rule, Joe's utility maximizing decision would be to use his income of $20 to consume two cups of coffee and four scones. What if he decided to experiment and reallocate his consumption while still spending only $20 on coffee and scones? For example, four cups of coffee (MU = 4) and three scones (MU = 20) fails our rule, but Joe still is spending $20. On closer inspection, this is a poor decision because total utility falls to 102.

Example:

Now the price of a cup of coffee falls to $1. Joe needs to reexamine his utility maximizing combination of coffee and scones.

$$MU_c/MU_s = \$1/\$4 = .25$$

Again, there are three possibilities, but only one uses exactly $20 of income. If Joe buys four cups of coffee (MU = 4) and four scones (MU = 16), he spends exactly his income and receives total utility of 118. The combination of three cups of coffee and two scones does not use all of the income, and the combination of five cups of coffee and six scones exceeds the income constraint.

Connection Back to Demand Curves

Joe, as a utility-maximizing consumer, chooses two cups of coffee at a price of $2 and four cups of coffee at a price of $1. This sounds familiar! What Joe has done, simply by responding in a utility-maximizing way, is illustrate the law of demand. The two combinations of price and quantity demanded are two points on Joe's coffee demand curve. By connecting these points, we trace out his demand curve (Figure 7.22).

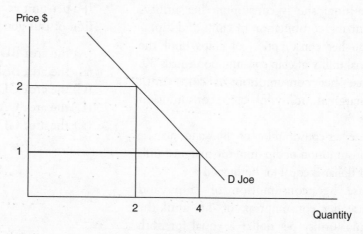

Figure 7.22

Individual and Market Demand Curves

We can take the individual decisions made by consumers like Joe and expand the analysis to build a market demand curve for coffee and other goods. This process is called **horizontal summation**. At every price, we would simply add the quantity demanded for all individual consumers.

- Utility-maximizing behavior of individuals creates individual demand curves.
- Summing the quantity demanded by individuals at each price creates market demand curves.

› Review Questions

1. If the price of corn rises 5 percent and the quantity demanded for corn falls 1 percent, then

   (A) $E_d = 5$ and demand is price elastic.
   (B) $E_d = 1/5$ and demand is price elastic.
   (C) $E_d = 5$ and demand is price inelastic.
   (D) $E_d = 1/5$ and demand is price inelastic.
   (E) $E_d = 5$ and corn is a luxury good.

2. A small business estimates price elasticity of demand for the product to be 3. To raise total revenue, owners should

   (A) decrease price as demand is elastic.
   (B) decrease price as demand is inelastic.
   (C) increase price as demand is elastic.
   (D) increase price as demand is inelastic.
   (E) do nothing; they are already maximizing total revenue.

3. Mrs. Johnson spends her entire daily budget on potato chips, at a price of $1 each, and onion dip at a price of $2 each. At her current consumption bundle, the marginal utility of chips is 12 and the marginal utility of dip is 30. Mrs. Johnson should

   (A) do nothing; she is consuming her utility-maximizing combination of chips and dip.
   (B) increase her consumption of chips until the marginal utility of chip consumption equals 30.
   (C) decrease her consumption of chips until the marginal utility of chip consumption equals 30.
   (D) decrease her consumption of chips and increase her consumption of dip until the marginal utility per dollar is equal for both goods.
   (E) increase her consumption of chips and increase her consumption of dip until the marginal utility per dollar is equal for both goods.

4. A consequence of a price floor is

   (A) a persistent shortage of the good.
   (B) an increase in total welfare.
   (C) a persistent surplus of the good.
   (D) elimination of deadweight loss.
   (E) an increase in quantity demanded and a decrease in quantity supplied.

Use the figure below to respond to the next two questions.

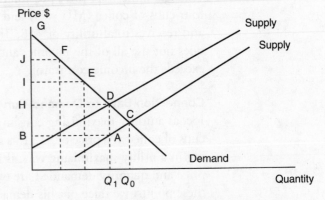

5. The competitive market equilibrium is at point C. If a per-unit excise tax is imposed on the production of this good, the deadweight loss is

   (A) the area BDE.
   (B) the area BADH.
   (C) the area GDH.
   (D) the area DAC.
   (E) the area GDAB.

6. The competitive market equilibrium is at point C. If a per-unit excise tax is imposed on the production of this good, the revenue collected by the government is

(A) the area BDE.
(B) the area BADH.
(C) the area GDH.
(D) the area DAC.
(E) the area GDAB.

› Answers and Explanations

1. D—You must know the formula for elasticity: $E_d = (\%\Delta Q_d)/(\%\Delta P) = 1/5$. Since $E_d < 1$, this is inelastic demand, and you can quickly eliminate any reference to elastic demand. Although calculators are not allowed on the AP exam, simple calculations can be made in the margins of your exam.

2. A—If you know your elasticity measures, you see that with $E_d = 3$, you can eliminate any reference to inelastic demand. Choice E is incorrect, as total revenue is maximized at the midpoint of the demand curve where $E_d = 1$. If $E_d > 1$, the firm increases total revenue by decreasing the price because the quantity demanded rises by a greater percentage than the fall in price.

3. D—Mrs. Johnson needs to find the combination of chips and dip where the ratio of marginal utility per dollar is equated. Currently, $MU_c/P_c = 12$ and $MU_d/P_d = 15$, so choice A is ruled out. Since she is receiving more "bang for her buck" from dip consumption, she increases dip consumption and therefore decreases chip consumption. MU_d falls and MU_c rises. She adjusts her spending until $MU_c/P_c = MU_d/P_d$.

4. C—Price floors are installed when the market equilibrium price is believed to be "too low." This price lies above the equilibrium price, decreasing Q_d and increasing Q_s, thus creating a surplus. Price controls worsen total welfare and create deadweight loss.

5. D—Deadweight loss is total welfare that used to be gained by society prior to the tax. When looking for deadweight loss, narrow your focus by comparing the quantity produced with and without the tax. The horizontal distance between Q_0 and Q_1 is the unattained output from the tax. The vertical distance between points D and A illustrates that MB > MC and is therefore an inefficient outcome.

6. B—Revenue collected by the government is equal to the per-unit tax multiplied by the new quantity. The vertical distance between supply curves is the tax.

› Rapid Review

Elasticity: Measures the sensitivity, or responsiveness, of a choice to a change in an external factor.

Price elasticity of demand (E_d): Measures the sensitivity of consumer quantity demanded for good X when the price of good X changes.

Price elasticity formula: $E_d = (\%\Delta Q_d)/(\%\Delta P)$. Ignore the negative sign.

Price elastic demand: $E_d > 1$ or the $(\%\Delta Q_d) > (\%\Delta P)$. Consumers are price sensitive.

Price inelastic demand: $E_d < 1$ or the $(\%\Delta Q_d) < (\%\Delta P)$. Consumers are not price sensitive.

Unit elastic demand: $E_d = 1$, meaning $(\%\Delta Q_d) = (\%\Delta P)$.

Perfectly inelastic: $E_d = 0$. In this special case, the demand curve is vertical and there is absolutely no response to a price change.

Perfectly elastic: $E_d = \infty$. In this special case, the demand curve is horizontal, meaning consumers have an instantaneous and infinite response to a price change.

Slope and elasticity: In general, the more vertical a good's demand curve, the more inelastic the demand for that good. The more horizontal a good's demand curve, the more elastic the demand for that good. Despite this generalization, be careful, as elasticities and slopes are *not* equivalent measures.

Determinants of elasticity: If a good has more readily available substitutes (luxuries versus necessities), it is likely that consumers are more price elastic for that good. If a high proportion of a consumer's income is devoted to a particular good, consumers are generally more price elastic for that good. When consumers have more time to adjust to a price change, their response is usually more elastic.

Total revenue and total spending: $TR = P \times Q_d = TS$

Total revenue test: Total revenue rises with a price increase if demand is price inelastic and falls with a price increase if demand is price elastic.

Elasticity and demand curves: At the midpoint of a linear demand curve, $E_d = 1$. Above the midpoint demand is elastic and below the midpoint demand is inelastic.

Income elasticity: A measure of how sensitive consumption of good X is to a change in the consumer's income.

Income elasticity formula: $E_I = (\%\Delta Q_d \text{ good X})/(\%\Delta \text{ income})$

Luxury: A good for which the income elasticity is greater than one.

Necessity: A good for which the income elasticity is above zero but less than one.

Values of Income Elasticity: If $E_I > 1$, the good is normal and a luxury. If $1 > E_I > 0$, the good is normal and income inelastic (necessity). If $E_I < 0$, the good is inferior.

Cross-price elasticity of demand: A measure of how sensitive consumption of good X is to a change in the price of good Y.

Cross-price elasticity formula: $E_{x,y} = (\%\Delta Q_d \text{ good X})/(\%\Delta \text{ price Y})$

Values of cross-price elasticity of demand: If $E_{x,y} > 0$, goods X and Y are substitutes. If $E_{x,y} < 0$, goods X and Y are complementary.

Price elasticity of supply: Measures the sensitivity of quantity supplied for good X when the price of good X changes.

Price elasticity of supply formula: $E_s = (\%\Delta Q_s)/(\%\Delta P)$

Excise tax: A per-unit tax on production results in a vertical shift upward in the supply curve by the amount of the tax.

Consumer's Incidence of Tax: The proportion of the tax paid by consumers in the form of a higher price for the taxed good is greater if demand for the good is inelastic and supply is elastic.

Deadweight Loss: The lost net benefit to society caused by a movement away from the competitive market equilibrium. Policies like excise taxes, subsidies, and price controls create lost welfare to society.

Subsidy: Has the opposite effect of an excise tax, as it has the effect of lowering the marginal cost of production, resulting in a downward vertical shift in the supply curve for good X.

Price floor: A legal minimum price below which the product cannot be sold. If a floor is installed at some level above the equilibrium price, it creates a permanent surplus.

Price ceiling: A legal maximum price above which the product cannot be sold. If a ceiling is installed at a level below the equilibrium price, it creates a permanent shortage.

Utility: Happiness, benefit, satisfaction, or enjoyment gained from consumption.

Total utility: Total happiness received from consumption of a number of units of a good.

Marginal utility: The incremental happiness received, or lost, when the consumer increases consumption of a good by one unit.

Utils: A unit of measurement often used to quantify utility. Also known as "happy points."

Law of diminishing marginal utility: In a given time period, the marginal (additional) utility from consumption of more and more of that item falls.

Constrained utility maximization: For a one-good case. Constrained by prices and income, a consumer stops consuming a good when the price paid for the next unit is equal to the marginal benefit received.

Utility maximizing rule: The consumer maximizes utility when they choose amounts of goods X and Y, with their limited income, so that the marginal utility per dollar spent is equal for both goods. Mathematically: $MU_x/P_x = MU_y/P_y$, or $MU_x/MU_y = P_x/P_y$.

Horizontal summation: The process of adding, at each price, the individual quantities demanded to find the market demand curve for a good.

Revenue tariff: An excise tax levied on goods not produced in the domestic market.

Protective tariff: An excise tax levied on a good that is produced in the domestic market so that it may be protected from foreign competition.

Import quota: A limitation on the amount of a good that can be imported into the domestic market.

CHAPTER 8

The Firm, Profit, and the Costs of Production

IN THIS CHAPTER

Summary: The previous chapter focused on the choices made by consumers and how external forces and microeconomic policies affected those choices. The chapter concluded with the concept of constrained utility maximization and the utility maximizing rule. Also known as the consumer's equilibrium, this concept goes a long way toward explaining demand for goods and services. This chapter examines the same ideas for firms, who are assumed to maximize profit by hiring the perfect combination of production inputs at the lowest cost. First the firm is introduced, along with the importance of opportunity costs and the economic view of profits. Then the short-run production function and several principles that flow from production are introduced. The discussion then turns to the short-run costs of employing inputs and important principles associated with costs. In particular, these concepts provide the foundation for the supply curve. Lastly, the analysis is extended into the long run.

Key Ideas
- Economic Profit
- Short Run Versus Long Run
- Production in the Short Run
- Law of Diminishing Marginal Returns
- Costs in the Short Run
- Costs in the Long Run

8.1 Firms, Opportunity Costs, and Profits

Main Topics: *The Firm, Profit and Cost: When CPAs and Economists Collide, Short-Run and Long-Run Decisions*

The Firm

When we talk about consumers, it's very easy to imagine yourself in the leading role. However, when the conversation switches to the firm, it is often much more difficult to visualize what it is or who we are talking about. The firm can bring to mind many things to many different people. The firm can be an independent bookstore in your town, or it can be Barnes & Noble. It can be a street vendor selling hot dogs, or it can be Oscar Mayer. Regardless of the size of the business, a **firm** is defined as: "An organization that employs factors of production to produce a good or service that it hopes to profitably sell."

Profit and Cost: When CPAs and Economists Collide

Before we launch into a technical discussion of production and costs, we need to take care of, well, a technicality. The bottom line is that the accountant sees profit differently than does the economist.

Example:

Upon completion of her undergraduate double major in accounting and economics, Molly creates a firm that sells lemonade on a busy street corner in her small town. Selling cups of lemonade at $1 each, Molly sells 1,000 cups per month. The accountant and the economist in her agree (imagine a little devil and little angel on each shoulder—you can decide which is the CPA) that monthly total revenues (TR) = $1 × 1,000 cups = $1,000.

Molly's accounting textbooks clearly state that profit (π) is calculated by subtracting total production costs (TC) from total revenue. She rents a table from her parents at $75 per month; spends $300 per month on lemons, sugar, and cups; and purchases a monthly vendor's license at $25. These direct, purchased, out-of-pocket costs are referred to as accounting costs, or the firm's **explicit costs**.

$$\text{Accounting } \pi = \text{TR} - \text{explicit costs} = \$1,000 - 75 - 300 - 25$$
$$= \$600, \text{ a tidy profit!}$$

The economist on Molly's other shoulder disagrees. Are these the only costs of running the lemonade stand? What about the opportunity costs of resources not accounted for above? For example, Molly has chosen to give up a monthly salary of $1,000 at a bank. The economist knows that this opportunity cost must be subtracted from total revenue to better measure profitability. These indirect, nonpurchased, opportunity costs are called economic costs, or the firm's **implicit costs**.

$$\text{Economic } \pi = \text{TR} - \text{explicit costs} - \text{implicit costs} = \$1,000 - 75 - 300 - 25 - 1,000$$
$$= -\$400, \text{ a painful loss!}$$

Other implicit costs borne by many entrepreneurs include the interest given up when savings are liquidated, or rent forgone if the individual works out of a home or garage. Here's one way to try to keep the firm's explicit and implicit costs straight:

- Were the dollars paid to outside resource suppliers (employees, a landlord, a wholesale food store)? Did money actually change hands? **Explicit.**
- Were the resources supplied by the entrepreneur herself (salary or interest given up)? **Implicit.**

So Which Should I Use?

This is an excellent question. The "quickie" answer is to turn to the title page of this book, and use that method. Of course, as a student of economics, you must include implicit economic costs in calculating economic profit. But why? Well, it's more accurate. An adept student of economics knows that the cost of something goes beyond the price tag. A friend of mine in graduate school once said that "nothing is free; it is just nonpriced." If you visit your AP teacher's office, you might not have to pay to pass through the door, but you could be doing something else with your time. This is a nonpriced economic cost. Molly's labor and effort at the lemonade stand appear to be free; this is why an accountant does not include that effort in calculating profit. An economist knows that it is not free—it is just nonpriced. An economist tries to quantify that price by using the value of Molly's efforts in her next best alternative as the banker. Throughout this book, costs refer to economic costs, and profits refer to economic profits.

Short-Run and Long-Run Decisions

The short run is a time when at least one production input is fixed and cannot be changed to respond to a change in product demand. During the holiday season a local gift shop extends hours and increases the workers hired. Much more difficult to change is the total capacity of the shop. The capacity of the shop is fixed in the short run but can be altered with enough time. The amount of time required to change the plant size is known as the **long run**. In other words, all inputs are variable in the long run. See Table 8.1.

Table 8.1

	PLANT SIZE (CAPITAL)	FIXED COSTS	VARIABLE COSTS	ENTRY/EXIT OF FIRMS
Short Run	Fixed	Some	Some	No
Long Run	Variable	None	All	Yes

Example:

When Molly pays $25 for a monthly vendor's license on January 1, she is committed for a month. She cannot receive a refund if she fails to operate the lemonade stand, and she does not have to pay more if she works 24 hours a day all month. For Molly, the long run is one month. On the other hand, at any point in the month, Molly can choose to purchase more lemons, cups, or sugar, or employ assistants if she is selling more cups of lemonade. This is a short-run decision.

8.2 Production and Cost

Main Topics: *Short-Run Production Functions, Law of Diminishing Marginal Returns, Short-Run Costs, Bridge over (Troubling) Economic Waters, Long-Run Costs, Economies of Scale*

Short-Run Production Functions

How do economic resources like labor, capital, natural resources, and entrepreneurial talent become a cup of lemonade, or a ton of copper, or a 30-second television commercial? A **production function** is the mechanism for combining production resources with existing technology into finished goods and services. In other words, a production function takes inputs and creates output. In a production function that uses only labor (L) and capital (K):

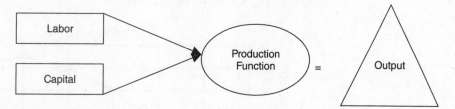

Fixed and Variable Inputs

The short run is a period of time too brief to change the plant capacity. This implies that some production inputs cannot be changed in the short run. These are **fixed inputs**. During the short run, firms can adjust production to meet changes in demand for their output. This implies that some inputs are **variable inputs**. Using only labor and capital, we assume that labor can be changed in the short run, but capital (i.e., the plant capacity) is fixed.

Short-Run Production Measures

By its very nature, production lends itself to be quantified, and as a result, you need to study these three production measures. To keep it simple, capital is assumed to be fixed while labor can be changed to produce more or less output.

1. **Total product of labor** (TP_L) is the total quantity, or total output, of a good produced at each quantity of labor employed.

2. **Marginal product of labor** (MP_L) is the change in total product resulting from a change in the labor input. $MP_L = \Delta TP_L/\Delta L$. If labor is changing one unit at a time, $MP_L = \Delta TP_L$.

3. **Average product of labor** (AP_L) is also a measure of average labor productivity and is total product divided by the amount of labor employed: $AP_L = TP_L/L$.

As you can see, MP_L and AP_L are both derived from TP_L. It is useful to see how these three measures are related with a numerical example.

Example:

In the production period of a month, Molly's lemonade stand combines variable inputs of her labor (and the raw materials) to the fixed inputs of her table and her license to operate. Molly adds employees to her stand (or we could call it the plant) and forecasts the change in production (cups per day) in Table 8.2.

Table 8.2

UNITS OF LABOR	TOTAL PRODUCT (TP_L)	MARGINAL PRODUCT (MP_L)	AVERAGE PRODUCT (AP_L)
0	0 cups		
1	5	5−0 = 5	5/1 = 5
2	15	10	7.5
3	30	15	10
4	40	10	10
5	45	5	9
6	40	−5	6.67
7	30	−10	4.29

As Molly employs more workers to the fixed plant capacity (the table on the corner), total product increases, eventually peaks, and then begins to fall. This production function can be seen in Figure 8.1.

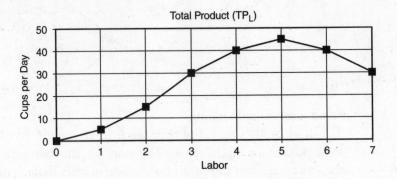

Figure 8.1

Law of Diminishing Marginal Returns

Imagine what happens to the lemonade stand as Molly adds more and more workers. At first, tasks are divided. (For example, Josh squeezes the lemons; Molly adds the sugar; Kelli stirs.) Specialization occurs. The marginal productivity of successive workers is rising in the early stage of production, but at some point, adding more workers increases the total product by a lesser amount. Maybe the fourth worker is pouring the lemonade and stocking while the fifth is taking money and making change. Beyond the fifth worker, the table is too crowded with employees, cups are spilled, product is wasted, and total production actually falls. The marginal contribution of these workers is negative. This illustrates one of the most important production concepts in the short run, the **law of diminishing marginal returns**, which states that *as successive units of a variable resource are added to a fixed resource, beyond some point the marginal product falls.*

- Increasing marginal returns: MP_L increases as L increases.
- Diminishing marginal returns: MP_L decreases as L increases.
- Negative marginal returns: MP_L becomes negative as L increases.

Graphically Speaking

Marginal product is the incremental change in total product as one more unit of labor is added. Marginal product is the geometric slope of total product. In Figure 8.1, the total product curve is initially getting steeper as more labor is added. This is seen in Figure 8.2 as increasing marginal product. From the third to the fifth worker, the slope of total product is still positive, but it is becoming less steep. In Figure 8.2, marginal product from workers 3 to 5 is still positive but is falling. Beyond the fifth worker, total product is falling and thus has a negative slope. This turn of events is seen below when marginal product becomes negative.

Average product, also plotted below, initially rises, reaches a peak, and then begins to fall. So long as the marginal (next) worker adds production that is above the current average, they are pulling the average up. This is why we see AP_L rising so long as MP_L is above AP_L. If the marginal worker adds production that is below the current average, the worker pulls the average down. Thus, when MP_L is below AP_L, you see that AP_L is falling. Logically then, MP_L intersects AP_L at the peak of AP_L. Average product cannot be negative.

- If $MP_L > AP_L$: AP_L is rising.
- If $MP_L < AP_L$: AP_L is falling.
- If $MP_L = AP_L$: AP_L is at the peak.

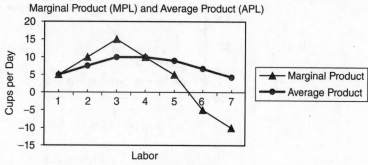

Figure 8.2

Short-Run Costs

It is important to note that we have discussed production theory without including the nagging necessity of paying for our hired inputs. For every employed input, fixed or variable, a cost is incurred.

Total Costs

In the short run, there is at least one input that is fixed and so these costs are also fixed. All inputs that are variable incur variable costs.

1. **Total fixed costs (TFC)** are those costs that do not vary with changes in short-run output. They must be paid even when output is zero. These include rent on building or equipment, insurance, or licenses.

2. **Total variable costs (TVC)** are those costs that change with the level of output. If output is zero, so are total variable costs. They include payment for materials, fuel, power, transportation services, most labor, and similar costs.

3. **Total cost (TC)** is the sum of total fixed and total variable costs at each level of output:

$$TC = TVC + TFC$$

Table 8.3

TOTAL PRODUCT CUPS PER MINUTE	TOTAL FIXED COST (TFC)	TOTAL VARIABLE COST (TVC)	TOTAL COST (TC = TFC + TVC)
0	$6	$0	$6
1	$6	$5	$11
2	$6	$8	$14
3	$6	$13	$19
4	$6	$19	$25
5	$6	$26	$32
6	$6	$34	$40
7	$6	$43	$49

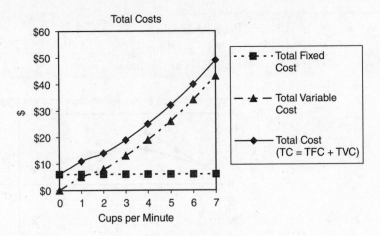

Figure 8.3

Table 8.3 summarizes Molly's costs of producing cups of lemonade per minute. Her total fixed costs are assumed to be $6 per minute, and total variable costs increase as production increases.

Figure 8.3 illustrates the three total cost functions. Total fixed cost is a constant at all levels of output. Total variable cost quickly rises at first, briefly slows, and then proceeds to increase at an increasing rate. Total cost is simply the sum of TFC and TVC at every level of output, and so it lies parallel to TVC. Thus, the vertical distance between TC and TVC is equal to TFC.

Table 8.4

TOTAL PRODUCT CUPS PER MINUTE	MARGINAL COST (MC)	AVERAGE FIXED COST (AFC)	AVERAGE VARIABLE COST (AVC)	AVERAGE TOTAL COST (ATC)
0				
1	$5	$6.00	$5.00	$11.00
2	$3	$3.00	$4.00	$7.00
3	$5	$2.00	$4.33	$6.33
4	$6	$1.50	$4.75	$6.25
5	$7	$1.20	$5.20	$6.40
6	$8	$1.00	$5.67	$6.67
7	$9	$0.86	$6.14	$7.00

Marginal and Average Costs

Similar to our discussion of production, we can derive marginal and per-unit measures of cost from the total cost functions. These are in Table 8.4.

1. **Marginal cost** is the additional cost of producing one more unit of output $MC = \Delta TC/\Delta Q$. Since TVCs are the only costs that change with the level of output, marginal cost is also calculated as $MC = \Delta TVC/\Delta Q$. If quantity is changing one unit at a time, $MC = \Delta TC = \Delta TVC$.

2. **Average fixed cost** (AFC) is total fixed cost divided by output: $AFC = TFC/Q$. It continuously falls as output rises.

3. **Average variable cost (AVC)** is total variable cost divided by output: $AVC = TVC/Q$.

4. **Average total cost (ATC)** is total cost divided by output $ATC = TC/Q$. Note that $ATC = AFC + AVC$.

Graphically Speaking

If marginal product is the slope of total product, it should be no surprise that marginal cost is the slope of total cost, or total variable cost. We can see that marginal cost initially falls due to specialization but soon begins to rise as more output is produced. This is the law of increasing costs and is a direct result of the law of diminishing marginal returns to production. Both being U-shaped curves, average variable and average total costs initially fall, hit a minimum point, and begin to rise. Average total cost is vertically above AVC by the amount of AFC. Figure 8.4 illustrates this.

Marginal cost and average variable and average total cost are related in much the same way as marginal product is related to average product of labor. When the marginal cost of producing another cup of lemonade exceeds the current average cost, the average is rising. When the marginal cost of producing another cup of lemonade falls below the current average cost, the average is falling. Therefore, marginal cost equals average total cost at the minimum of ATC and equals average variable cost at the minimum of AVC.

When drawing a graph similar to the one in Figure 8.4, it is important that you show an upward-sloping MC curve intersecting AVC and ATC at the *minimum* of those U-shaped curves. You can lose free-response points for sloppy graphs that show MC intersecting AVC and ATC at a point that is not *clearly* the minimum point, or bottom of the U-shaped curves.

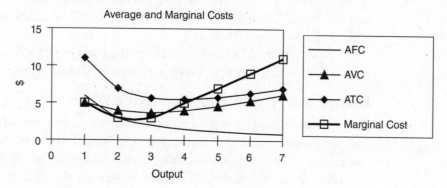

Figure 8.4

Here are three easy steps to drawing a clean graph that avoids any lost graphing points:

- Draw the upward-sloping curve and label it MC.
- Draw a downward-sloping curve that stops at the MC curve. Lift your pen from the paper. Trust me, if you try to draw the U in one smooth movement, you are more likely to lose this point.
- Beginning at the point where your downward-sloping curve intersects MC, draw an upward-sloping curve to complete the U-shaped ATC curve. You can repeat these steps to draw the AVC curve that lies below the ATC curve.

The mathematical relationship between total costs and per-unit (or average) costs is rather straightforward: divide the total dollars of cost by the output produced, and you get average dollars spent on a unit of output. These relationships can also be seen in a graph similar to the one in Figure 8.4, and recent free-response and multiple choice questions have tested these relationships by asking students to use an average-cost graph like the one in Figure 8.5 to identify a total cost concept.

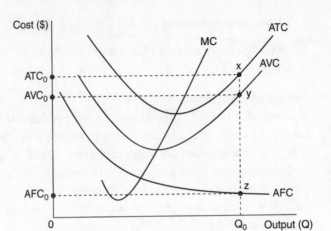

Figure 8.5

Suppose the firm is producing Q_0 units of output. How can we determine total cost (TC_0), total variable cost (TVC_0), and total fixed cost (TFC_0) from the information in Figure 8.5? Let's take the relationship between ATC and TC as an example. Remember that average total cost is computed as

$$ATC_0 = TC_0/Q_0$$

so $TC_0 = ATC_0 \times Q_0$. In Figure 8.5, TC_0 is the area of a rectangle with a width of Q_0 units and a height of ATC_0. Using the notation in the graph, this area would be identified by the area $0ATC_0xQ_0$. In a similar way, the TVC_0 would be identified by the area $0AVC_0yQ_0$, and TFC_0 by the area $0AFC_0zQ_0$.

If you know the relationships between total and per-unit costs, and you can identify the area in a graph like Figure 8.5, you are prepared to earn some valuable points.

Bridge over (Troubling) Economic Waters

Many students think that production and cost concepts are two sets of theoretical topics. This separation creates the impression that "there's twice as much to remember." These students are surprised to find out that production and cost are closely connected.

Think about it from Molly's point of view. If the next worker employed has a high marginal product, then the marginal cost of producing that increased product must be quite low. When things are going well with production, they must be going well with cost. Try to see the concepts of production and cost not as two isolated bodies of theory but as two related sets of concepts that just need to be bridged. Let us try to build this bridge with a little algebra.

Marginal Product and Marginal Cost

$MC = \Delta TVC/\Delta Q$, and since the only variable input is labor being paid a fixed wage w,
$MC = w\Delta L/\Delta Q$, which can be modified as
$MC = w/(\Delta Q/\Delta L) = w/MP_L$. MC and MP_L are inverses of each other!

- As MP_L is falling (diminishing marginal returns), MC is rising.
- As MP_L is rising (increasing marginal returns), MC is falling.
- When MP_L is highest, MC is lowest.

Average Product and Average Variable Cost

$AVC = TVC/Q$ and with the only variable input being labor paid a fixed wage w,
$AVC = wL/Q$, which can be modified as
$AVC = w/(Q/L) = w/AP_L$. AVC and AP_L are inverses of each other!

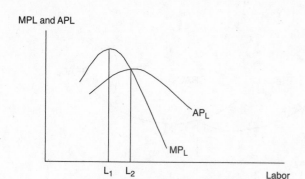

Figure 8.6

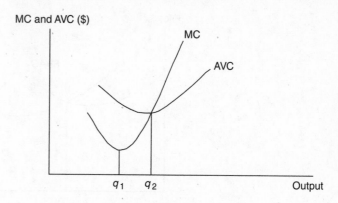

Figure 8.7

KEY IDEA

- As AP_L is falling, AVC is rising.
- As AP_L is rising, AVC is falling.
- When AP_L is highest, AVC is lowest.

If we put smoother versions of our production and cost figures together, we can see these relationships in Figures 8.6 and 8.7.

Long-Run Costs

Since all inputs are variable in the long run, discussion of production levels isn't so much about output per hour or day; it's more a question of plant size or capacity. In the short run, the firm asks, "With our current plant size, how much must we produce today?" The long run is long enough to adjust the plant capacity, so the issue is really one of scale. The firm might ask itself, "At what scale do we want to operate?"

Long-Run Average Cost

I like to think of the firm's short-run average costs as a snapshot of the firm's ability to produce efficiently *at the fixed plant size*. Over time, the firm may grow and expand the plant size and begin to produce efficiently, but at the larger fixed plant size, giving us another snapshot. This process repeats itself as the firm expands or contracts and each time we receive another short-run snapshot of average cost. If we could put these short-run snapshots together into a kind of motion picture, we would see a more continuous long-run home movie of the firm's average costs. The example and Figure 8.8 illustrate the connection between short- and long-run average costs.

> "Make sure you know the definition for the Law of Diminishing Marginal Returns. It could appear in lots of different questions."
> —Cassie, AP Student

> "Make sure you can differentiate between long-run and short-run curves." —Kristy, AP Student

Example:
- In year one, Molly's firm operates at a "small" scale, producing on $SRAC_1$.
- In year two, Molly could expand and operate at a "medium" scale, producing on $SRAC_2$, but only if she can sell more than 100 gallons of lemonade. At quantities below 100, $SRAC_1 < SRAC_2$, so expansion would not be wise.
- In year three, Molly might expand to operate at a "large" scale and move to $SRAC_3$, but only if she can sell more than 250 gallons.
- Beyond the "large" scale exists a "grand" scale, but very quickly $SRAC_4 > SRAC_3$ and so this plant capacity actually begins to incur rising per-unit costs.

Each of these four short-run snapshots of average costs can be smoothed out into the home movie long-run average cost curve, which is composed of sections of each short-run average cost curve at each of the four plant sizes that Molly might choose for her firm. In Figure 8.8, the long-run average cost curve would lie along the segments a→b→c→d→e.

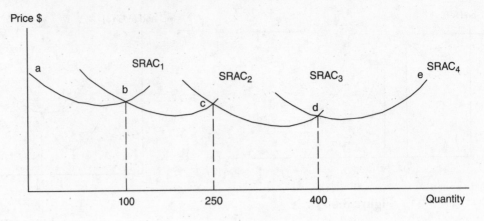

Figure 8.8

Economies of Scale

Construction of a smoother version of Figure 8.8 allows us to see more easily some important stages of the long-run average cost curves (Figure 8.9).

1. **Economies of scale** are advantages of increased plant size and are seen on the downward part of the LRAC curve. LRAC falls as plant size rises.
   a. Labor and managerial specialization is one reason for this.
   b. Ability to purchase and use more efficient capital goods also can explain economies of scale.
   c. The plant size that marks the lowest point on the long-run average cost curve is called **minimum efficient scale**. Because minimum efficient scale is associated with small per-unit costs, firms will do their best to expand the plant size to that level of output, and this has a big role in shaping what the industry looks like. If the minimum efficient scale represents a small plant size, the industry is likely to be populated with many small firms. However, if the minimum efficient scale represents a giant-sized firm, the industry almost assuredly includes just a small number of enormous companies.

2. **Constant returns to scale** can occur when LRAC is constant over a variety of plant sizes.

3. **Diseconomies of scale** are illustrated by the rising part of the LRAC curve and can occur if a firm becomes too large.
   a. Some reasons for this include distant management, worker alienation, and problems with communication and coordination.

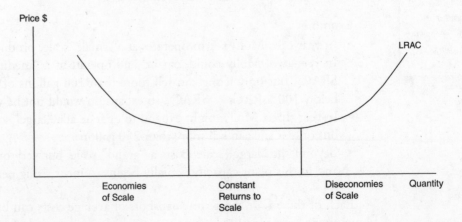

Figure 8.9

Another Bridge between Production and Cost

You might be thinking, "I've heard about scale economies, but my teacher was talking about production, not cost. I'm so confused!" You're right; it can be confusing when similar-sounding economic phrases are tossed around in seemingly different contexts. If you remember the "bridge" between costs and production, you might recall that when something is happening with regard to cost, a similar thing is happening in the production realm. They are very much connected in both the short run and the long run. Let's look at a quick example.

Remember that, in the long run, the firm can adjust all inputs to produce more or less output. Let's suppose that the firm initially has one unit of both labor (L) and capital (K), these inputs are producing one unit of output (Q), and the price of labor and capital is $1 each. With these input prices, the firm is spending a total of $2 ($1 for labor plus $1 for capital) in total cost (TC) and the average total cost (ATC) is also $2 (TC/Q). This is summarized in the first row of Table 8.5.

Table 8.5

QUANTITY OF LABOR (L)	QUANTITY OF CAPITAL (K)	OUTPUT PRODUCED (Q)	TOTAL COST (TC)	LONG-RUN AVERAGE TOTAL COST (LRAC) = TC/Q
1	1	1	$2	$2
2	2	4	$4	$1
4	4	8	$8	$1
8	8	12	$16	$1.33

In the second row of Table 8.5, let's see what happens if the firm doubles both labor and capital in the long run, and the output more than doubles (increases from one to four units). When this happens in the production function, the firm is said to experience **increasing returns to scale**. And notice what happens to long-run average total cost; it falls. This tells us that if the firm is experiencing increasing returns to scale in production (a good thing), they are also experiencing economies of scale in costs (also a good thing).

If we double our inputs again, and output exactly doubles, it is said that the firm has **constant returns to scale** in production. In this case, long-run average total costs remain at $1, and this is also described as constant returns to scale in costs. This is seen as the horizontal region of the LRAC curve.

Finally, if we double our inputs one last time, and output increases by less than double (not a desired outcome), we say that the firm has **decreasing returns to scale** in production. When this happens, the long-run average total costs increase to $1.33. Once again we see that if something bad is happening in production, something undesirable is happening with long-run average costs; they are rising.

Table 8.6 summarizes these long-run production and cost concepts in a way that might help you see that they are not really different.

Table 8.6

WHEN ALL INPUTS ARE DOUBLED AND...	OUTPUT INCREASES BY...	WE CALL THIS...	AT THE SAME TIME, LRAC IS...	AND WE CALL THIS...
	More than double	Increasing returns to production	falling	Economies of scale
	Exactly double	Constant returns to scale in production	horizontal	Constant returns to scale
	Less than double	Decreasing returns to scale in production	rising	Diseconomies of scale

› Review Questions

1. Which of the following is most likely an example of production inputs that can be adjusted in the long run, but not in the short run?

   (A) Amount of wood used to make a desk.
   (B) Number of pickles put on a sandwich.
   (C) The size of a McDonald's kitchen.
   (D) Number of teachers' assistants in local high schools.
   (E) The amount of electricity consumed by a manufacturing plant.

2. The law of diminishing marginal returns is responsible for

   (A) AVC that first rises, but eventually falls, as output increases.
   (B) AFC that first rises, but eventually falls, as output increases.
   (C) MP that first falls, but eventually rises, as output increases.
   (D) MC that first falls, but eventually rises, as output increases.
   (E) ATC that first rises, but eventually falls, as output increases.

3. Which of the following cost and production relationships is inaccurately stated?

   (A) $AFC = AVC - ATC$
   (B) $MC = \Delta TVC/\Delta Q$
   (C) $TVC = TC - TFC$
   (D) $AP_L = TP_L/L$
   (E) $MC = w/MP_L$

4. If the per-unit price of labor, a variable resource, increases, it causes which of the following?

   (A) An upward shift in AFC.
   (B) An upward shift in MP_L.
   (C) A downward shift in ATC.
   (D) An upward shift in MC.
   (E) A downward shift in AFC.

Use the following figure to respond to questions 5 and 6.

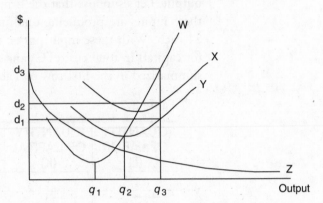

5. The curves labeled W, X, Y, Z refer to which respective cost functions?

   (A) MC, AVC, ATC, and AFC.
   (B) MC, TC, TVC, and AFC.
   (C) MC, ATC, AVC, and AFC.
   (D) MC, ATC, AVC, and TFC.
   (E) ATC, AVC, AFC, and MC.

6. At the q_3 level of output,

   (A) $AFC = \$d_2 - \$d_1$.
   (B) $MC = \$d_2$.
   (C) $TVC = \$d_2$.
   (D) $ATC = \$d_3$.
   (E) $AFC = \$d_3 - \$d_2$.

› Answers and Explanations

1. **C**—The short run is a period of time too short to increase the plant size. All other choices involve decisions that could increase production almost immediately, with no change in the size of the facility. Increasing the size of a McDonald's kitchen takes quite some time and represents an increase in the total capacity of the kitchen to produce.

2. **D**—The law of diminishing marginal returns says that MP_L eventually falls as you add more labor to a fixed plant. This question tests you on the important connection between production and cost. Remember that we derived this "bridge" and found that $MC = w/MP_L$. So when MP_L is initially rising, MC is falling. Eventually when MP_L is falling, MC is rising. Choices A, B, and E are just flat wrong. All three average costs begin by falling. AFC continues to fall, but AVC and ATC eventually rise.

3. **A**—AFC plus AVC equals ATC. If you do the subtraction, AFC = ATC − AVC, making choice A the only incorrect statement. If you have studied your production and cost relationships, you recognize that choices B, C, D, and E are all stated correctly.

4. **D**—When labor is more expensive, the MC of producing the good increases, so the MC curve shifts upward. The price of a variable input has increased, so easily rule out any reference to fixed costs. Because of the inverse relationship between marginal cost and marginal product of labor, a higher wage shifts MP_L downward.

5. **C**—You must be familiar with the graphical representation of marginal and average cost functions.

6. **A**—The vertical distance between ATC and AVC is AFC at any level of output.

› Rapid Review

The firm: An organization that employs factors of production to produce a good or service that it hopes to profitably sell.

Accounting profit: The difference between total revenue and total explicit costs.

Economic profit: The difference between total revenue and total explicit and implicit costs.

Explicit costs: Direct, purchased, out-of-pocket costs paid to resource suppliers outside the firm. Also referred to as *accounting costs*.

Implicit costs: Indirect, nonpurchased, or opportunity costs of resources provided by the entrepreneur. Also called *economic costs*.

Short run: A period of time too short to change the size of the plant, but many other, more variable resources can be adjusted to meet demand.

Long run: A period of time long enough to alter the plant size. New firms can enter the industry and existing firms can liquidate and exit.

Production function: The mechanism for combining production resources, with existing technology, into finished goods and services. Inputs are turned into outputs.

Fixed inputs: Production inputs that cannot be changed in the short run. Usually this is the plant size or capital.

Variable inputs: Production inputs that the firm can adjust in the short run to meet changes in demand for their output. Often this is labor and/or raw materials.

Total Product of Labor (TP_L): The total quantity, or total output, of a good produced at each quantity of labor employed.

Marginal Product of Labor (MP_L): The change in total product resulting from a change in the labor input. $MP_L = \Delta TP_L/\Delta L$, or the slope of total product.

Average Product of Labor (AP_L): Total product divided by labor employed: $AP_L = TP_L/L$.

Law of diminishing marginal returns: As successive units of a variable resource are added to a fixed resource, beyond some point the marginal product of the variable resource declines.

Total fixed costs (TFC): Costs that do not vary with changes in short-run output. They must be paid even when output is zero.

Total variable costs (TVC): Costs that change with the level of output. If output is zero, so are total variable costs.

Total cost (TC): The sum of total fixed and total variable costs at each level of output: TC = TVC + TFC.

Marginal cost (MC): The additional cost of producing one more unit of output. MC = ΔTC/ΔQ = ΔTVC/ΔQ or the slope of total cost and total variable cost.

Average fixed cost (AFC): Total fixed cost divided by output: AFC = TFC/Q.

Average variable cost (AVC): Total variable cost divided by output: AVC = TVC/Q.

Average total cost (ATC): Total cost divided by output. ATC = TC/Q = AFC + AVC.

Relationship between MP_L and MC: If labor is the variable input being paid a fixed wage (w), MC and MP_L are inverses of each other. MC = $w/(\Delta Q/\Delta L)$ = w/MP_L.

Relationship between AP_L and AVC: In the simplified case where labor is the variable input being paid a fixed wage (w), AVC and AP_L are inverses of each other. AVC = $w/(Q/L)$ = w/AP_L.

Economies of scale: The downward part of the LRAC curve where LRAC falls as plant size increases. This is the result of specialization, lower cost of inputs, or other efficiencies from larger scale.

Minimum efficient scale: The plant size at which the LRAC first reaches its minimum point.

Constant returns to scale: Occurs when LRAC is constant over a variety of plant sizes.

Diseconomies of scale: The upward part of the LRAC curve where LRAC rises as plant size increases. This is usually the result of the increased difficulty of managing larger firms, which results in lost efficiency and rising per-unit costs.

Increasing returns to scale in production: The long-run outcome when output more than doubles from a doubling of all inputs.

Constant returns to scale in production: The long-run outcome when output exactly doubles from a doubling of all inputs.

Decreasing returns to scale in production: The long-run outcome when output less than doubles from a doubling of all inputs.

Market Structures, Perfect Competition, Monopoly, and Things Between

IN THIS CHAPTER

Summary: Chapter 7 presented the relationship between product demand, elasticity, and total revenue. Chapter 8 introduced the concept of economic profit and presented the theory behind production and costs. This chapter puts revenue and cost together to examine how a firm chooses the profit-maximizing level of output and price of the product. But this profit-maximizing decision depends on the structure in which the firm operates. At one extreme there are many perfectly competitive firms, each too small to have a measurable impact on market price, much less each other. At the other extreme there is one firm, a monopolist, that absolutely controls the industry price and output. In between are various shades of each extreme, some closer to monopoly, and some closer to perfect competition. It is important to realize that there is no "representative" industry, or market structure, so we focus on four general models and study how firms in these structures determine price and output. In addition to the extremes of perfect competition and monopoly, we cover the models of monopolistic competition and oligopoly. This chapter also introduces you to some basic game theoretic models.

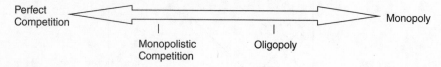

Perfect Competition ⟷ Monopoly

Monopolistic Competition   Oligopoly

Key Ideas

- ✪ Perfect Competition
- ✪ Monopoly
- ✪ Monopolistic Competition
- ✪ Oligopoly

9.1 Perfect Competition

Main Topics: *Structural Characteristics of Perfect Competition, Demand for the Firm, Profit Maximization, Short-Run Profit and Loss, Decision to Shut Down, Long-Run Adjustment*

Structural Characteristics of Perfect Competition

Each market structure is defined by structural characteristics. These characteristics determine, among other things, how the profit-maximizing price and quantity are set in the short run, as well as how profits might be maintained in the long run. Perfect competition is typically described by four characteristics:

- *Many small independent producers and consumers.* Each firm is too small to have an impact on market price. No one firm can drive up the price by restricting supply, or drive down the price by flooding the market with output. No one consumer can, by changing the amount of the good that they consume, impact the price.
- *Firms produce a standardized (or homogeneous) product.* There exist no real differences between one firm's output and the next.
- *No barriers to entry or exit.* There exist no significant obstacles to the entry of new firms into, or the exit of existing firms out of, this industry. Profitability, or lack thereof, determines whether the industry is expanding or contracting.
- *Firms are "price takers."* This characteristic is actually a result of the first three. Because all firms are too small to affect the price, they must accept the market price and produce as much as they wish at that price. Even if they *could* change the price, they would not do so. To see this, suppose that the market determined the competitive price of barley is $5. If farmer Katie increased the price to $5.01, she would now be the high-price supplier of barley, with thousands of competitors producing an identical product at a lower price; Katie is likely to lose all of her customers. If she lowers her price to $4.99, she would seemingly clean up her competition. But, remember, the price-taking characteristic tells us that Katie can sell all she wants at the market price of $5. If you can sell all you want at $5, why would Katie sell even one unit at $4.99?

> "In order to keep the different types of firms straight, make a table including the firm's definition, what kind of product they produce, barriers, and how they control price. It is the best way to study."
> —Kristy, AP Student

All four of the characteristics of perfect competition are rarely found in today's industries, but agricultural commodities are usually regarded as approximately perfectly competitive.

Demand for the Firm

Each perfectly competitive firm produces a standardized, or homogenous, product. Because each firm's output is such a small share of the total market supply, the demand for each firm's output is perfectly elastic. Perfectly competitive firms have no effect on the market price; they simply produce as much as they can at the going price. This implies a horizontal demand curve for their product. This does *not* imply that the market demand curve is

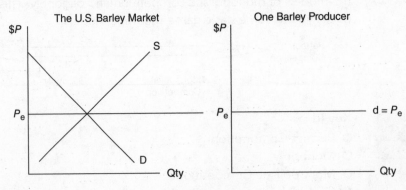

Figure 9.1

horizontal. If the market price of barley falls, quantity demanded rises. Figure 9.1 illustrates the difference between market demand (D) and the demand for one firm's product (d).

Profit Maximization

Let's get one thing straight. When we say firms *maximize* economic profit, this means they are not going to settle for anything less than the highest possible difference between total revenue and total economic cost. If an additional dollar of profit is to be earned, they take that opportunity. If the maximum profit possible is actually zero, or even negative dollars, they accept this short-run outcome. There are two equivalent ways to maximize economic profit.

The Method of "Totals"

The perfectly competitive firm cannot change the price; it can only adjust output. To maximize profit, the firm selects the output to maximize:

$$\text{Economic profit } (\pi) = \text{Total revenue} - \text{Total economic cost}$$

An example should help to illustrate how a firm goes about maximizing profit.

Example:

A carrot farmer operates in a perfectly competitive market. The going price for a bushel of carrots is $11. Table 9.1 summarizes how total revenue, total cost, and profit differ at various levels of output. Because it is the short run, there exist $16 of fixed costs. All costs reflect the explicit and implicit costs of hiring a resource.

Table 9.1

DAILY BUSHELS OF CARROTS (q)	PRICE (P)	TOTAL REVENUE (TR)	TOTAL COST (TC)	PROFIT (π)
0	$11	$0	$16	−$16
1	$11	$11	$22	−$11
2	$11	$22	$27.50	−$5.50
3	$11	$33	$34	−$1
4	$11	$44	$42	$2
5	$11	$55	$53	$2
6	$11	$66	$65	$1

Because the firm is a price taker, the level of output does not affect the going price. Total costs rise as production increases, a concept seen in the previous chapter. As a profit maximizer, our carrot farmer would choose to produce five bushels per day and earn $2 in daily economic profit. Note, when there are two quantities that produce the same amount of profit, like four and five bushels, we select the larger of the two quantities. This method of profit maximization is much like trial and error and is a bit cumbersome. Let's explore an equivalent and easier way.

The Method of "Marginals"

Throughout this book we have seen illustrations of marginal analysis, and this situation is no different. You'll recall that rational decision making implies the following:

- If MB > MC, do more of it.
- If MB < MC, do less of it.
- If MB = MC, stop here.

Since the only decision to be made by the perfectly competitive firm is to choose the optimal level of output, the firm's rule is as follows:

TIP

• **Choose the level of output where MR = MC.**

Table 9.2 can be modified to show the marginal revenue and marginal cost of selling additional bushels of carrots.

"If you only remember one thing, remember this! MR = MC."
—Kristy, AP Student

Table 9.2

DAILY BUSHELS OF CARROTS (q)	PRICE (P)	TOTAL REVENUE (TR)	TOTAL COST (TC)	PROFIT (o)	MARGINAL REVENUE (MR)	MARGINAL COST (MC)
0	$11	$0	$16	−$16		
1	$11	$11	$22	−$11	$11	$6
2	$11	$22	$27.50	−$5.50	$11	$5.50
3	$11	$33	$34	−$1	$11	$6.50
4	$11	$44	$42	$2	$11	$8
5	*$11*	*$55*	*$53*	*$2*	*$11*	*$11*
6	$11	$66	$65	$1	$11	$12

Notice that in perfect competition, the price is equal to marginal revenue. This is fairly simple if you recall the assumptions of the model. Farmers can sell as much as they want at the market price. If a farmer sells one more bushel, total revenue increases by the price of the bushel, $11 in this case. Sell another bushel; earn another marginal revenue of $11. Price is also equivalent to **average revenue** (AR), or total revenue per unit. These relationships can be seen in Figure 9.2.

TIP

• $MR = \Delta TR/\Delta Q = P \times \Delta Q/\Delta Q = P$
• $AR = TR/Q = P \times Q/Q = P$
• $P = MR = AR =$ Demand for the firm's product
• Total revenue ($P \times q$) equal to $55 can be seen as the area of the rectangle with a height of $P = \$11$ and width of $q_e = 5$.

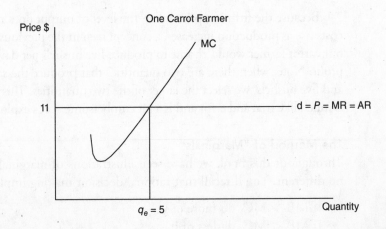

Figure 9.2

Short-Run Profit and Loss

To maximize profit, the firm must choose the level of output (q_e) where MR = MC. But how can we use Figure 9.2 to identify these profits? A little algebra goes a long way.

$\pi = \text{TR} - \text{TC} = P \times q_e - \text{TC}$. If you divide both terms by quantity and remember that $\text{TC}/q = $ Average total cost (ATC), you have

$$\pi = q_e \times (P - \text{ATC}).$$

The term $(P - \text{ATC})$ is the per-unit difference between what the firm receives from the sale of each unit and the average cost of producing it, or profit per unit. When you multiply this per-unit profit by the number of units (q_e) produced, you have total profit. Table 9.3 and Figure 9.3 incorporate the ATC into our carrot farmer's profit-maximizing decision table.

Table 9.3

DAILY BUSHELS OF CARROTS (q)	PRICE (P)	TOTAL COST (TC)	AVERAGE TOTAL COST (ATC)	(P − ATC)	PROFIT (Π) = q × (P − ATC)
0	$11	$16			−$16
1	$11	$22	$22	−$11	−$11
2	$11	$27.50	$13.75	−$2.75	−$5.50
3	$11	$34	$11.33	−$.33	−$1
4	$11	$42	$10.50	$.50	$2
5	*$11*	*$53*	*$10.60*	*$.40*	*$2*
6	$11	$65	$10.83	$.17	$1

> "This is a great analogy to remember."
> —AP Teacher

Profit Rectangles and Flying Monkeys

Everyone remembers *The Wizard of Oz* and the critical instructions that the people of Munchkinland gave Dorothy and Toto as they set off to find the Wizard: "Follow the yellow brick road." And when Dorothy, Toto, and friends stayed on the yellow brick road,

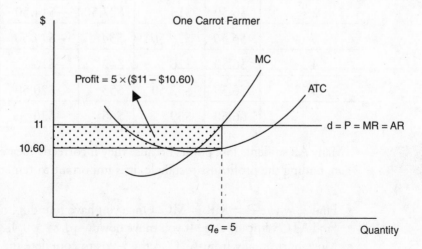

Figure 9.3

they were fine. Whenever they ignored these cautionary words and left the yellow brick road, bad things happened—the scariest being the arrival of the flying monkeys. The flying monkeys tore the Scarecrow limb from limb and set the Scarecrow's straw innards on fire. Very bad things happen when you leave the yellow brick road.

When you find the profit-maximizing level of production, q_e, you are locating the yellow brick road for this firm. *Never* leave this level of output or bad things happen. Finding q_e is the first step in calculating profit with a "profit rectangle." The area of the shaded rectangle is 5 bushels wide, multiplied by 40 cents high. In our case, the price $11 in Figure 9.3 is above the average total cost $10.60, so we have positive economic profits of $2. This does not always occur in the short run. Another look at our per-unit equation tells us:

- If $P > \text{ATC}$, $\pi > 0$.
- If $P < \text{ATC}$, $\pi < 0$.
- If $P = \text{ATC}$, $\pi = 0$.

Short-Run Losses

While firms would love to maintain the above scenario where $P > \text{ATC}$ and positive economic profits are made, it might not always turn out that way. Due to a failure of the Bugs Bunny diet fad, the market for carrots suffers a dramatic decrease in demand. Plummeting demand decreases the market price to $6.50 per bushel, and firms must readjust their profit-maximizing output decision.

As seen in Table 9.4, at the much lower price of $6.50, the firm now finds that MR = MC at an output of three bushels per day. Not surprisingly, the opportunity for positive economic profit has been eliminated. The profit-maximizing, or loss-minimizing, output of three bushels provides the best possible scenario for the firm; but that scenario involves economic losses of $14.50. The rectangle can still be seen in Figure 9.4, where average total cost is $11.33 per bushel.

Table 9.4

DAILY BUSHELS OF CARROTS (Q)	PRICE (P)	TOTAL REVENUE (TR)	TOTAL COST (TC)	PROFIT (π)	MARGINAL REVENUE (MR)	MARGINAL COST (MC)
0	$6.50	$0	$16	−$16		
1	$6.50	$6.50	$22	−$15.50	$6.50	$6
2	$6.50	$13	$27.50	−$14.50	$6.50	$5.50
3	*$6.50*	*$19.50*	*$34*	*−$14.50*	*$6.50*	*$6.50*
4	$6.50	$26	$42	−$16	$6.50	$8
5	$6.50	$32.50	$53	−$20.50	$6.50	$11
6	$6.50	$39	$65	−$26	$6.50	$12

- Many AP students lose points because they incorrectly locate and label profit. When you are finding the profit/loss rectangle, it is important to remember the following.

- Find q_e where $P = \text{MR} = \text{MC}$. Once you have found q_e, never leave it.
- Find ATC vertically at q_e. If you move downward, $\pi > 0$. If you move upward, $\pi < 0$.
- Move horizontally from ATC to the y-axis to complete the rectangle, and clearly label it as positive or negative.

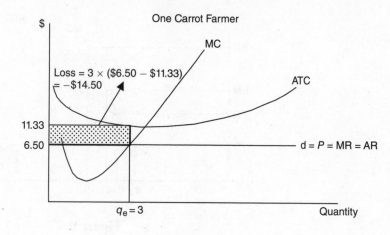

Figure 9.4

Decision to Shut Down

Firms obviously do not enjoy producing at a loss and desperately hope that the market price improves so that profits are possible. However, if firms are incurring losses, they must decide whether it is economically rational to operate at all. The decision to shut down, or produce zero, in the short run is sometimes the optimal strategy. To see why, consider what happens when a firm begins to produce. When a perfectly competitive firm decides to produce any level of output greater than zero, two things happen:

1. It collects total revenue (TR) = $P \times q_e$.
2. It incurs variable costs (TVC). Of course, the firm also incurs total fixed costs, but it incurs those costs anyway, regardless of the level of output.

"This has great potential to be asked on both sections of the exam."
—*AP Teacher*

If the firm, by producing in the short run, can collect total revenues that at least exceed the total variable costs, then it continues to produce, even at a loss. However, if producing output incurs more variable cost than revenue collected, why bother? Shut down, hope for better times, and suffer losses equal to TFC. This comparison provides us a decision rule for shutting down in the short run:

- If $TR \geq TVC$, the firm produces q_e where $MR = MC$.
- If $TR < TVC$, the firm shuts down and $q = 0$.

The Shutdown Point

We can see the shutdown point in Figure 9.5 by converting the above decision rule into a per-unit comparison. Dividing total revenue and total variable cost by q tells us to shut down if $P < AVC$. This is the identical decision rule; it is just a per-unit comparison of revenue and variable cost:

- If $P \geq AVC$, the firm produces q_e where $MR = MC$.
- If $P < AVC$, the firm shuts down and $q = 0$.

In Figure 9.5, there are four prices shown:

- PH is the highest price. At q_h, the firm earns enough total revenue to cover all costs. $\pi > 0$.
- PM is the middle price. At q_m, the firm's TR exceeds TVC but only covers part of the TFC. $\pi < 0$.
- PD is the shutdown price. At q_d, the firm's TR just covers TVC and the firm is at the shutdown point. If price falls any lower, the firm does not produce.
- PL is the lowest price. At q_1, the firm's TR cannot even cover TVC, and so the firm shuts down, producing $q = 0$. $\pi = -TFC$.

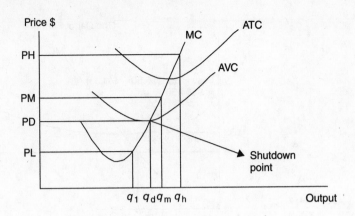

Figure 9.5

Short-Run Supply

As you can see in Figure 9.5, when the price fluctuates between PH and PD, the firm finds a new profit-maximizing quantity where P = MR = MC. If price increases, quantity supplied increases. If price decreases, quantity supplied decreases. This is a restatement of the law of supply. This movement upward and downward along the marginal cost curve implies that MC serves as the supply curve for the perfectly competitive firm. The only exception is when the price falls below the shutdown point (minimum of AVC) and the firm quickly decides to produce nothing. The market supply curve is simply the horizontal summation of all firms' MC curves.

- The MC curve above the shutdown point serves as the supply curve for each perfectly competitive firm.
- The market supply curve is therefore the horizontal sum of all of the MC curves: $S = \Sigma MC$.

Long-Run Adjustment

The short run is a period of time too brief for firms to change the size of their plants. This means that it is also too short for existing firms to exit the industry in bad times and too short for new entrepreneurs to enter the industry in good times. The "free entry and exit" characteristic of perfect competition assures us that in the long run, we can expect to see firms either exiting or entering, depending on whether profits or losses are being made in the short run. We'll first examine the case where short-run positive profits are made in the carrot industry. Then we'll look at the situation where short-run losses are incurred.

- In most of the past AP Microeconomics exams, free-response questions have appeared that test the students' knowledge of perfect competition and the difference between the short- and long-run equilibria.

Short-Run Positive Profits

Figure 9.6 illustrates the perfectly competitive carrot industry where the market price is above average total cost. Firms are earning positive short-run profits, as illustrated by the shaded rectangle.

So what next? Well, many entrepreneurs on the outside of this market are attracted by the positive short-run profits being made by carrot producers. Given sufficient time (i.e., the long run), these new firms enter the market. With more carrot producers, the market supply curve shifts outward, driving down the price. As the price falls, the profit rectangle gets smaller and smaller until it actually disappears. At the point where $P = MR = MC = ATC$, each carrot farmer is now breaking even with $\pi = 0$. Would the next potential carrot farmer enter the market? Unlikely, as the entry of one more firm pushes the price down just enough to where losses are actually incurred. Thus,

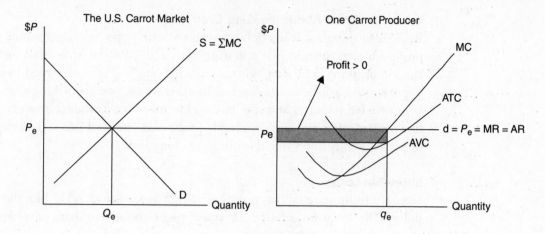

Figure 9.6

this breakeven point is described as the long-run equilibrium. The market quantity has increased, and each firm produces less at the lower price. Figure 9.7 illustrates the movement toward the long-run equilibrium.

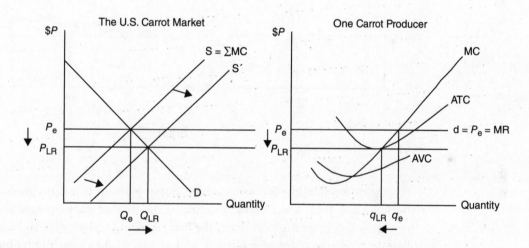

Figure 9.7

- Entry of new firms attracted by economic $\pi > 0$.
- Increase in market supply.
- A decrease in the market price to P_{LR}.
- Profits fall to the breakeven point, $P_{LR} = MR = MC = ATC$ and economic $\pi = 0$.
- Market quantity increases.
- Individual producer output falls.
- Many FRQs ask you to draw perfect competition with side-by-side graphs of the market and the typical firm. In addition to knowing perfect competition inside and out, you must be very careful to follow all instructions in the prompt. For example, questions often say, "Label output in the market Q_m and output for the typical firm Q_f." Following these instructions exactly can prevent unnecessary errors that will cost you easy graphing points.

What's So Great About Breaking Even?

Remember there is a distinction between accounting profit and economic profit. Economic profit subtracts the next best opportunity costs of your resources from total revenue. If you are still breaking even after subtracting what you might have earned in all of those other opportunities, you can't feel cheated. In other words, you are making a fair rate of return on your invested resources and you have no incentive to take them elsewhere. Sure, you would like to earn more than zero economic profit (aka "**normal profit**"), but the characteristics of perfect competition rule this out in the long run.

Short-Run Losses

Figure 9.8 illustrates short-run losses with a price below ATC but above the shutdown point. The long-run adjustment story might sound familiar, only with market forces moving in the opposite direction.

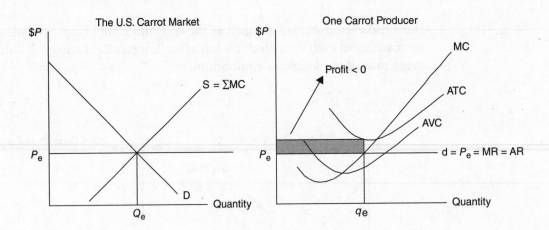

Figure 9.8

Again, we should ask "What next?" Some existing firms in this market begin to exit the industry. With fewer carrot producers, the market supply curve shifts leftward, driving up the price. As the price rises, the loss rectangle gets smaller and smaller until again it disappears. At the point where $P_{LR} = MR = MC = ATC$, each remaining carrot farmer is now breaking even with $\pi = 0$. Would another carrot farmer exit the market? Possibly, but the exit of one more firm bumps up the price just enough so that a small positive profit is earned, prompting one firm to enter and get us back to the breakeven point. Arrival at the breakeven point is once again the long-run equilibrium. The market quantity has decreased, but each surviving firm produces more at the higher price. Figure 9.9 illustrates the movement toward the long-run equilibrium.

The long-run adjustment to short-run losses can be summarized as:

- Exit of existing firms prompted by economic $\pi < 0$.
- Decrease in market supply.
- An increase in the market price to P_{LR}.
- Profits increase to the breakeven point, $P_{LR} = MR = MC = ATC$ and economic $\pi = 0$.
- Market quantity decreases.
- Individual producer output rises.

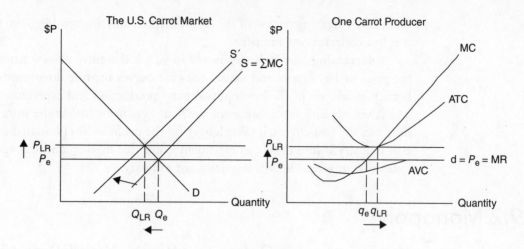

Figure 9.9

Table 9.5 provides a summary of the four possible short-run scenarios and resulting long-run adjustments to the perfectly competitive equilibrium, which always ends in the same place.

Table 9.5

WHEN THE SHORT RUN …	THE FIRM PRODUCES WHERE …	SHORT-RUN ECONOMIC PROFITS ARE …	IN THE LONG RUN …	THE LONG-RUN OUTCOME IS …
$P > \text{ATC}$	MR = MC	Positive	Firms enter	$P_{LR} = \text{MR} = \text{MC} = \text{ATC}$ and $\pi = 0$
$P = \text{ATC}$	MR = MC	Zero, break even	No entry or exit	$P_{LR} = \text{MR} = \text{MC} = \text{ATC}$ and $\pi = 0$
$\text{AVC} < P < \text{ATC}$	MR = MC	Negative $0 > \pi > -\text{TFC}$	Firms exit	$P_{LR} = \text{MR} = \text{MC} = \text{ATC}$ and $\pi = 0$
$P < \text{AVC}$	Zero, shut down	Negative $(= -\text{TFC})$	Firms exit	$P_{LR} = \text{MR} = \text{MC} = \text{ATC}$ and $\pi = 0$

Are There Variations on This Story and Do I Need to Know Them?

The answer to these questions are yes, and maybe. Throughout this section we have made an assumption that entry and exit of firms has no impact on the cost curves of firms in the market. In other words, we have been assuming a **constant cost industry**. Recent AP Microeconomics exams have made references to constant cost industries and (maybe) caused unnecessary confusion for test takers. It is always possible that future exams will refer to constant, increasing, or decreasing cost industries, so you should probably become familiar with these terms. A quick explanation and you will not be one of the confused.

Suppose that entry of new firms into a profitable carrot market increases the demand for key resources like land, labor, and capital. Increased demand for these resources might increase the cost of employing those resources. When this happens, the cost curves for firms in the carrot industry start to shift upward. This situation is described as an **increasing cost industry**. Graphing this situation gets sticky, but if you follow the logic, you will be fine. The entry of new firms drives down the price of the output *and* increases the cost curves, so the profit is eliminated more quickly than with our constant cost industry. Fewer firms eventually enter this version of the carrot market, and the new long-run price is higher than it is in a constant cost industry.

A **decreasing cost industry** is one in which the entry of new firms actually decreases the price of key inputs and causes the cost curves to shift downward. This might occur because producers of the key inputs expand production and experience economies of scale and lower per-unit costs. Since the entry of new firms lowers the price of the output *and* decreases the cost curves, it takes longer for the profit to be eliminated than in our constant cost industry. More firms can eventually enter this market, and the new long-run price is lower than it would be in a constant cost industry.

9.2 Monopoly

Main Topics: *Structural Characteristics of Monopoly, Monopoly Demand, Profit Maximization, Efficiency Analysis, Price Discrimination*

Structural Characteristics of Monopoly

Since monopoly is the very opposite of perfect competition in the range of market structures, we can expect that the structural characteristics are also quite different.

- *A single producer.* This is pretty self-explanatory, but a strict definition of monopoly requires that there are no other firms in the industry.
- *No close substitutes.* Consumers cannot find a similar product in other markets.
- *Barriers to entry.* Perhaps the most important characteristic of monopoly is that there exists something that prevents rival firms from entering the market to provide competition to the monopolist and choice to consumers.
- *Market power.* This is the result of the first three characteristics. With no competition and barriers to entry, the unregulated monopolist has **market power**, or monopoly price-setting ability.

Again, it is rare to find a firm that satisfies all of the characteristics of monopoly, but the De Beers firm holds a near monopoly on global diamond production. The only gas station or bank in a small town might also act as a local monopolist.

Barriers to Entry

If there were no barrier to entry, a monopolist earning positive economic profits would be history and this chapter would be done. So before moving on to the behavior of monopoly, let's talk a little more about this necessary condition for the existence of monopoly.

- *Legal barriers.* In your local television market, only one firm is given the right to broadcast on a specific frequency. There might be only one firm given the right to sell liquor in a small community. There are patents, trademarks, and copyright laws to protect inventions and intellectual property. These legal protections do not provide for absolute monopoly, for there are often viable substitutes available to consumers.
- *Economies of scale.* In Chapter 8, this concept was introduced. As a firm grows larger in the long run, average total costs fall, providing the larger firm a cost advantage over smaller firms. If extensive economies of scale exist, an industry could evolve into one with only one enormous producer. A **natural monopoly** is a case where economies of scale are so extensive that it is less costly for one firm to supply the entire range of demand. Power plants are a good example of natural monopoly within a local area.
- *Control of key resources.* If a firm controlled most of the available resources in the production of a good, it would be very difficult for a competitor to enter the market. For example, if a

producer of granulated sugar wanted to monopolize the market, the firm might wish to control all of the sugarcane plantations.

Monopoly Demand

The perfectly competitive firm is a price taker and faces perfectly elastic demand for their product. The firm sells all it wants at the going market price; this decision does not affect the market price. The monopolist is the only provider of that good, making the demand for their product the market demand for that product. The monopolist must pay attention to the law of demand, which means that if it wishes to sell more, the monopolist must decrease the price.

Demand, Price, and Marginal Revenue

Price exceeds marginal revenue because the monopolist must lower price to boost sales. The added revenue from selling one more unit is the price of the last unit less the sum of the price cuts that must be taken on all prior units of output. For example, the demand curve for the monopolist's product is $P = 7 - Q_d$.

The monopolist begins at a price of $6 and sells one unit of the good (see Table 9.6). A price cut to $5 results in one more unit sold, so total revenue increases by $5 on this second unit. However, the first unit, previously sold at $6, must also now be sold at $5, which costs the firm $1 in total revenue. With $5 gained ($P$) from the second and $1 lost in total revenue from the first unit, the net or marginal increase (MR) in total revenue is $4 for the second unit. Graphically we can see the revenue effect of selling the second unit in Figure 9.10.

KEY IDEA

Chapter 7 examined the effect that price elasticity of demand (E_d) has on total revenue. Demand is elastic above the midpoint of a linear demand curve like the one in Figure 9.10, so cuts in price increase total revenue. Demand is inelastic below the midpoint; further cuts in price decrease total revenue. At the midpoint, total revenue is maximized and demand is unit elastic. Recognizing this connection, the price-making monopolist is going to avoid the inelastic portion of the demand curve and operate at some point to the left of the midpoint. Figure 9.11 combines demand, marginal revenue, and the total revenue function. You can see that when total revenue is at the maximum, marginal revenue is zero and further price cuts decrease total revenue, making marginal revenue negative.

Table 9.6

P	Q	TR	MR
7	0	0	
6	1	6	6
5	2	10	4
4	3	12	2
3	4	12	0
2	5	10	-2
1	6	6	-4
0	7	0	-6

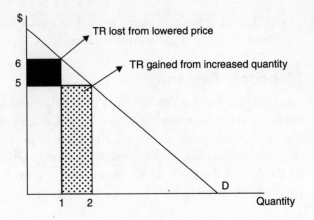

Figure 9.10

- Demand is horizontal, and $P = $ MR in perfect competition.
- Demand is downward sloping, and $P > $ MR in monopoly.
- The monopolist operates in the elastic (or upper) range of demand.

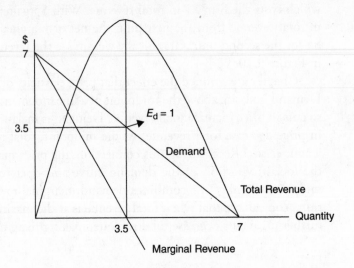

Figure 9.11

Profit Maximization

While demand looks different for the monopolist, the mechanism for maximizing profit is the same for both the monopolist and the perfectly competitive firm. **The firm must set output at the level where MR = MC. At this level of output (Q_m), the monopolist sets the price (P_m) from the demand curve.** Profit is found in the same way by creating the profit rectangle with average total cost. This is seen in Figure 9.12.

The positive monopoly profits illustrated in Figure 9.12 are likely, due to the entry barrier, to last into the long run. Though $\pi > 0$ is usually the case for a monopoly firm, you might imagine a case where demand plummets, or perhaps production costs increase, to the point where $P <$ ATC and losses are incurred. In the event of persistent losses, we expect the monopolist to exit the industry.

"Understand the profit max rule well. It will help you throughout economics."
—Nick,
AP Student

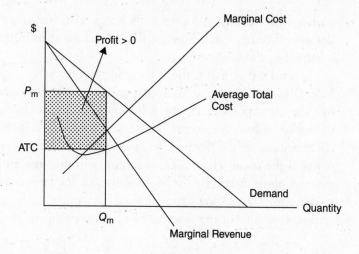

Figure 9.12

- Find Q_m where MR = MC. Once you have found Q_m, never leave it.
- Find P_m vertically from the demand curve above MR = MC.
- Find ATC vertically at Q_m. If you move downward, $\pi > 0$. If you move upward, $\pi < 0$.
- Move horizontally from ATC to the y-axis to complete the rectangle and clearly label it as positive or negative.

Efficiency Analysis

We refer to efficiency in a couple of different sections of this book, and now that we have compared perfect competition to monopoly, it is time for another discussion. **Allocative efficiency** is achieved when the market produces a level of output where the marginal cost (MC) to society exactly equals the marginal benefit (P) received by society. Total welfare to society is maximized at this outcome, so any movement away from this level of output results in deadweight loss. **Productive efficiency** is achieved if society has produced a level of output with the lowest possible cost. In perfect competition, the long-run market outcome achieves both of these criteria for efficiency. Figure 9.13 illustrates the competitive and

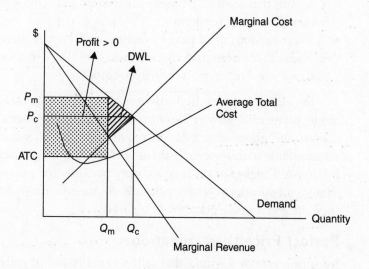

Figure 9.13

monopoly outcomes. Allocative efficiency exists because $P_c = MR = MC$ at Q_c, and productive efficiency exists because firms produce at minimum ATC, once entry or exit has occurred in the long term.

On the other hand, the monopolist produces at a quantity Q_m where $P_m > MR = MC$. This result tells us that consumers would like to consume more of the product; but the monopolist does not produce as much as consumers want. This is an example of market failure, a concept introduced back in Chapter 5. Failing to achieve allocative efficiency creates the deadweight loss (DWL) shown in Figure 9.13. The monopoly output is not at the point where ATC is minimized; thus the monopolist is not productively efficient. A profit earned by the monopolist is a transfer of consumer surplus from consumers to the firm. To see what happens to output, price, profit, and efficiency after a tax has been imposed, see one of the practice FRQs later in this book.

- $Q_m < Q_c$.
- $P_m > P_c$.
- $P_m > MC$ so monopoly is not allocatively efficient.
- Deadweight loss exists with monopoly.
- $P_m >$ minimum ATC so monopoly is not productively efficient.
- $\pi_m > 0$ is a transfer of lost consumer surplus from consumers to the firm.

Price Discrimination

Though the name implies a nasty stereotype, **price discrimination** is the selling of the same good at different prices to different consumers. Successful price discrimination is possible if three conditions exist:

1. The firm has monopoly pricing power.

2. The firm is able to identify and separate groups of consumers.

3. The firm is able to prevent resale between consumers.

Common examples of price discrimination include the following:

- Child and senior discounts at the movie theater or restaurants
- Airline tickets that are bought three weeks in advance compared to tickets bought one hour in advance
- Coupons that separate price-sensitive consumers (those who use the coupon) from those who are less price sensitive
- A lower per-unit price paid by consumers who buy items in large quantities (like a case of soda) than those paid by consumers who buy in lesser quantities (like a six-pack of soda, or one can from a vending machine)

The airline industry is clearly not perfectly competitive, so there must be a degree of monopoly pricing power. The firm creates groupings based on when consumers purchase tickets. The photo identification requirement for all passengers is an important security measure, but it also prevents the resale of a low-priced ticket to a consumer who is willing to pay a higher price. If resale were possible, the pricing system might break down. It should not surprise you that price discrimination allows firms to earn more profit than if they charged a single price.

Perfect Price Discrimination

Imagine a monopoly shop that sells a certain kind of gadget, but there is something odd about the way these gadgets are priced. When a customer walks into the shop, a sign above the door flashes a number that only the shopkeeper can see; this number is the highest price this particular customer is willing to pay (WTP) for a gadget. Because each customer has a different budget, and different tastes and preferences, each customer has a different WTP. The shopkeeper, knowing the customer's willingness to pay, charges a price exactly equal to this customer's WTP. For example, if Becky's WTP is $8, that's the price she would be charged for a gadget. If Jamaal's WTP is $9.50, that's the price he would be charged.

This unique kind of price discrimination is called **perfect price discrimination** and is seen in Figure 9.14. The demand curve and marginal revenue are now the same ($P =$ MR), and the firm will continue selling gadgets until the marginal revenue from the last sale is equal to the marginal cost of a gadget. There is no single equilibrium price, because each customer was charged a different price. There are two other key outcomes to see here. First, because each customer pays a price exactly equal to their WTP, there is no consumer surplus; the monopolist takes all of it as producer surplus. Second, because the last unit sold is the one for which $P =$ MC, this outcome is allocatively efficient.

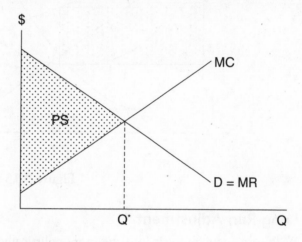

Figure 9.14

9.3 Monopolistic Competition

Main Topics: *Structural Characteristics, Short-Run Profit Maximization, Long-Run Adjustment*

Structural Characteristics

Sharing some of the characteristics of both perfect competition and monopoly, the market structure of monopolistic competition provides a description of many modern industries.

- *Relatively large number of firms.* Rather than the thousands of perfectly competitive firms, in monopolistic competition there are perhaps dozens, each with a fairly small share of the total market.
- *Differentiated products.* This characteristic makes monopolistic competition stand out as different from the perfectly competitive market structure and gives firms their ability to set the price above the competitive level.
- *Easy entry and exit.* There are very few barriers to entry in monopolistic competition, perhaps the largest being the need to provide sufficient marketing to differentiate a new firm's product from that of the existing rivals.

The market for shoes closely fits the description of monopolistic competition. While all shoes serve the same basic purpose, to cover and protect the feet, a running shoe, a hiking boot, and a flip-flop are very different and are made by many firms in the global market. The book publishing and local restaurant markets are also described as monopolistically competitive.

Short-Run Profit Maximization

Like the monopoly, the firm in monopolistic competition faces a downward-sloping demand curve for its differentiated product. Because there are many similar substitutes available to consumers, the demand is fairly elastic. In a recurring theme for profit-maximizing behavior, the firm sets Q_{mc} where $MR = MC$ and sets the price from the demand curve. Figure 9.15 illustrates a monopolistically competitive firm that is earning positive short-run economic profits.

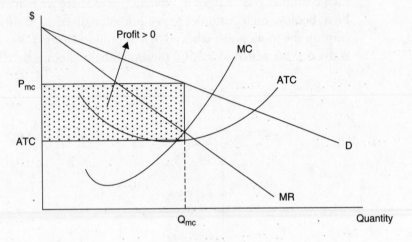

Figure 9.15

Long-Run Adjustment

With easy entry and exit into the monopolistically competitive industry, short-run positive profits like those in Figure 9.15 are not going to last for long. As new firms enter this industry, the market share of all existing firms begins to fall. Graphically we see this as a leftward shift in the demand curve. As the price begins to fall, the profit rectangle begins to shrink. Entry stops when profits are zero and $P_{mc} = ATC$, or when the demand curve is just tangent to ATC. This adjustment is seen in Figure 9.16.

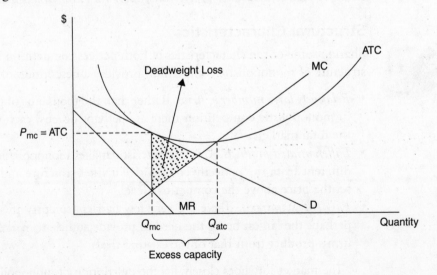

Figure 9.16

"What About Advertising to Maintain Profits?"

Because easy entry of competitors drives profits down to breakeven levels, monopolistically competitive firms typically engage in extensive amounts of advertising to slow down, and even reverse, declining market share. This advertising is realistically only a short-run "fix," as there is no reason to believe that barriers to entry suddenly emerge to prevent the eventual return to breakeven profit levels.

Efficiency and Excess Capacity

In long-run monopolistic competition, the firm earns $\pi = 0$, a characteristic shared by the perfectly competitive firm. But because of the differentiated products, $P > MR = MC$, allocative efficiency is not achieved. The deadweight loss is the shaded area in Figure 9.16. Though the firms are breaking even, they are not operating at the minimum of ATC; productive efficiency is also not achieved. The difference between the monopolistic competition output Q_{mc} and the output at minimum ATC is referred to as **excess capacity**. Excess capacity is underused plant and equipment that is the result of producing at an output less than that which minimizes ATC. The market is overpopulated with firms, each producing enough to break even in the long run, but so many firms means that each produces below full capacity.

- $Q_{mc} < Q_c$.
- $P_{mc} > P_c$.
- $P_{mc} > MC$ so monopolistic competition is not allocatively efficient.
- Deadweight loss exists, but not as much as with monopoly.
- $P_m > $ minimum ATC so monopolistic competition is not productively efficient.
- $\pi_{mc} = 0$ in the long run.
- Excess capacity is $Q_{atc} - Q_{mc}$.

9.4 Oligopoly

Main Topics: *Structural Characteristics, Industry Concentration, Game Theory and the Prisoner's Dilemma, Is Every Game a Prisoner's Dilemma?, Collusive Pricing*

Oligopoly markets are typically further from perfect competition than the monopolistic market structure, although there is no one model of oligopoly. A couple of oligopoly models are presented, but keep in mind that if one little assumption is relaxed, the predictions of the model can be radically different. For the AP exam, you will likely face only these basics.

Structural Characteristics

You can see from these characteristics that oligopoly shares more common ground with monopoly, but these are flexible enough to describe many different and diverse industries:

- *A few large producers.* Can it get more vague than this? Think of the American auto industry, with the "Big 3" producers, or cell phone providers, an industry dominated by four huge firms. If the distribution of market share in an industry is top-heavy with a few large firms, the industry is described as oligopolistic.
- *Differentiated or standardized product.* Oligopoly industries can come in both flavors. Crude oil is a fairly standard product, but it is very much an oligopoly of large producers. Automobiles, beer, and soft drinks are also oligopoly markets, but with more differentiated products.
- *Entry barriers.* If these industries were fairly easy to enter, we would not see them dominated by a few huge producers.
- *Mutual interdependence.* Because a few large producers control these industries, the action of one firm (price setting or advertising) is likely to affect the others and prompt

a response. A good example of this is your local gasoline market. This is very much an oligopoly; when one gas station lowers prices by one cent per gallon, the others usually quickly follow.

Industry Concentration

How does an industry become classified as an oligopoly? Economists have tried to get more specific than a "few large producers" by developing ways to measure how much market share is held by, or concentrated in, the largest of the firms. One way to gauge how powerful the largest of firms might be is to sum up the market share of the top 4, or 8, or 12 firms and create a **concentration ratio**. If the top four firms in the breakfast cereal industry have a combined market share of 85 percent, we say that the four-firm concentration ratio is 85. Some economists use a four-firm concentration ratio of 40 percent or greater as a rough guideline for identifying an oligopolistic industry. We predict that as this concentration ratio increases, the degree of monopoly price-setting power increases.

Game Theory and the Prisoner's Dilemma

Imagine a case where a two-firm oligopoly (a duopoly) engages in a daily pricing decision. Each firm knows that if it sets a price higher than the rival's, it loses sales. Likewise, if it sets a price below the rival's, it steals sales. This noncollusive model of pricing, called the **prisoner's dilemma,** emerges from the following scenario that any fan of *Law and Order* or a similar crime drama quickly recognizes.

Example:

A college professor suspects two students (Jack and Diane) of cheating on a take-home final exam, but she cannot prove guilt with enough certainty to fail both students in the course or expel them from the school. Without a confession, she will give each student a D in the course. With a confession from one student but not the other, she can reward the confessor with a B. The professor brings both students, one at a time, into her office and gives each the following deal:

- If you remain silent and do not confess, and your classmate implicates you, I will expel you from school and give your friend a B.
- If you confess to cheating and implicate your silent classmate, I will pass you with a B and expel your friend from school.

These options are depicted in the following matrix:

		JACK'S CHOICES	
		Confess	*Stay Silent*
DIANE'S CHOICES	*Confess*	D: Fail the course J: Fail the course	D: Gets a B J: Expelled from school
	Stay Silent	D: Expelled from school J: Gets a B	D: Gets a D J: Gets a D

Diane doesn't know what Jack is going to do when he is in the professor's office. But whatever Jack's decision, Diane should confess. She might be thinking that Jack is going to confess. If so, she confesses because staying silent will get her expelled from school. Maybe she thinks that Jack is going to stay silent. If true, the choice is between a B and a D in the course. Diane would be wise to confess. For Diane, confessing is a **dominant strategy** because no matter what Jack does, confession is always better than staying silent. Likewise, for Jack, the dominant strategy is to confess.

The outcome of the game (both students confess) is called a "**Nash equilibrium**" after the late Dr. John Nash, a mathematician at Princeton, who won the Nobel Prize in Economics in 1994. The premise is quite simple: the outcome of the game is a Nash equilibrium if each player's strategy maximizes their payoff, given the strategies used by the rival players. In other words, Jack's decision to confess ensures his best outcome, *given he knows that Diane is also going to confess*. And the same is true of Diane's decision. In other words, the decision to confess is the best response to what the other player is going to do.

This is certainly a dilemma, because if Jack and Diane could only agree to give the professor the silent treatment, they would both walk away with a D, which is much better than failing the course or expulsion from school. Without such a binding agreement, cheating on the pact would be quite tempting, maybe even fairly predictable.

Example:

The owners of two gas stations operate on opposite corners of a busy intersection. Every morning each owner goes out to the sign and sets the price of gasoline, either high or low. Consumers are concerned only about the lowest price of gas. The following matrix summarizes the daily revenues for each station:

		STATION Y	
		Price High	*Price Low*
STATION X	*Price High*	X: $2,000 Y: $2,000	X: $500 Y: $3,000
	Price Low	X: $3,000 Y: $500	X: $1,000 Y: $1,000

Can you see the dilemma? Both stations would love to set a high price of gas so that they could earn $2,000 in daily revenue. But if the rival were to set the low price, the high price station would be stuck with $500 while the other station cleans up with $3,000. Since both firms recognize that pricing low is the dominant strategy, both earn only $1,000 every day. This outcome, where both firms set the low price, is the Nash equilibrium. A collusive agreement might emerge.

Use of the previous game matrices assumes that both players in the game make simultaneous choices. Many games involve a series of stages where one player moves first. The second player observes the choice made by the first and then reacts to it. These sequential games are typically seen as a game tree rather than a game matrix.

Let's convert the previous game to a sequential game where gas station X gets to move first, as shown in Figure 9.17. Station Y sees the choice of station X and then sets the price high or low. Payoffs are given at the end of the tree.

Can you see how this game will play out? Gas station X knows that its rival, station Y, still has a dominant strategy of setting a low price. No matter what the initial decision of station X, station Y would always see that a low price beats a high price. Because station X knows this about its rival, it will select a low price at the beginning of the game. In 2007, the AP Microeconomics exam included simple game theory on the free-response section for the very first time. Since 2007, this area of microeconomics has been repeatedly tested, and I predict that the degree of difficulty will gradually increase.

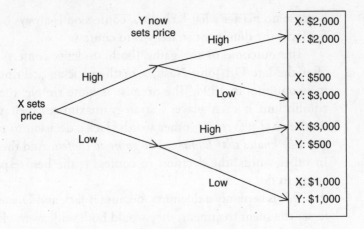

Figure 9.17

Is Every Game a Prisoner's Dilemma?

Absolutely not. Several recent AP Microeconomics exams have included FRQs that are not simple examples of a prisoner's dilemma.

Example:

Suppose there are two hamburger stands in town, Stinky's and Sloppy's, and each firm sells what it considers to be the best burger in town. Both burger stands are considering a move to offer hot dogs on the menu, or they could do nothing and continue to offer only burgers. The following payoff matrix shows payoffs as daily profits for Stinky's, followed by daily profits for Sloppy's.

		SLOPPY'S CHOICES	
		Burgers Only	*Add Hot Dogs*
STINKY'S CHOICES	*Burgers Only*	$500, $300	$400, $400
	Add Hot Dogs	$600, $200	$500, $100

In this game, Stinky's has a dominant strategy of adding hot dogs to the menu. No matter what Sloppy's does, Stinky's earns more money by making this choice. However, Sloppy's does not have a dominant strategy. If Stinky's were to offer only burgers, Sloppy's should add hot dogs ($400 is better than $300). But if Stinky's were to add hot dogs to its menu, Sloppy's should continue to offer only burgers ($200 is better than $100).

So where is the dominant strategy? Sloppy's will recognize that Stinky's is going to add hot dogs to the menu, so Sloppy's will respond by maintaining a burgers-only menu. The Nash equilibrium combination of payoffs is $600 for Stinky's and $200 for Sloppy's. This is not a prisoner's dilemma, because there is no alternative outcome that would, with prior collusion, increase profits for *both* firms.

Can there ever be more than one Nash equilibrium?

Yes, more than one Nash equilibrium is possible, and the Course and Exam Description for AP Micro does leave open the possibility that you might encounter such a situation. In fact, there was a recent FRQ that included a game matrix that had two equilibria. This can be a little confusing, so let's look at an example.

Harper and Hayden are rival owners of dance studios. They can each choose to advertise (A) on local media, or not advertise (DA). The payoff matrix is below, with Harper's payoffs first and Hayden's payoffs second. We assume that they make their choices simultaneously and the game is only played once.

		HAYDEN'S STUDIO	
		ADVERTISE (A)	DON'T ADVERTISE (DA)
HARPER'S STUDIO	ADVERTISE (A)	$50, $50	$75, $25
	DON'T ADVERTISE (DA)	$25, $75	$100, $100

Neither player has a dominant strategy because their best response to the rival's choice changes. For example, if Hayden chooses A, Harper's best response is to also choose A ($50 > $25). But if Hayden were to choose DA, Harper's best response is to choose DA ($100 > $75). The payoffs are the same for Hayden, so we have two Nash equilibria: both advertise and neither advertise.

Of course, the option that maximizes their combined payoffs is for neither to advertise; they would each earn $100. But since neither has a dominant strategy, achieving this outcome would require a collusive agreement before choices are made.

 If a FRQ asks you to identify the "equilibrium or equilibria," spend a little time investigating whether there are indeed two equilibria.

Collusive Pricing

Explicit **collusive** behavior between direct competitors is an illegal business practice, but it does happen (surprise!) from time to time. More common is a kind of tacit, or understood, collusion. Two competitors over time figure out that repeated attempts to undercut the price of their rivals is counterproductive. Eventually they understand that if both set the price high, both firms win. When one cheats on this "understanding," the other inflicts punishment with a retaliatory price cut.

Cartels are more organized forms of collusive oligopoly behavior. Cartels are groups of firms that create a formal agreement not to compete with each other on the basis of price, production, or other competitive dimensions. The general idea of the cartel is that rather than act independently to maximize individual profits, they collectively operate as a monopolist to maximize their joint profits. Each cartel member agrees to a limited level of output, and this results in a higher cartel price. Joint profits are maximized and distributed to each member.

In addition to the pesky illegality of forming cartels, these entities face three challenges that are completely unrelated to the Attorney General:

1. Difficulty in arriving at a mutually acceptable agreement to restrict output. Have you ever tried to order pizza or binge-watch a TV series with more than two other friends? If so, you get the idea.

2. Punishment mechanism. If the cartel can restrict output and increase the price above the current competitive level, cartel members have an incentive to cheat by producing more than their allotment. There must be some kind of deterrent to cheating.

3. Entry of new firms. If the cartel members are successful in creating monopoly profits, they are faced with new firms eager to enter. If entry occurs, the cartel loses monopoly power and profit.

› Review Questions

1. For a competitive firm, what is the most important thing to consider in deciding whether to shut down in the short run?

   (A) Compare AVC to MR.
   (B) Compare TR to TC.
   (C) Do not produce if the TFC is not covered by revenue.
   (D) Produce the highest quantity demanded regardless of price.
   (E) Compare P to ATC.

2. Which characteristic is likely a part of a monopoly market but not of monopolistic competition?

   (A) Differentiated products
   (B) Patents and copyrights
   (C) Possibility of profit in the short run
   (D) Deadweight loss exists
   (E) None of the above

3. If the perfectly competitive price is currently above minimum ATC, we can expect which of the following events in the long run?

   (A) Price rises as firms enter the industry.
   (B) Market equilibrium quantity rises as firms exit the industry.
   (C) Nothing. The industry is currently in long-run equilibrium.
   (D) Profits fall as the market price rises.
   (E) Price falls as firms enter the industry.

4. Which of these situations is not an example of price discrimination?

   (A) Brent works nights, so he chooses to buy bread at 7 a.m. rather than at 7 p.m.
   (B) Bob and Nancy each receive a "$1 off" coupon in the mail, but Bob redeems it while Nancy does not.
   (C) Katie buys 12 Cokes for $3, and Josh buys one Coke at a time for $1.
   (D) Velma likes to go to the movies at the lower afternoon matinee price, and Rosemary would rather pay more for the evening show.
   (E) Jason and Jen go to a popular nightclub. Because it is "Ladies' Night," Jen pays no cover charge, but Jason must pay to enter the club.

Two competing firms are deciding whether to launch a huge costly advertising campaign or maintain the status quo. Use the following matrix showing the profits of this duopoly to respond to question 5.

		FIRM Y	
		Advertise	Status Quo
FIRM X	Advertise	X: $4.5 million Y: $4.5 million	X: $1 million Y: $6 million
	Status Quo	X: $6 million Y: $1 million	X: $5 million Y: $5 million

5. If these firms do not collude, the outcome will be that

   (A) both firms maintain the status quo.
   (B) both firms advertise.
   (C) Firm X advertises and Firm Y maintains the status quo.
   (D) Firm Y advertises and Firm X maintains the status quo.
   (E) Firm X advertises and Firm Y alternates between the status quo and advertising.

6. Deadweight loss occurs in

   (A) monopolistic competition as $P > MC$.
   (B) monopoly markets because $P > MC$.
   (C) oligopoly markets because $P > MC$.
   (D) All of the above
   (E) None of the above

› Answers and Explanations

1. **A**—The firm only operates if the total revenue is at least as great as total variable cost. On a per-unit basis, the firm must receive a $P = MR$ that is at least as great as AVC. Since firms pay TFC regardless of production, they are not a factor in whether you should shut down. Choices B, C, and E are wrong because TC and ATC include the fixed costs. Choice D is incorrect because it might not be the profitable strategy, and it is irrelevant to the shutdown decision.

2. **B**—Monopoly has barriers to entry (e.g., patents) and the monopolistic competitive firm does not. Choices A, C, and D are true of monopolistic competition and monopoly.

3. **E**—With $P > ATC$, you should recognize that positive economic profits exist. Firms enter and price falls toward the breakeven point, so any mention of exit or rising prices can be eliminated. Entry also increases the market quantity of the good produced.

4. **A**—If Brent chooses to buy his bread early in the morning rather than in the evening, this is not price discrimination. The other choices describe buying in bulk, redeeming a coupon, or paying a lower price because of the time in which one consumes the good. The nightclub example is price discrimination based on gender.

5. **A**—For each firm, choosing the status quo is the dominant strategy.

6. **D**—Allocative inefficiency and deadweight loss in *any* market structure is when $P > MC$.

› Rapid Review

Perfect competition: The most competitive market structure is characterized by many small price-taking firms producing a standardized product in an industry in which there are no barriers to entry or exit.

Profit maximizing rule: All firms maximize profit by producing where MR = MC.

Breakeven point: The output in perfect competition where ATC is minimized and economic profit is zero.

Shutdown point: The output where AVC is minimized. If the price falls below this point, the firm chooses to shut down or produce zero units in the short run.

Perfectly competitive long-run equilibrium: Occurs when there is no more incentive for firms to enter or exit. $P = MR = MC = ATC$ and $\pi = 0$.

Normal profit: Another way of saying that firms are earning zero economic profits or a fair rate of return on invested resources.

Constant cost industry: Entry (or exit) of firms does not shift the cost curves of firms in the industry.

Increasing cost industry: Entry of new firms shifts the cost curves for all firms upward.

Decreasing cost industry: Entry of new firms shifts the cost curves for all firms downward.

Monopoly: The least competitive market structure; it is characterized by a single producer, with no close substitutes, barriers to entry, and price-making power.

Market power: The ability to set the price above the perfectly competitive level.

Natural monopoly: The case where economies of scale are so extensive that it is less costly for one firm to supply the entire range of demand.

Monopoly long-run equilibrium: $P_m > MR = MC$, which is not allocatively efficient and deadweight loss exists. $P_m > ATC$, which is not productively efficient. $\pi_m > 0$ so consumer surplus is transferred to the monopolist as profit.

Price discrimination: The practice of selling essentially the same good to different groups of consumers at different prices.

Perfect price discrimination: The type of price discrimination in which each consumer pays exactly their maximum willingness to pay. Consumer surplus is eliminated, yet the allocatively efficient output is produced.

Monopolistic competition: A market structure characterized by a few small firms producing a differentiated product with easy entry into the market.

Monopolistic competition long-run equilibrium: $P_{mc} > MR = MC$ and $P_{mc} >$ minimum ATC, so the outcome is not efficient, but $\pi_{mc} = 0$.

Excess capacity: The difference between the monopolistic competition output Q_{mc} and the output at minimum ATC. Excess capacity is underused plant and equipment.

Oligopoly: A very diverse market structure characterized by a small number of interdependent large firms, producing a standardized or differentiated product in a market with a barrier to entry.

Four-firm concentration ratio: A measure of industry market power. If the combined market share of the four largest firms is above 40 percent, it is a good indicator of oligopoly.

Noncollusive oligopoly: Models where firms are competitive rivals seeking to gain at the expense of their rivals.

Prisoner's dilemma: A game where the two rivals achieve a less desirable outcome because they are unable to coordinate their strategies.

Dominant strategy: A strategy that is always the best strategy to pursue, regardless of what a rival is doing.

Nash equilibrium: The outcome of a game for which each player's strategy maximizes their payoff, given the strategies used by the rival players.

Collusive oligopoly: Models where firms agree to mutually improve their situation.

Cartel: A group of firms that agree not to compete with each other on the basis of price, production, or other competitive dimensions. Cartel members operate as a monopolist to maximize their joint profits.

CHAPTER 10

Factor Markets

IN THIS CHAPTER

Summary: We have invested significant time reviewing the forces of supply and demand in the competitive market for goods and services. In addition, we have investigated the theory behind production and cost, but have not brought market forces to bear on those input, or factor, markets. We begin with the demand for inputs in a perfectly competitive input market, and then move to the supply of inputs and construct a model of wage and employment. We tweak the competitive model by allowing for some monopoly hiring behavior. Will wages for nurses be rising or falling? Can we predict whether employment of steel workers is going to grow or decline? A study of input markets sheds some light on many important microeconomic issues that have critical macroeconomic implications.

Key Ideas
- Factor Demand
- Least-Cost Hiring of Inputs
- Factor Supply
- Equilibrium in Competitive Factor Markets
- Noncompetitive Factor Markets
- Minimum Wages

10.1 Factor Demand

Main Topics: *Competitive Factor Markets, Marginal Revenue Product, Profit-Maximizing Resource Employment, MRP$_L$ as Demand for Labor, Derived Demand, Determinants of Resource Demand*

The theory of factor (or resource, or input) demand is applicable to any factor of production, but it is more intuitive if we focus on labor, the production input with which we are all most comfortable. Because we are most familiar with it, most examples below address labor, but later in the chapter we will also look at the market for capital.

Competitive Factor Markets

To best see the theory of factor demand, we assume the simplest market structure. First, we'll assume that the firms are price takers in the product (output) market. Second, we'll assume that they are price takers in the factor (input) market. This means that they cannot impact either the price of their product or the price they must pay to employ more of an input. In a competitive labor market, they can employ as much labor as they wish at the going market-determined wage.

Marginal Revenue Product

Here's a difficult question for any employee to ask: What am I worth to my employer? Sure, I'm a snazzy dresser; I can tell a humorous joke, and my personal hygiene is top-notch. However, the bottom line to my employer is probably more important than these civilities. To build a model of factor demand, economists assert that the demand for a unit of labor is a function of two things important to employers. First, employers are very interested in the marginal productivity of the next unit of labor. If the next worker is going to greatly contribute to the firm's total production, he is likely to be a good hire for the firm. Second, the firm must then receive good value for the production. The value of this production to the firm is the additional, or marginal, revenue that it brings to the firm. Combining the necessary components of marginal productivity of labor and marginal revenue provides **marginal revenue product of labor (MRP$_L$)**, a measure of what the next unit of a resource, such as labor, brings to the firm. With the assumption of a perfectly competitive output market, the marginal revenue is simply the price of the product. Some textbooks will refer to marginal revenue product as the value of the marginal product (VMP$_L$), while others will reserve VMP$_L$ for the case where price and marginal revenue are not the same. Consult your textbook to see which approach that author prefers.

$$MRP_L = \frac{\text{Change in total revenue}}{\text{Change in resource quantity}} = MR \times MP_L = P \times MP_L$$

In our examples, we change the resource (labor) by a quantity of one. Table 10.1 revises the hourly production function for Molly's lemonade stand. Recall that in the short run she hires additional units of labor to a fixed level of capital. The competitive price of a cup of lemonade is 50 cents.

Table 10.1

LABOR INPUT (WORKERS PER HOUR)	TOTAL PRODUCT (TP$_L$) (CUPS PER HOUR)	MARGINAL PRODUCT (MP$_L$)	MARGINAL REVENUE (MR = P)	MARGINAL REVENUE PRODUCT (MRP$_L$ = MP$_L$ × MR)
0	0			
1	25	25	$.50	$12.50
2	45	20	$.50	$10.00
3	60	15	$.50	$7.50

Table 10.1—cont'd

LABOR INPUT (WORKERS PER HOUR)	TOTAL PRODUCT (TP$_L$) (CUPS PER HOUR)	MARGINAL PRODUCT (MP$_L$)	MARGINAL REVENUE (MR = P)	MARGINAL REVENUE PRODUCT (MRP$_L$ = MP$_L$ × MR)
4	70	10	$.50	$5.00
5	75	5	$.50	$2.50
6	70	−5	$.50	−$2.50
7	60	−10	$.50	−$5.00

Profit-Maximizing Resource Employment

Yet again, we are faced with a decision that must be based on marginal benefits and marginal costs. Our decision rule is, and has always been:

- If MB > MC, do more of it.
- If MB < MC, do less of it.
- If MB = MC, stop here.

In the case of resource hiring, the marginal benefit is **MRP$_L$**. The marginal cost of resource hiring is **marginal resource cost (MRC)**, a measure of how much cost the firm incurs from using an additional unit of an input. When the firm is hiring labor in a competitive labor market, MRC is equal to the wage (w).

Some textbooks refer to this as the **marginal factor cost (MFC)** or, when the factor is labor, the **marginal cost of labor (MC$_L$)**. No matter what label your textbook might use, the concept is the same and the labels are often used interchangeably.

$$MRC = \frac{\text{Change in total resource cost}}{\text{Change in resource quantity}} = \text{Wage}$$

With this measure of marginal cost, the profit-maximizing employer of labor would hire to the point where MRP$_L$ = MRC = Wage. Table 10.2 adds a competitive $7.50 hourly wage to Molly's table of lemonade production. At this wage, Molly should employ three hourly workers to her fixed capital.

Table 10.2

TOTAL LABOR INPUT (WORKERS PER HOUR)	PRODUCT (TP$_L$) (CUPS PER HOUR)	MARGINAL PRODUCT (MP$_L$)	MARGINAL REVENUE (MR = P)	MARGINAL REVENUE PRODUCT (MRP$_L$ = MP$_L$ × MR)	MARGINAL RESOURCE COST (MRC = WAGE)
0	0				
1	25	25	$.50	$12.50	$7.50
2	45	20	$.50	$10.00	$7.50
3	60	15	$.50	$7.50	$7.50
4	70	10	$.50	$5.00	$7.50
5	75	5	$.50	$2.50	$7.50
6	70	−5	$.50	−$2.50	$7.50
7	60	−10	$.50	−$5.00	$7.50

MRP$_L$ as Demand for Labor

If the hourly wage were to rise to $10, Molly would reduce her employment to two workers per hour. If the wage decreases to $5 per hour, she would employ four workers. All else equal, as the price of labor increases, the employment falls and as the price of labor decreases, employment rises. This is the law of demand again! Figure 10.1 illustrates the MRP$_L$ and Molly's hiring at three wages.

Molly's demand for labor is actually represented by the MRP$_L$. It is downward sloping, like any demand curve would be, because of the diminishing marginal productivity of labor in the short run. To move from Molly's demand for labor to the overall market demand for labor, we simply sum up all of the individual firms' MRP$_L$ curves: Market D$_L$ = ΣMRP$_L$.

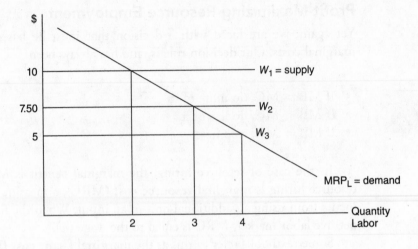

Figure 10.1

Market Wage as Supply of Labor

Under the assumptions of a perfectly competitive labor market, the supply of labor to the individual firm is perfectly elastic and equal to the wage. This means that the firm can employ all of the workers it desires at the going market wage.

- In competitive markets, MRP$_L$ is the firm's downward-sloping labor demand curve.
- In competitive markets, wage is the firm's horizontal labor supply curve.

Derived Demand

Economists say that the demand for an input like labor is derived from the demand for the goods produced by the input. If the weather is hot and demand for lemonade rises, local economists might predict a stronger demand for production resources like lemonade workers, lemons, and sugar. An increase in the demand for a resource means that at any wage, the firm wishes to employ more of that resource. If the demand for lemonade increases and the price rises to $1 per cup, the MRP$_L$ increases at all quantities of labor. This is seen in Figure 10.2. At the market wage of $10, the firm would increase hiring from two to three workers.

- You are *very* likely to see the topic of derived demand on the AP exam. To avoid losing points on the free-response question, you *must* make the connection between the price of the product rising and the increased demand for the labor.
- ↑D for product, ↑price of product, ↑MRP$_L$, ↑hiring of labor at the current wage.

Determinants of Resource Demand

The demand for the goods themselves is an important determinant of resource demand, but not the only determinant.

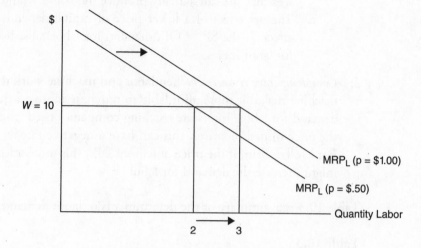

Figure 10.2

- *Product demand.* An increase in the demand for textiles—towels, for example—results in an increased price of those goods. The higher price increases the marginal revenue product of resources used in the production of textiles (e.g., textile workers), and this shifts the demand for those resources to the right. Of course, this works in the opposite direction and is probably a more accurate story of what has happened to textile workers in the United States.
- *Productivity* (*output per resource unit*). If the productivity of the resource increases, the firm has a profit motive to take advantage of that heightened productivity, and the demand for the resource should increase. Productivity of a resource is affected by a few different factors:

  1. *Quantity of other resources.* Give workers more equipment to help production and labor's productivity can be increased. If Molly were to provide her workers with a larger workspace or more manual juicers or pitchers or stirring spoons or measuring cups, they might achieve increased output per worker.
  2. *Technical progress.* Better technology with which to work can increase labor's productivity. Rather than using manual lemon squeezers, Molly invests in electric squeezers that allow for a given number of employees to produce more lemonade every hour.
  3. *Quality of variable resources.* Fertile farmland in the Midwest is a huge productivity advantage over the same acreage of farmland in Nevada. A more educated and trained workforce is an improvement in the quality of the labor and therefore provides more productivity. Maybe Molly employs only those who have completed daylong training at the local community college.

- *Prices of other resources.* Employers hire several different resources, so the demand for one (labor) often depends on the prices of the others.

  1. *Substitute resources.* If the price of a substitute resource—machinery, for example—falls, it has two competing effects on the demand for labor.

     a. Substitution effect (SE). Because machinery is now relatively less expensive, the firm uses more machinery and decreases demand for labor. For Molly, a lower price of electric lemon squeezers would put pressure on her to decrease the demand for labor.

b. Output effect (OE). Lower machine prices lower production costs (a downward shift in MC), which increases output for the firm and prompts an increased demand for labor. With the lower marginal cost of producing lemonade, Molly sees that she can actually produce more and would therefore need more labor.

c. The net effect of a lower price of capital depends on the magnitude of each effect. If the SE > OE, demand for labor falls. If the OE > SE, the demand for labor increases.

2. *Complementary resources.* When labor and machine work together, a lower price of the machine makes it more affordable to purchase more machinery but also increases the demand for labor. Interstate trucking companies need trucks, fuel, and drivers. When the price of fuel increases, this can have a negative impact on the demand for drivers. For Molly's firm, if the price of lemons falls, this more affordable complement to labor might increase the demand for labor.

Table 10.3 is a summary of the determinants of labor demand.

Table 10.3

LABOR DEMAND INCREASES IF . . .	LABOR DEMAND DECREASES IF . . .
Demand for the product increases, increasing the price.	Demand for the product decreases, decreasing the price.
The labor becomes more productive, either with more resources available, better technology, or a higher quality workforce.	The labor becomes less productive, either with fewer resources available, lessened technology, or a lower quality workforce.
The price of a substitute resource falls and the OE > SE.	The price of a substitute resource falls and the SE > OE.
The price of a substitute resource rises and the SE > OE.	The price of a substitute resource rises and the OE > SE.
The price of a complementary resource falls.	The price of a complementary resource rises.

10.2 Least-Cost Hiring of Multiple Inputs

Main Topic: *The Least-Cost Hiring Rule*

Finding the best way to cope with scarcity really excites economists. We found that consumers needed to find the best (utility-maximizing) combination of two goods, given the prices and an income constraint. For producers, we would like to find the best (cost-minimizing) combination of two inputs, given the prices and production constraint. To do this, we use the consumer's decision as a model for the producer's decision. The consumer's utility maximizing rule said to find the combination of good X and good Y so that $MU_x/P_x = MU_y/P_y$ while spending exactly the consumer's income and paying prices P_x and P_y.

Least-Cost Hiring Rule

For a producer, we can express the constraint in two equivalent ways. Remember the bridge between production and cost?

1. You must produce Q^* units of output. Now find the least-cost ($TC) way of doing so.

2. You can only spend \$TC. Now find the highest level of output (Q^*).

There is only one combination of two resources (we'll use labor and capital) that satisfies either of these two constraints, and it is found by using this **least-cost rule**. The price of labor is P_L and the price of capital (K) is P_K.

$$MP_L/P_L = MP_K/P_K, \text{ or equivalently, } MP_L/MP_K = P_L/P_K$$

Example:

If each of the inputs is hired at \$1 per unit and at the current amount of labor and capital you have employed, the $MP_L = 100$ and the $MP_K = 10$, clearly, the least-cost rule is not satisfied:

$$100 \text{ units}/\$1 > 10 \text{ units}/\$1$$

If you could spend \$1 more on labor, you would see output increase by 100 units. That extra \$1 would come from spending \$1 less on capital, which would decrease output by 10 units. So you spend the same amount of money but get 90 more units of output.

Great deal! In situations like this, where $MP_L/P_L > MP_K/P_K$, the firm is going to find it in its best interest to increase spending on L and decrease spending on K. The law of diminishing marginal returns predicts that as you increase L, MP_L falls. And as you decrease K, MP_K rises. The substitution of labor for capital ceases to be a great deal at the combination of L and K where the ratios of marginal product per dollar are equal again.

SITUATION	FIRM WILL . . .	WHICH CAUSES . . .	AND . . .	UNTIL
$MP_L/P_L > MP_K/P_K$	↑L and ↓K	↓MP_L	↑MP_K	$MP_L/P_L = MP_K/P_K$
$MP_L/P_L < MP_K/P_K$	↑K and ↓L	↓MP_K	↑MP_L	$MP_L/P_L = MP_K/P_K$

Example:

A producer of gadgets pays \$5 for each hour of labor and \$10 for each hour of capital employed. Table 10.4 describes the marginal products of each at various levels of employment. Told that you must produce $Q = 360$ gadgets, find the least-cost combination of labor and capital.

Table 10.4

# OF L EMPLOYED	MPL	# OF K EMPLOYED	MPK
1	50	1	100
2	40	2	90
3	30	3	80
4	20	4	60
5	10	5	45
6	5	6	30

Find all of the combinations of L and K where our rule is satisfied:

$$MP_L/P_L = MP_K/P_K$$
$$\text{or } MP_L/MP_K = \$5/\$10 = .5$$

There are three possibilities where the MP_L is one-half the size of MP_K:

- L = 1, K = 1. Total Product = 50 + 100 = 150
- L = 2, K = 3. Total Product = (50 + 40) + (100 + 90 + 80) = 360
- L = 3, K = 4. Total Product = (50 + 40 + 30) + (100 + 90 + 80 + 60) = 450

The best way to produce 360 gadgets is to hire two units of labor and three units of capital at a total cost of TC = $5 × 2 + $10 × 3 = $40. The same problem could have been modified to use a cost constraint rather than an output constraint.

Told that you can only spend $40, find the combination of labor and capital that maximizes production. Of course, the solution is again $L = 2$, $K = 3$, and output is 360 gadgets.

10.3 Factor Supply and Market Equilibrium

Main Topics: *Supply of Labor, Wage and Employment Determination, What About Other Resources?*

If you have ever had a job, you have been a small part of the labor supply curve. We quickly investigate labor supply and combine it with labor demand to complete a labor market. It is in this competitive market that wage and employment are determined.

Supply of Labor

Economic theory predicts that as the price of a good increases, suppliers of that good increase the quantity supplied. This is the **law of supply**. If the price of labor (wage) increases, more hours of labor should be supplied. For the most part, this is true, and the market labor supply curve slopes upward. If the hourly wage increased from $5 to $8, most people respond by working more hours, earning more income ($320 per 40-hour workweek), and consuming more goods.

Wage and Employment Determination

Assuming competitive output and input markets, the competitive wage is found at the intersection of labor demand and labor supply. Changing demand and supply influences this wage, and the equilibrium quantity of labor that accompanies it.

Example:

The aging population in the United States is giving a boost to the market for nurses. An increase in the demand for nurses increases both the wage and employment of nurses. This is seen in Figure 10.3.

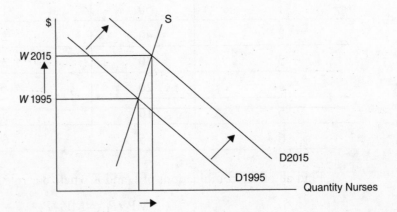

Figure 10.3

What About Other Resources?

Labor is the resource with which most people identify because we have all been, or expect to be, units of labor in a labor market. However, we can use the theory of resource demand to predict how the market for capital (or any other resource) would behave. For example, suppose that the market for capital is also perfectly competitive. If so, then each firm's demand for capital is also derived from the marginal revenue product of capital (MRP_K)

$$MRP_K = P \times MP_K.$$

And because the marginal product of capital diminishes, the demand for capital is downward sloping. In a competitive resource market, the firm can hire all of the capital it wants at the marginal factor cost equal to the rental rate of capital (r^*).

Each firm hires the profit-maximizing quantity of capital (K^*) at the point where the MRP_K is equal to the rental rate (r^*). We can see this hiring decision in Figure 10.4.

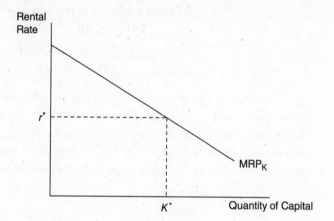

Figure 10.4

But where does this rental price of capital come from? With many firms hiring capital in this competitive market, the market demand for capital is downward sloping. The market supply curve for capital is upward sloping, and the market determines the competitive price of capital (r^*). This is seen in Figure 10.5.

Market forces, just as in the labor market, would cause the rental rate and quantity of capital to change. For example, if the demand for capital increases, perhaps because of a strong economy and positive corporate expectations, the equilibrium price and quantity of capital in the market would be expected to increase.

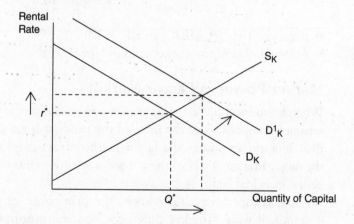

Figure 10.5

10.4 Imperfect Competition in Product and Factor Markets

Main Topics: *Market Power in Product Markets, Market Power in Factor Markets*

We saw in the previous chapter that perfectly competitive markets might not always exist. After all, the conditions for perfect competition are rather strict and not often observed in the "real world." In the sections that follow, we assume that the firm has some market power, first in the product market and then in the factor (labor) market. To no surprise, the outcome of wage and employment differs from the competitive outcome described previously.

Market Power in Product Markets

Perhaps the most important result seen from a firm that has the ability to be a price setter is that the price exceeds marginal revenue. Because $MR < P$ with market power, this has an impact on the marginal revenue product function.

Under perfectly competitive price-taking conditions:
$$MRP_c = MR \times MP_L = P \times MP_L$$

Under conditions of market power:
$$MR < P: MRP_m = MR \times MP_L < MRP_c$$

The result of a lower marginal revenue product function is that the optimal amount of employment falls at all wages. Figure 10.6 illustrates this. In other words, the monopolist hires lesser amounts of all resources, including labor. This should make sense if you recall that monopoly markets produce less output than the competitive market. If the market produces less output, it makes sense that the market would employ fewer resources.

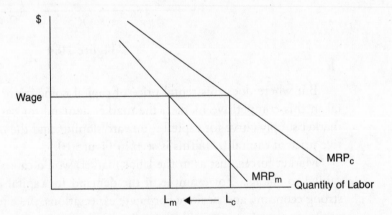

Figure 10.6

- Because $MR < P$, $MRP_m = MR \times MP_L < MRP_c$.
- A monopoly output market employs fewer workers than the competitive output market.

Market Power in Factor Markets

When a producer has extreme market power in the product market, we label them a price-setting monopolist, and the price of the product is set above marginal revenue. Let's turn this situation around to the factor market. If an employer has extreme market power in the factor market, we label them a wage-setting monopsonist, and we observe the wage set below marginal factor cost.

In a competitive labor market, the firm could employ all it wanted at the market-determined wage. The key difference between **monopsony** and a perfectly competitive labor market is that the employer must increase the wage to increase the quantity of labor that is supplied. In other words, the labor supply to the firm is upward sloping, not horizontal. Marginal factor cost is now greater than the wage. Table 10.5 illustrates how this happens.

Table 10.5

LABOR SUPPLIED TO THE FIRM (L_s)	NECESSARY HOURLY WAGE (W)	TOTAL WAGE BILL = $L_s \times W$	MARGINAL FACTOR COST (MFC)
0		$0	
1	$4	$4	$4
2	$5	$10	$6
3	$6	$18	$8
4	$7	$28	$10
5	$8	$40	$12
6	$9	$54	$14

Example:

Molly's lemonade conglomerate can employ more workers but must increase the wage to do so. However, not only does she have to increase the wage for additional workers but also to her current workers. This creates a situation where MFC > W. See Figure 10.7. Molly still chooses to employ where MRP_L = MFC, but the wage is determined from the labor supply curve. Graphically the MFC curve lies above the labor supply curve, which means that labor is paid below their MRP_L. If this employer was hiring at the competitive level, she would employ more workers (L_c) and pay a higher wage (W_c).

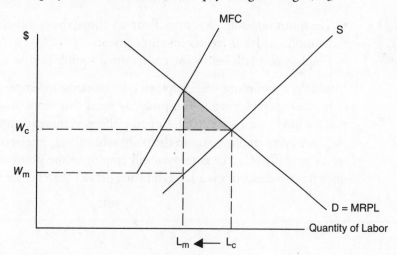

Figure 10.7

- Under monopsony, employers hire $L_m < L_c$.
- Monopsony firms pay $W_m < W_c = MRP_L$.
- Because monopsony hiring falls below the competitive level, deadweight loss exists. This can be seen as the gray shaded triangle in Figure 10.7.

Remember that MRP_L measures the value of the last worker to the firm. The outcome that workers receive less than their value to the firm might be alarming. Does this happen? If you doubt that an employer can get away with such rampant exploitation, I give you a four-letter response: N-C-A-A. A big-time college star athlete might produce, over the course of a four-year career, millions of dollars in revenue to a university. Even if we include the value of four years of tuition, room, and board, star athletes are compensated well below their marginal revenue product. Is it so crazy that many talented college athletes make an early jump to a professional league or in some cases skip college all together?

10.5 Minimum Wages

Minimum wages are a price floor in a labor market; employers are not legally allowed to pay a wage below it. We saw in Chapter 7 that price floors create a surplus in the market, and this is true of minimum wages in labor markets.

Figure 10.8 shows a competitive labor market with an equilibrium wage of W_e and equilibrium employment of L_e. The minimum wage W_{min} is set above W_e, creating a surplus of labor as the quantity of labor supplied is greater than the quantity that is demanded. In a labor market, this surplus can also be labeled as the unemployment of workers. Employment falls from L_e to L_d.

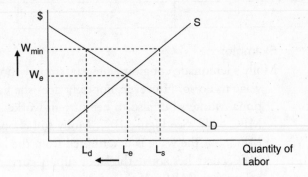

Figure 10.8

- The minimum wage is a price floor set above the competitive equilibrium wage.
- A surplus of labor creates unemployment.
- Employment falls below the competitive equilibrium level.

Ironically, a minimum wage imposed on a monopsony employer can have the opposite effect of increasing employment. You probably recall that monopsonies pay wages below the competitive level. See Figure 10.9. Suppose the government imposed a minimum wage above W_m. For every employee up to the point where W_{min} intersects the labor supply curve, W_{min} serves as the MFC. The employer will employ at the point where W_{min} intersects the labor demand curve and this is a level of hiring greater than before the minimum wage.

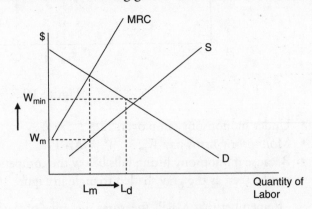

Figure 10.9

- The minimum wage is a price floor set above the monopsony wage and acts as the MRC to the point where it intersects the labor supply curve.
- The firm hires to the point where the minimum wage intersects the labor demand curve.
- A minimum wage can increase hiring in a monopsony labor market.

› Review Questions

1. Your aunt runs a small firm from her home making apple pies. She hires some friends to help her. Which of the following situations would most likely increase her demand for labor?

   (A) The price of apple peelers/corers rises.
   (B) Your aunt's friends gossip all day, slowing their dough-making process.
   (C) There is a sale on ovens.
   (D) A new study reveals that apples increase your risk of cancer.
   (E) The price of apples increases.

2. The price of labor is $2, and the price of capital is $1. The marginal product of labor is 200, and the marginal product of capital is 50. What should the firm do?

   (A) Increase capital and decrease labor so that the marginal product of capital falls and the marginal product of labor rises.
   (B) Increase capital and decrease labor so that the marginal product of capital rises and the marginal product of labor falls.
   (C) Decrease capital and increase labor so that the marginal product of capital rises and the marginal product of labor falls.
   (D) Decrease capital and increase labor so that the marginal product of capital falls and the marginal product of labor rises.
   (E) Increase both capital and labor until the ratio of marginal products per dollar is equal.

3. A competitive labor market is currently in equilibrium. Which of the following most likely increases the market wage?

   (A) More students graduate with the necessary skills for this labor market.
   (B) Demand for the good produced by this labor is stronger.

   (C) The price of a complementary resource increases.
   (D) The Department of Labor removes the need for workers to pass an exam before they can work in this field.
   (E) Over time, one large employer grows to act as a monopsonist.

Use Table 10.6 to respond to questions 4 and 5.

Table 10.6

WAGE (W)	QUANTITY OF LABOR SUPPLIED	MARGINAL FACTOR COST OF LABOR (MFC)	MARGINAL REVENUE PRODUCT OF LABOR (MRP$_L$)
$3	0		
$4	1	$4	$10
$5	2	$6	$9
$6	3	$8	$8
$7	4	$10	$7

4. If a firm is hiring labor in the perfectly competitive labor market, the wage and employment are

   (A) $3 and 0.
   (B) $4 and 1.
   (C) $5 and 2.
   (D) $6 and 3.
   (E) $7 and 4.

5. If a firm hires labor in a monopsony labor market, the wage and employment are

   (A) $3 and 0.
   (B) $8 and 3.
   (C) $5 and 2.
   (D) $6 and 3.
   (E) $7 and 4.

❯ Answers and Explanations

1. **C**—Since ovens would be a less expensive complementary resource (with more ovens, they can bake more pies), your aunt needs more employees to go along with the extra ovens. Apple corers and peelers are complements, but even if you think they are substitutes, the impact on labor demand is uncertain because of the competing output and substitution effects.

2. **C**—Do a quick ratio of marginal product per dollar. When you see that the $MP_L/P_L > MP_K/P_K$, you notice that the firm is getting more "bang for the buck" with labor. Immediately rule out any choice that says they hire less labor. The only way that MP_L/P_L falls to equal MP_K/P_K is to decrease the capital and increase the labor, causing the MP_K to rise and the MP_L to fall. The firm does this until the marginal products divided by the prices are equal.

3. **B**—The equilibrium wage rises with stronger demand or lessened supply of labor. The stronger demand for the product increases the wage as the demand for labor increases. All other choices either increase the labor supply or decrease the demand, thus decreasing the wage. Emergence of monopsony decreases the wage below competitive levels.

4. **E**—In a competitive labor market, equilibrium is where $W = MRP_L$.

5. **D**—In a monopsony labor market, equilibrium is where $MFC = MRP_L$.

❯ Rapid Review

Marginal revenue product (MRP): Measures the value of what the next unit of a resource (e.g., labor) brings to the firm. $MRP_L = MR \times MP_L$. In a perfectly competitive product market, $MRP_L = P \times MP_L$. In a monopoly product market, $MR < P$ so $MRP_m < MRP_c$.

Marginal resource cost (MRC): Measures the cost the firm incurs from using an additional unit of an input. In a perfectly competitive labor market, MRC = Wage. In a monopsony labor market, MRC > Wage.

Profit-maximizing resource employment: The firm hires the profit-maximizing amount of a resource at the point where MRP = MRC.

Demand for labor: Labor demand for the firm is the MRP_L curve. The labor demand for the entire market $D_L = \Sigma MRP_L$ of all firms.

Derived demand: Demand for a resource like labor is derived from the demand for the goods produced by the resource.

Determinants of labor demand: One of the external factors that influences labor demand. When these variables change, the entire demand curve shifts to the left or right.

Least-cost rule: The combination of labor and capital that minimizes total costs for a given production rate. Hire L and K so that $MP_L/P_L = MP_K/P_K$ or $MP_L/MP_K = P_L/P_K$.

Monopsonist: A firm that has market power in the factor market, i.e., a wage setter.

CHAPTER 11

Public Goods, Externalities, and the Role of Government

IN THIS CHAPTER

Summary: One of the recurring themes of the first half of this book is that the competitive marketplace provides the most efficient societal outcome where goods are produced at the point where MB = MC, or at the intersection of market supply and market demand. We have not, however, explored the possibility that the demand curve might not capture all of the benefits to society from the consumption of a good. There is also the possibility that the supply curve might not capture all of the costs to society from the production of the good. If these benefits and/or costs are indeed not reflected in the market equilibrium price and quantity, then we conclude that the market has failed to provide the efficient outcome. When this occurs, the government usually needs to step in.

KEY IDEA

Key Ideas
- ✪ Public and Private Goods
- ✪ Positive and Negative Externalities
- ✪ Income Distribution
- ✪ Tax Structures

11.1 Public Goods and Spillover Benefits

Main Topics: *Private and Public Goods, Spillover Benefits and Positive Externalities*

Private and Public Goods

So far, when discussing goods and services, we have focused on private goods and services. **Private goods** are goods that are both rival and excludable. A bag of potato chips and a cup of herbal tea are both private goods. These are rival in that only one person can consume the good, and so consumption by one consumer necessarily means another cannot. Private goods are excludable in that consumers who do not pay for the good are excluded from consumption.

Public goods, however, are special cases where the goods are both nonrival and nonexcludable. These characteristics mean that one person's consumption does not prevent another from also consuming the good. If a public good is provided to some, it is necessarily provided to all, even if they do not pay for the good. Common examples of public goods are national defense, local fire and police services, space exploration, and environmental protection.

Who Pays?

In the case of private goods, each individual decides whether they are going to pay the going price. If the marginal benefit to me is at least as high as the price, I might decide to purchase and consume the good. For private goods, those who want the good badly enough, and can afford the price, are the ones who pay.

Maybe you have confronted the difficulty in paying for a public good if you have been assigned a group project in school. If each group member receives the same grade, regardless of their level of effort, some members of the group might slack off and benefit from the hard work of the others. If this sounds familiar, you have experienced the **free-rider problem**. The free-rider problem pops up whenever some members of the community understand that they can consume the public good while others provide for it.

A small town has a community meeting to decide how to pay for local police protection. The mayor passes a collection plate around the room, and we each make a voluntary donation toward this public good. There are some difficulties with paying for a public good in this way. How much do I use or value the next unit of police services in my protection? Is this more than, less than, or the same as my neighbor's use and value of police protection? It is impossible to answer this question, and even if it were possible to determine how much my neighbor values police service, maybe he won't pay his fair share. After all, if police protection is going to be provided to the entire community, and this protection cannot be denied to anyone, some members of the community might become **free riders**. The free-rider problem and the nonexcludable nature of public goods require that the government collect taxes to pay for their provision.

Spillover Benefits and Positive Externalities

In graduate school I rented a small house on a dead-end street. On the other side of the street, an older couple had an immaculately landscaped yard with gorgeous rosebushes. Riding my mountain bike home from campus, I was happy to see, and smell, the results of their hard yard work. I'm sure that I was not the only neighbor who felt that way. When one person's consumption of a good provides utility to a third party who has not directly purchased the good, there exist **spillover benefits** that are not reflected in the market price of that good. In my case, my neighbors went to the trouble, expense, and effort to beautify their yard. In the process, they beautified the neighborhood and provided benefits to those of us who received utility from the landscaping and the roses. This situation is described as a **positive externality** and is illustrated in Figure 11.1.

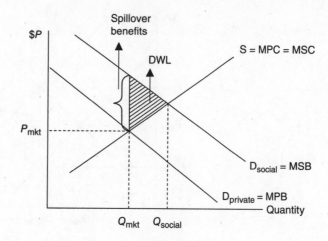

Figure 11.1

The market demand curve D_{private} for roses (labeled MPB for marginal private benefits) captures the private benefits received by consumers of roses but does not capture the additional benefits received by neighbors of those who consumed roses. Figure 11.1 incorporates the spillover benefits to the market for roses. The private demand curve, which does not include the spillover benefits, lies below the societal demand curve (labeled MSB for marginal social benefits) by an amount equal to the per-unit spillover benefits. The market produces only Q_{mkt} roses, but the optimal amount is greater at Q_{social}. Because the market produces less than the socially optimal amount, it is said that there is an underallocation of resources to rose production and deadweight loss is the result. In other words, society wants more than the market provides.

- The existence of spillover benefits in a market results in an underallocation of resources in that market. In other words, there is not enough of a good thing.
- In the presence of a positive externality, at Q_{mkt}, the MSB is greater than MPB due to spillover benefits. At the market quantity, MSB > MSC.
- Because the market ignores the spillover benefits, deadweight loss exists and is seen as the shaded area between MSB and MPB and between Q_{social} and Q_{mkt}. There is no deadweight loss at the socially optimal output where MSC = MSB.

The couple who lived across the street from my house were essentially providing a public good that we might call "community beautification," and the rest of us were free riding on their activity. How could we have contributed to the provision of the public good? Maybe we could have brought them cash donations, or we could have volunteered our labor. Each of these gestures would have lessened their burden and freed up their private resources to provide even more landscaping for the neighborhood.

Subsidies

On a larger scale, this type of market failure can be remedied through government intervention. Our goal as economic policy makers is to move the equilibrium quantity from Q_{mkt} to Q_{social}. One solution might be to provide a subsidy to gardeners equal to the amount of the spillover benefit that their activity provides to the community. By sending a check (or voucher) to the couple, they would have increased their demand for roses and other landscaping and shifted the private demand out to equal the social demand. This is seen in Figure 11.2. The price received by the firm has risen to P_{firm}, but when the consumer applies the voucher, the actual price to the consumer is lower at P_{cons}.

Another possibility is to provide a subsidy to producers of roses. This type of subsidy would result in an outward shift in the supply curve so that the equilibrium quantity of roses would be at Q_{social}. This policy is seen in Figure 11.3. The price to consumers, P_{cons}, is also lower in this case, while producers receive, with the subsidy, P_{firm}.

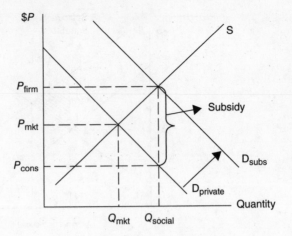

Figure 11.2

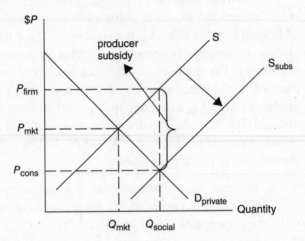

Figure 11.3

11.2 Pollution and Spillover Costs

Main Topics: *Spillover Costs and Negative Externalities*

Another kind of market failure occurs when there are additional costs associated with production of a good that are not reflected in the market price. Pollution of all kinds is a classic example.

Spillover Costs and Negative Externalities

Almost anyone who has walked down a busy street has experienced secondhand smoke. Even nonsmokers, having spent just a minute walking next to a smoker, can smell smoke on their clothes. While the smoker has chosen to pay the market price of tobacco, the nonsmoker also pays a price for that choice, either in minor disutility or worsened health. When the exchange of a good imposes disutility on a third party who has not directly purchased the good, there exist **spillover costs** that are not reflected in the market price of that good. A situation in which polluters impose costs upon third parties is called a **negative externality**.

The existence of spillover costs from a negative externality means that not all of the costs of production are captured by the market supply curve S$_{private}$. In much of the world, the burning of coal produces most electricity. The private cost of electricity production includes the coal, the labor, and capital at the plant. But the burning of coal imposes environmental costs in the form of air, water, and land pollution. These costs actually make people, not to mention the planet, sick! These societal costs are not found in the market price (P_{mkt}) of charging your cell phone or running the dishwasher. The difference between the private cost and the societal cost of producing electricity is seen in Figure 11.4. The private supply curve (labeled MPC for marginal private cost), which does not include the spillover costs, lies below the societal supply curve (labeled MSC for marginal social cost). The market produces Q_{mkt} units of electricity, but the optimal amount is less at Q_{social}. Because the market produces more than the socially optimal amount, it is said that there is an overallocation of resources to electricity production, so a deadweight loss exists. In other words, society wants less than the market provides.

- The existence of spillover costs in a market results in an overallocation of resources in that market. In other words, there is too much of a bad thing.
- In the presence of a negative externality, at Q_{mkt}, the MSC is greater than MPC due to spillover costs. At the market quantity, MSC > MSB.
- Because the market ignores the spillover costs, deadweight loss exists and is seen as the shaded area between MSC and MPC and between Q_{social} and Q_{mkt}. At the socially efficient quantity, MSC = MSB, and there is no deadweight loss.

> "I was always told to make big graphs to keep things clear. It ended up saving me from many careless errors."
> —Ross, AP Student

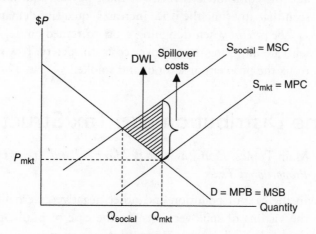

Figure 11.4

So how could cigarette smokers alleviate the discomfort that they impose upon their nonsmoking citizens? How could coal-burning power plants compensate the planet for the damage they do to it? The aim of any such policy is to try to move the spillover costs away from the third-party victims and back upon those who produce the externality.

Pollution Taxes

Rather than allow the spillover costs to fall externally on members of society, the goal of pollution taxes is to internalize these costs by imposing a tax on the production or consumption of goods that create negative externalities. Our goal is to move the market equilibrium quantity closer to the socially optimal quantity of electricity. Suppose government imposes a tax, equal to the spillover cost, on every unit of coal that our power plant uses to produce electricity. This pollution tax results in an inward, or upward, shift of the private supply curve so that it equals the social supply curve. See Figure 11.5. The price of running the dishwasher has increased, but now that price incorporates all of the costs of electricity, including the effects of pollution on the environment and human health.

In some cases, a tax may be imposed on consumers, if they are responsible for the negative externality. For example, in major metropolitan areas, traffic is a serious problem and millions of commuters create significant amounts of pollution. We might increase the auto-

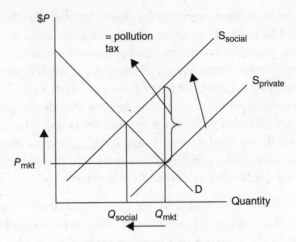

Figure 11.5

mobile registration tax or create a system of toll highways so that the users of automobiles and the commuters themselves must pay an additional price for that behavior. We have seen that any time the price increases, quantity demanded (in this case, driving) must fall.

Be careful when designing a tax to remedy a negative externality. We must tax those who are imposing the spillover costs on society. It would not be fair to tax the nonsmoker to fix the problem of secondhand smoke.

11.3 Income Distribution and Tax Structures

Main Topics: *Equity as a Goal; Marginal and Average Tax Rates; Progressive, Regressive, and Proportional Taxes*

In the case of pollution and other negative externalities, the marketplace fails to protect the victims of spillover costs. In the case of public goods or other positive externalities, the market fails to provide an adequate quantity to satisfy the needs of society. As we saw previously, the government is called to action to move the market outcome closer to the societal efficient outcome. The government is also called to action to remedy issues of equity, or fairness. This section discusses equity, distribution of income, and tax structures to move closer to a more equitable outcome.

Equity as a Goal

While we tout the efficiency of competitive markets with a fervor that approaches deification, the one thing even the most efficient market does not do is provide equity, or fairness. Some consumers can afford a new Mercedes; some cannot. Yet I doubt that this is a good example of the unfairness of markets. But some consumers cannot afford pediatric services for their infant children. Even if these services are exchanged at the efficient quantity where the marginal social benefit is equal to the marginal social cost, even the most die-hard advocates of the free market can see that it is an outcome that should be remedied through some form of income redistribution.

An Equal Share?

There are some who propose that the economic resources should be equally divided among all members of society. This egalitarian, or equal-share, view seems fair but has at least one serious criticism. **Egalitarianism** suffers from an issue of compensation that fails to match productivity. In other words, the incentives to work hard, take risks, and seek a competitive advantage are greatly reduced. If you were guaranteed an equal share of the resources, how hard would you work?

Example:

All students in your class are assured of being compensated with a B, regardless of the effort and productivity that might merit a B. C-level students lack the motivation to become more productive because they are guaranteed compensation above their productivity. A-level students lack the motivation to produce A-level work because they know compensation falls below that. The high-productivity students get disenchanted and disgruntled, and work even less.

Productivity Share?

If egalitarianism suffers from a lack of productivity incentives, maybe everyone's share of economic resources should be based on individual productivity. In other words, this **marginal productivity theory** says your wage is a function of your marginal revenue product. If markets are competitive, this can be quite efficient. In theory, this could even be fair. The flaw in this method of income distribution is that not all citizens are given a fair shake at demonstrating to the labor market their true marginal revenue product. Think of all of the advantages, large or small, that you were lucky enough to be born with. Now imagine all of them being removed from your past and present. Productive individuals who have few advantages can overcome obstacles with hard work, but some societal barriers (e.g., discrimination, a disability) prevent them from ever receiving a compensation equal to their productivity.

How Do We Measure the Income Distribution?

There are a couple of common ways to see a nation's income distribution. Whether or not we think this is "fair" is another question entirely.

1. *Quintiles.*

Economists sort households from the lowest incomes to the highest incomes and then divide that range into fifths, or **quintiles**. In each quintile lies 20 percent of all households. Table 11.1 illustrates the income distribution in 2000, 2010, and 2020 as estimated and published by the Census Bureau. If income were perfectly distributed, each 20 percent of the families in the United States would have 20 percent of the total income.

Table 11.1

QUINTILE	% OF TOTAL INCOME (2000)	% OF TOTAL INCOME (2010)	% OF TOTAL INCOME (2020)
Lowest 20%	3.6%	3.3%	3%
Second 20%	8.9%	8.5%	8.1%
Third 20%	14.8%	14.6%	14%
Fourth 20%	23.0%	23.4%	22.6%
Highest 20%	49.8%	50.2%	52.2%
Total	100.0%	100.0%	100%

2. *Lorenz Curve and Gini Ratio.*

The above quintile distribution can be graphically illustrated with a **Lorenz curve** (see Figure 11.6). The farther the Lorenz curve lies below the hypothetical line of perfect equality, the more unequal the distribution of income. This distance of the actual distribution of income from the line of perfect equality is calculated by constructing a **Gini ratio**, the area of the gap between the perfect equality line and the Lorenz curve (A) as a ratio of the entire area (A + B). The closer the Gini ratio is to zero, the more equal the distribution. The closer to one, the more unequal the income distribution. In the United States, the Gini ratio was estimated to be .489 in 2020. The Gini ratio was equal to .43 in 2010, which indicates that the distribution of income is becoming less equal.

$$\text{Gini ratio} = \text{Area A}/(\text{Area A} + \text{Area B})$$

- The closer the Gini ratio gets to zero, the more equal the distribution of income.
- The closer the Gini ratio gets to one, the more unequal the distribution of income.

What Are the Sources of Inequality?

The market is not always a good mechanism for distributing income equally. There are some commonly accepted factors for income inequality:

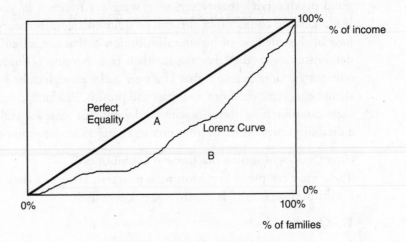

Figure 11.6

- *Ability.* Because natural ability is not distributed equally, income is not distributed equally. This factor would explain why some quarterbacks or artists are more highly paid than other quarterbacks or artists.
- *Human capital.* Individuals augment their ability with education and training, resulting in higher income. Not everyone attains the same level of human capital, so income is not equally distributed.
- *Discrimination.* Despite social progress, discrimination is a hurdle that might not be surmountable even with high levels of ability and human capital.
- *Preferences.* Some individuals, even with high ability and human capital, prefer to maximize utility with more leisure and less labor.
- *Market power.* We learned that monopoly and monopsony markets are detrimental to consumers and workers. The more market power held in the hands of the few, the more unequal the distribution of income.
- *Luck and connections.* Some are born into prosperity, and some are lucky enough to stumble upon the right connections.

Can Income Be Redistributed?

The economic system in the United States emphasizes a productivity-based distribution of resources, but we know that this system does not overcome all of the equity issues that are theoretically solved by egalitarianism. We have decided that the government should have a role in income distribution. The idea behind redistribution of income is that the government collects taxes from one segment of society and transfers it to another. These transfers come in the form of social programs like government housing, Medicare, or public education. And while most agree that these programs are essentially good, how government decides to tax is a hotly debated issue along philosophical and political grounds. We summarize the nature of progressive, regressive, and proportional taxes, and use the marginal and average concepts again in this new context.

Marginal and Average Tax Rates

Marginal tax rate is the rate paid on the last dollar earned. This is found by taking the ratio of the change in taxes divided by the change in income:

$$\text{Marginal tax rate} = (\Delta \text{ taxes due})/(\Delta \text{ taxable income})$$

Example:

If my income rises by $100 and the taxes that I owe the government rise by $25, the marginal tax rate is 25 percent on those additional $100.

Average tax rate is the proportion of total income paid to taxes. It is calculated by dividing the total taxes owed by the total taxable income:

$$\text{Average tax rate} = (\text{Total taxes due})/(\text{Total taxable income})$$

Example:

If my monthly taxable income is $1,000 and $200 is deducted for taxes, my average tax rate is 20 percent.

Progressive, Regressive, and Proportional Taxes

The way in which a redistributive tax works depends on how the average tax rate changes as income changes.

A Progressive Tax

A **progressive tax** exists if as income increases, the average tax rates increase. The federal income tax works this way. If your household income is above a certain minimum level but below a certain maximum level (a tax bracket), you might pay an average of 20 percent of your income in taxes. If your household income rises above that upper limit and falls into a higher tax bracket, your average tax rate might increase to 24 percent. A **tax bracket** is a range of income on which is applied a given marginal tax rate. This structure is designed so that the lowest incomes pay taxes at a much lower rate than the highest incomes.

A Regressive Tax

A tax is **regressive** if the average tax rate falls as income rises. A sales tax on consumption is a good example of a regressive tax.

Example:

Two unmarried consumers with no children both shop at the grocery store in a state with a 5 percent sales tax. One consumer, Bill, earns a modest $20,000 and spends $10,000 annually on food at the store. He pays $500 in sales tax. A second consumer, Mary, earns $200,000, or 10 times as much as Bill. Can we expect her to spend 10 times as much on food? Doubtful. Let's be generous and say that Mary spends $20,000 annually on food at the grocery store and pays $1,000 in sales tax. Everyone in the state pays 5 percent sales tax on their consumption spending, but as a percentage of income, Bill pays a much higher average tax rate.

$$\text{Bill's average tax rate} = \$500/\$20,000 = 2.5\%$$

$$\text{Mary's average tax rate} = \$1,000/\$200,000 = .5\%$$

A Proportional Tax

A proportional tax exists if a constant tax rate is applied regardless of income. Many politicians, on the grounds of a more streamlined way of taxing the population, have proposed this kind of "flat tax." Some U.S. states have adopted a proportional income tax rather than the more traditional progressive tax on income.

Example:
Melanie and Max earn $30,000 and $60,000, respectively. A proportional tax of 10% would require that Melanie pays $300 and Max pays $600 in taxes.

› Review Questions

1. In the figure below, X represents

   (A) spillover benefits.
   (B) a potential producer subsidy to eliminate an externality.
   (C) a potential consumer subsidy to eliminate an externality.
   (D) both A and C.
   (E) A, B, and C.

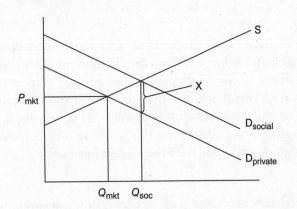

2. Which of the following scenarios best describes a negative externality?

   (A) A roommate has an extensive music library, and you share the same taste in music.
   (B) Your neighbor has a swimming pool, and you have an open invitation to come on over for a pool party.

   (C) Your neighbor has a swimming pool, and her six-year-old child has his first-grade friends over every day for a pool party.
   (D) Your roommate's mom has decided that your apartment needs cable TV and pays for it.
   (E) Your dad has purchased a new sports coupe and has agreed that you can drive it to the prom.

3. Which of the following is the best example of a public good?

   (A) A lighthouse on a rocky coastline
   (B) Tickets to the Super Bowl
   (C) A granola bar
   (D) A cup of coffee
   (E) A magazine subscription

4. Production of energy (i.e., electricity, natural gas, heating oil) creates a negative externality in the form of air pollution blown to communities downwind from the source of the pollution. Of the choices below, which is the most appropriate policy to remedy this negative externality?

   (A) a per-unit tax on consumers of subway tickets and city bus passes
   (B) a per-unit tax on producers of energy
   (C) a per-unit subsidy for energy consumers
   (D) a per-unit tax on consumers of energy-efficient lightbulbs
   (E) a per-unit subsidy for energy producers

5. Jason earns $1,000 a week and pays a total of $200 in taxes. Jennifer earns $2,000 a week and pays a total of $300 in taxes. We can conclude from this information that their income is taxed with a(n)

(A) progressive tax.
(B) proportional tax.
(C) regressive tax.
(D) tax bracket.
(E) egalitarian tax.

6. You learn that one nation has a Gini ratio of .25 and another nation has a Gini ratio of .85. Based on this you might conclude

(A) the nation with the higher Gini ratio has a more equal distribution of wealth and income.
(B) the nation with the higher Gini ratio has a more unequal distribution of citizens with college degrees.
(C) the nation with the lower Gini ratio has more societal barriers like discrimination.
(D) the nation with the higher Gini ratio has fewer societal barriers like discrimination.
(E) the nation with the lower Gini ratio has more oligopolistic industries.

› Answers and Explanations

1. **E**—This vertical distance between society's demand curve and the market demand curve represents spillover benefits, or additional benefits to society not captured by market demand. However, it could also be the amount of a producer or consumer subsidy if the government chose to eliminate the externality.

2. **C**—A negative externality is a situation where a third party is harmed by the actions of consumers and/or producers. The first-grade pool party is the best candidate for such a situation, as all of the other choices are likely to benefit you, rather than impose cost upon you.

3. **A**—A public good is a good that is nonrival and nonexcludable. In other words, if one person consumes it, all others can still consume it.

4. **B**—The presence of the negative externality should rule out any choice that refers to a subsidy of either producers or consumers of energy. To reduce consumption and production, we must reduce the market quantity, not encourage more of it. Subsidies could be used to encourage more energy-efficient behavior, but choices A and D would actually inhibit this kind of action. The per-unit tax on producers of the negative externality is the most appropriate choice, as the tax shifts the market supply inward, making it closer to the socially optimal supply of energy.

5. **C**—Jennifer's weekly income is twice Jason's, yet she pays less than double his taxes. This is a regressive tax. A proportional tax would require Jennifer to pay $400, and a progressive tax would require that she pay more than $400 in weekly taxes.

6. **B**—The distribution of human capital is a factor in determining the distribution of income and wealth. A nation that has a more unequal distribution of educational attainment would therefore likely have a more unequal distribution of income.

› Rapid Review

Private goods: Goods that are both rival and excludable. Only one person can consume the good at a time, and consumers who do not pay for the good are excluded from consumption. Examples include a tube of toothpaste or an airline ticket.

Public goods: Goods that are both nonrival and nonexcludable. One person's consumption does not prevent another from also consuming the good, and if it is provided to some, it is necessarily provided to all, even if they do not pay for the good. Examples are local police services and national defense.

Free-rider problem: In the case of a public good, some members of the community know that they can consume the public good while others provide for it. This results in a lack of private funding for the good and requires that the government provide it.

Spillover benefits: Additional benefits to society, not captured by the market demand curve from the production of a good, result in a price that is too high and a market quantity that is too low. Resources are underallocated to the production of this good.

Positive externality: Exists when the production of a good creates utility (the spillover benefits) for third parties not directly involved in the consumption or production of the good.

Marginal private benefit curve (MPB): The MPB reflects the additional benefit received by actual consumers of a good; the market demand curve.

Marginal social benefit curve (MSB): The MSB reflects the additional benefit received by all members of society, including both those who actually consume the good and those who receive spillover benefits from that consumption; the socially optimal demand curve.

Spillover costs: Additional costs to society, not captured by the market supply curve from the production of a good, result in a price that is too low and market quantity that is too high. Resources are overallocated to the production of this good.

Negative externality: Exists when the production of a good imposes disutility (the spillover costs) upon third parties not directly involved in the consumption or production of the good.

Marginal private cost curve (MPC): The MPC reflects the additional cost incurred by actual producers of a good; the market supply curve.

Marginal social cost curve (MSC): The MSC reflects the additional cost incurred by all members of society, including those who actually produce the good and those who incur spillover costs from that production; the socially optimal supply curve.

Egalitarianism: The philosophy that all citizens should receive an equal share of the economic resources.

Marginal productivity theory: The philosophy that a citizen should receive a share of economic resources proportional to the marginal revenue product of their productivity.

Marginal tax rate: The rate paid on the last dollar earned. This is found by taking the ratio of the change in taxes divided by the change in income.

Average tax rate: The proportion of total income paid to taxes. It is calculated by dividing the total taxes owed by the total taxable income.

Progressive tax: The proportion of income paid in taxes rises as income rises. An example is the personal income tax.

Tax bracket: A range of income on which a given marginal tax rate is applied.

Regressive tax: The proportion of income paid in taxes decreases as income rises. An example is a sales tax.

Proportional tax: A constant proportion of income is paid in taxes no matter the level of income. An example is a "flat tax" or the corporate income tax.

Lorenz curve: A graphical representation of a nation's income distribution.

Gini ratio: A measure of a nation's income inequality. This measure uses a scale between zero and one. The closer it lies to zero, the more equal the distribution of income.

STEP 5

Build Your Test-Taking Confidence

AP Microeconomics Practice Exam 1
AP Microeconomics Practice Exam 2

AP Microeconomics Practice Exam 1

SECTION I: Multiple-Choice Questions
ANSWER SHEET

1 Ⓐ Ⓑ Ⓒ Ⓓ Ⓔ   21 Ⓐ Ⓑ Ⓒ Ⓓ Ⓔ   41 Ⓐ Ⓑ Ⓒ Ⓓ Ⓔ
2 Ⓐ Ⓑ Ⓒ Ⓓ Ⓔ   22 Ⓐ Ⓑ Ⓒ Ⓓ Ⓔ   42 Ⓐ Ⓑ Ⓒ Ⓓ Ⓔ
3 Ⓐ Ⓑ Ⓒ Ⓓ Ⓔ   23 Ⓐ Ⓑ Ⓒ Ⓓ Ⓔ   43 Ⓐ Ⓑ Ⓒ Ⓓ Ⓔ
4 Ⓐ Ⓑ Ⓒ Ⓓ Ⓔ   24 Ⓐ Ⓑ Ⓒ Ⓓ Ⓔ   44 Ⓐ Ⓑ Ⓒ Ⓓ Ⓔ
5 Ⓐ Ⓑ Ⓒ Ⓓ Ⓔ   25 Ⓐ Ⓑ Ⓒ Ⓓ Ⓔ   45 Ⓐ Ⓑ Ⓒ Ⓓ Ⓔ
6 Ⓐ Ⓑ Ⓒ Ⓓ Ⓔ   26 Ⓐ Ⓑ Ⓒ Ⓓ Ⓔ   46 Ⓐ Ⓑ Ⓒ Ⓓ Ⓔ
7 Ⓐ Ⓑ Ⓒ Ⓓ Ⓔ   27 Ⓐ Ⓑ Ⓒ Ⓓ Ⓔ   47 Ⓐ Ⓑ Ⓒ Ⓓ Ⓔ
8 Ⓐ Ⓑ Ⓒ Ⓓ Ⓔ   28 Ⓐ Ⓑ Ⓒ Ⓓ Ⓔ   48 Ⓐ Ⓑ Ⓒ Ⓓ Ⓔ
9 Ⓐ Ⓑ Ⓒ Ⓓ Ⓔ   29 Ⓐ Ⓑ Ⓒ Ⓓ Ⓔ   49 Ⓐ Ⓑ Ⓒ Ⓓ Ⓔ
10 Ⓐ Ⓑ Ⓒ Ⓓ Ⓔ   30 Ⓐ Ⓑ Ⓒ Ⓓ Ⓔ   50 Ⓐ Ⓑ Ⓒ Ⓓ Ⓔ
11 Ⓐ Ⓑ Ⓒ Ⓓ Ⓔ   31 Ⓐ Ⓑ Ⓒ Ⓓ Ⓔ   51 Ⓐ Ⓑ Ⓒ Ⓓ Ⓔ
12 Ⓐ Ⓑ Ⓒ Ⓓ Ⓔ   32 Ⓐ Ⓑ Ⓒ Ⓓ Ⓔ   52 Ⓐ Ⓑ Ⓒ Ⓓ Ⓔ
13 Ⓐ Ⓑ Ⓒ Ⓓ Ⓔ   33 Ⓐ Ⓑ Ⓒ Ⓓ Ⓔ   53 Ⓐ Ⓑ Ⓒ Ⓓ Ⓔ
14 Ⓐ Ⓑ Ⓒ Ⓓ Ⓔ   34 Ⓐ Ⓑ Ⓒ Ⓓ Ⓔ   54 Ⓐ Ⓑ Ⓒ Ⓓ Ⓔ
15 Ⓐ Ⓑ Ⓒ Ⓓ Ⓔ   35 Ⓐ Ⓑ Ⓒ Ⓓ Ⓔ   55 Ⓐ Ⓑ Ⓒ Ⓓ Ⓔ
16 Ⓐ Ⓑ Ⓒ Ⓓ Ⓔ   36 Ⓐ Ⓑ Ⓒ Ⓓ Ⓔ   56 Ⓐ Ⓑ Ⓒ Ⓓ Ⓔ
17 Ⓐ Ⓑ Ⓒ Ⓓ Ⓔ   37 Ⓐ Ⓑ Ⓒ Ⓓ Ⓔ   57 Ⓐ Ⓑ Ⓒ Ⓓ Ⓔ
18 Ⓐ Ⓑ Ⓒ Ⓓ Ⓔ   38 Ⓐ Ⓑ Ⓒ Ⓓ Ⓔ   58 Ⓐ Ⓑ Ⓒ Ⓓ Ⓔ
19 Ⓐ Ⓑ Ⓒ Ⓓ Ⓔ   39 Ⓐ Ⓑ Ⓒ Ⓓ Ⓔ   59 Ⓐ Ⓑ Ⓒ Ⓓ Ⓔ
20 Ⓐ Ⓑ Ⓒ Ⓓ Ⓔ   40 Ⓐ Ⓑ Ⓒ Ⓓ Ⓔ   60 Ⓐ Ⓑ Ⓒ Ⓓ Ⓔ

AP Microeconomics Practice Exam 1

SECTION I

Multiple-Choice Questions
Time—1 hour and 10 minutes
60 questions

For the multiple-choice questions that follow, select the best answer and fill in the appropriate letter on the answer sheet.

1. At the birthday party of your best friend, you see Skylar help himself to a second piece of cake. For this individual, it must be the case that

   (A) the marginal benefit of the second piece of cake is less than the marginal cost.
   (B) the total benefit received from eating cake is falling.
   (C) the ratio of marginal benefit over marginal cost is less than one.
   (D) the marginal benefit of the second piece of cake is greater than the marginal cost.
   (E) Skylar is irrationally consuming too much cake.

2. Nancy has the choice to spend one hour studying for an exam, mowing the lawn for one hour at a wage of $6, or babysitting her niece for one hour at a wage of $8. If we know that Nancy has chosen to study for the exam, which of the following is true?

   (A) The benefit received from studying is greater than the opportunity cost of $8.
   (B) The opportunity cost of studying is $14, which is less than the benefit received from studying.
   (C) Nancy is indifferent to both studying and mowing the lawn.
   (D) Nancy's behavior is irrational, since babysitting was clearly superior to all other options.
   (E) Nancy is indifferent to both babysitting and mowing the lawn.

3. Suppose the market for roses is currently in equilibrium. If the supply of roses falls, while at the same time the demand for roses rises, what can you say about the price and quantity of roses in the market?

   (A) Price and quantity both rise.
   (B) Price rises, but the change in quantity is ambiguous.
   (C) Price and quantity both fall.
   (D) Quantity rises, but the change in price is ambiguous.
   (E) Neither price nor quantity change, as these shifts offset one another.

4. The United States is trading salmon to Peru in exchange for anchovies. If these nations are trading based on relative opportunity costs, what must be the case?

   (A) The United States has comparative advantage in anchovy production, and Peru has comparative advantage in salmon production.
   (B) The United States has comparative advantage in salmon production, and Peru has comparative advantage in anchovy production.
   (C) The United States has absolute advantage in anchovy production, and Peru has absolute advantage in salmon production.
   (D) The United States has absolute advantage in salmon production, and Peru has absolute advantage in anchovy production.
   (E) The United States has comparative advantage in salmon production, and Peru has absolute advantage in anchovy production.

5. Which of the following is the best example of a public good?

   (A) Private violin lessons
   (B) The volunteer fire department in your community
   (C) A $1 ticket for admission to a museum
   (D) A bag of potato chips
   (E) A history textbook

6. A typical characteristic of capitalist market economies is

   (A) government ownership of land and capital.
   (B) extensive price controls.
   (C) centralized government decision making to determine production limits.
   (D) an absence of scarcity.
   (E) private ownership of economic resources.

Questions 7 to 9 refer to the graph below.

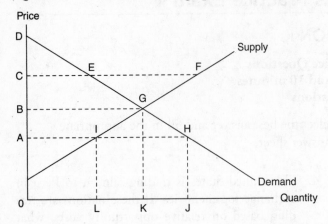

7. Assuming no government involvement in this market, if the current price were at the level of 0A, we would expect

(A) a surplus in the market to be eliminated by rising prices.
(B) a shortage in the market to be eliminated by falling prices.
(C) a surplus in the market to be eliminated by falling prices.
(D) a shortage in the market to be eliminated by rising prices.
(E) a decrease in quantity supplied and an increase in quantity demanded as the price rises.

8. If the market is initially in equilibrium, which of the following would create a new equilibrium at point H?

(A) A decrease in consumer income if this good is normal
(B) An increase in the price of a substitute for this good
(C) A decrease in the cost of a production input for this good
(D) An increase in the number of consumers of this good
(E) An increase in consumer income if this good is normal

9. If the price were to rise from 0B to 0C,

(A) dollars spent on this good would increase if demand for the good were price elastic.
(B) dollars spent on this good would decrease if demand for the good were price inelastic.
(C) dollars spent on this good would increase if demand for the good were price inelastic.
(D) dollars spent on this good would increase if demand for the good were unitary price elastic.
(E) dollars spent on this good would decrease if demand for the good were unitary price elastic.

10. Every day Melanie spends her lunch money consuming apples, at $1 each, and oranges, at $2 each. At her current level of consumption, Melanie's marginal utility of apples is 12 and her marginal utility of oranges is 18. If she has already spent all of her lunch money, how should Melanie change her consumption decision to maximize utility?

(A) She should make no changes; she is consuming the utility maximizing combination of apples and oranges.
(B) She should increase her apple consumption and decrease her orange consumption until the marginal utility per dollar is equal for both.
(C) She should decrease her apple consumption and increase her orange consumption until the marginal utility per dollar is equal for both.
(D) She should increase her apple consumption and decrease her orange consumption until the marginal utility is equal for both.
(E) She should decrease her apple consumption and increase her orange consumption until the marginal utility is equal for both.

11. When the production or consumption of a good creates a positive externality, it is deemed a market failure because at the market quantity

(A) the marginal social benefit exceeds the marginal social cost.
(B) the marginal social cost exceeds the marginal social benefit.
(C) society produces too much of the good.
(D) the private benefits from consuming the good exceed the social benefits.
(E) a surplus of the good always exists without government intervention.

12. Which of the following would best complete a short definition of economics? "Economics is the study of . . ."

   (A) how unlimited resources are allocated between scarce wants.
   (B) how money is circulated through the economy.
   (C) how corporations maximize the share price of their stock.
   (D) how nations trade goods and services in a global marketplace.
   (E) how scarce resources are allocated to satisfy unlimited wants.

13. Suppose the price elasticity of demand for cigarettes is less than one. When an excise tax is imposed on cigarette production, it changes the price, quantity, and consumer spending in which of the following ways?

	PRICE	QUANTITY	SPENDING
(A)	Decrease	Increase	Increase
(B)	Decrease	Decrease	Decrease
(C)	Increase	Decrease	Decrease
(D)	Increase	Decrease	Increase
(E)	Increase	Increase	Increase

14. Which of the following is true of a price floor?

   (A) The price floor shifts the demand curve to the left.
   (B) An effective floor creates a shortage of the good.
   (C) The price floor shifts the supply curve of the good to the right.
   (D) To be an effective floor, it must be set above the equilibrium price.
   (E) The government sets the price floor to assist consumers who are exploited at the equilibrium price.

15. You are told that the income elasticity for skateboards is +1.5. This means that

   (A) a 10-percent increase in income produces a 15-percent increase in consumption of skateboards. Skateboards are a normal luxury good.
   (B) a 10-percent increase in income produces a 15-percent increase in consumption of skateboards. Skateboards are an inferior good.
   (C) a 10-percent increase in income produces a 15-percent decrease in consumption of skateboards. Skateboards are an inferior good.
   (D) a 10-percent increase in the price of skateboards produces a 15-percent decrease in consumption of skateboards. Skateboards are a price elastic good.
   (E) a 10-percent increase in the price of skateboards produces a 15-percent decrease in consumption of skateboards. Skateboards are a price inelastic good.

16. Which of the following causes the supply curve of paper to shift to the left?

   (A) Paper producers expect lower paper prices in the months ahead.
   (B) The price of pencils, a complement to paper, increases.
   (C) Improvements are made in the technology used to produce paper.
   (D) Household income falls.
   (E) Environmental concerns reduce the yearly amount of timber that can be harvested.

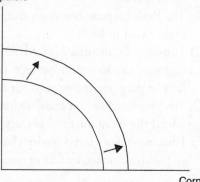

17. Using the diagram above, which of the following might have caused the outward movement of the production possibility frontier?

   (A) A decrease in the availability of fertile farmland
   (B) A plague of destructive grasshoppers
   (C) An increase in the productivity of the labor force
   (D) A severe and long-lasting drought
   (E) A decline in the rate of technological improvements

18. Suppose the county government sends each parent a coupon that can be used to subsidize the cost of sending each child to daycare. What would you expect to occur in the market for daycare services?

    (A) The demand for daycare falls, lowering the market price.
    (B) The demand for daycare rises, increasing the market price.
    (C) The supply of daycare rises, lowering the market price.
    (D) The supply of daycare falls, increasing the market price.
    (E) A permanent shortage of daycare services exists.

19. Monopoly deadweight loss is the result of

    (A) setting the price above marginal cost.
    (B) setting the price above average total cost.
    (C) monopoly output being greater than the competitive output.
    (D) long-run normal profits.
    (E) marginal revenue equaling marginal cost.

20. The market for Cincinnati Reds baseball tickets is currently in equilibrium. Which of the following events would most likely increase the consumer surplus received by Reds fans?

    (A) The Reds offer discounted parking for all home games.
    (B) The Reds increase hot dog prices to reflect a higher cost of buns.
    (C) The city of Cincinnati is undertaking a huge highway construction project that strands fans in pregame traffic jams for hours.
    (D) The Reds must increase ticket prices to afford the most talented players.
    (E) Fans must pay a steep service charge in order to purchase tickets online or over the phone.

21. If Matt's total utility from consuming bratwurst increased at a constant rate, no matter how many bratwurst Matt consumed, what would Matt's demand curve for bratwurst look like?

    (A) Vertical
    (B) Horizontal
    (C) Downward sloping
    (D) Upward sloping
    (E) First upward, but eventually downward sloping

22. When a firm is earning a normal profit from the production of a good, it is true that

    (A) total revenues from production are equal to explicit costs.
    (B) explicit costs are equal to implicit costs.
    (C) total revenues from production are equal to implicit costs.
    (D) total revenues from production are equal to the sum of explicit and implicit costs.
    (E) implicit costs are greater than explicit costs.

23. You are told that the cross-price elasticity between goods X and Y is +2.0. This means that

    (A) goods X and Y are normal goods.
    (B) goods X and Y are inferior goods.
    (C) goods X and Y are complementary goods.
    (D) goods X and Y are substitute goods.
    (E) demand for good X is twice as elastic as demand for good Y.

24. Which of the following is an example of a long-run adjustment for the owners of a small café?

    (A) The owners switch from whole wheat to sourdough bread.
    (B) The owners hire several part-time workers to cover the dinner shifts.
    (C) The owners work overtime on a busy weekend.
    (D) The owners install more energy-efficient lightbulbs in all of the light fixtures.
    (E) The owners buy the office next door, and this doubles the customer seating.

25. If total product of labor is rising at an increasing rate,

    (A) marginal product of labor is rising.
    (B) marginal product of labor is at its minimum.
    (C) marginal product of labor is at its maximum.
    (D) marginal cost is rising.
    (E) average product of labor is at its minimum.

26. The demand curve for a perfectly competitive firm's product is

    (A) downward sloping and equal to the market demand curve.
    (B) perfectly elastic.
    (C) perfectly inelastic.
    (D) "kinked" at the going market price.
    (E) the same as the firm's marginal cost curve.

27. Which of the following is true in the long run in perfect competition?

(A) $P = MR = MC = ATC$
(B) $P = MR = MC > ATC$
(C) $P > MR = MC = ATC$
(D) $P = MR > MC = ATC$
(E) $P > MR = MC > ATC$

28. If the market price is above the perfectly competitive firm's average total cost curve, we expect that in the long run,

(A) the industry contracts as firms exit the market.
(B) the industry expands as firms exit the market.
(C) the industry contracts as firms enter the market.
(D) the industry expands as firms enter the market.
(E) the government seeks to regulate the market to ensure efficient outcomes.

29. If a market is organized by a cartel, we can expect

(A) normal profits for all cartel firms.
(B) an incentive for cartel firms to cheat on the cartel agreement.
(C) profit maximization by individual firms in the cartel.
(D) allocative efficiency.
(E) perfectly competitive prices.

30. Jason cleans swimming pools in a perfectly competitive local market. A profit maximizer, he can charge $10 per pool to clean 9 pools per day, incurring total variable costs of $80 and total fixed costs of $20. Which of the following is true?

(A) Jason should shut down in the short run, with economic losses of $20.
(B) Jason should shut down in the short run, with economic losses of $10.
(C) Jason should clean 9 pools per day, with economic losses of $20.
(D) Jason should clean 9 pools per day, with economic losses of $10.
(E) Jason should clean 9 pools per day, with economic profits of $10.

31. Which of the following might explain how a price decrease might cause a decrease in quantity demanded and an upward-sloping demand curve?

(A) The good is inferior and the income effect is stronger than the substitution effect.
(B) The good is normal and the income effect is stronger than the substitution effect.
(C) The good is normal and the income effect is weaker than the substitution effect.
(D) The good is inferior and a luxury.
(E) The good is highly subsidized, creating a large increase in marginal utility per dollar.

32. For the perfectly competitive firm, the profit-maximizing decision to shut down is made when the price

(A) falls below minimum average total cost.
(B) is greater than minimum average variable cost, but lower than minimum average total cost.
(C) falls below minimum average variable cost.
(D) is equal to minimum average total cost.
(E) is equal to average fixed cost.

33. Declining populations of tuna in the Atlantic Ocean have likely had which of the following impacts on the wages of tuna fishers, the employment of tuna fishers, and real estate prices in New England fishing towns?

	FISHER WAGES	EMPLOYMENT OF FISHERS	REAL ESTATE PRICES
(A)	Decrease	Increase	Increase
(B)	Decrease	Decrease	Decrease
(C)	Decrease	Decrease	Increase
(D)	Increase	Decrease	Decrease
(E)	Increase	Increase	Increase

34. Which of the following is true of monopoly markets?

(A) Deadweight loss exists in the short run, but not in the long run.
(B) A homogenous product allows for long-run entry of competing firms.
(C) Collusion between close rivals creates pricing above marginal cost.
(D) Barriers to entry allow for the power to set prices above marginal cost.
(E) Allocative efficiency is guaranteed because marginal revenue equals marginal cost.

Questions 35 and 36 refer to the graph below.

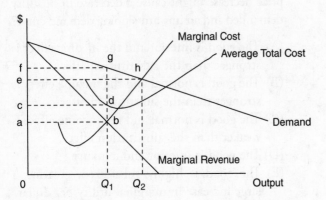

35. If this firm were a profit-maximizing monopolist, the price and output would be which of the following?

(A) 0a and $Q1$
(B) 0c and $Q1$
(C) 0e and $Q1$
(D) 0e and $Q2$
(E) 0f and $Q1$

36. Deadweight loss is equal to which of the following areas?

(A) abcd
(B) cdfg
(C) $0abQ1$
(D) $Q1Q2gh$
(E) bdgh

Two competing firms are deciding whether to enter a new market or maintain the status quo. Use the following profit matrix to respond to question 37.

		FIRM Y	
		Enter Market	**Status Quo**
FIRM X	**Enter Market**	X: $3 million Y: $3 million	X: $1 million Y: $6 million
	Status Quo	X: $6 million Y: $1 million	X: $5 million Y: $5 million

37. If these firms do not collude, the outcome will be

(A) both firms maintain the status quo.
(B) both firms enter the market.
(C) Firm X enters the market and Firm Y maintains the status quo.
(D) Firm Y enters the market and Firm X maintains the status quo.
(E) both firms alternate between entering the market and maintaining the status quo.

38. When the marginal product of labor is equal to the average product of labor,

(A) marginal product of labor is at its maximum.
(B) marginal cost of production is at its minimum.
(C) marginal cost is equal to minimum average variable cost.
(D) average total cost is at its minimum.
(E) total product of labor is at its maximum.

Questions 39 to 41 refer to the graph below.

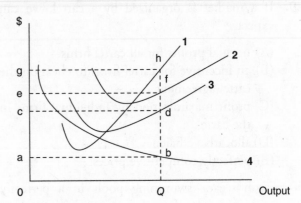

39. The area $0abQ$ is equal to

(A) total cost.
(B) total variable cost.
(C) total fixed cost.
(D) marginal cost.
(E) average product of labor.

40. The curve labeled 1 represents which of the following?

(A) Marginal cost
(B) Marginal product of labor
(C) Average total cost
(D) Average variable cost
(E) Average fixed cost

41. If this firm was operating in a perfectly competitive market, and the price was equal to 0g, economic profit would be equal to which of the following areas?

    (A) abcd
    (B) cdgh
    (C) cdef
    (D) eghf
    (E) abgh

42. Which is true of monopolistic competition?

    (A) Firms earn long-run economic profits.
    (B) $P = MR = MC = ATC$.
    (C) Firms spend money to differentiate and advertise their products.
    (D) In the long run the market is allocatively efficient.
    (E) Excess capacity is eliminated in the long run.

43. If firms are entering an industry that is monopolistically competitive, we would expect

    (A) the demand for existing firms to shift rightward.
    (B) the market price of the product to increase.
    (C) the demand for existing firms to become more inelastic.
    (D) economic profits to rise for all firms.
    (E) the demand for existing firms to shift leftward.

44. Monopolistic competition is said to be productively inefficient because

    (A) the long-run price is above minimum average total cost.
    (B) long-run profits are positive.
    (C) firms engage in collusive behavior.
    (D) there exist no barriers to entry.
    (E) there exist diseconomies of scale.

45. One of the reasons that the government discourages and regulates monopolies is that

    (A) producer surplus is lost and consumer surplus is gained.
    (B) monopoly prices ensure productive efficiency but cost society allocative efficiency.
    (C) monopoly firms do not engage in significant research and development.
    (D) consumer surplus is lost with higher prices and lower levels of output.
    (E) lower prices and higher levels of output create deadweight loss.

46. What is one reason why the government discourages collusion between large firms in the same industry?

    (A) Collusive output levels tend to increase, driving the price above competitive levels.
    (B) Consumer surplus falls as the price is driven downward.
    (C) Collusive output levels tend to decrease, driving the price down to competitive levels.
    (D) Joint profit maximization drives profits downward, forcing colluding firms to exit the industry.
    (E) Joint profit maximization costs society consumer surplus as the price rises above competitive levels.

47. In a competitive labor market for housepainters, which of the following would increase the demand for housepainters?

    (A) An effective minimum wage imposed on this labor market
    (B) An increase in the price of gallons of paint
    (C) An increase in the construction of new houses
    (D) An increase in the price of mechanical painters so long as the output effect exceeds the substitution effect
    (E) An increase in home mortgage interest rates

48. If a monopsony labor market suddenly were transformed into a perfectly competitive labor market, how would the wage and employment change?

    (A) Both would increase.
    (B) Both would decrease.
    (C) The wage would remain constant, but employment would increase.
    (D) The wage would fall, but employment would increase.
    (E) The wage would rise, but employment would decrease.

49. Which of the following is most likely to be true in the long run for a monopoly firm?

    (A) $P = MR = MC = ATC$
    (B) $P = MR = MC > ATC$
    (C) $P > MR = MC = ATC$
    (D) $P = MR > MC = ATC$
    (E) $P > ATC > MR = MC$

Questions 50 and 51 refer to the table below, which describes employment and production of a firm.

UNITS OF LABOR	TOTAL PRODUCT	PRICE OF OUTPUT
0	0	$2
1	8	$2
2	20	$2
3	30	$2
4	38	$2
5	44	$2

50. The marginal revenue product of the fourth unit of labor is equal to

(A) $19.
(B) $16.
(C) $8.
(D) $20.
(E) $2.

51. If the wage paid to all units of labor is $20, how many units of labor are employed?

(A) 1
(B) 2
(C) 3
(D) 4
(E) 5

52. An industry described as an oligopoly would most likely have

(A) normal profits in the long run.
(B) no opportunities for collusive behavior.
(C) significant barriers to entry.
(D) price-taking behavior.
(E) one firm with no close rivals.

53. An effective minimum wage in the competitive market for fast-food workers is likely to produce

(A) an increase in the demand for fast-food workers.
(B) a decrease in the supply of fast-food workers.
(C) a shortage of fast-food workers.
(D) a lower price of fast-food products.
(E) a surplus of fast-food workers.

54. In order to hire the least-cost combination of labor and capital, the firm must do which of the following?

(A) Find the combination of labor and capital where the marginal product of labor is equal to the marginal product of capital.
(B) Find the combination of labor and capital where the ratio of the marginal product of labor to the marginal product of capital is equal to one.
(C) Find the combination of labor and capital where the marginal product of labor divided by the price of labor is equal to the marginal product of capital divided by the price of capital.
(D) Find the combination of labor and capital where the price of labor is equal to the price of capital.
(E) Find the combination of labor and capital where the marginal revenue product of labor is equal to the marginal revenue product of capital.

55. More college students are graduating with BA degrees in economics. Given this trend, we would expect the wage of economists, the employment of economists, and the demand for economics textbooks to change in which of the following ways?

	ECONOMIST WAGES	EMPLOYMENT OF ECONOMISTS	DEMAND FOR ECONOMICS TEXTBOOKS
(A)	Decrease	Increase	Increase
(B)	Decrease	Decrease	Decrease
(C)	Increase	Decrease	Decrease
(D)	Increase	Decrease	Increase
(E)	Increase	Increase	Increase

56. Which of the following is the best example of a negative externality and the appropriate plan for eliminating it?

   (A) Air pollution from a factory blows downwind and harms children in a small community. Tax the citizens of the community.
   (B) Your neighbor plants a fragrant blooming cherry tree in her front yard. Give a tree subsidy to your neighbor.
   (C) The waste from a hog farm pollutes a neighbor's drinking water. Give a subsidy to the hog farmer.
   (D) Diesel-burning cars, trucks, and buses are creating smog in your city. Eliminate a subsidy for people who purchase electric vehicles.
   (E) Air pollution from a power plant is blowing downwind and harming the trees in your community. Tax the production of electricity.

57. A perfectly competitive employer hires labor up to the point where

   (A) wage = marginal factor cost.
   (B) wage = marginal product of labor.
   (C) wage = marginal revenue.
   (D) wage = marginal revenue product of labor.
   (E) wage = price of the good produced by the labor.

58. The sales tax that you pay at a clothing store is commonly labeled a

   (A) progressive tax.
   (B) regressive tax.
   (C) wage tax.
   (D) excise tax.
   (E) tax bracket.

59. Which of the following is the best example of the free-rider effect?

   (A) You and a friend take a road trip to Florida in your friend's car. You pay for the gas.
   (B) In exchange for tutoring your friend in economics, she helps you with your geometry assignment.
   (C) You have paid for a streaming television service, and several of your buddies show up unannounced to watch it at your place.
   (D) You buy your date dinner, but your date insists on leaving a tip for the server.
   (E) A local Girl Scout troop is giving a "free" carwash. You give them a $5 donation.

Question 60 refers to the graph below.

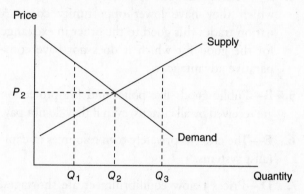

60. If the market for this good was in equilibrium at $Q2$ but the socially optimal output was $Q1$, the government could best remedy this _____ of resources by legislating a _____ on _____ of the good.

   (A) underallocation, per-unit tax, consumers
   (B) overallocation, per-unit subsidy, consumers
   (C) underallocation, per-unit tax, producers
   (D) overallocation, per-unit subsidy, producers
   (E) overallocation, per-unit tax, producers

› Answers and Explanations

1. **D**—You have to assume that Skylar evaluated the marginal benefits and marginal costs of the second piece of cake and decided that he should consume it.

2. **A**—The opportunity cost is the value of the most attractive alternative (in this case, the babysitting wage).

3. **B**—If demand increases and supply decreases, the price definitely rises. The quantity is ambiguous and depends on which effect is stronger. Draw these shifting curves in the margin of your exam book.

4. **B**—Trading nations specialize in the good in which they have lower opportunity costs. A nation trades this good to the other in exchange for the good for which it does not have comparative advantage.

5. **B**—Public goods like police and fire protection are received by all citizens, even if they do not pay.

6. **E**—The citizens privately own resources in capitalist systems.

7. **D**—Prices below equilibrium create shortages, but they do not last.

8. **C**—A rightward shift in supply would move the market to point H and lower input prices would do just that.

9. **C**—If $E_d < 1$, a given percent increase in the price outweighs the percent decrease in quantity demanded, thus increasing total dollars spent on the good.

10. **B**—The utility maximizing rule requires that MU/P is equal for both goods. Now the MU/P is greater for apples than for oranges. Melanie consumes more apples and fewer oranges, which lowers MU of apples and increases the MU of oranges.

11. **A**—Market equilibrium occurs where marginal private benefit equals marginal cost to society. With a positive externality, the MSB > MPB at the market quantity.

12. **E**—This is the definition of economics!

13. **D**—Excise taxes shift a supply curve leftward, increase price, and decrease quantity. If $E_d < 1$, cigarette consumers spend more on cigarettes.

14. **D**—Price floors are legal minimum prices so they are set above equilibrium. A surplus results.

15. **A**—When $E_I > 0$, it is a normal good. When $E_I > 1$, it is a luxury good.

16. **E**—Restricting the supply of a raw material to paper would increase the price of the production input and decrease the supply of paper.

17. **C**—Economic growth is the result of better, or more economic, resources or more technological progress. A more productive labor force increases the PPF for both goods.

18. **B**—A subsidy given to consumers acts as an increase in income. Demand for daycare rises, raising the price of daycare.

19. **A**—If $P = MC$, the market is allocatively efficient and there is no deadweight loss. If the monopoly $P > MC$, DWL emerges.

20. **A**—Anything that effectively lowers the price of attending the Reds game increases CS.

21. **B**—Downward-sloping demand is the result of diminishing marginal utility. This consumer's MU is constant, so the demand curve for bratwurst is horizontal.

22. **D**—Normal profits are also thought of as break-even economic profits.

23. **D**—If $E_{xy} > 0$, goods are substitutes.

24. **E**—Long-run adjustments change the production capacity of a firm.

25. **A**—MP_L tells you how TP_L is changing when more labor is hired. If more labor is increasing TP_L at a faster and faster rate, MP_L is rising.

26. **B**—Perfectly competitive firms are price takers, so demand for each firm's product is horizontal: $E_d = \infty$.

27. **A**—A defining outcome of long-run equilibrium in perfect competition.

28. **D**—If $P > ATC$, positive short-run economic profits exist. Long-run entry expands the market.

29. **B**—Cartels are illegal collusive agreements to lower output, raise the price, and maximize joint profits. Each member has an incentive to cheat by producing a little more.

30. **D**—TR > TVC, so Jason does not shut down. Subtracting all costs from TR, he is losing $10 per day.

31. **A**—Income and substitution effects work in opposite directions for inferior goods. A lower price prompts a substitution effect, increasing quantity demanded of the good. A lower price increases purchasing power, and for an inferior good, it decreases consumption. If the income effect outweighs the substitution effect, we can see an upward-sloping demand curve.

32. **C**—This is the shutdown point.

33. **B**—Decreased labor demand lowers wage and employment. Lower incomes and higher unemployment decrease real estate prices.

34. **D**—Barriers to entry are the key to monopoly pricing power.

35. **E**—Find the output where MR = MC and the price is found vertically at the demand curve.

36. **E**—DWL is the area above MC and below the demand curve, between the monopoly output and the perfectly competitive output.

37. **A**—Keeping the status quo is a dominant strategy for both firms.

38. **C**—MC and AVC are inverses of MP_L and AP_L. Because $MP_L = AP_L$ at the maximum of AP_L, MC = AVC at the minimum of AVC.

39. **C**—Familiarity with cost curves identifies curve 4 as AFC. The area of this rectangle is $Q \times AFC = TFC$.

40. **A**—Quickly recognize this as MC.

41. **D**—The profit rectangle is the quantity multiplied by the vertical distance between price and ATC.

42. **C**—With product differentiation, monopolistically competitive firms spend money to promote their product as different from the others.

43. **E**—Entry of new firms takes market share from existing firms, so demand curves begin to shift to the left.

44. **A**—Profits are normal and P = ATC, but unlike perfect competition, P > minimum ATC, so the industry is not productively efficient.

45. **D**—Lost CS is a big reason why government keeps an eye on the monopoly power of firms.

46. **E**—Colluding members of an oligopoly act as a monopolist, restraining competition, restricting output, and increasing the price.

47. **C**—This is the idea of derived demand.

48. **A**—Monopsony lowers both wage and employment when compared to the competitive labor market.

49. **E**—Like the competitive firm, the monopolist produces where MR = MC, but P > ATC, which is most likely even further above MR = MC.

50. **B**—MRP = MP × P. Calculate MP by looking at the difference in TP as one more unit of labor is hired.

51. **C**—Labor is hired to the point where W = MRP, so quickly find the point in the table where MP = 10, which when multiplied by P = $2 gives you MRP = $20.

52. **C**—This is a main identifier of oligopoly.

53. **E**—Minimum wages are price floors in a labor market. A surplus results.

54. **C**—This choice describes the least-cost rule for hiring inputs.

55. **A**—Increased labor supply lowers the wage, increases employment, and increases demand for goods that are "tools of the trade."

56. **E**—The appropriate fix to a negative externality is to tax either the producers or the consumers of electricity.

57. **D**—This describes the choice that is made by employers in competitive labor markets.

58. **B**—Sales taxes are typical examples of regressive taxes.

59. **C**—Free riders receive the benefit of a public good without contributing to its production.

60. **E**—If equilibrium output exceeds the socially desirable output, resources are overallocated to production of this good. This negative externality can be fixed with a tax on producers or sometimes on consumers.

AP Microeconomics Practice Exam 1

SECTION II

Free-Response Questions
Planning time—10 minutes
Writing time—50 minutes

At the conclusion of the planning time, you have 50 minutes to respond to the following three questions. Approximately half of your time should be given to the first question, and the second half should be divided evenly between the remaining two questions. Be careful to clearly explain your reasoning and to provide clear labels to all graph axes and curves.

1. The soybean market is a constant cost industry and Bob's Beans is a perfectly competitive soybean producer. The market price of soybeans is currently below average total cost, but above Bob's shutdown point.

   (A) Using two correctly labeled graphs, show the soybean market side by side with Bob's Beans. Clearly indicate which graph represents the market and which represents Bob's Beans. In your graphs, identify

      i. the equilibrium price and quantity in the soybean market, labeled P_{mkt} and Q_{mkt}, respectively.
      ii. the profit-maximizing quantity produced by Bob's Beans, labeled Q_b.
      iii. the area of economic profit or loss for Bob's Beans.

   (B) Will the number of firms in the soybean market increase, decrease, or stay the same in the long run? Explain.

   (C) Suppose now that Bob's Beans is a monopoly producer of soybeans currently setting a price that exceeds average total cost. In a correctly labeled graph, show a profit-maximizing monopolist and indicate each of the following:

      i. The profit-maximizing monopoly output, labeled Q_m
      ii. The monopoly price, labeled P_m
      iii. The area of economic profit or loss for Bob's Beans

2. Eli's lemonade stand employs only labor and lemons to produce lemonade. The table below shows how total production changes at different combinations of labor and lemons. Lemonade sells in a competitive market at $1 per cup.

HOURS OF LABOR	TOTAL PRODUCTION	POUNDS OF LEMONS	TOTAL PRODUC-TION
0	0	0	0
1	12	1	9
2	22	2	17
3	30	3	23
4	36	4	27
5	39	5	29
6	40	6	30

   (A) In competitive input markets, each hour of labor costs $6 to employ and each pound of lemons costs $2 to employ. If Eli has a $14 budget for hiring inputs, identify the least-cost combination of labor and lemons.

   (B) At the least-cost combination of labor and lemons, calculate each of the following:

      i. The output produced. Show your work.
      ii. The economic profit earned. Show your work.

   (C) Now suppose that the market demand for lemonade shifts to the right.
      i. All else equal, how does this change in lemonade demand affect Eli's demand for labor? Explain.
      ii. Will Eli's employment of labor increase, decrease, or stay the same?

3. Assume that the market for pork is perfectly competitive, but the production of pork on hog farms generates pollution that seeps into the ground and can pollute the local well-water supply.

(A) In a correctly labeled graph, illustrate the market for pork and identify:

i. The market equilibrium price and quantity of pork, labeled P_{mkt} and Q_{mkt}, respectively.

(B) Assuming that local residents do not enjoy having polluted drinking water, in your graph in part (A), show each of the following.

i. The marginal social cost curve, labeled MSC

ii. The marginal social benefit curve, labeled MSB

iii. The deadweight loss, if any, shaded completely

(C) Suppose the government grants a subsidy to pork consumers equal to the marginal external cost of the polluted water. Will this increase, decrease, or have no effect on the deadweight loss? Explain.

› Free-Response Grading Rubric

Note: Based on my experience, these point allocations roughly approximate the weighting on similar questions on the AP examinations. I have also tried to provide you with notations on where points would likely be deducted for responses that were not acceptable enough for full credit. However, be aware that every year the point allocations change and partial credit is awarded differently.

Question 1 (10 points)

Part (A): 4 points
These points are graphing points.

- One point is earned for drawing a correctly labeled graph of the soybean market with P_{mkt} and Q_{mkt}. The market demand curve must be downward sloping and the market supply curve must be upward sloping.
- One point is earned for showing a horizontal demand curve on the firm's graph extended from the market equilibrium price, P_{mkt}.
- One point is earned for identifying the firm's profit-maximizing quantity, Q_b, at marginal cost equal to marginal revenue.
- One point is earned for showing the firm's average total cost (ATC) curve and marginal cost (MC) passing through the minimum point of ATC, and P < ATC and P > AVC, at Q_b.

You cannot have a downward-sloping MR curve here.

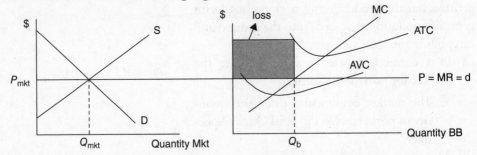

 TIP 1: On graphing problems, you can lose a point for not indicating which variables lie on each graphical axis. In this case, it would be as simple as a $ and a Q.

TIP 2: When asked to identify equilibrium price and quantity, make it clear to the reader that you know where these are found. The preferred way to do this is to use dashed lines from the intersection to the axes. You should also use the labeling given to you in the prompt. If you are told to label the market output Q_m and the firm's output Q_f, you are wise to play along.

TIP 3: Draw your graphs large enough for you to clearly identify the area of profit/loss. If your graph is the size of a postage stamp, it becomes more difficult for you to identify all relevant parts. It is also very tough for the reader to find all of the points.

When completing graphs, label everything and indicate direction of change and you will lose fewer points.

Part (B): 2 points

i. One point is earned for stating that the number of firms will decrease.
   One point is earned for explaining that because of short-run losses, firms will begin to exit the soybean market.

Part (C): 4 points

- One point is earned for drawing a correctly labeled graph of the monopoly showing downward-sloping demand (D) and marginal revenue (MR) curves with the MR curve below the demand curve.
- One point is earned for showing the profit-maximizing quantity, labeled Q_M, where $MR = MC$.
- One point is earned for both showing the profit-maximizing price, labeled P_M, from the demand curve at Q_M, and above the average total cost (ATC) curve.
- One point is earned for shading the correct area of economic profit.

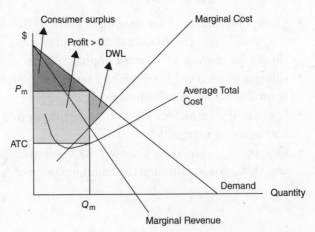

Note: I've also shaded the areas of consumer surplus and deadweight loss, which were not required in this practice problem. Because a more thorough analysis of monopoly has been asked on recent exams, be sure that you can identify monopoly profit, deadweight loss, and consumer surplus.

Question: So I've messed up the monopoly quantity; have I lost all points in part (C)?

Answer: Again, maybe not, but the rest of your response must be consistent with the incorrectly labeled output. In the figure below I have tried to replicate one possible incorrectly identified output, but consistent price and profit.

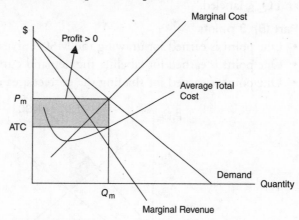

An Alternative Scoring for Part (C).

This graph shows output where demand intersects MC, not where MR = MC. This response cannot be given the point for a correct level of output. However, you would likely get a point for a correctly drawn monopoly figure, a price P_m that is consistent with the Q_m in this figure, and a profit area that is also consistent with Q_m and P_m.

Question 2 (5 points)

Part (A): 1 point

One point is earned for stating that Labor = 1, Lemons = 4.

TIP: Quickly write down the marginal products and highlight the options that satisfy the least-cost condition that states that the ratio of the (MPL/MPK) must be equal to the ratio of the input prices (PL/PK). With the price of labor being $6 and the price of lemons $2, find those ratios that are 3:1 and ignore all other possibilities.

Part (B): 2 points

i. One point is earned for calculating Output = 39 (12 from 1 labor and 27 from 4 lemons).
ii. One point is earned for calculating Total revenue = $1 × 39 = $39
   − Total cost = $6 × 1 + $2 × 4 = $14
   Economic profit = $25.

If you do not show your work, you will *not* earn these points.

Note: If you happened to pick an incorrect combination of labor and lemons in part (A), it may be possible to receive both points in part (B) if you find the consistent level of output and profit.

Part (C): 2 points
- One point is earned for stating that Eli's demand for labor will increase and for the explanation that the increase in the price of lemonade increases the marginal revenue product of labor ($MRP_L = P \times MP_L$).
- One point is earned for stating that Eli's employment of labor will increase.

Question 3 (5 points)

Part (A): 1 point
One point is earned for drawing a correctly labeled supply and demand graph with P_{Mkt} and Q_{mkt} labeled.

Part (B): 3 points
- One point is earned for drawing the MSC curve above the MPC, or supply curve.
- One point is earned for labeling the demand curve MSB.
- One point is earned for shading the correct area of the deadweight loss.

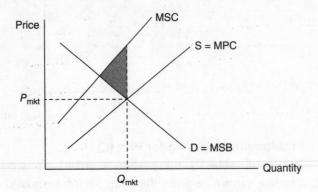

Part (C): 1 point
One point is earned for stating that the subsidy would increase the deadweight loss and for the explanation that a subsidy will increase the quantity of pork exchanged in the market. Since the market already produces more than the socially optimal quantity of pork, a subsidy will only worsen this over-allocation of resources.

Scoring and Interpretation

AP Microeconomics Practice Exam 1

Multiple-Choice Questions:

Number of correct answers: _____
Number of incorrect answers: _____
Number of blank answers: _____
Did you complete this part of the test in the allotted time? <u>Yes/No</u>

Free-Response Questions:

1. _____/10
2. _____/5
3. _____/5

Did you complete this part of the test in the allotted time? <u>Yes/No</u>

Calculate Your Score:

Multiple-Choice Questions:

$$\frac{}{\text{(\# right)}} = \frac{}{\text{MC raw score}}$$

Free-Response Questions:

Free-Response Raw Score = $(1.50 \times \text{Score 1}) + (1.50 \times \text{Score 2}) + (1.50 \times \text{Score 3}) = $ _____

Add the raw scores from the multiple-choice and free-response sections to obtain your total raw score for the practice exam. Use the table below to determine your grade, remembering these are rough estimates using questions that are not actually from AP exams, so do not read too much into this conversion from raw score to AP score.

| MICROECONOMICS #1 ||
RAW SCORE	APPROXIMATE AP GRADE
73–90	5
58–72	4
45–57	3
33–44	2
0–32	1

AP Microeconomics Practice Exam 2

SECTION I: Multiple-Choice Questions

ANSWER SHEET

1 Ⓐ Ⓑ Ⓒ Ⓓ Ⓔ	21 Ⓐ Ⓑ Ⓒ Ⓓ Ⓔ	41 Ⓐ Ⓑ Ⓒ Ⓓ Ⓔ
2 Ⓐ Ⓑ Ⓒ Ⓓ Ⓔ	22 Ⓐ Ⓑ Ⓒ Ⓓ Ⓔ	42 Ⓐ Ⓑ Ⓒ Ⓓ Ⓔ
3 Ⓐ Ⓑ Ⓒ Ⓓ Ⓔ	23 Ⓐ Ⓑ Ⓒ Ⓓ Ⓔ	43 Ⓐ Ⓑ Ⓒ Ⓓ Ⓔ
4 Ⓐ Ⓑ Ⓒ Ⓓ Ⓔ	24 Ⓐ Ⓑ Ⓒ Ⓓ Ⓔ	44 Ⓐ Ⓑ Ⓒ Ⓓ Ⓔ
5 Ⓐ Ⓑ Ⓒ Ⓓ Ⓔ	25 Ⓐ Ⓑ Ⓒ Ⓓ Ⓔ	45 Ⓐ Ⓑ Ⓒ Ⓓ Ⓔ
6 Ⓐ Ⓑ Ⓒ Ⓓ Ⓔ	26 Ⓐ Ⓑ Ⓒ Ⓓ Ⓔ	46 Ⓐ Ⓑ Ⓒ Ⓓ Ⓔ
7 Ⓐ Ⓑ Ⓒ Ⓓ Ⓔ	27 Ⓐ Ⓑ Ⓒ Ⓓ Ⓔ	47 Ⓐ Ⓑ Ⓒ Ⓓ Ⓔ
8 Ⓐ Ⓑ Ⓒ Ⓓ Ⓔ	28 Ⓐ Ⓑ Ⓒ Ⓓ Ⓔ	48 Ⓐ Ⓑ Ⓒ Ⓓ Ⓔ
9 Ⓐ Ⓑ Ⓒ Ⓓ Ⓔ	29 Ⓐ Ⓑ Ⓒ Ⓓ Ⓔ	49 Ⓐ Ⓑ Ⓒ Ⓓ Ⓔ
10 Ⓐ Ⓑ Ⓒ Ⓓ Ⓔ	30 Ⓐ Ⓑ Ⓒ Ⓓ Ⓔ	50 Ⓐ Ⓑ Ⓒ Ⓓ Ⓔ
11 Ⓐ Ⓑ Ⓒ Ⓓ Ⓔ	31 Ⓐ Ⓑ Ⓒ Ⓓ Ⓔ	51 Ⓐ Ⓑ Ⓒ Ⓓ Ⓔ
12 Ⓐ Ⓑ Ⓒ Ⓓ Ⓔ	32 Ⓐ Ⓑ Ⓒ Ⓓ Ⓔ	52 Ⓐ Ⓑ Ⓒ Ⓓ Ⓔ
13 Ⓐ Ⓑ Ⓒ Ⓓ Ⓔ	33 Ⓐ Ⓑ Ⓒ Ⓓ Ⓔ	53 Ⓐ Ⓑ Ⓒ Ⓓ Ⓔ
14 Ⓐ Ⓑ Ⓒ Ⓓ Ⓔ	34 Ⓐ Ⓑ Ⓒ Ⓓ Ⓔ	54 Ⓐ Ⓑ Ⓒ Ⓓ Ⓔ
15 Ⓐ Ⓑ Ⓒ Ⓓ Ⓔ	35 Ⓐ Ⓑ Ⓒ Ⓓ Ⓔ	55 Ⓐ Ⓑ Ⓒ Ⓓ Ⓔ
16 Ⓐ Ⓑ Ⓒ Ⓓ Ⓔ	36 Ⓐ Ⓑ Ⓒ Ⓓ Ⓔ	56 Ⓐ Ⓑ Ⓒ Ⓓ Ⓔ
17 Ⓐ Ⓑ Ⓒ Ⓓ Ⓔ	37 Ⓐ Ⓑ Ⓒ Ⓓ Ⓔ	57 Ⓐ Ⓑ Ⓒ Ⓓ Ⓔ
18 Ⓐ Ⓑ Ⓒ Ⓓ Ⓔ	38 Ⓐ Ⓑ Ⓒ Ⓓ Ⓔ	58 Ⓐ Ⓑ Ⓒ Ⓓ Ⓔ
19 Ⓐ Ⓑ Ⓒ Ⓓ Ⓔ	39 Ⓐ Ⓑ Ⓒ Ⓓ Ⓔ	59 Ⓐ Ⓑ Ⓒ Ⓓ Ⓔ
20 Ⓐ Ⓑ Ⓒ Ⓓ Ⓔ	40 Ⓐ Ⓑ Ⓒ Ⓓ Ⓔ	60 Ⓐ Ⓑ Ⓒ Ⓓ Ⓔ

AP Microeconomics Practice Exam 2

SECTION I

Multiple-Choice Questions
Time—1 hour and 10 minutes
60 questions

For the multiple-choice questions that follow, select the best answer and fill in the appropriate letter on the answer sheet.

1. Land, labor, capital, and entrepreneurial talent are often referred to as

   (A) production possibilities.
   (B) goods and services.
   (C) unlimited human wants.
   (D) opportunity costs.
   (E) scarce economic resources.

2. The law of increasing costs is useful in describing

   (A) a demand curve.
   (B) a marginal benefit curve.
   (C) a linear production possibility frontier.
   (D) a concave production possibility frontier.
   (E) a total fixed costs curve.

3. Which of the following is likely to have a demand curve that is the least elastic?

   (A) Demand for the perfectly competitive firm's output
   (B) Demand for the oligopoly firm's output with a homogenous product
   (C) Demand for the oligopoly firm's output with a differentiated product
   (D) Demand for the monopolistically competitive firm's output
   (E) Demand for the monopoly firm's output

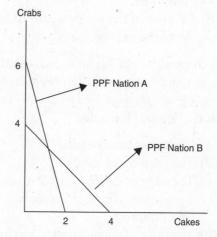

4. The figure above shows the production possibility frontiers (PPFs) for two nations that produce crabs and cakes. If these nations specialize and trade based on the principle of comparative advantage, which of the following trade agreements benefit both nations?

   (A) Nation A trades three crabs to Nation B in exchange for two cakes.
   (B) Nation A trades three cakes to Nation B in exchange for three crabs.
   (C) Nation A trades one cake to Nation B in exchange for two crabs.
   (D) Nation A trades one crab to Nation B in exchange for two cakes.
   (E) Nation A trades four crabs to Nation B in exchange for six cakes.

5. Which of the following scenarios would increase a nation's production possibility frontier (PPF)?

   (A) The nation's system of higher education slowly declines in quality.
   (B) The nation invests in research and development of new technology.
   (C) The nation's infant mortality rate increases.
   (D) Environmental pollution severely damages the health of the population.
   (E) Mineral reserves are exhausted.

6. A rational consumer who is eating Girl Scout cookies stops eating when

   (A) the total benefit equals the total cost of eating cookies.
   (B) the marginal benefit equals the marginal cost of the next cookie.
   (C) the marginal cost of eating cookies is maximized.
   (D) the marginal benefit of eating cookies is minimized.
   (E) the price of the cookie equals the total benefit of the next cookie.

7. A competitive market for coffee, a normal good, is currently in equilibrium. Which of the following would most likely result in an increase in the demand for coffee?

   (A) Consumer income falls.
   (B) The price of tea rises.
   (C) The wage of coffee plantation workers falls.
   (D) Technology in the harvesting of coffee beans improves.
   (E) The price of coffee brewing machines rises.

8. Which of the following certainly lowers the equilibrium price of a good exchanged in a competitive market?

   (A) The demand curve shifts to the right.
   (B) The supply curve shifts to the left.
   (C) The demand curve shifts to the left, and the supply curve shifts to the right.
   (D) The demand curve shifts to the right, and the supply curve shifts to the left.
   (E) Both the demand and supply curves shift to the left.

9. An effective price ceiling in the market for good X likely results in

   (A) a persistent surplus of good X.
   (B) a persistent shortage of good X.
   (C) an increase in the demand for good Y, a substitute for good X.
   (D) a decrease in the demand for good Z, a complement with good X.
   (E) a rightward shift in the supply curve of good X.

10. Which of the following goods is likely to have the most elastic demand curve?

    (A) Demand for white Ford minivans
    (B) Demand for automobiles
    (C) Demand for Ford automobiles
    (D) Demand for American-made automobiles
    (E) Demand for a Ford minivan

11. Which of the following is a fundamental aspect of the free market system?

    (A) A high degree of government involvement
    (B) Public ownership of resources
    (C) Private property
    (D) Central planners set wages and prices
    (E) Employers consult government agencies for guidance in hiring workers with appropriate job skills

12. The elasticity of supply is typically greater when

    (A) producers have fewer alternative goods to produce.
    (B) producers have less time to respond to price changes.
    (C) producers are operating near the limits of their production.
    (D) producers have less access to raw materials necessary for production.
    (E) producers have more time to respond to price changes.

13. Good X is exchanged in a competitive market. Which of the following is true if an excise tax is now imposed on the production of good X?

    (A) If the demand curve is perfectly elastic, the price rises by the amount of the tax.
    (B) The consumer's burden of the tax rises as the demand curve is more elastic.
    (C) Consumer surplus rises as a result of the tax.
    (D) The consumer's burden of the tax rises as the demand curve is less elastic.
    (E) If the demand curve is perfectly inelastic, the price does not rise as a result of the tax.

14. Which of the following is an implicit cost for the owner of a small store in your hometown?

    (A) The wage that is paid to the assistant manager
    (B) The cost of purchasing canned goods from a wholesale food distributor
    (C) The value placed on the owner's skills in an alternative career
    (D) The cost of cooling the refrigerated meat display
    (E) The price of placing an advertisement in the local newspaper

15. Suppose a price floor is installed in the competitive market for coffee. One result of this policy would be

    (A) a decrease in the demand for coffee-brewing machines.
    (B) a persistent shortage of coffee in the market.
    (C) an increase in consumer surplus due to lower coffee prices.
    (D) an increase in the demand for coffee.
    (E) a decrease in the producer surplus for the suppliers of coffee.

Questions 16 and 17 refer to the table below, which describes employment and production of a firm that hires labor and produces output in competitive markets. The competitive price of the product is $.50.

UNITS OF LABOR	TOTAL PRODUCT
0	0
1	11
2	20
3	27
4	32
5	35

16. Which unit of labor has marginal revenue product equal to $1.50?

    (A) 1st
    (B) 2nd
    (C) 3rd
    (D) 4th
    (E) 5th

17. If the wage paid to all units of labor is $4.50, how many units of labor are hired?

    (A) 1
    (B) 2
    (C) 3
    (D) 4
    (E) 5

18. Which of the following is true of the perfectly competitive firm in the short run?

    (A) The firm earns a normal profit.
    (B) The firm shuts down if the price falls below average total cost.
    (C) The firm earns positive economic profit.
    (D) The firm maximizes profit by producing where the price equals marginal revenue.
    (E) The firm may earn positive, negative, or normal profits.

Questions 19 to 21 refer to the figure below.

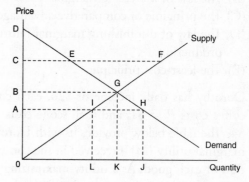

19. If the current price is 0B, we would expect

    (A) a surplus in the market to be eliminated by rising prices.
    (B) a shortage in the market to be eliminated by falling prices.
    (C) a surplus in the market to be eliminated by falling prices.
    (D) quantity demanded to be equal to quantity supplied as the market is in equilibrium.
    (E) a shortage in the market to be eliminated by rising prices.

20. If the price were to fall from 0C to 0A, which of the following would be true?

    (A) Dollars spent on this good would increase if demand for the good were price inelastic.
    (B) Dollars spent on this good would decrease if demand for the good were price elastic.
    (C) Dollars spent on this good would increase if demand for the good were price elastic.
    (D) Dollars spent on this good would increase if demand for the good were unitary price elastic.
    (E) Dollars spent on this good would decrease if demand for the good were unitary price elastic.

21. If the market is in equilibrium, which of the following areas corresponds to producer surplus?

    (A) BGD
    (B) 0AHJ
    (C) 0DGK
    (D) 0BG
    (E) 0BGK

22. The downward-sloping demand curve is partially explained by which of the following?

    (A) Substitution effects and income effects
    (B) The law of increasing marginal costs
    (C) The principle of comparative advantage
    (D) The law of diminishing marginal returns to production
    (E) The least-cost principle

23. Dorothy has daily income of $20, each cup of coffee costs $P_c = \$1$, and each scone costs $P_s = \$4$. The table below provides us with Dorothy's marginal utility (MU) received in the consumption of each good. As a utility-maximizing consumer, which combination of coffee and scones should Dorothy consume each day?

CUPS OF COFFEE	MU OF COFFEE	# OF SCONES	MU OF SCONES
1	10	1	30
2	8	2	24
3	6	3	20
4	4	4	16
5	2	5	14
6	1	6	8

    (A) 2 coffee and 2 scones
    (B) 5 coffee and 6 scones
    (C) 3 coffee and 2 scones
    (D) 4 coffee and 4 scones
    (E) 4 coffee and 16 scones

24. You are told that the Gini coefficient of income inequality has risen from .35 to .85. Which of the following is a likely cause of this change?

    (A) Market power in the factor and output markets has increased.
    (B) Labor market discrimination has been eliminated.
    (C) The distribution of wealth and property has become more equitable.
    (D) The vast majority of adults have achieved at least a college degree.
    (E) The tax system has become even more progressive.

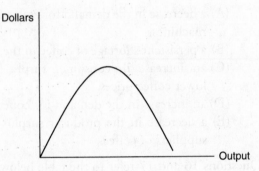

25. The figure above best represents which of the following functions?

    (A) Total product of labor
    (B) Total revenue
    (C) Total cost
    (D) Total utility
    (E) Total short-run economic profits

26. If it is true that bacon and eggs are complementary goods, then

    (A) the income elasticity of bacon is positive and the income elasticity for eggs is negative.
    (B) the price elasticity for eggs is greater than the price elasticity for bacon.
    (C) the cross-price elasticity between bacon and eggs is negative.
    (D) the income elasticity of bacon is negative and the income elasticity for eggs is positive.
    (E) the cross-price elasticity between bacon and eggs is positive.

27. A firm employs variable amounts of labor to a fixed amount of capital to produce output. If the daily wage paid to labor increases, how does this affect the firm's costs?

	TOTAL VARIABLE COST	TOTAL FIXED COST	TOTAL COST
(A)	Decrease	No change	Decrease
(B)	Decrease	Decrease	Decrease
(C)	Increase	Decrease	No change
(D)	Increase	No change	Increase
(E)	Increase	Increase	Increase

28. Diminishing marginal returns to short-run production begin when

(A) the average product of labor begins to fall.
(B) the total product of labor begins to fall.
(C) marginal product of labor becomes negative.
(D) average variable cost begins to rise.
(E) marginal product of labor begins to fall.

29. Which of the following is a characteristic of perfect competition?

(A) Firms produce a homogeneous product.
(B) Barriers to entry exist.
(C) Firms are price-setting profit maximizers.
(D) The government regulates the price so that deadweight loss is eliminated.
(E) Long-run positive profits are available.

UNITS OF LABOR	TOTAL PRODUCT (TP$_L$)
0	0 cups
1	5
2	15
3	30
4	40
5	45
6	40
7	30

30. The table above shows how hiring increasing amounts of labor to a fixed amount of capital affects the hourly output of Eli's lemonade stand. Based on this table of production data, which of the following can be said?

(A) Diminishing marginal returns begins with the first worker hired.
(B) Marginal cost begins to rise at the sixth worker hired.
(C) Total product is maximized at the third worker hired.
(D) Average product begins to decline with the first worker hired.
(E) Diminishing marginal returns begins with the fourth worker hired.

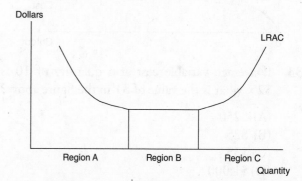

31. The figure above shows the long-run average cost curve of a competitive firm. Which of the following choices best describes Region B in the diagram?

(A) Economies of scale
(B) Diseconomies of scale
(C) Constant returns to scale
(D) Diminishing returns to scale
(E) Increasing returns to scale

32. The market for good X is currently in equilibrium. Which of the following choices would *not* cause both a decrease in the equilibrium price of good X and a decrease in the equilibrium quantity of good X?

(A) A decrease in consumer income and good X is a normal good.
(B) An increase in consumer income and good X is an inferior good.
(C) An increase in the price of good Y, a complement for good X.
(D) A decrease in the price of good Y, a substitute for good X.
(E) An increase in the number of consumers in the market for good X.

Questions 33 and 34 refer to the figure below, which shows cost curves for a competitive firm.

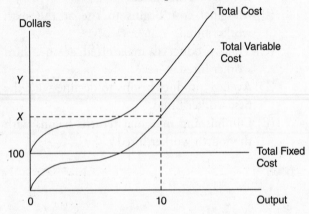

33. If average variable cost at a quantity of 10 is $25, what is the value of Y in the figure above?

(A) $250
(B) $25
(C) $35
(D) $1,000
(E) $350

34. At a quantity of 10, what is the value of $(Y - X)$?

(A) $100
(B) $25
(C) $10
(D) $35
(E) $350

35. The demand for labor falls if

(A) labor productivity falls.
(B) the price of the good produced by labor rises.
(C) the price of a complementary input falls.
(D) demand for the good produced by labor rises.
(E) a minimum wage is removed from the labor market.

Questions 36 and 37 refer to the graph below.

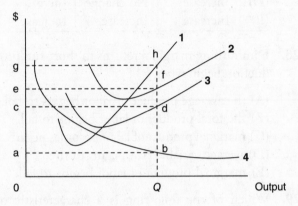

36. The curve labeled 4 represents which of the following?

(A) Marginal cost
(B) Marginal product of labor
(C) Average total cost
(D) Average fixed cost
(E) Average variable cost

37. Where is the shutdown point for this perfectly competitive firm?

(A) Any price below curve 4
(B) Any price below 0c
(C) Any price below curve 3
(D) Any price below curve 2
(E) Any quantity less than Q

38. If a market for a good is producing a negative externality,

(A) at the market output the marginal costs to society exceed the private marginal costs of production.

(B) at the market output the marginal benefits to society exceed the private marginal costs of production.

(C) at the market output the marginal costs to society exceed the total benefits to society.

(D) at the market output the private marginal costs of production exceed the marginal costs to society.

(E) at the market output the marginal benefits to society exceed the marginal costs to society.

39. Which of the following is a characteristic of a monopoly market?

(A) Firms produce a homogeneous product.

(B) Barriers to entry exist.

(C) Firms are price-taking profit maximizers.

(D) Deadweight loss is eliminated through entry of competing firms in the long run.

(E) In the long run the firm earns normal profits.

40. A monopolist may be able to maintain long-run positive profit due to

(A) deadweight loss.

(B) economies of scale in production.

(C) a price that is set equal to average total cost.

(D) perfectly elastic demand for the product.

(E) entry of new firms that keep the price high.

Questions 41 and 42 refer to the graph below.

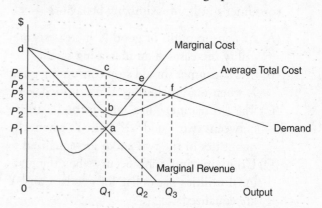

41. If this firm were a profit-maximizing monopolist, the price, output, and profit would be

	PRICE	OUTPUT	PROFIT
(A)	$P5$	$Q1$	$Q1 \times (c-b)$
(B)	$P5$	$Q1$	$Q1 \times P1$
(C)	$P4$	$Q2$	$Q2 \times (P4-P1)$
(D)	$P1$	$Q1$	$Q1 \times (P5-P1)$
(E)	$P3$	$Q3$	$Q3 \times P3$

42. Consumer surplus in the monopolist market is equal to the area

(A) abce.

(B) abcf.

(C) $P5$cd.

(D) $0Q1aP1$.

(E) $P1P5$ca.

43. The top six firms in an oligopolistic industry have market shares of 25%, 25%, 15%, 10%, 6%, and 3%. Many smaller firms split the rest of the market. What is the value of the four-firm concentration ratio?

(A) 65%

(B) 54%

(C) 75%

(D) 34%

(E) 50%

44. Which of the following statements is true of a consumer's utility-maximizing behavior?

    (A) As consumption of good X increases, total utility increases at an increasing rate.
    (B) The consumer should stop consuming good X when marginal utility is maximized.
    (C) The consumer has maximized utility between two goods X and Y when the quantities of the two goods are equalized.
    (D) Utility maximization occurs when the marginal utilities per dollar for goods X and Y are equalized.
    (E) As consumption of good X increases, the marginal utility per dollar spent on good X also increases.

45. Oligopoly has at times been the subject of government antitrust regulation. Which of the following is a reason for this government regulation?

    (A) Price is approximately equal to marginal cost.
    (B) Price is approximately equal to average total cost.
    (C) Deadweight loss lessens over time.
    (D) Consumer surplus is lost as market power increases.
    (E) Market efficiency is maximized.

46. The production of chicken often results in offending odors that are picked up by the wind and blown over rural communities. This is an example of a _____ externality, the result of which are spillover _____ and an _____ of resources to chicken production.

    (A) negative, costs, underallocation
    (B) negative, benefits, overallocation
    (C) negative, benefits, underallocation
    (D) positive, costs, overallocation
    (E) negative, costs, overallocation

47. Which of the following choices is true of both perfectly competitive firms and monopolistically competitive firms?

    (A) Barriers to entry
    (B) Homogenous products
    (C) Normal profits in the long run
    (D) Excess capacity
    (E) Price-setting behavior

48. The monopolistically competitive price is above marginal revenue because

    (A) firms have differentiated products.
    (B) firms are price takers.
    (C) firms produce a homogenous product.
    (D) the market is allocatively efficient.
    (E) profits are normal in the long run.

49. Deadweight loss in industries with market power is a result of

    (A) profit-maximizing output occurs where price equals marginal revenue.
    (B) profit-maximizing output occurs where price exceeds marginal cost.
    (C) profit-maximizing output occurs where price equals marginal cost.
    (D) profit-maximizing output occurs where price exceeds average total cost.
    (E) profit-maximizing output occurs where price equals average total cost.

50. If the government wishes to regulate a natural monopoly so that it earns a normal profit, it sets

    (A) Price = Marginal cost.
    (B) Marginal revenue = Marginal cost.
    (C) Price = Average total cost.
    (D) Price = Marginal revenue.
    (E) Marginal revenue = Average total cost.

51. Which of the following would improve the efficiency of a monopoly market?

(A) The government regulates the monopolist to produce the output where marginal revenue equals marginal cost.

(B) The government provides additional legal barriers to entry.

(C) The government subsidizes the monopolist so that they achieve even greater economies of scale.

(D) The government eliminates trade barriers on potential foreign producers.

(E) The government regulates the monopolist to produce the output where monopoly profits are maximized.

52. Which of the following increases the demand for interstate truck drivers?

(A) An increase in the wage of truck drivers

(B) An increase in the supply of truck drivers

(C) An increase in the price of diesel fuel, which is used to power semitrucks

(D) A decrease in the demand for interstate shipping

(E) A decrease in the price of semitrucks

53. A monopsony employer hires labor up to the point where

(A) wage = marginal factor cost.

(B) marginal factor cost = marginal product of labor.

(C) marginal factor cost = marginal revenue product of labor.

(D) wage = marginal revenue product of labor.

(E) wage = price of the good produced by the labor.

54. The price of labor is $5 and the price of capital is $10 per unit. Using the table below, what is the least-cost combination of labor and capital that should be hired to produce 18 units of output?

UNITS OF LABOR	MARGINAL PRODUCT OF LABOR	UNITS OF CAPITAL	MARGINAL PRODUCT OF CAPITAL
1	6	1	8
2	4	2	6
3	3	3	5
4	2	4	4
5	1	5	2

(A) 1 Labor and 2 Capital

(B) 4 Labor and 8 Capital

(C) 2 Labor and 1 Capital

(D) 5 Labor and 5 Capital

(E) 3 Labor and 2 Capital

55. A cartel is often the result of

(A) perfectly competitive firms that agree to produce a homogenous product.

(B) oligopoly competitors that agree to restrict output to maximize joint profits.

(C) a monopoly that has been regulated by the government.

(D) a natural monopoly that has evolved into a perfectly competitive industry.

(E) monopolistically competitive firms that have agreed to earn normal profits in the long run.

56. Suppose the state requires hairdressers and manicurists to pass a series of exams to be certified cosmetologists. How does this policy change the supply of cosmetologists, the equilibrium wage, and the price of a manicure?

	SUPPLY OF COSMETOLOGISTS	WAGE	PRICE OF MANICURES
(A)	Decrease	Increase	Increase
(B)	Decrease	Decrease	Decrease
(C)	Increase	Decrease	Decrease
(D)	Increase	Decrease	Increase
(E)	Increase	Increase	Increase

57. The local market for bankers is currently in equilibrium. Which of the following increases the local wage paid to bankers?

(A) Internet banking at home is becoming more popular.

(B) More college students are majoring in finance and economics, majors that make them attractive as bank employees.

(C) The price of banking software, a complementary resource to bankers, rises.

(D) Several banks in the local market merge and consolidate many operations.

(E) The price of automatic teller machines, a substitute for bankers, decreases and the output effect is greater than the substitution effect.

58. The U.S. government collects tax revenue, buys military equipment from many private firms, and uses this equipment to provide national defense to all Americans. This is a good example of

(A) a natural monopoly.

(B) an excise tax on military equipment.

(C) a regressive tax.

(D) a public good.

(E) deadweight loss.

59. Which of the following scenarios is the best example of a positive externality?

(A) Your neighbor has a swimming pool and throws loud late-night parties.

(B) Your neighbor has a swimming pool and allows you free access.

(C) Your neighbor has a swimming pool and the powerful chlorine odor blows into your open dining room window.

(D) Your neighbor has a swimming pool and allows you to use it in exchange for letting his kids use your swing.

(E) Your neighbor has a swimming pool that is conducive for the breeding of mosquitoes.

60. Because of the free-rider effect, the private marketplace tends to

(A) provide the allocatively efficient amount of a public good.

(B) produce too much of a public good, requiring the government to intervene and tax the production of it.

(C) produce a public good in the amount where the marginal benefit to society equals the marginal cost to society.

(D) produce too little of the public good, requiring the government to intervene and provide it for all.

(E) produce too little of the public good, requiring the government to intervene and ban it.

› Answers and Explanations

1. **E**—Know the four scarce economic resources.

2. **D**—A concave PPF exhibits the law of increasing costs. As more of a good is produced, opportunity costs rise. This is because resources are not perfectly substitutable between the production of different goods.

3. **E**—Demand is more elastic if there are more substitute goods. A monopolist has no close substitutes so is likely the least elastic demand.

4. **A**—Nation A has comparative advantage in crab production, and Nation B has comparative advantage in cake production. Nation A specializes in crabs and Nation B specializes in cakes, so avoid any option suggesting the opposite. Choice A is the only one that allows both to consume beyond the PPF.

5. **B**—Nations that invest in research and technology expect the PPF to expand, the key to economic growth.

6. **B**—Rational decision makers consume right up to the point where the MB of the next cookie is exactly equal to the MC of the next cookie.

7. **B**—Tea is a coffee substitute. Higher tea prices increase coffee demand.

8. **C**—Leftward demand shifts coupled with rightward supply shifts put downward pressure on prices.

9. **B**—Price ceilings are legal maximum prices set below the equilibrium price. A shortage results.

10. **A**—The more narrowly a good is defined, the more elastic demand.

11. **C**—Private property is fundamental to the free market economy.

12. **E**—The supply curve is more elastic as more time elapses.

13. **D**—If the demand curve is more inelastic (more vertical), a greater burden of an excise tax falls upon consumers and less upon producers.

14. **C**—The opportunity cost of starting a small store is the salary given up in the next best alternative for the entrepreneur's skills.

15. **A**—A price floor is a legal minimum price set above the equilibrium price. Higher coffee prices decrease the demand for complementary goods like coffee machines.

16. **E**—$P \times MP_L = MRP_L$.

17. **B**—At the second worker, wage = MRP_L.

18. **E**—In perfect competition, short-run profits may be positive or negative, or normal, but long-run profits are always normal.

19. **D**—This is the equilibrium price.

20. **C**—When the price falls and quantity demanded rises, consumer spending on the good ($P \times Q$) can change in two directions. If $E_d > 0$, a percent decrease in price increases quantity demanded by a greater percent, increasing spending on the good.

21. **D**—PS is the area under the price and above supply.

22. **A**—Substitution and income effects explain the law of demand.

23. **D**—Using the utility maximizing rule, set $MU_c/\$1 = MU_s/\$4$. There are three options where the MU_c is four times the MU_s, and only one of those options uses exactly $20 of daily income.

24. **A**—The Gini coefficient measures income inequality. The closer it gets to one, the more unequal the income distribution. One explanation for inequality is more market power in product and input markets. This redistributes CS to monopoly producers and/or employers.

25. **B**—Quickly look at the graph to eliminate some possibilities. With dollars on the y-axis, this curve cannot represent TP_L (output on the y-axis) or total utility (utility on the y-axis). The other key is that this curve has a value of zero dollars at an output of zero. TC = TFC at zero output and short-run economic losses equal TFC at zero output.

26. **C**—If the price of eggs rises, demand for bacon falls if they are complementary; $E_{xy} < 0$.

27. **D**—Labor is a variable cost so there is no change in TFC, but an increase in TVC and TC.

28. **E**—This defines diminishing marginal returns and is often missed by students, who make the mistake of identifying falling TP_L, rather than falling MP_L, with diminishing returns.

29. **A**—Know the characteristics of all market structures.

30. **E**—The fourth worker is the first to have lower MP_L than the worker before.

31. **C**—Constant returns exist when a larger firm has constant LRAC.

32. **E**—All other choices *would* produce a decrease in the demand for good X and would therefore decrease both the price and quantity. You are looking for the only choice that would *not*. More consumers for good X would increase demand and increase both the price and quantity.

33. **E**—Since you know that AVC is $25 at $Q = 10$, TVC is $250. Adding this to the given $100 of TFC produces $350 of total cost at $Q = 10$.

34. **A**—The vertical distance between TC and TVC is TFC.

35. **A**—Demand for labor is the MRP_L curve. Higher labor productivity increases labor demand.

36. **D**—AFC declines as output rises.

37. **C**—The shutdown point is at $P < AVC$.

38. **A**—With no externality, MSB = MSC. With a negative externality, MSC > MPC = MSB for the good.

39. **B**—Barriers to entry are a defining characteristic of monopoly.

40. **B**—Economies of scale are a common barrier to entry; a key to maintaining long-run positive profits.

41. **A**—Find the output level where MR = MC and locate the price from the demand curve. Profit is equal to $Q \times (P - ATC)$ at that output.

42. **C**—CS is the area above price and under demand.

43. **C**—A four-firm concentration ratio is the sum of the market share of the four largest firms in an industry.

44. **D**—Utility-maximizing consumers do not equate the units of two goods, they equate MU/P for each good.

45. **D**—As industries approach monopoly, prices rise, lowering CS.

46. **E**—Negative externalities, like "fowl" odors, impose spillover costs upon third parties. These costs, ignored by the market, reflect an overallocation of resources to chicken production.

47. **C**—Know the characteristics of all market structures.

48. **A**—Product differentiation results in a small degree of price-setting ability and downward-sloping demand curves for the firms. $P = ATC$ and profits are normal in the long run, and this output level does not occur where ATC is minimized. This defines excess capacity.

49. **B**—DWL emerges when output is moved away from where $P = MC$.

50. **C**—If $P = ATC$, economic profit is zero, or normal.

51. **D**—Allowing more foreign competition lessens market power of a monopolist and improves efficiency as the price falls closer to MC.

52. **E**—Semitrucks are a complementary resource to the truck drivers. If the price falls, demand for the labor rises.

53. **C**—The monopsony hiring decision.

54. **C**—Use the least-cost rule of $MP_L/\$5 = MP_K/\$10$ to find the optimal combination of labor and capital. There are three combinations of labor and capital where the MP_K is twice the MP_L, but only one choice produces 18 units of output. Remember that adding the marginal products provides the total product.

55. **B**—This describes a cartel.

56. **A**—Certification exams decrease labor supply and raise the wage in the market. A higher wage increases the MC of producing the good, which raises the price of the good.

57. **E**—If the price of a substitute resource falls, labor demand can increase if the output effect is greater than the substitution effect.

58. **D**—Know your public goods.

59. **B**—You are the recipient of a spillover benefit from your neighbor's purchase of a pool.

60. **D**—The private marketplace underprovides for a public good because free riders benefit from the good without paying for it. Government must provide the public good.

AP Microeconomics Practice Exam 2

SECTION II

Free-Response Questions
Planning time—10 minutes
Writing time—50 minutes

At the conclusion of the planning time, you have 50 minutes to respond to the following three questions. Approximately half of your time should be given to the first question, and the second half should be divided evenly between the remaining two questions. Be careful to clearly explain your reasoning and to provide clear labels to all graph axes and curves.

1. The graph below shows a firm that has monopolized the market for gadgets.

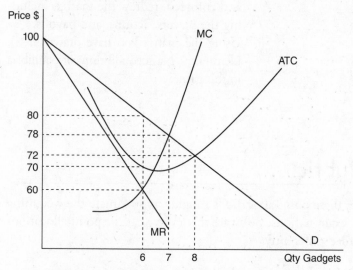

(A) Using the values in the graph, identify the following:

   i.   The profit-maximizing quantity
   ii. The price of a gadget when the monopolist has maximized profit
   iii. The allocatively efficient output

(B) Using the values in the graph, calculate the following and show your work:

   i. Monopoly profit
   ii. Consumer surplus

(C) Suppose the government levies a lump-sum tax on the monopolist.

   i.   Will output increase, decrease, or stay the same? Explain.
   ii. Will deadweight loss increase, decrease, or stay the same? Explain.
   iii. Will profit increase, decrease, or stay the same?

2. Assume the following about the market for gizmos:

   • Gizmos are sold in a competitive market.
   • Gizmos have no close substitute.
   • The demand for gizmos is price inelastic but not perfectly inelastic.

Suppose now that the government imposes a per-unit excise tax on producers of gizmos.

(A) Using a correctly labeled graph, show the impact of the excise tax on each of the following in the gizmos market:

   i.   The change to price and quantity, after the tax
   ii. The area of tax revenue collected by the government
   iii. Deadweight loss from the tax

(B) Given that demand for gizmos is price inelastic, will consumer spending on gizmos increase, decrease, or remain constant after the tax is imposed? Explain.

3. There are two bakeries in the Burg, Best Buns and Doughbody's Business, and both firms are considering new strategies to take effect at the beginning of the year. Best Buns can pay for advertising or choose to not advertise. Doughbody's Business can begin to deliver to customers or choose to not deliver. The payoff matrix below shows the annual profits for each bakery. The first value is the profit for Best Buns and the second value is the profit for Doughbody's Business. Choices are made simultaneously and independently.

		DOUGHBODY'S BUSINESS	
		Delivery (D)	No Delivery (ND)
Best Buns	Advertise (A)	$100, $100	$250, $75
	Don't Advertise (DA)	$75, $250	$300, $300

(A) Does Best Buns have a dominant strategy? Explain using values in the payoff matrix.
(B) Identify the Nash equilibrium or equilibria in this game.
(C) If these two bakeries could collude without fear of legal penalties, what choices would they make to maximize their combined profits?
(D) Suppose the bakeries made an agreement without fear of legal penalties. Best Buns will choose advertising and Doughbody's Business will choose delivery. If a firm cheats on the agreement, they must donate $75 of their profit to charity.

   i. Assuming the agreement was in effect and enforced, redraw the matrix, including the players, actions, and payoffs.
   ii. Using the matrix you have drawn in (i), identify the Nash equilibrium or equilibria in this game.

› Free-Response Grading Rubric

Note: Based on my experience, these point allocations roughly approximate the weighting on similar questions on the AP examinations. Be aware that every year the point allocations differ and partial credit is awarded differently.

Question 1 (10 points)

Part (A): 3 points

   i. One point is earned for identifying 6 as the profit maximizing output.
   ii. One point is earned for identifying $80 as the price.
   iii. One point is earned for identifying that 7 units would be allocatively efficient (where $P = MC$).

Part (B): 2 points

   i. One point is earned for calculating, with work shown, that $\pi = 6 \times (\$80 - \$70) = \$60$.
   ii. One point is earned for calculating, with work shown, that $CS = .5 \times 6 \times \$20 = \$60$.

Part (C): 5 points

   i. One point is earned for stating that output will not change.
One point is earned for explaining that the lump-sum tax does not affect marginal revenue or marginal cost.
   ii. One point is earned for stating that deadweight loss doesn't change.
One point is earned for explaining that because output doesn't change, and the demand curve still intersects MC at 7 units, the difference between profit maximizing and allocatively efficient output levels is the same.
   iii. One point is earned for stating that profit decreases.

Question 2 (5 points)

Part (A): 4 points

These are all graphing points, so to get all points, you must perfectly identify all curves, axes, and directional shifts.

One point is earned for drawing a correctly labeled graph showing the supply curve shifting upward by the amount of a tax.

When you are given the flexibility to use your own labeling, use arrows to clearly demonstrate that you know that price is rising and quantity is falling.

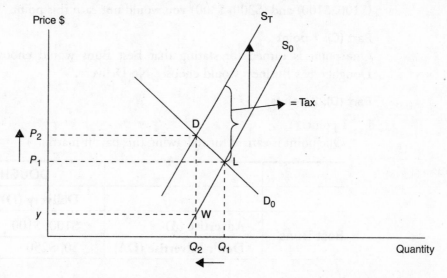

   i. One point is earned for showing that the price increases and quantity decreases after the tax.

   ii. One point is earned for identifying tax revenue as the area of the rectangle yP_2DW.

   iii. One point is earned for showing deadweight loss as the area of the triangle DWL shown above.

TIP: In a question like this, there are very few partial credit possibilities. You either get the graphing points or you do not.

Part (B): 1 point

One point is earned for stating that consumer spending increases because the percent increase in the price is greater than the percent decrease in quantity. It is also accurate to refer to proportional changes.

TIP: This explanation point is the more difficult of the two necessary parts of the correct answer and serves to differentiate students. In the past you might have also received credit for saying "a *large* increase in the price outweighs a *small* decrease in quantity." It is much more accurate to refer to proportional or percentage changes, and in recent years, the rubric has been more stringent on this point.

Question 3 (5 points)

Part (A): 1 point

One point is earned for stating that Best Buns does not have a dominant strategy and providing a thorough explanation that uses values from the payoff matrix.

If Doughbody's Business chooses "Delivery," Best Buns should choose "Advertising" because they would earn $100 rather than $75. If Doughbody's Business chooses "No

Delivery," Best Buns should choose "No Advertising" because they would earn $300 rather than $250.

TIP: If you are instructed to use values in the matrix, you will not earn this point if those are missing from your response.

Part (B): 1 point

One point is earned for stating that there are two Nash equilibria in this game: (Advertising, Delivery) and (No Advertising, No Delivery).

TIP: A Nash equilibrium is a conversion of actions taken, not the payoffs. If you answered ($100, $100) and ($300, $300) you would not earn this point.

Part (C): 1 point

One point is earned for stating that Best Buns would choose "No Advertising" and Doughbody's Business would choose "No Delivery."

Part (D): 2 points

i. 1 point
    One point is earned for redrawing this payoff matrix.

		DOUGHBODY'S BUSINESS	
		Delivery (D)	**No Delivery (ND)**
Best Buns	**Advertise (A)**	$100, $100	$250, $0
	Don't Advertise (DA)	$0, $250	$225, $225

ii. 1 point
    One point is earned for stating that the Nash equilibrium is that Best Buns will choose "Advertise" and Doughbody's Business will choose "Delivery."

Scoring and Interpretation

AP Microeconomics Practice Exam 2

Multiple-Choice Questions:

Number of correct answers: _____
Number of incorrect answers: _____
Number of blank answers: _____

Did you complete this part of the test in the allotted time? Yes/No

Free-Response Questions:

1. _____/10
2. _____/5
3. _____/5

Did you complete this part of the test in the allotted time? Yes/No

Calculate Your Score:

Multiple-Choice Questions:

$$\frac{}{\text{(\# right)}} = \frac{}{\text{MC raw score}}$$

Free-Response Questions:

Free-Response Raw Score $= (1.50 \times \text{Score 1}) + (1.50 \times \text{Score 2}) + (1.50 \times \text{Score 3}) = $ _____

Add the raw scores from the multiple-choice and free-response sections to obtain your total raw score for the practice exam. Use the table below to determine your grade, remembering these are rough estimates using questions that are not actually from AP exams, so do not read too much into this conversion from raw score to AP score.

MICROECONOMICS #2	
RAW SCORE	APPROXIMATE AP GRADE
73–90	5
58–72	4
45–57	3
33–44	2
0–32	1

5 Minutes to a 5

90 AP Microeconomics Activities and Questions in

5 Minutes a Day

INTRODUCTION

Welcome to *5 Minutes to a 5: 180 Questions and Activities*! This bonus section is another tool for you to use as you work toward your goal of achieving a 5 on the AP exam(s) in May. Since AP Macroeconomics and AP Microeconomics courses are typically taught in concurrent semesters, students often find themselves preparing for these exams in the span of one school year. As such, in this section you will find 90 questions and activities that pertain to the AP Macroeconomics course and 90 questions and activities that pertain to the AP Microeconomics course. These questions cover the most essential material in each course and will guide you in preparation for either one or both exams.

One of the secrets to excelling in your AP class is spending a bit of time *each day* studying the subject(s). The questions and activities offered here are designed to be done one per day, and each should take 5 minutes or so to complete. (Although there might be exceptions. Depending on the exam—some exercises may take a little longer, some a little less.) You will encounter stimulating questions to make you think about a topic in a big way, and some very subject-specific activities, which cover the main book's chapters; some science subjects will offer at-home labs, and some humanities subjects will offer ample chunks of text to be read on one day, with questions and activities for follow-up on the following day(s). There will also be suggestions for relevant videos for you to watch, websites to visit, or both. Most questions and activities are linked to the specific chapters of your book, so you are constantly fortifying your knowledge.

Remember, approaching this section for 5 minutes a day is much more effective than bingeing a week's worth in one sitting! So if you practice all the extra exercises in this section and reinforce the main content of this book, we are certain you will build the skills and confidence needed to succeed on your exam. Good luck!

—Editors of McGraw-Hill

Check off each activity as it is completed.

1. ❑	24. ❑	47. ❑	70. ❑
2. ❑	25. ❑	48. ❑	71. ❑
3. ❑	26. ❑	49. ❑	72. ❑
4. ❑	27. ❑	50. ❑	73. ❑
5. ❑	28. ❑	51. ❑	74. ❑
6. ❑	29. ❑	52. ❑	75. ❑
7. ❑	30. ❑	53. ❑	76. ❑
8. ❑	31. ❑	54. ❑	77. ❑
9. ❑	32. ❑	55. ❑	78. ❑
10. ❑	33. ❑	56. ❑	79. ❑
11. ❑	34. ❑	57. ❑	80. ❑
12. ❑	35. ❑	58. ❑	81. ❑
13. ❑	36. ❑	59. ❑	82. ❑
14. ❑	37. ❑	60. ❑	83. ❑
15. ❑	38. ❑	61. ❑	84. ❑
16. ❑	39. ❑	62. ❑	85. ❑
17. ❑	40. ❑	63. ❑	86. ❑
18. ❑	41. ❑	64. ❑	87. ❑
19. ❑	42. ❑	65. ❑	88. ❑
20. ❑	43. ❑	66. ❑	89. ❑
21. ❑	44. ❑	67. ❑	90. ❑
22. ❑	45. ❑	68. ❑	
23. ❑	46. ❑	69. ❑	

CHAPTER 5 – USING THE FOUR ECONOMIC RESOURCES IN THE KITCHEN

Suppose you are going to make dinner for a friend. List the four economic resources that you would use to complete the dinner. Be as specific as possible.

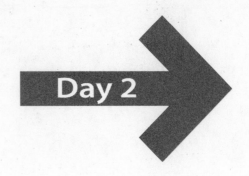

THE OPPORTUNITY COST OF GOING TO THE MOVIES

You're going to go see a movie at a nearby cinema. What is the opportunity cost of this activity?

You will need to do a little research on all of the costs involved. This might be done by searching the cinema's website or visiting it in person to record the necessary information.

1. Select a movie and determine the price of a ticket.

2. Will you buy snacks or drinks? Record those prices.

3. Will you require transportation to get to the cinema? If you are using a car, estimate the amount of gasoline you will require and the local price of that gasoline.

4. Determine how much time, including the transportation time, you will need to watch the movie. What is the value of your time as measured by an hourly wage you could receive if you had worked instead?

5. Use all of this information to determine the total opportunity cost of going to the movie.

Day 3

HOW MANY SLICES OF PIZZA WILL YOU EAT?

Imagine a day when you've skipped lunch, and you're very hungry for dinner. You know a pizza place that sells pizza by the slice at $2 each. In this hypothetical situation, how many slices of pizza do you think you would purchase and eat?

Now with this number in mind, draw a graph of marginal benefit and marginal cost curves that shows your decision to stop buying pizza.

YOUR PRODUCTION POSSIBILITIES

Suppose that each day you have 16 waking hours to divide between studying (measured in pages read) and socializing (measured in text messages sent).

a. Assuming constant opportunity costs, draw your production possibility curve (PPC) with pages read on the *x*-axis and text messaging on the *y*-axis.

b. Now suppose you complete a speed-reading course that increases the number of pages you can read in an hour. Adjust your PPC from part (a).

c. How has the opportunity cost of socializing changed? Can you explain *why* it has changed?

COMPARATIVE ADVANTAGE AROUND THE HOUSE

Let's say that there are two tasks that need to be performed around the house: folding clean towels in the laundry and washing dirty plates in the sink. Information below summarizes how many towels could be folded and how many plates could be washed by two kids in the household.

Hourly Output for Eli: 20 towels and 0 plates, or 0 towels and 10 plates
Hourly Output for Theodore: 6 towels and 0 plates, or 0 towels and 6 plates

a. If Eli and Theodore each split their time equally between folding towels and washing plates, what is their combined output in 1 hour?

b. If Eli and Theodore specialized their tasks based on comparative advantage, what is their combined output in 1 hour?

ALLOCATIVE EFFICIENCY, PRODUCTIVE EFFICIENCY, AND EQUITY

Suppose you were going to bake a dozen cookies for yourself and three friends. When the cookies are done, you will also determine how many cookies each person receives.

1. How would these cookies be baked if you were productively efficient in the kitchen? Hint: It might be easier to think of a situation where the cookies were produced inefficiently.

2. How might the dozen cookies be distributed if your goal was an equitable distribution?

3. Suppose your goal was an allocatively efficient distribution of the dozen cookies. How might you change your equitable distribution from part 2 to reflect this new goal?

CONSTANT, INCREASING, AND DECREASING OPPORTUNITY COSTS

In the production possibilities model, there is more than one way to draw the PPC. Assume that we can use economic resources in our economy to produce only shoes and pizza. In each of the following scenarios, sketch a graph of the PPC. In each case, what must we assume about the substitutability of our resources? Which graph more accurately depicts the trade-offs we face when producing more output?

a. The opportunity cost of producing more pizza is a constant number of shoes.
b. The opportunity cost of producing more pizza is an increasing number of shoes.
c. The opportunity cost of producing more pizza is a decreasing number of shoes.

GROWTH

Imagine an economy that produces only two items: automobiles (representing the manufacturing sector) and wheat (representing the agricultural sector). For the sake of simplicity, we will assume there are constant opportunity costs along the production possibility curve. Our initial PPC has been drawn as follows.

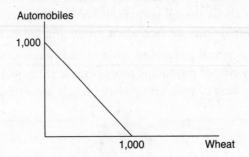

a. Adjust the PPC to reflect new technology that increases maximum automobile production by 20% but has no impact on wheat production. How does this affect the opportunity cost of wheat?

b. Adjust the PPC to reflect a crippling drought that decreases maximum wheat production by 25% but has no impact on automobile production. How does this affect the opportunity cost of automobiles?

c. Adjust the PPC to reflect new technology that increases maximum auto production by 20% and also increases maximum wheat production by 50%. How does this affect the opportunity cost of wheat?

Day 9

A CHANGING PPC OVER TIME

When a nation's stock of economic resources increases, the PPC shifts outward. To get a sense of how this has happened in the United States, you will need to find some data.

A. Labor Force

The civilian labor force is measured as the total number of people (over the age of 16) working plus the number of people not working but trying to find work. The size of the labor force can be found at the following website:

http://www.bls.gov/cps/lfcharacteristics.htm#laborforce

Look for links to "Database: Retrieve historical data series" and "Top Series," and ultimately find the seasonally adjusted civilian labor force. Try to find data going back as far as it exists. Calculate the percentage change in the labor force over this time period. Note: If you're pretty good with using Excel, create a graph that shows the change over time.

B. Capital Stock

A nation's stock of capital (equipment and buildings) is also very important in producing goods and services. If a nation invests in new capital, and replaces the capital that wears out (depreciation), then the stock of capital increases, and the PPC shifts outward.

The Federal Reserve Bank of St. Louis, or the FRED, has a website with lots of data, and there are many ways to access it. You'll begin exploring the FRED's site here: https://fred.stlouisfed.org/.

Search for "capital stock" and you'll get many results, but you should focus on data that is measured in "constant dollars." This simply means that the data have been adjusted for inflation over time. Once you find your data, the FRED will also likely produce a graph for you. Again, calculate the percentage change in the nation's capital stock.

Day 10

CHAPTER 6 – ARE FREE THINGS REALLY FREE?

We often find ourselves enjoying some "free" leisure time by watching a television show, texting with friends, or just reading. We do these things because they are enjoyable, but are they really free? Economists know that nothing is truly free, because there is always a second activity that was sacrificed in order to pursue the first activity.

In this exercise, we will try to figure out a way to put a price on both the enjoyment of an activity and the cost of pursuing it.

Measuring Benefit

Your task is to find someone who is enjoying some leisure. Maybe you can locate a family member or friend who is watching TV, playing a video game, texting or chatting on their phone, or reading a book, magazine, or newspaper.

Suppose you find someone watching a TV show. Your economic brain tells you that this person is choosing to watch TV because they believe the benefit exceeds the cost. How can we measure the benefit?

Measuring Cost

Let's return to our person watching TV. Ask the person, "If our cable/satellite/internet connection suddenly stopped, what would you do instead?" Make sure that the person provides you with their *next best* choice for the use of this time. How can we measure the cost of skipping that second-best activity?

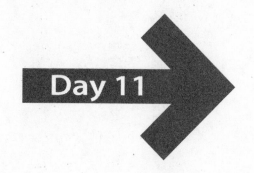

Day 11

BUILDING A FRIENDLY DEMAND CURVE

Think of a good or a service that you and your friends buy on a regular basis. For the sake of this example, let's say that this good is a ticket to a movie. Each individual has an individual demand curve for movie tickets, and this demand curve shows us the relationship between a variety of prices and the quantity of movie tickets a person would demand in a period of time, say, a month.

Use a table like the following to collect data from yourself and at least five friends. You might begin by asking each friend, "If the price of a movie ticket were $10, how many tickets would you be willing and able to buy in a month?" Record their responses, and repeat with higher and lower prices.

Use the data to construct a demand curve for the product you have chosen.

PRICE PER MOVIE TICKET	QUANTITY DEMANDED BY YOU	QUANTITY DEMANDED FOR FRIEND 1	QUANTITY DEMANDED FOR FRIEND 2	QUANTITY DEMANDED FOR FRIEND 3	QUANTITY DEMANDED FOR FRIEND 4	QUANTITY DEMANDED FOR FRIEND 5
$6						
$8						
$10						
$12						
$14						

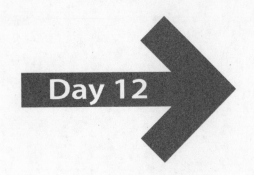

DEMAND DETERMINANTS (CURVE SHIFTERS)

It is critical that you have a solid grasp of the factors that shift demand curves to the left or to the right.

For each of the following, describe how the demand for orange juice will be affected. Be sure to determine which, if any, of the demand shifters is at work.

a. The *New York Times* reports that drinking orange juice will lower your risk of cancer, increase your IQ, and increase your life expectancy.
b. The price of apple juice increases.
c. The economy goes into a recession, and orange juice is a normal good.
d. Consumers expect the price of orange juice to rise in the future because a hurricane damaged the orange crop in Florida.
e. The price of orange juice drops.

MORE DEMAND DETERMINANTS

For each of the following, how will the U.S. demand for 1-pound blocks of cheddar cheese be affected? Your response must include (1) which, if any, of the demand shifters is at work and (2) which direction, if any, the demand for cheddar cheese is shifting.

a. The price of 1-pound blocks of Swiss cheese is rising.
b. The price of 1-pound blocks of cheddar cheese is falling.
c. The average household income in the United States is rising.
d. An outbreak of "mad cow" disease creates a widespread fear of eating dairy products.
e. The price of crackers is rising.

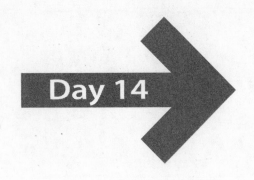

A FRIENDLY SUPPLY CURVE

With the help of several friends, your goal is to construct a supply of labor curve. Each individual worker makes a decision on how many hours (e.g., in a week) of work to supply at different hourly wages. When we combine all of these individual supply decisions, we have a market supply of labor.

Use a table like this one to collect data from yourself and at least five friends. Begin by asking each friend, "If you could receive an hourly wage of $10, how many hours of work would you supply in a week?" Record their response and repeat with higher and lower wages.

Use the data to construct a labor supply curve for the market.

HOURLY WAGE	QUANTITY OF HOURS SUPPLIED BY YOU	QUANTITY OF HOURS SUPPLIED BY FRIEND 1	QUANTITY OF HOURS SUPPLIED BY FRIEND 2	QUANTITY OF HOURS SUPPLIED BY FRIEND 3	QUANTITY OF HOURS SUPPLIED BY FRIEND 4	QUANTITY OF HOURS SUPPLIED BY FRIEND 5
$6						
$8						
$10						
$12						
$14						

SUPPLY DETERMINANTS

It is very important that you have a solid grasp of the determinants of supply.

For each of the following, describe how the supply of academic textbooks will be affected. Be sure to determine which, if any, of the supply shifters is at work.

a. Publishers have developed a more efficient way of mass-producing textbooks.
b. The price of paper has increased.
c. A boom in the market for self-help books has increased the price consumers are willing to pay for self-help books.
d. Several publishing companies have failed and have left the industry.
e. The government provides a $5 subsidy to every new textbook produced.

MORE SUPPLY DETERMINANTS

Here's even more practice with your supply determinants.

For each of the following, describe how the *supply* of pumpkin pie will be affected. Be sure to identify which, if any, of the supply shifters is at work.

a. All else equal, the price of pumpkins is falling.
b. All else equal, the price of apple pies is increasing.
c. All else equal, bakeries are able to bake more pies each day in larger ovens.
d. All else equal, the price of pumpkin pies is falling.
e. All else equal, several new pumpkin pie bakeries have just begun to operate.

SHORTAGES AND SURPLUSES

The following table shows the quantity of Cheezbows that are demanded (Q_d) and supplied (Q_s) at several prices.

PRICE	Q_d	Q_s	
$10	20	110	
9	25	100	
8	30	90	
7	35	80	
6	40	70	
5	45	60	
4	50	50	
3	55	40	
2	60	30	
1	65	20	

At each price, determine whether there exists a shortage or a surplus of Cheezbows, and calculate the size of the shortage or surplus.

WHAT DOES THE DEMAND CURVE TELL US?

It's easy to learn the law of demand and understand that higher prices, all else equal, are associated with lower quantities demanded. You also know that shifts of the demand curve are the result of a change in one of those other variables, but it's instructive to gain a little more understanding of what these demand curves are telling us.

Let's use a simple linear demand equation to demonstrate what this is all about.

Demand equation:

$$P = 50 - 2Q_d$$

a. In a correctly labeled graph, draw this demand curve, being careful to label the vertical and horizontal intercepts.

b. At any price, the demand curve tells us how many units of the product consumers are willing and able to purchase. If the current price is $30, how many units will be demanded? Add this point to the graph.

c. At any quantity, the demand curve tells us the highest price consumers would be willing to pay for this product. If the current quantity is 15 units, what is the highest price consumers would pay? Add this point to the graph.

d. Now suppose the demand for this product increases and the new demand equation is:

$$P = 100 - 2Q_d$$

Add the new demand curve to the graph, again being sure to label the intercepts.

e. Redo part (b). How does your new quantity demanded reflect the shift in demand?

f. Redo part (c). How does your new price reflect the shift in demand?

Day 19

CHANGES TO MARKET EQUILIBRIUM

Suppose the competitive market for apples is in equilibrium. Given the following scenarios, you must: (1) identify the specific shifter that is happening, (2) state which direction a curve is shifting, and (3) predict changes to the equilibrium price and quantity of apples.

   Note: A diagram is not required to answer these questions, but might be useful to you.

   a. All else equal, the cost of labor used in picking apples has decreased.
   b. All else equal, the *New York Times* reports that eating apples increases the likelihood of contracting Ebola, a deadly virus.
   c. All else equal, the price of oranges has increased.
   d. All else equal, combine the effects of parts (a) and (b).

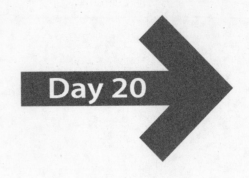

MORE CHANGES TO MARKET EQUILIBRIUM

Suppose the competitive market for pumpkin pie is in equilibrium. Given the following scenarios, predict changes to the equilibrium price and quantity of pumpkin pie. Be sure to determine which of the market shifters is at work. A diagram is not required but might be useful to you.

  a. All else equal, the economy is robust and consumer purchasing power has increased.
  b. All else equal, the price of apple pies has decreased.
  c. All else equal, five small pumpkin pie bakeries merge into one bakery.
  d. All else equal, combine the events from parts (a) and (c).

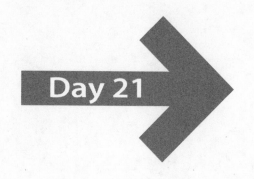

CONSUMER SURPLUS FROM GROCERY RECEIPTS

Consumer surplus is the difference between that maximum price you would have paid for an item (this is called willingness to pay) and the actual price you paid for an item. Your task here is to compute a friend's or family member's consumer surplus from a recent shopping trip that person made. Complete a table like the following. Find a person who has recently gone to the grocery store (or any store or restaurant for that matter), purchased a few items, and has the receipt. With the receipt as your guide, try to elicit from this person how much they would have paid for each item.

ITEM PURCHASED	HIGHEST PRICE SHOPPER WOULD HAVE PAID (WTP)	ACTUAL PRICE PAID (P)	CONSUMER SURPLUS EARNED (CS = WTP – P)
			$\sum$ CS =

CALCULATING CONSUMER SURPLUS

Suppose the demand curve for Gizmos is given by the following equation:

$$P = 250 - 3Q_d$$

The current price of a Gizmo is $100.

Draw this demand curve, and calculate consumer surplus at the current price.

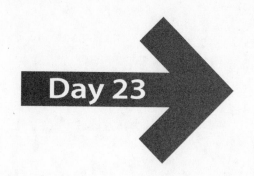

CALCULATING PRODUCER SURPLUS

Suppose the supply curve of Whodats is given by the following equation:

$$P = 100 + \tfrac{1}{2}Q_s$$

The current price of a Whodat is $200.

Draw this supply curve, and calculate producer surplus at the current price.

CALCULATING MARKET EQUILIBRIUM

It's a useful exercise to employ a little bit of algebra to calculate equilibrium price and quantity, and it can be useful in seeing how a demand or supply shift affects price and quantity.

Suppose that the market for Snarrs is given by the following demand and supply equations:

Demand

$$P = 700 - 2Q_d$$

Supply

$$P = 100 + Q_s$$

a. Calculate equilibrium quantity and price in the Snarr market.
b. Now suppose the supply curve shifts to the left so that the new supply curve is:

$$P = 160 + Q_s$$

First, predict the change in price and quantity after a decrease in supply; then calculate the new price and new quantity in the market for Snarrs.

   c. Let's assume the supply of Snarrs has returned to the original equation. Now the demand has shifted to the right, so that the new demand curve is:

$$P = 760 - 2Q_d$$

First predict the change in price and quantity after an increase in demand; then calculate the new price and new quantity in the market for Snarrs.

CALCULATING CONSUMER AND PRODUCER SURPLUS IN EQUILIBRIUM

Let's say that the market for Whoopsidoos has demand and supply equations that look like this:

Demand

$$P = 12 - \tfrac{1}{4} Q_d$$

Supply

$$P = 3 + \tfrac{1}{2} Q_s$$

a. Solve for market equilibrium price and quantity.
b. In equilibrium, calculate consumer and producer surplus. Note: It may help to draw the market, including the vertical intercepts.

EFFICIENCY AND INEFFICIENCY IN THE MARKET

Competitive markets are said to be efficient because the equilibrium outcome maximizes the sum of consumer and producer surplus. Your task is to show this in a neatly drawn graph.

a. Draw market equilibrium and label the equilibrium price P_e and equilibrium quantity Q_e.

b. Shade the areas of consumer and producer surplus.

c. Now suppose a law limited the quantity of this product to about half of Q_e. Add this regulated quantity to the graph and label it Q_r.

d. At quantity Q_r, show the area of consumer and producer surplus that would *not* be earned if this law were in place.

CHAPTER 7 – BASIC ELASTICITY OF DEMAND

For each of the following scenarios, calculate the price elasticity of demand and determine whether demand for the product is elastic, inelastic, or unit elastic.

a. The price of gasoline increases by 5%, and the gallons of gasoline demanded falls by 3%.

b. The price of broccoli decreases by 6%, and the quantity of broccoli demanded rises by 9%.

c. The price of wool socks increases by 7.5%, and the quantity of wool socks demanded falls by 7.5%.

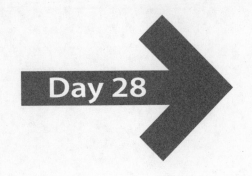

PRICE ELASTICITY OF DEMAND AROUND THE HOUSE

Think of something that your family purchases on a regular basis. Ask someone (maybe a parent) in the house how many of these products are purchased in a typical month. Then ask the same person how many would be purchased if the price increased by 50%. Use this person's responses to calculate the price elasticity of demand for this product, at least in your household.

Tip: If the person you are interviewing finds it difficult to answer the second question, you might have to give that person a specific price increase of 50% to make it more real, and less hypothetical, for them. For example, you might say, "Movie tickets usually cost us $12, so a 50% increase would make the new price of a movie ticket $18."

DRAWING DEMAND CURVES WITH VARYING ELASTICITIES

Without consulting your textbook or class notes, draw four demand curves in one graph.

    a. A perfectly inelastic demand curve, labeled D_{PI}

    b. A perfectly elastic demand curve, labeled D_{PE}

    c. A relatively elastic, but not perfectly elastic, demand curve, labeled D_E

    d. A relatively inelastic, but not perfectly inelastic, demand curve, labeled D_I

USING THE MIDPOINT FORMULA

Suppose the demand curve for a hoozit is given by the following equation:

$$P = 100 - 2Q_d$$

The current price of a hoozit is $40, but management is considering lowering the price to $20.

a. Use the midpoint formula to calculate the price elasticity of demand between these two prices on the demand curve.

b. Interpret your result from part (a).

DEMAND, TOTAL REVENUE, AND ELASTICITY

The following table shows a demand schedule for a hypothetical product. Your task is to complete the table. When it comes to computing the price elasticity of demand, use the midpoint formula between two adjacent prices. For example, at a price of $7, use the midpoint between $8 and $7. For this reason, there is a shaded cell of the table at $8.

PRICE PER UNIT	QUANTITY OF THE GOOD DEMANDED	TOTAL REVENUE $= P \times Q_d$	PRICE ELASTICITY OF DEMAND
$8	0		
$7	1		
$6	2		
$5	3		
$4	4		
$3	5		
$2	6		
$1	7		
$0	8		

THE TOTAL REVENUE TEST

We start with the completed table from the previous day. Can you explain, in your own words, why the total revenue initially rises when the price falls, but eventually total revenue begins to fall with further decreases in the price? Hint: It has everything to do with what is happening with price elasticity of demand when the price falls.

PRICE PER UNIT	QUANTITY OF THE GOOD DEMANDED	TOTAL REVENUE $= P \times Q_d$	PRICE ELASTICITY OF DEMAND
$8	0	$0	
$7	1	$7	15.00
$6	2	$12	4.33
$5	3	$15	2.20
$4	4	$16	1.29
$3	5	$15	0.78
$2	6	$12	0.45
$1	7	$7	0.23
$0	8	$0	0.07

ELASTICITY AND REVENUE

Dr. Susan DeBeers, the president of a local college, is facing a shortfall of total revenue from student tuition at the college. She believes that if the college lowers tuition by 5%, total revenues will increase. She has asked you for your economic advice. You know, from your research, that the price elasticity of demand for similar colleges is approximately equal to 0.50. In a short paragraph, report to Dr. DeBeers on how her plan will or will not achieve her goal of increasing total revenue to the college. She has never had a class in microeconomics, so be sure to explain your reasoning, and include any specific estimates that might help her understand the analysis.

INCOME ELASTICITY

For each of the following goods, determine whether the good is normal or inferior, and interpret what each income elasticity actually tells us.

GOOD OR SERVICE	INCOME ELASTICITY OF DEMAND (E_i)	NORMAL OR INFERIOR?
Eggs	0.35	
Flour	−0.37	
Margarine	−0.21	
Furniture	1.47	

SUBSTITUTES OR COMPLEMENTS?

For each pair of goods, identify which goods are substitutes for each other and which are complements of each other. Then interpret each cross-price elasticity of demand.

GOOD	CROSS ELASTICITY WITH RESPECT TO A CHANGE IN THE PRICE OF:	CROSS ELASTICITY	SUBSTITUTES OR COMPLEMENTS?
Beef	Pork	0.27	
Cereal	Milk	−0.90	
Butter	Margarine	0.67	
Potatoes	Meat	−0.50	

INCOME ELASTICITY OF DEMAND AROUND THE HOUSE

Once again, it's time to think of something that your family purchases on a regular basis. Ask someone (maybe a parent) in the house how many of these products are purchased in a typical month. Then ask the same person how many would be purchased if household income increased by 50%. Use this person's responses to calculate the income elasticity of demand, at least in your household, for this product.

Note: Alternatively, you could ask how this person would respond if household income were decreased by 50% (or cut in half).

COMBINING PRICE AND CROSS-PRICE ELASTICITY OF DEMAND

Suppose that the cross-price elasticity of breakfast cereal with respect to a change in the price of milk is equal to –0.80. Suppose also that the price elasticity of demand for cereal is 0.45 and the price elasticity of demand for milk is 0.20.

Assume that conditions in the market for milk have resulted in a decrease in milk supply, and the price of milk has risen by 10%.

a. Calculate how this will affect the quantity of milk demanded.
b. Calculate how this will affect the quantity of cereal demanded.
c. Calculate how much the price of cereal needs to be changed to offset the impact of the higher milk prices.

ELASTICITY OF FARM SUPPLY

> Farmer Liz raises turkeys, and each young turkey requires about nine months to mature to the point where it is ready to be sold. Suppose you tell Liz that you've heard that turkey prices have significantly risen, and you think she should take advantage of these high prices and sell a lot more turkeys. Liz thinks about it for a moment and then replies, "I can't right now, but I will certainly take your advice in nine months."
>
> Draw a supply curve that reflects Liz's comment about her ability to supply more turkeys now and label it S_{SR}. In the same graph, draw a supply curve that reflects Liz's comment about her willingness to supply more turkeys in nine months and label it S_{LR}. How do these supply curves relate to the price elasticity of supply for Liz's turkeys?

DRAWING AN EFFECTIVE PRICE CEILING

The market for gazjabs is in equilibrium, and the government decides to create a price ceiling for this product.

a. In a correctly labeled graph of the gazjab market, show the equilibrium price (P_e) and quantity (Q_e).

b. Add an effective price ceiling in the market and label the price P_c.

c. Does this create a shortage or a surplus of gazjabs? Show this in your graph.

DRAWING AN EFFECTIVE PRICE FLOOR

The market for doozles is in equilibrium, and the government decides to create a price floor for this product.

   a. In a correctly labeled graph of the doozle market, show the equilibrium price (P_e) and quantity (Q_e).

   b. Add an effective price floor in the market and label the price P_f.

   c. Does this create a shortage or a surplus of doozles? Show this in your graph.

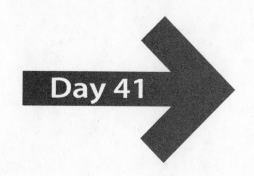

DEADWEIGHT LOSS OF A PRICE CEILING

The following graph shows a price ceiling (P_c) in a competitive market. The graph also shows the areas of consumer and producer surplus if the market did *not* have a price ceiling and came to equilibrium.

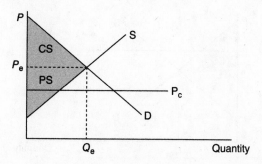

After the price ceiling is in place, identify the new areas of consumer surplus (CS), producer surplus (PS), and deadweight loss (DWL).

DEADWEIGHT LOSS OF A PRICE FLOOR

The following graph shows a price ceiling (P_f) in a competitive market. The graph also shows the areas of consumer and producer surplus if the market did *not* have a price floor and came to equilibrium.

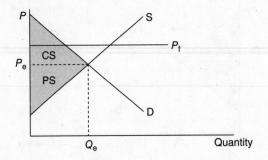

After the price floor is in place, identify the new areas of consumer surplus (CS), producer surplus (PS), and deadweight loss (DWL). Assume that the surplus units will *not* be purchased by the government.

5 Minutes to a 5

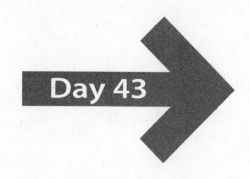

SHOWING THE IMPACT OF AN EXCISE TAX

The market for snaghozzles is competitive, has come to equilibrium, and is shown as follows. The consumer and producer surplus in the market is also shown.

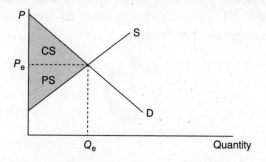

Now suppose the government has levied an excise tax of T on the supply of snaghozzles. In a new graph of the market, show the following:

- The new supply curve that reflects the tax of T (S_t)
- The new quantity of snaghozzles exchanged in the market (Q_t)
- The new price paid by buyers (P_b) of snaghozzles
- The new price sellers receive after paying the tax (P_s)
- Consumer surplus (CS) and producer surplus (PS)
- Tax revenue collected by the government (G)
- Deadweight loss (DWL)

INFERRING THE INCIDENCE OF A TAX

One product that has an excise tax levied on it is tobacco. Suppose you hear that a tax sufficient to increase the price of cigarettes by 10% reduces adult consumption of cigarettes by about 4%. What does this information say about the likely incidence of the tax between consumers and producers?

THE INCIDENCE OF A TAX ON ELECTRICITY PRODUCTION

Some economists argue that a tax should be levied on electricity production, especially if it is generated by fossil fuels (i.e., coal) to reduce pollution and greenhouse gas emissions. Suppose you read in the newspaper that the president of an electricity provider claims that any tax on electricity production "will simply be passed on to the consumers." If this is true, what must be true of the demand for electricity? Do you think the president of the company is correct in this assertion?

SHOWING THE IMPACT OF A PER-UNIT SUBSIDY

The market for snaghozzles is competitive, has come to equilibrium, and is shown as follows. A subsidy on each snaghozzle produced is being proposed. This subsidy of $S would allow for production and consumption of Q_s snaghozzles. Your job is to analyze the social welfare of such a program. Complete the following table. The competitive market outcome has been completed for you.

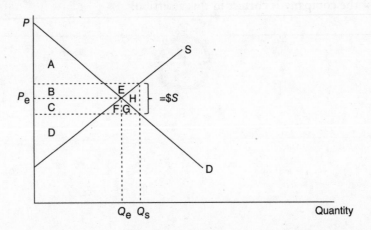

	BEFORE THE SUBSIDY	AFTER THE SUBSIDY
Consumer surplus	A + B	
Producer surplus	C + D	
Government spending	0	
Total surplus	A + B + C + D	
Deadweight loss	0	

THE IMPACT OF INTERNATIONAL TRADE IN A MARKET

The domestic market for jaggnods is shown as follows. Because international trade is prohibited, the domestic price is P_d, and the quantity exchanged in the domestic market is Q_d.

Suppose that the world price of jaggnods is P_w, and it is significantly lower than P_d. If international trade in jaggnods is allowed, identify the units demanded in the domestic market (Q_1), the units supplied by domestic producers (Q_2), and the total amount of jaggnods imported from foreign producers (I).

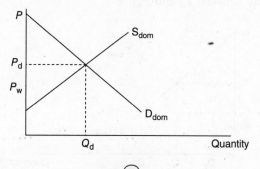

SHOWING THE IMPACT OF A TARIFF

The domestic market for quizbogs is shown as follows. If international trade is prohibited, the domestic price is P_d, and the quantity exchanged in the domestic market is Q_d.

Suppose that the world price of quizbogs is P_w, and it is significantly lower than P_d. When international trade in quizbogs is allowed, the units demanded in the domestic market (Q_1) exceeds the units supplied by domestic producers (Q_2), and the total amount of quizbogs imported from foreign producers (I) is the difference.

Now the domestic government is planning to impose an import tariff on each quizbog imported into the domestic market. The new domestic price (P_T) would be approximately halfway between P_d and P_w.

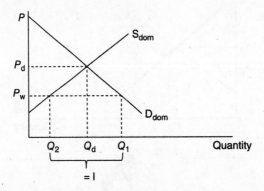

In a new graph, use arrows to show how the tariff impacts domestic consumption and domestic production and the impact on the domestic price. Label the new quantity of quizbogs imported, and government tariff revenue (G). Finally, identify the deadweight loss (DWL) from the tariff.

WINNERS AND LOSERS FROM TRADE RESTRICTIONS

If you want to see real-world examples of import tariffs, go to the website for the U.S. International Trade Commission and their Harmonized Tariff Schedule:

https://usitc.gov/tata/hts/bychapter/index.htm

You will see many different product categories and can select any of them to see how much of an import tariff is levied by the U.S. government. For example, if you select Chapter 9, you will discover that there is no tariff levied on imported coffee, but there is a 6.4% tariff on imported green tea.

Make a short list of who you think benefits from an import tariff on a product like green tea and who is harmed by such tariffs.

TOTAL AND MARGINAL UTILITY

Max likes chocolate, but his utility rises at a decreasing rate as more chocolate is eaten. If he eats more than seven pieces of chocolate, he knows that he will get sick.

Draw two graphs. The first is Max's total utility from eating chocolate, and the second is his marginal utility from eating chocolate. Be sure to show in each graph the point at which he stops eating chocolate.

THE DISUTILITY FROM CONSUMPTION

Interview a friend or family member, and try to find a good or service that this person would absolutely not consume, even if it was free, because they really, *really* do not enjoy it. You might try asking, "Are there any foods that you just cannot or will not eat?" or "Is there a type of music or a specific singer/band that you just cannot stand?" Once you have found something that this person detests so much that they wouldn't consume even one unit at a price of zero, try to draw this person's total utility curve for this product.

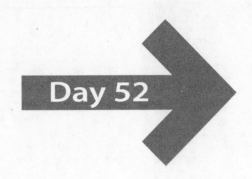

Day 52

UTILITY MAXIMIZATION 1

Suppose that Mary spends her entire income of $250 on goods X and Y. The price of X is $10 and the price of Y is $30. The table shows how Mary's marginal utility changes as she increases her consumption of each good.

a. The combination of 1X and 8Y is affordable. How much total utility is Mary enjoying at this combination of X and Y? Use the utility maximization rule to explain why this could not be the preferred combination of these two goods. How would Mary adjust her consumption?

# OF UNITS OF GOOD X CONSUMED	MARGINAL UTILITY OF GOOD X	# OF UNITS OF GOOD Y CONSUMED	MARGINAL UTILITY OF GOOD Y
1	10	1	30
2	7	2	28
3	6	3	24
4	5	4	21
5	4	5	18
6	3	6	16
7	2	7	15
8	1	8	14

b. Assuming she maximizes her utility, how many units of each good should she purchase? How much total utility is Mary enjoying at this combination?

5 Minutes to a 5

UTILITY MAXIMIZATION 2

Theo has $50 to spend on jellybeans (B) and crackers (C). The price of jellybeans is $10 per bag and the price of crackers is $5 per box.

Refer to the following table of utility that Theo would receive from various combinations of crackers and jellybeans.

QTY OF CRACKERS	TOTAL UTILITY FROM CRACKERS	QTY OF JELLYBEANS	UTILITY FROM JELLYBEANS
0	0	0	0
2	70	1	80
4	130	2	150
6	180	3	210
8	220	4	260
10	250	5	300

a. Focusing only on the combinations that use all of his income, complete the following table to find the combination that maximizes Theo's total utility.

# CRACKERS	# JELLYBEANS	TOTAL UTILITY
0	5	
2	4	
4	3	
6	2	
8	1	
10	0	

b. Now maximize Theo's utility by finding the marginal utility of each product and then finding the marginal utility per dollar spent on each product. Note: Theo's consumption of crackers is rising by two boxes at a time.

QTY OF CRACKERS	UTILITY FROM CRACKERS	MU$_C$	MU$_C$/P$_C$	QTY OF JELLYBEANS	UTILITY FROM JELLYBEANS	MU$_B$	MU$_B$/P$_B$
0	0			0	0		
2	70			1	80		
4	130			2	150		
6	180			3	210		
8	220			4	260		
10	250			5	300		

Using this approach, what is the utility maximizing combination of crackers and jellybeans? How much utility is he enjoying?

CHAPTER 8 – ECONOMIC AND ACCOUNTING PROFIT

You own and operate a skateboard shop. Each year, you receive revenue of $250,000 from your skateboard sales, and it costs you $130,000 to obtain the skateboards. In addition, you pay $40,000 for electricity, taxes, and other expenses each year. Instead of running the skateboard shop, you could become an accountant and receive a yearly salary of $50,000. A large clothing retail chain wants to expand and offers to rent the shop from you for $40,000 per year. How do you explain to your friends that despite making a profit, it is too costly for you to continue running your shop? Support your explanation with necessary computations.

FIXED AND VARIABLE COSTS OF DRIVING

Let's consider the ownership of a car and the output of car ownership measured as miles driven in a month. Make a list of variable costs of producing miles driven and another list of fixed costs.

FIXED AND VARIABLE COSTS OF LIVING

Let's consider living in a house or apartment and the output of living in the residence measured as nights slept in the residence. Make a list of variable costs of producing nights slept in the residence and another list of fixed costs.

TOTAL, MARGINAL, AND AVERAGE PRODUCTS OF LABOR

A local cabinet maker can employ carpenters, and a fixed amount of capital equipment, to assist him in building cabinets for kitchens and bathrooms. The following table gives some information on his monthly short-run production function.

# OF CARPENTERS	TOTAL PRODUCT (# OF CABINETS PER MONTH)	MARGINAL PRODUCT	AVERAGE PRODUCT
0	0	X	X
1			8
2	18		
3		8	
4	32		
5			7.2
6	38		
7		-2	

a. Complete the table.
b. Ignoring for now the cost of employing carpenters, how many carpenters should this owner hire? Explain.

EXPLAINING DIMINISHING MARGINAL RETURNS IN PRODUCTION

Without looking at your class notes or a textbook, can you explain why economists think that the marginal product of labor diminishes as more labor is hired in the short run?

THE RELATIONSHIP BETWEEN TOTAL PRODUCT AND MARGINAL PRODUCT OF LABOR CURVES

The following three graphs show three different short-run total product of labor curves.

Using the shapes of these TP_L curves, draw the MP_L curve that would be derived from each of them. Which of these TP_L curves makes the most economic sense?

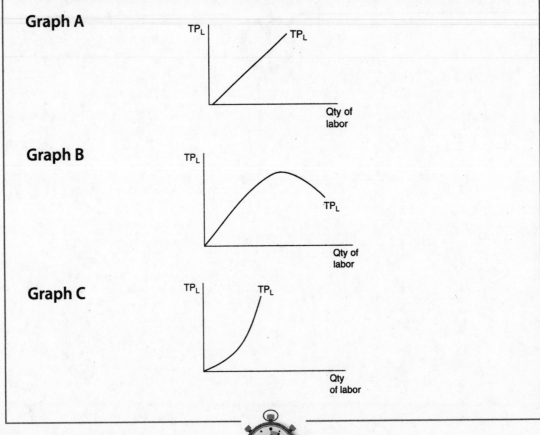

SHORT-RUN COSTS OF PRODUCTION

Melanie's apparel shop makes women's accessories in a perfectly competitive market.

Some of the production costs for Melanie's shop are given as follows. You will need to complete the table.

PRODUCTION (Q)	TFC	TVC	TC	MC
0	$5			N/A
1		$6		
2			$14	
3		$13		
4			$23	
5				$7
6		$34		
7		$45		
8			$63	

GRAPHING THE SHORT-RUN TOTAL AND MARGINAL COSTS

PRODUCTION (Q)	TFC	TVC	TC	MC
0	$5	$0	$5	N/A
1	5	6	11	6
2	5	9	14	3
3	5	13	18	4
4	5	18	23	5
5	5	25	30	7
6	5	34	39	9
7	5	45	50	11
8	5	58	63	13

In one graph, plot the TFC, TVC, and TC curves.

In another graph, plot the MC curve.

AVERAGE COSTS IN THE SHORT RUN

Hint: If you're good at using Excel, you can do these quickly. If not, maybe try using a calculator.

Complete the following table.

PRODUCTION (Q)	TFC	TVC	TC	MC	AFC	AVC	ATC
0	$5	$0	$5		XX	XX	XX
1	$5	$6	$11	$6			
2	$5	$9	$14	$3			
3	$5	$13	$18	$4			
4	$5	$18	$23	$5			
5	$5	$25	$30	$7			
6	$5	$34	$39	$9			
7	$5	$45	$50	$11			
8	$5	$58	$63	$13			

GRAPHING THE SHORT-RUN AVERAGE COSTS CURVES

PRODUCTION (Q)	MC	AFC	AVC	ATC
0		XX	XX	XX
1	$6	$5.00	$6.00	$11.00
2	$3	$2.50	$4.50	$7.00
3	$4	$1.67	$4.33	$6.00
4	$5	$1.25	$4.50	$5.75
5	$7	$1.00	$5.00	$6.00
6	$9	$0.83	$5.67	$6.50
7	$11	$0.71	$6.43	$7.14
8	$13	$0.63	$7.25	$7.88

In one graph, plot the AFC, AVC, ATC, and MC curves.

Hint: If you're good at using Excel, you can do these quickly. If not, maybe try using graph paper.

NAME THAT CURVE!

The following short-run cost curves are unnamed. Your job is to correctly identify them, without the use of your books and/or class notes.

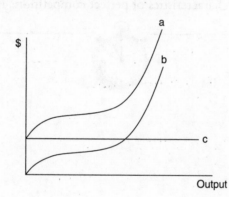

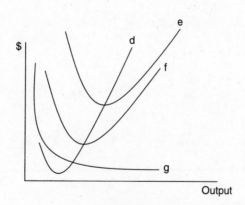

CHAPTER 9 – THE CHARACTERISTICS OF PERFECT COMPETITION

Quick! Can you list the characteristics of perfect competition? Ready, set, go!

MAXIMIZING PROFIT IN THE SHORT RUN IN PERFECT COMPETITION

Suppose grapes are grown in a perfectly competitive market. Short-run costs for a grape farmer are given in the following table.

OUTPUT (Q)	TFC	TVC	TC
0	$500	$0	$500
1	$500	$150	$650
2	$500	$200	$700
3	$500	$260	$760
4	$500	$340	$840
5	$500	$450	$950
6	$500	$590	$1,090
7	$500	$770	$1,270
8	$500	$1,000	$1,500
9	$500	$1,290	$1,790
10	$500	$1,650	$2,150

If the price of a bushel of grapes is $230, find the profit maximizing level of output. If there are two output levels that provide the same maximum profit, we choose the greater of the two outputs. Compute the level of profit each producer would earn.

OUTPUT (Q)	TOTAL REVENUE = P × Q	PROFIT (+) OR LOSS (−) = TR − TC
0		
1		
2		
3		
4		
5		
6		
7		
8		
9		
10		

Suppose the price of grapes drops to $180. How much would the firm produce, and how much short-run profit would be earned?

THE PROFIT-MAXIMIZATION RULE

Suppose grapes are grown in a perfectly competitive market. Short-run costs for a grape farmer are given in the following table.

OUTPUT (Q)	TFC	TVC	TC
0	$500	$0	$500
1	$500	$150	$650
2	$500	$200	$700
3	$500	$260	$760
4	$500	$340	$840
5	$500	$450	$950
6	$500	$590	$1,090
7	$500	$770	$1,270
8	$500	$1,000	$1,500
9	$500	$1,290	$1,790
10	$500	$1,650	$2,150

If the price of a bushel of grapes is $290, use the profit-maximization rule to find the profit maximizing level of output. Compute the level of profit each producer would earn.

If the price of grapes fell to $80 per bushel, determine how many bushels the farmer should supply in the short run and compute profit.

5 Minutes to a 5

THE SIDE-BY-SIDE GRAPHS OF PERFECT COMPETITION PROFIT

There will come a time when you will need to throw down your high-level ninja graphing skills, and there is nothing more ninja-like than a perfect side-by-side representation of perfect competition in the short run.

Here's the situation. A market is perfectly competitive in the short run, and the typical firm is earning positive economic profit. In the side-by-side graphs, show equilibrium in the market, output for the typical firm, and the area of economic profit. Everything must be perfectly labeled.

THE SIDE-BY-SIDE GRAPHS OF PERFECT COMPETITION LOSSES

Again, you must have these graphing skills down.

Here's the situation. A market is perfectly competitive in the short run, and the typical firm is earning negative economic profit (losses), but is not in a shutdown situation. In the side-by-side graphs, show equilibrium in the market, output for the typical firm, and the area of economic losses. Everything must be perfectly labeled.

LONG-RUN ADJUSTMENT TO EQUILIBRIUM IN PERFECT COMPETITION

a. A perfectly competitive market is in short-run equilibrium, and firms are earning positive economic profit. Describe how this market and the typical firm will adjust in the long run.

b. A perfectly competitive market is in short-run equilibrium, and firms are earning negative economic profit. Describe how this market and the typical firm will adjust in the long run.

c. In the side-by-side graphs of perfect competition, show long-run equilibrium in the market, price, and output for the typical firm. Everything must be perfectly labeled.

THE CHARACTERISTICS OF MONOPOLY

> Quick! Can you list the characteristics of monopoly? Ready, set, go!

MONOPOLY PROFIT MAXIMIZATION

A monopolist has the following total cost data and demand schedule:

OUTPUT (UNITS)	PRICE ($)	TOTAL COST ($)
0	12	5
1	11	10
2	10	15
3	9	20
4	8	25
5	7	30
6	6	35
7	5	40
8	4	45
9	3	50
10	2	55
11	1	60
12	0	65

a. If this monopolist is unregulated, find the profit-maximizing quantity, price, and profit.
b. Suppose that the government imposes a lump-sum tax of $1 that increases total fixed cost by $1. Find the new profit-maximizing quantity, price, and profit.
c. Now suppose the lump-sum tax from part (b) is eliminated, but the government wishes to regulate this monopolist to produce at the level of output where there is zero deadweight loss. How will this affect the output, price, and profit realized by the monopolist? Be specific.

DRAWING MONOPOLY

Eli is a profitable monopolist seller of doodads. In a correctly labeled graph, draw Eli's profit-maximizing level of output, the price he would charge, and his area of monopoly profit.

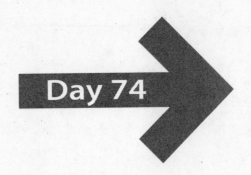

CHARACTERISTICS OF MONOPOLISTIC COMPETITION

Quick! Can you list the characteristics of monopolistic competition? Ready, set, go!

LONG-RUN ADJUSTMENTS IN MONOPOLISTIC COMPETITION

a. A monopolistically competitive market is in short-run equilibrium, and firms are earning positive economic profit. Describe how this market and the typical firm will adjust in the long run.

b. A monopolistically competitive market is in short-run equilibrium, and firms are earning negative economic profit. Describe how this market and the typical firm will adjust in the long run.

c. In a graph of one firm in monopolistic competition, show long-run equilibrium price and output. Everything must be perfectly labeled.

A GAME THEORY PROBLEM

Hamm and Rye are two oligopolistic widget manufacturers engaged in bitter competition with one another. Each firm is deciding whether to build a new factory in a neighboring state. The following table shows profit payoffs for the firms (Hamm, Rye) under various scenarios:

		RYE	
		BUILD	DON'T BUILD
Hamm	Build	5, 5	3, 7
	Don't build	6, 1	4, 2

a. Does either firm have a dominant strategy? Explain why or why not.
b. What is the Nash equilibrium of this game? Explain how you came to this conclusion.
c. Is this a prisoner's dilemma? Explain how you came to this conclusion.

Day 77

ONLINE PRISONER'S DILEMMA

Your assignment is to play a game against a computer-simulated opponent. The following three links should take you to different simulated prisoner's dilemma games. Play the games a few times, experiment with strategies, and try to beat your opponent. What seems to work, and what does not?

https://www.gametheory.net/applets/prisoners.html

https://serendipstudio.org/playground/pd.html

http://www.iterated-prisoners-dilemma.net/

CHAPTER 10 – THE MRP$_L$ AND HIRING DECISION

Hamilton's Pizza Parlor has the production function per hour shown in the following table. The hourly wage rate for each worker is $8, and each pizza sells for $2.

QUANTITY OF LABOR (WORKERS)	QUANTITY OF PIZZA	
0	0	
1	9	
2	15	
3	20	
4	24	
5	27	
6	29	
7	30	

a. Hamilton is an economics major and describes herself as a "price taker and a wage taker." What does this mean?

b. Calculate the value of the marginal revenue product of labor (MRP$_L$), and add this to the table.

c. How many units of labor should Hamilton employ? Illustrate this hiring decision in a correctly labeled graph.

d. Now suppose that the price of pizza rises to $4. How does this affect Hamilton's hiring decision? Show this in the graph from part (c).

CHANGES IN FACTOR MARKETS

Let's assume that the markets for labor, land, and capital are all perfectly competitive. For each of the following scenarios, predict what would happen in the factor market, and predict changes in equilibrium price and quantity of that factor.

a. The factor market: semitruck drivers

The event: the price of diesel fuel falls

b. The factor market: elementary school teachers

The event: the government requires two more years of education before a person can become a teacher

c. The factor market: capital equipment

The event: interest rates are rising

d. The factor market: beachfront property

The event: the sea level continues to rise

DOING SOME RESEARCH ON AN OCCUPATION

Go to the following link for the *Occupational Outlook Handbook* (*OOH*):

http://www.bls.gov/ooh/

Browse the many different occupations, or search for something specific, and read about the occupation. Report on the following:

- What do these people do?
- What kind of education or training would you need?
- What are the current pay levels?
- What is the growth outlook (jobs and percentage change) from 2020–2030?

Investigate several different occupations that might interest you, and see if there are qualities that are encouraging or maybe discouraging your interest in that occupation.

LEAST-COST AND PROFIT-MAXIMIZING COMBINATION OF INPUTS

In the following table are the marginal product schedules for two resources, labor and capital. Both resources are variable and are employed in purely competitive resources markets. The price of the output, which is sold in a perfectly competitive output market, is $0.50. The price of labor is $1 and the price of capital is $2.

QTY OF LABOR EMPLOYED	MARGINAL PRODUCT OF LABOR	MRP OF LABOR	QUANTITY OF CAPITAL EMPLOYED	MARGINAL PRODUCT OF CAPITAL	MRP OF CAPITAL
1	20		1	20	
2	16		2	18	
3	12		3	16	
4	10		4	12	
5	8		5	8	
6	4		6	6	
7	2		7	4	
8	1		8	2	

a. Complete the table by computing the MRP for each resource.
b. What is the least-cost combination of labor and capital that would enable the firm to produce 144 units of output?
c. What is the profit-maximizing combination of labor and capital?
d. What is the total output and profit when the firm is employing the profit-maximizing combinations of labor and capital?

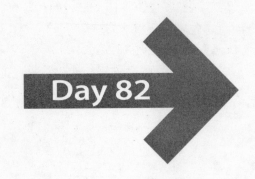

CHAPTER 11 – PRIVATE AND PUBLIC GOODS

Review the concepts of excludability and rivalry that identify the difference between private and public goods. Use these concepts to classify the following goods and services.

   a. A gallon of milk
   b. Streetlamps along a highway
   c. An hour of legal advice from an attorney
   d. Lobsters in the Atlantic Ocean

A TRAGEDY OF THE COMMONS

A special kind of environmental and economic problem is when a common resource is overexploited, often to the point of ruin, because of the nonexcludable and rival characteristics of it. There are many examples of this "tragedy of the commons," but one of the best-known cases is that of overfishing the world's oceans. To see how this happens, go to the following website and play the Tragedy of the Fish Game. https://cloudinstitute.org/fish-game

Read the instructions, and play the game. When you're done, watch the Fish Game Video Debrief. Why do you think that common resources (like fish in the ocean) are so commonly overexploited?

GRAPHING A POSITIVE EXTERNALITY

Suppose that snaghorns are exchanged in a perfectly competitive market, and the consumption of snaghorns provides utility to third parties who are not consuming this fine product. In a correctly labeled graph, show the following:

- The quantity produced by the market (Q_m) and the market price (P_m)
- The spillover benefit received by the third parties on each snaghorn consumed
- The socially efficient quantity (Q_e) and the efficient price (P_e)
- The area of deadweight loss to society from not producing the efficient quantity of snaghorns

BEES AND APPLES

Quinton is a beekeeper who has several beehives, and he makes a living selling honey at the farmers' market. Quinton's neighbor is Payton, and she owns an apple orchard and makes a living selling apples at the same farmers' market. One day at the farmers' market, an economist named Fernando is buying both apples and honey. He tells Payton that she should really send Quinton some money so he can install more beehives. Why would an economist make such a suggestion? Or is he just delirious from grading papers and should be completely ignored? Explain.

GRAPHING A NEGATIVE EXTERNALITY

Suppose that goosedumples are exchanged in a perfectly competitive market, and the production of goosedumples imposes costs on third parties who are not involved in the exchange of this product. In a correctly labeled graph, show the following:

- The quantity produced by the market (Q_m) and the market price (P_m)
- The spillover cost imposed on the third parties on each goosedumple produced
- The socially efficient quantity (Q_e) and the efficient price (P_e)
- The area of deadweight loss to society from not producing the efficient quantity of goosedumples

PROGRESSIVE INCOME TAX BRACKETS

In the United States, personal income is taxed with a system of progressive tax rates, or tax brackets. As your taxable income rises, so does the marginal tax rate that you pay. Go to the following link to see tax brackets for 2021. https://www.irs.com/articles/2021-federal-income-tax-rates-brackets-standard-deduction-amounts/

Use these tax brackets to compute the amount of taxes a single person would pay if she had a taxable income of $60,000.

YOUR LOCAL ENVIRONMENT

Pollution is a perfect example of a negative externality. Do you know how much pollution is in your zip code? What chemicals are ending up in your water? Where is it coming from? The Environmental Protection Agency has a great way of answering these questions.

Go to the following website:

https://www.epa.gov/environmental-topics/location-specific-environmental-information

Go to the section titled "Find Local Data." Enter the zip code of your choice, and explore the environmental quality of this area. Find the following information.

- Find the current air quality index (AQI) at the nearest air quality monitoring station to your zip code. Is it safe to go outside?
  You can find more specific AQI information here:
  https://www.airnow.gov/about-airnow/
- Under the water quality menu, look for "Water Quality Assessment." Is there a body of water that is listed as impaired in any way? How so? What's wrong with it?
- Find the link for My WATERS Mapper. You might have to enter your zip code again. On the right side look for "Water Impairments." Select one or all of the three options and report what you find. You might have to adjust the zoom of the map. Any streams, rivers, or lakes that are impaired?
- Now select the "My Land" menu. Another map will pop up. On the left side, show the layers of the map and on the right side, select the Hazardous Waste box. You will probably see several locations show up in your map. Select one of those locations. What type of business is this? What can you discover about their toxic waste? Are there any concerns about specific chemicals or compounds?
- Go to the "My Health" menu. What kind of cancer risk exists in this community? What is the main cause of this cancer risk? How does infant mortality compare in your chosen zip code to the state average and national average? Do the same comparison for low birth weight.

A REGRESSIVE SALES TAX

Most U.S. states have legislated a sales tax on most purchases. Some cities have also created higher sales taxes than other parts of the state. For example, the 2016 sales tax in Illinois is 6.25%, but the state grants counties and cities the flexibility to increase the local sales tax. In Chicago, the sales tax in 2016 was 10.25%.

A sales tax is considered a regressive tax because the tax payment is a smaller share of income as income rises. Let's see how this works.

Melanie earns $2,000 per week, and Eric earns $1,000 per week. Suppose each of these consumers is shopping for $100 of clothing in Indiana, a state with a sales tax rate of 7%.

Compute the amount of sales tax each shopper will pay, and then compute what fraction of weekly income this sales tax amounts to.

INCOME DISTRIBUTION

The Census Bureau of the United States collects data on many things, including how income is distributed across households. The distribution is divided into fifths, or quintiles, so that the households that earn less than 80% of all households fall into the bottom quintile, and the households that earn more than 80% of all households fall into the top quintile. Select the following link provided, and then choose table H-2 "All races." This will download a file in Excel, and you can see data going back to the late 1960s.

http://www.census.gov/data/tables/time-series/demo/income-poverty/historical-income-households.html

From the same page above, you can download table H-4 to see a Gini index for the United States for the same period of time. The Gini ratio is a measure of how equally income is distributed across a nation's households. The closer the Gini ratio is to zero, the more equally income is distributed. The closer it is to 1 (or 100 if you multiply the index by 100), the more unequally it is distributed.

The United Nations produces a "Human Development Report," and part of that report is a statistic called a "Human Development Index." Values close to 1 indicate a highly developed nation with strong institutions, health, and prosperity for the citizens. Part of this HDI is the Gini coefficient measure of income equality. The following link allows you to see estimates of a Gini coefficient for many nations. Notice that the report shows both the HDI and the "inequality adjusted HDI" that accounts for several measures of inequality within the nation.

http://hdr.undp.org/en/content/latest-human-development-index-ranking

Questions

- What has happened to income equality in the United States since the late 1960s? Are there any possible explanations for what you see in the data?
- How does the United States compare to other nations in the Gini coefficient, and how is this reflected in the inequality adjusted HDI?

Answers

Day 1

1. Labor: Your efforts in buying the groceries, **preparing and cooking** the food, serving the meal

2. Capital: The knives, pans, oven, or any other **equipment** you would need to cook the meal

3. Natural resources: The raw ingredients (meat, **vegetables**, spices, etc.)

4. Entrepreneurial ability: Your know-how and creativity in bringing all of the other resources together to make the meal

Day 2

Note: The following numbers are hypothetical but **give you an idea** of how to compute your *actual* opportunity cost.

1. I selected *Star Trek Beyond*, and the local price of a ticket is $10.

2. Yes, I will buy popcorn and a drink, and this will **cost about another** $10.

3. The nearest cinema is 6 miles away, so I would **drive 12 total miles.** My car gets about 24 miles per gallon, so I would use ½ gallon of gas. Local prices are about $2 per gallon, so my driving costs are about $1.

4. The movie lasts 122 minutes, and the drive is estimated to be 9 minutes each way, for a total of 140 minutes, or 2.33 hours. If I could receive a wage of $10 per hour, I could have earned $23.33 (ignoring taxes) during the movie.

5. Total opportunity cost of this movie = $10 + $10 + $1 + $23.33 = $44.33

Day 3

Since each slice of pizza costs $2, the marginal cost curve should be drawn horizontal at $2. The marginal benefit curve is drawn downward sloping because the next slice of pizza provides less additional benefit. After all, your hunger is partially satisfied with each slice, so the next slice isn't quite as great as the one that came before.

So if your hypothetical number of pizza slices was 4, the graph should look something like this:

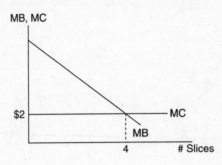

Day 4

a. A PPC with constant opportunity costs should be drawn as a straight line.

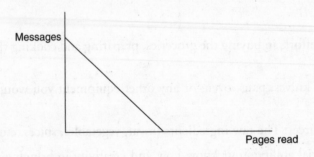

b. Since the speed-reading course allows you to read more pages in an hour, the PPC should move outward along the *x*-axis but not along the *y*-axis.

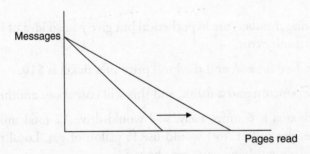

c. The opportunity cost of socializing has now increased. Remember that opportunity cost of an activity, socializing in this case, is what you have given up to engage in that activity. Now that you are a speed-reader, every hour spent socializing comes at a greater sacrifice in the number of pages you could have been reading.

Day 5

a. If Eli splits his time equally, he can fold 10 towels and wash 5 plates.

If Theodore does the same, he can fold 3 towels and wash 3 plates.

Total output: 13 towels + 8 plates = 21

b. A person is said to have comparative advantage in a task if they can perform that task at a lower opportunity cost.

For every plate that Eli washes, he gives up 2 towels folded, so that is his opportunity cost of washing plates. On the other hand, for every towel that he folds, he gives up washing ½ plate.

For every plate that Theodore washes, he gives up 1 towel folded. And for every towel he folds, he gives up 1 washed plate.

So we can see that Theodore has a lower opportunity cost of washing plates (1 towel) when compared to Eli's opportunity cost of washing plates (2 towels). Theodore has comparative advantage in washing plates. On the other hand, Eli has the comparative advantage in folding towels because he gives up ½ washed plate while Theodore gives up 1 washed plate.

If they specialize based on comparative advantage, Eli should spend all of his time folding towels and Theodore should spend all of his time washing plates.

Total output with specialization: 20 towels + 6 plates = 26

Day 6

1. Productive efficiency is achieved when you produce the maximum amount of output for a given level of technology and resources. If you were inefficient in the kitchen, you might use the correct quantity of ingredients but produce only 10 cookies. Another way of being productively inefficient would be to produce a dozen cookies, but waste some of the ingredients in the process (like dropping an egg on the floor or spilling some flour).

2. Most people, if equity were the goal, would give each person three cookies. Of course, this outcome depends on how you define "equitable." Rather than this egalitarian outcome, another might define equitable by giving the most cookies to the person with the highest GPA or other arbitrary measure of merit. This is similar to saying that the highest wages should be paid to those who are most productive.

3. Allocative efficiency would be achieved if the cookies were distributed to maximize the happiness of the four people eating them. One way to do this would be to give the most cookies to the person who most desired them (or was the hungriest) and the fewest cookies to the person who had the least desire for cookies. Alternatively, you could give each person three cookies and then allow them to trade cookies among themselves. When there are no more trades to be made, it's likely you have found an efficient allocation.

Day 7

For all three graphs, I will put units of pizza on the horizontal axis and units of shoes on the vertical axis. The slope of the PPC always gives you the opportunity cost of the good on the horizontal axis, while the inverse of the slope gives you the opportunity cost of the good on the vertical axis.

a. Constant opportunity cost is described by a straight line (constant slope). If the PPC is linear, it implies that resources are perfectly substitutable in producing pizza and shoes. No matter where you are on the PPC, increasing pizza production will always cost the same number of shoes.

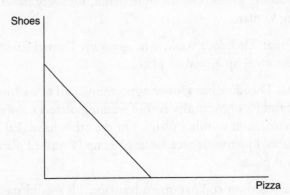

b. A PPC with increasing opportunity costs is drawn with a bowed-outward shape to it, flatter at the top and steeper at the bottom. This shape implies that there are some resources particularly suited to pizza production (like an oven) and some that are better for shoe production (like sewing machines). As we move resources down the PPC to produce more pizza, we would be smart to first allocate the best pizza resources (and weakest shoe resources), thus making our increased pizza big but lost shoe production small. However, when we get closer to maximum shoe production, the only resources we have left are best at shoe-making, so we will gain very few pizzas but lose many shoes. One way to think about this shape is that it gets more difficult (i.e., more costly) to produce something as we produce more of it. Because we see these differences in resources in the real world, this is likely the most realistic depiction of the PPC.

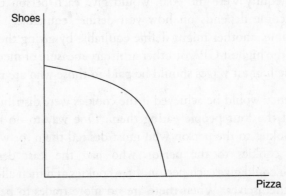

c. If a PPC exhibits decreasing opportunity cost, then it should be drawn as bowed-inward; steeper at the top and flatter at the bottom. This shape also implies that resources are not perfectly substitutable, but it also implies that we would do something counterintuitive when reallocating resources to pizza production: We would select the resources

Answers →

best suited for *shoe* production and use them first for *pizza* production. This decision would cause a sharp decline in shoe production with a very small gain in pizza production. The opportunity cost of making pizza declines as we get closer to the bottom of the PPC, because now we are finally sending strong pizza-making resources to the pizza parlor, thus losing very little shoe production. Because it doesn't make sense to allocate resources in this way, and because we seldom observe opportunity costs falling rather than rising, you would almost never see a PPC drawn this way.

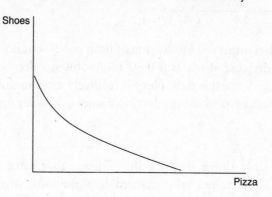

Day 8

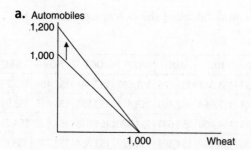

A 20% increase in maximum automobile production moves the vertical intercept up to 1,200 automobiles. Remember that the slope of the PPC gives us the opportunity cost of wheat. Prior to the technology, 1 unit of wheat costs 1 automobile, but now 1 unit of wheat costs 1.2 automobiles. Because automobile-producing technology has improved, devoting resources to wheat costs society more automobiles that could have been produced.

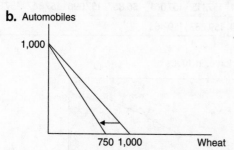

A 25% decrease in maximum wheat production moves the horizontal intercept down to 750 units of wheat. Remember that the inverse of the slope of the PPC gives us the opportunity cost of automobiles. Prior to the drought, 1 automobile costs 1 unit of wheat, but now 1 automobile costs 0.75 units of wheat. Because of the drought that has hampered wheat production, devoting resources to automobiles costs society fewer units of wheat that could have been produced.

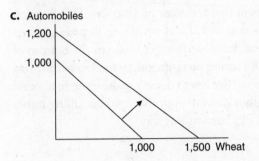

c. Automobiles

Better technology has improved production of both goods, but not by the same degree. The new opportunity cost of wheat is 0.80 automobiles, a decrease from the original cost of 1 automobile. Since this technology is relatively more useful for growing wheat, devoting more resources to wheat production comes at a lower opportunity cost.

Day 9

A. The following table shows data for the civilian labor force from January 2006 to August 2016. These values are measured in thousands, so the actual value for August 2016 is about 159,463,000 people in the labor force. The percentage change is: $100 \times (159,463 - 150,214)/150,214 = 6.2\%$.

If you found data going back to 1948, you would calculate the percentage change to be about 165%.

YEAR	JAN	FEB	MAR	APR	MAY	JUN	JUL	AUG	SEP	OCT	NOV	DEC
2006	150,214(1)	150,641	150,813	150,881	151,069	151,354	151,377	151,716	151,662	152,041	152,406	152,732
2007	153,144(1)	152,983	153,051	152,435	152,670	153,041	153,054	152,749	153,414	153,183	153,835	153,918
2008	154,063(1)	153,653	153,908	153,769	154,303	154,313	154,469	154,641	154,570	154,876	154,639	154,655
2009	154,210(1)	154,538	154,133	154,509	154,747	154,716	154,502	154,307	153,827	153,784	153,878	153,111
2010	153,484(1)	153,694	153,954	154,622	154,091	153,616	153,691	154,086	153,975	153,635	154,125	153,650
2011	153,263(1)	153,214	153,376	153,543	153,479	153,346	153,288	153,760	154,131	153,961	154,128	153,995
2012	154,351(1)	154,695	154,768	154,557	154,859	155,084	154,943	154,753	155,168	155,539	155,356	155,597
2013	155,666(1)	155,313	155,034	155,365	155,483	155,753	155,662	155,568	155,749	154,694	155,352	155,083
2014	155,285(1)	155,560	156,187	155,376	155,511	155,684	156,090	156,080	156,129	156,363	156,442	156,142
2015	157,025(1)	156,878	156,890	157,032	157,367	156,984	157,115	157,061	156,867	157,096	157,367	157,833
2016	158,335(1)	158,890	159,286	158,924	158,466	158,880	159,287	159,463				

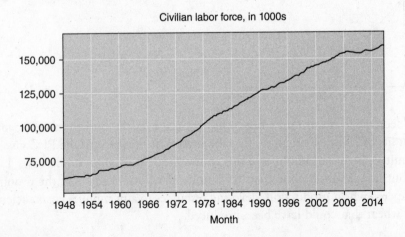

Civilian labor force, in 1000s

Month

B. If you found the capital stock data from this data series:

https://fred.stlouisfed.org/series/RKNANPUSA666NRUG#0

then you would see the following graph. These values are measured in millions of 2011 dollars.

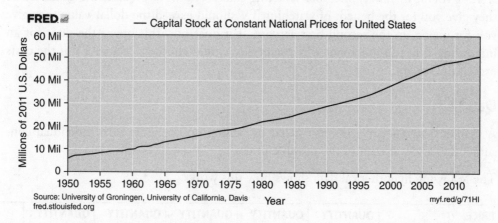

Source: University of Groningen, University of California, Davis
fred.stlouisfed.org

The percentage change in the capital stock from 1950 to 2014 is equal to: $100 \times (51{,}190{,}644.0 - 5{,}684{,}549.5)/5{,}684{,}549.5 = 800.5\%$.

We can see that over a comparable period of time, the stock of capital in the United States has increased by a much larger percentage than has the nation's labor force. Increases in both of these critical economic resources have contributed to the great expansion of the U.S. production possibilities.

Day 10

To measure the benefit of an activity that has no price tag, economists can try to create a hypothetical auction.

Ask this person, "How much money would I need to pay you to stop watching TV and forgo the enjoyment (utility) you are receiving from it? Would you take $1, $5, $10?" Keep increasing the bid until this person accepts a hypothetical compensation to give up doing something they enjoy: watching TV. Once you reach this number, you know how much economic value (money) this person places on watching TV. After all, if the person would accept $20 to turn off the TV, watching TV must be worth $20 to them.

We can do a similar exercise to try to measure the opportunity cost of not doing a second-best use of our time. You have asked a person to tell you what they would be doing if the TV signal suddenly ended and the person could not watch TV during this time. Of course, this person could give you any of dozens of possible activities, but suppose the person tells you that they would be playing a game on their phone. Now ask this person, "If you were playing a game on your phone, how much money would I need to pay you to stop?" Begin the auction at $1 and gradually raise the hypothetical price until the person accepts a value that would compensate them for turning off the game.

Answers

If the person would need to be paid $10 to turn off the game, this is the value they place on playing the game. Because the person is watching TV at the moment, and not playing the game, then missing the game means the person is sacrificing $10 of potential enjoyment. This is the opportunity cost of watching TV.

If your friend or family member is acting like economists predict, the dollar value they give you for the benefit of watching TV should exceed the dollar value they give you for giving up the second-best activity. If it does not, this opens the door for an interesting conversation about why the person would choose to watch TV if the costs exceed the benefit.

Day 11

A market demand curve is constructed by adding up the units each individual consumer demands, at each of the possible prices.

The following hypothetical data shows how this works.

PRICE PER MOVIE TICKET	QUANTITY DEMANDED BY YOU	QUANTITY DEMANDED FOR FRIEND 1	QUANTITY DEMANDED FOR FRIEND 2	QUANTITY DEMANDED FOR FRIEND 3	QUANTITY DEMANDED FOR FRIEND 4	QUANTITY DEMANDED FOR FRIEND 5	TOTAL Q_d
$6	8	6	10	5	4	2	35
$8	7	5	8	4	3	1	28
$10	6	4	6	3	2	0	21
$12	5	3	4	2	1	0	15
$14	4	2	0	1	0	0	7

You can take the prices in the first column and the total quantity demanded in the last column and draw out the demand curve for the selected good or service. The demand curve for the hypothetical movie ticket example looks like:

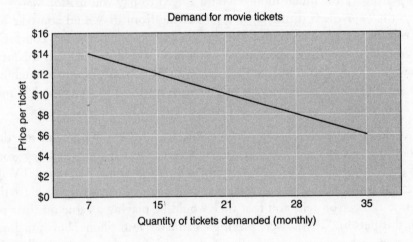

Demand for movie tickets

Day 12

a. This is an increase in tastes and preferences, so demand for OJ shifts to the right.

b. This is an increase in the price of a substitute, so demand for OJ shifts to the right.

c. This is a decrease in income, so because OJ is a normal good, demand shifts to the left.

d. An expectation of a higher price of OJ in the future causes demand to shift to the right now.

e. This will not cause a shift in the demand for OJ; it will cause the quantity of OJ to increase downward along the demand curve.

Day 13

a. If we consider Swiss cheese to be a substitute good, a higher price of Swiss will increase demand for cheddar. The demand for cheddar shifts to the right.

b. This is not a shifter. When the price of cheddar falls, the quantity of cheddar demanded increases. This is a movement downward along the curve. Be careful not to call this an "increase in demand," as this would describe a shift.

c. Assuming cheddar is a normal good, higher incomes will shift demand for cheddar to the right. If you argue that cheddar is an inferior good, then you predict a leftward shift.

d. Fear of getting sick weakens the tastes and preferences for cheddar, and this would decrease demand.

e. If you think that crackers are a complementary good to cheddar, then higher cracker prices should decrease the demand for cheddar.

Day 14

A market supply of labor curve is constructed by adding up the hours each individual worker supplies, at each of the possible wages.

The hypothetical data that follows shows how this works.

HOURLY WAGE	QUANTITY OF HOURS SUPPLIED BY YOU	QUANTITY OF HOURS SUPPLIED BY FRIEND 1	QUANTITY OF HOURS SUPPLIED BY FRIEND 2	QUANTITY OF HOURS SUPPLIED BY FRIEND 3	QUANTITY OF HOURS SUPPLIED BY FRIEND 4	QUANTITY OF HOURS SUPPLIED BY FRIEND 5	TOTAL Q_S (HOURS)
$6	6	10	0	12	0	10	38
$8	10	15	10	17	4	20	76
$10	20	20	20	22	15	30	127
$12	25	25	30	27	20	40	167
$14	30	30	40	32	23	50	205

You can take the wages in the first column and the total quantity supplied in the last column and draw out the supply curve for the labor market. The supply curve for the hypothetical data looks like:

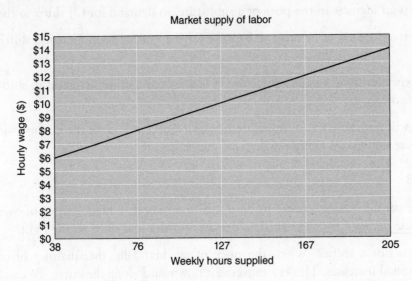

Market supply of labor

Day 15

a. Better technology shifts supply to the right.

b. A higher input price (the paper) shifts supply to the left.

c. The higher price of a related output (self-help books) would decrease the supply of textbooks.

d. Having fewer sellers shifts the supply to the left.

e. This effectively makes it less costly to produce each textbook, so it acts in the same way as a decrease in the price of an input, shifting supply to the right.

Day 16

a. Pumpkins are a key input, so this will increase the supply of pumpkin pies.

b. If apple pies are a substitute output, the supply of pumpkin pies will decrease.

c. Better production technology increases the supply of pumpkin pie.

d. This is not going to shift the supply curve; it will decrease the quantity supplied along the supply curve.

e. With more producers, the supply of pumpkin pie increases.

Day 17

A surplus exists when quantity supplied exceeds quantity demanded, and these are seen at all prices above $4. The size of the surplus is equal to Q_s minus Q_d.

A shortage exists when quantity demanded exceeds quantity supplied, and these are seen at all prices below $4. The size of the shortage is equal to Q_d minus Q_s.

The only price where there is neither a shortage nor a surplus is $4, and this is the market equilibrium price.

PRICE	Q_d	Q_s	SHORTAGE OR SURPLUS
$10	20	110	Surplus = 90 units
$9	25	100	Surplus = 75 units
$8	30	90	Surplus = 60 units
$7	35	80	Surplus = 45 units
$6	40	70	Surplus = 30 units
$5	45	60	Surplus = 15 units
$4	50	50	Equilibrium, $Q_d = Q_s$
$3	55	40	Shortage = 15 units
$2	60	30	Shortage = 30 units
$1	65	20	Shortage = 45 units

Day 18

a. To find the vertical intercept, use $Q_d = 0$ and solve for $P = \$50$. To find the horizontal intercept, use $P = 0$ and solve for $Q_d = 25$.

b. Using $P = \$30$, solve for $Q_d = 10$.

c. Using $Q_d = 15$, solve for $P = \$20$.

d. The new demand curve has a vertical intercept of $100 and a horizontal intercept of 50 units.

e. With the new demand curve, a price of $30 will result in 35 units demanded. This tells us that, holding the price constant, consumers are now willing and able to purchase more of the product.

f. With the new demand curve, a quantity of 15 units results in a price of $70. This tells us that, holding quantity constant, consumers are now willing to pay a higher price for the product.

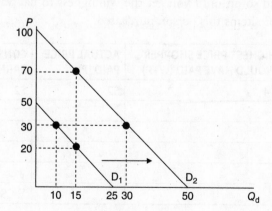

Day 19

a. The price of a key input is falling, so this would shift the supply of apples to the right, causing a decrease in the price and increase in quantity.

b. A health warning would decrease tastes and preferences for apples, causing a decrease in the demand and eventual decrease in both price and quantity.

c. The price of a substitute good is rising, so demand for apples will increase, causing an increase in both price and quantity.

d. When we combine an increase in the supply with a decrease in the demand for apples, the price will certainly fall, but the change in market quantity will depend on which shift is larger. If the supply shift is larger, quantity will rise. If the demand shift is larger, quantity will fall.

Day 20

a. With more income, assuming pumpkin pie is a normal good, demand for it will shift to the right, increasing price and quantity in the market.

b. If apple pies are a substitute good, demand for pumpkin pies will decrease, causing a decrease in price and quantity.

c. With fewer suppliers, the supply of pumpkin pie will shift to the left, causing an increase in price and decrease in quantity.

d. When we combine an increase in demand with a decrease in supply, the market price will definitely increase. However, the change in quantity depends on which of the shifts is larger. If the demand shift is larger, the quantity will rise. If the supply shift is larger, the quantity will fall.

Day 21

For example, you might ask, "You bought a tube of toothpaste for $2. What is the most you would have paid for the same tube?" A common response might be, "I have no idea." At this point, begin a downward auction by asking, "Would you have paid $6? $5? $4.50?," and so on until you get the willingness to pay value. Complete the table with a few more items this person purchased.

ITEM PURCHASED	HIGHEST PRICE SHOPPER WOULD HAVE PAID (WTP)	ACTUAL PRICE PAID (P)	CONSUMER SURPLUS EARNED (CS = WTP − P)
Toothpaste	$4	$2	$2
			Σ CS =

Day 22

Consumer surplus is the area below the demand curve and above the price. When the demand curve is a straight line, we can calculate consumer surplus as the area of a triangle; we just need to know the dimensions (height and width) of the triangle. To get the height, we need the vertical intercept and the price. The vertical intercept, the price when quantity is zero, is $250, and the current price is given to you as $100. To get the width, we need the quantity of Gizmos demanded. Using a price of $100 in the demand equation, we solve for a quantity of 50 units.

Calculate CS = ½ × ($150)(50) = $3,750

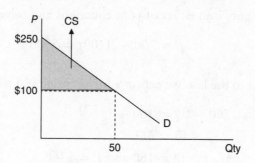

Day 23

Producer surplus is the area above the supply curve and below the price. When the supply curve is a straight line, we can calculate producer surplus as the area of a triangle; we just need to know the dimensions (height and width) of the triangle. To get the height, we need the vertical intercept and the price. The vertical intercept, the price when quantity is zero, is $100, and the current price is given to you as $200. To get the width, we need the quantity of Whodats supplied. Using a price of $200 in the supply equation, we solve for a quantity of 200 units.

Calculate PS = ½ × ($100)(200) = $10,000

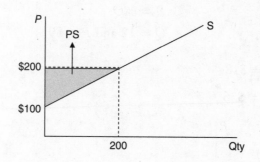

Day 24

a. To solve for equilibrium, we simply need to set the equations equal to each other. After all, the price from the demand curve will be the same as the price from the supply curve in equilibrium. You could also rearrange each equation for quantity and set those quantities equal to each other because $Q_d = Q_s$ in equilibrium.

$$700 - 2Q = 100 + Q \quad \text{(Note: There is no need for subscripts on the}$$
$$Q \text{ variable, as they are the same in equilibrium.)}$$

$$600 = 3Q$$
$$Q = 200$$

Substitute this quantity into either of your equations and solve for price.

$$P = 700 - 2(200) = \$300$$

b. When supply shifts to the left, we expect a higher price and a lower quantity.

$$700 - 2Q = 160 + Q$$
$$540 = 3Q$$
$$Q = 180 \text{ and } P = \$340$$

c. When demand shifts to the right, we expect a higher price and higher quantity.

$$760 - 2Q = 100 + Q$$
$$660 = 3Q$$
$$Q = 220 \text{ and } P = \$320$$

Day 25

a. Set the price from the demand curve equal to the price from the supply curve.

$$12 - \tfrac{1}{4}Q = 3 + \tfrac{1}{2}Q$$
$$9 = \tfrac{3}{4}Q$$
$$Q = 12 \text{ and } P = \$9$$

b. CS = ½($3)(12) = \$18

PS = ½ ($6)(12) = \$36

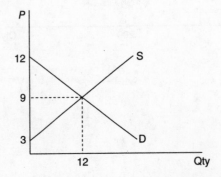

Day 26

Competitive markets are said to be efficient because the equilibrium outcome maximizes the sum of consumer and producer surplus. Your task is to show this in a neatly drawn graph.

a. Draw market equilibrium and label the equilibrium price Pe and equilibrium quantity Qe.

b. Shade the areas of consumer and producer surplus.

c. Now suppose a law limited the quantity of this product to about half of Qe. Add this regulated quantity to the graph and label it Qr.

d. At quantity Qr, show the area of consumer and producer surplus that would not be earned if this law was in place.

Answers:

a. and b. are shown in the graph below

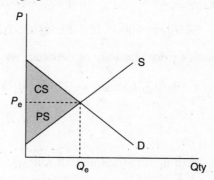

c. and d. are shown in the graph below. Because the shaded area represents consumer and producer surplus that is lost, economists call it "deadweight loss." This is a concept you will see in other chapters as you review AP Microeconomics.

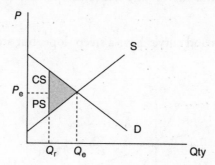

Day 27

It is very important to know how the price elasticity of demand is calculated:

$$E_d = (\%\Delta Q_d)/(\%\Delta P)$$

This value will almost always be less than zero because price and quantity demanded go in opposite directions, so we just ignore the negative sign.

a. Gasoline: $E_d = 3\%/5\% = 0.60$, and this is inelastic (less than 1)

b. Broccoli: $E_d = 9\%/6\% = 1.50$, and this is elastic (greater than 1)

c. Wool socks: $E_d = 7.5\%/7.5\% = 1$, and this is unit elastic (equals 1)

Day 28

For this example, I will use restaurant meals as a product that is commonly purchased in a household. Suppose the person you interview estimates that in a typical month about eight restaurant meals are purchased. Then suppose that if the price of dining out at restaurants increased by 50%, this person responds that only three meals would be purchased at restaurants in a month.

$$E_d = (\%\Delta Q_d)/(\%\Delta P)$$

We have already stated that the hypothetical price increase is 50%, so we need to calculate the percentage change in quantity demanded. To calculate the percentage change in quantity demanded, use this formula:

$$\%\Delta Q_d = 100 \times (\text{New } Q_d - \text{Old } Q_d)/(\text{Old } Q_d)$$

Using my hypothetical example,

$$\%\Delta Q_d = 100 \times (3 - 8)/(8) = -62.5\%$$

To complete the calculation of price elasticity of demand, we have:

$$E_d = (\%\Delta Q_d)/(\%\Delta P) = 62.5\%/50\% = 1.25$$

Day 29

Your graph should look something like the one that follows.

a. Perfectly inelastic demand curves are vertical.

b. Perfectly elastic demand curves are horizontal.

c. Relatively elastic demand curves have a small slope, but are still downward sloping (not horizontal).

d. Relatively inelastic demand curves have a steep slope, but are still downward sloping (not vertical).

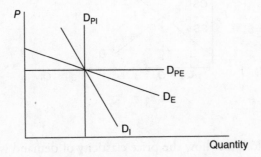

Day 30

a. First we need to determine the quantity of hoozits that would be demanded at each price. To do this, we just use the demand equation provided.

When $P = \$40$,

$$40 = 100 - 2Q_d \text{ and } Q_d = 30.$$

When $P = \$20$,

$$20 = 100 - 2Q_d \text{ and } Q_d = 40.$$

The midpoint approach to calculating price elasticity of demand uses the average price and average quantity between two points on the demand curve. Now that we have our two price and quantity combinations, we can use the price elasticity of demand midpoint formula:

$$E_d = (\Delta Q_d / \Delta P) \times (P_{avg} / Q_{avg})$$

The average price between $40 and $20 is $P_{avg} = \$30$, and the average quantity between 30 and 40 hoozits is $Q_{avg} = 35$.

$$E_d = (10/\$20) \times (\$30/35) = 0.43$$

b. The value of 0.43 tells us that between these two prices the demand is price-inelastic. In fact, it tells us that if the price were to increase by 1%, that quantity of hoozits demanded would decrease by only 0.43%.

Day 31

The completed table is shown as follows. To calculate the total revenue column, you simply multiply price and quantity demanded.

The midpoint approach to calculating price elasticity of demand uses the average price and average quantity between two points on the demand curve.

$$E_d = (\Delta Q_d / \Delta P) \times (P_{avg} / Q_{avg})$$

For example, the average price between $7 and $8 is $7.50, and the average quantity between 0 and 1 is 0.50 units. This leads us to calculate the price elasticity of demand between $7 and $8 as

$$E_d = (\Delta Q_d / \Delta P) \times (P_{avg} / Q_{avg}) = (1/\$1) \times (\$7.50/0.50) = 15$$

PRICE PER UNIT	QUANTITY OF THE GOOD DEMANDED	TOTAL REVENUE $= P \times Q_d$	PRICE ELASTICITY OF DEMAND
$8	0	$0	
$7	1	$7	15.00
$6	2	$12	4.33
$5	3	$15	2.20
$4	4	$16	1.29
$3	5	$15	0.78
$2	6	$12	0.45
$1	7	$7	0.23
$0	8	$0	0.07

Day 32

In the top half of the demand curve (above a price of $4), when the price falls the total revenue rises. The reason this happens is because there is an elastic response to a lower price. For every 1% decrease in the price, quantity demanded rises by *more than* 1%.

In the lower half of the demand curve (below $4), lower prices cause total revenue to fall. This happens because there is an inelastic response to a lower price. For every 1% decrease in the price, quantity demanded rises by *less than* 1%.

Total revenue $= P \times Q_d$, but downward sloping demand curves tell us that price and quantity demanded go in separate directions. When the percentage increase in Q_d outweighs the percentage decrease in P, total revenue will rise. But when the percentage decrease in P is greater than the percentage increase in Q_d, total revenue will fall.

Day 33

Dr. DeBeers, this planned decrease in tuition will not increase total revenue to the college; in fact, total revenue will fall! The price elasticity of demand measures how sensitive consumers, in this case students, are to a change in the price. It is computed with this formula:

$$E_d = (\%\Delta Q_d)/(\%\Delta P)$$

and my research tells me that this is equal to about 0.50. This value tells me that for every 1% decrease in the price (tuition), the quantity demanded (enrollment of students) increases by only 0.5%. In other words, your proposed 5% cut in tuition would increase student enrollment by 2.5%.

Total revenue is computed by this formula:

$$TR = P \times Q_d$$

If your price is falling by 5% and quantity demanded is rising by a lesser amount, 2.5%, then total revenue will fall by approximately 2.5%. What you should consider to increase total revenue is a tuition increase, because your customers are not very sensitive to a price change.

Day 34

Remember that the income elasticity of demand tells us how responsive consumers are to a 1% change in income:

$$E_I = (\%\Delta Q_d)/(\%\Delta I)$$

If this value is positive, it means that greater income is associated with greater quantities demanded: a normal good. If it turns out negative, it means that rising income is associated with fewer units demanded: an inferior good.

This allows us to classify eggs and furniture as normal goods, while flour and margarine are inferior goods.

GOOD OR SERVICE	INCOME ELASTICITY OF DEMAND (E_I)	NORMAL OR INFERIOR?
Eggs	0.35	Normal
Flour	−0.37	Inferior
Margarine	−0.21	Inferior
Furniture	1.47	Normal

Interpretations:

- If income rises by 1%, the quantity of eggs demanded will rise by 0.35%.
- If income rises by 1%, the quantity of flour demanded will fall by 0.37%.
- If income rises by 1%, the quantity of margarine demanded will fall by 0.21%.
- If income rises by 1%, the quantity of furniture demanded will rise by 1.47%.

Day 35

The cross-price elasticity of demand tells us how consumers respond in consumption of one product to a change in the price of a second product. The cross-price is calculated with this formula:

$$E_{x,y} = (\%\Delta Q_d \text{ of good } x)/(\%\Delta P \text{ of good } y)$$

If this turns out to be positive, the products are substitutes; if it is negative, the products are complements.

GOOD	CROSS ELASTICITY WITH RESPECT TO A CHANGE IN THE PRICE OF:	CROSS ELASTICITY	SUBSTITUTES OR COMPLEMENTS?
Beef	Pork	0.27	Substitutes
Cereal	Milk	−0.90	Complements
Butter	Margarine	0.67	Substitutes
Potatoes	Meat	−0.50	Complements

Interpretations:

- If the price of pork rises by 1%, the quantity of beef demanded rises by 0.27%.
- If the price of milk rises by 1%, the quantity of cereal demanded falls by 0.90%.
- If the price of margarine rises by 1%, the quantity of butter demanded rises by 0.67%.
- If the price of meat rises by 1%, the quantity of potatoes demanded falls by 0.50%.

Day 36

For this example, I will use tickets to see a movie as a product that is commonly purchased in a household. Suppose the person you interview estimates that in a typical month, the family goes to two movies. If household income were to rise by 50%, suppose this person responds that the family would go to four movies in a month.

$$E_I = (\%\Delta Q_d)/(\%\Delta I)$$

We have already stated that the hypothetical income increase is 50%, so we need to calculate the percentage change in quantity demanded. As a reminder, when we need to calculate the percentage change in quantity demanded, we use this formula:

$$\%\Delta Q_d = 100 \times (\text{New } Q_d - \text{Old } Q_d)/(\text{Old } Q_d)$$

Using my hypothetical example,

$$\%\Delta Q_d = 100 \times (4 - 2)/(2) = 100\%$$

To complete the calculation of price elasticity of demand, we have:

$$E_d = (\%\Delta Q_d)/(\%\Delta P) = 100\%/50\% = 2$$

Day 37

We need to use the price elasticity and cross-price elasticity of demand formulas for each of these problems.

The formulas are:

$$E_d = (\%\Delta Q_d)/(\%\Delta P) \text{ (Recall that we typically ignore the negative sign.)}$$

$$E_{x,y} = (\%\Delta Q_d \text{ of good } x)/(\%\Delta P \text{ of good } y)$$

a. $\%\Delta Q_d/10\% = 0.20$

When we solve for $\%\Delta Q_d = 2\%$, this tells us what happens to the quantity of milk demanded.

b. $E_{x,y} = (\%\Delta Q_d \text{ of good } x)/(\%\Delta P \text{ of good } y) = (\%\Delta Q_d \text{ of cereal})/10\% = -0.80$

Solving for the numerator informs us that cereal consumption will fall by 8% if the price of milk rises by 10%.

c. $E_d = (\%\Delta Q_d)/(\%\Delta P) = 8\%/\%\Delta P = 0.45$

When we solve for the denominator, we see that breakfast cereal manufacturers would need to decrease the price of cereal by about 17.8% to offset the 8% decrease in quantity demanded that was the result of higher milk prices.

Day 38

The price elasticity of supply measures how responsive suppliers are to a change in the price. If the quantity of a product supplied rises greatly with a small increase in the price, we would describe the supply curve as elastic. If the quantity supplied rises by very little or not at all with an increase in the price, we would describe it as inelastic.

The formula is:

$$E_s = (\%\Delta Q_s)/(\%\Delta P)$$

Liz says that she can't do anything about the higher turkey prices right now, presumably because the turkeys are too immature for sale, which tells us that her short-run supply curve is vertical (S_{SR}). However, in nine months, the turkeys will be ready, and she can increase her quantity supplied. This long-run supply curve (S_{LR}) will be upward sloping.

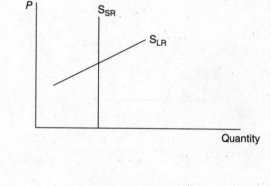

Quantity

Day 39

a. Equilibrium is found at the intersection of supply and demand.

b. Because a price ceiling is a legal maximum price (like rent control), an effective price ceiling must lie below the equilibrium price.

c. At the price ceiling, $Q_d > Q_s$, so a shortage exists.

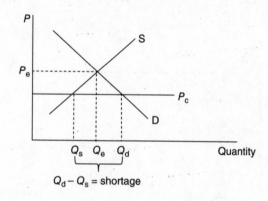

$Q_d - Q_s$ = shortage

Day 40

a. Equilibrium is found at the intersection of supply and demand.

b. Because a price floor is a legal minimum price (like a minimum wage), an effective price floor must lie above the equilibrium price.

c. At the price floor $Q_d < Q_s$, so a surplus exists.

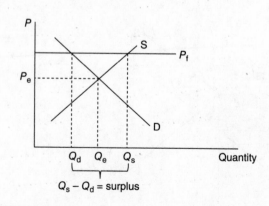

$Q_s - Q_d$ = surplus

Day 41

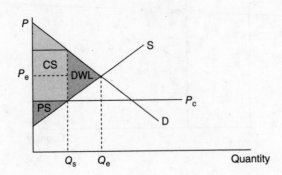

Because the price ceiling is below the equilibrium price (P_e), producers will restrict quantity supplied to Q_s.

Consumer surplus: the area under the demand curve and above P_c.

Producer surplus: the area above the supply curve and below P_c.

Deadweight loss: the area between the demand and supply curves and between Q_s and Q_e.

Day 42

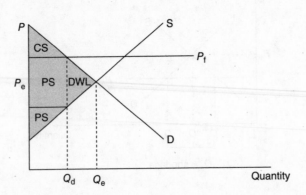

Because the price ceiling is below the equilibrium price (P_e), consumers will wish to buy only quantity demanded of Q_d.

Consumer surplus: the area under the demand curve and above P_f.

Producer surplus: the area above the supply curve and below P_f.

Deadweight loss: the area between the demand and supply curves and between Q_d and Q_e.

Day 43

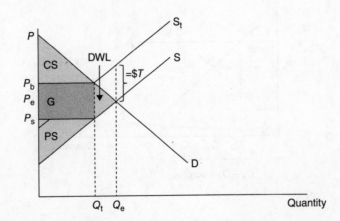

Day 44

This information tells us that demand for cigarettes is price inelastic. When a 10% increase in the price reduces consumption by 4%, the price elasticity of demand is about 0.40. Although there is no information about the price elasticity of supply, when demand for a product like cigarettes is price inelastic, consumers tend to bear a higher incidence of the tax. Of course, the opposite would be true if we discovered that the price elasticity of supply was actually smaller than the price elasticity of demand.

Day 45

If the excise tax on electricity is entirely passed on to the consumers of electricity, the demand curve must be vertical. In the following graph, we see that the original price of electricity is P_e. After a tax of $\$T$ is imposed, the price rises by exactly $\$T$; consumers pay the entire incidence of the tax.

While the demand for electricity, especially in the short run, is very likely inelastic, it is unlikely to be perfectly inelastic. In other words, the demand curve is probably steep, but still downward sloping. If so, the largest share of the tax will fall on the consumers, but not 100% of it.

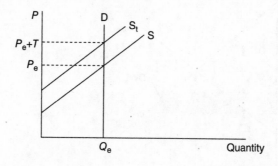

Day 46

	BEFORE THE SUBSIDY	AFTER THE SUBSIDY
Consumer surplus	A + B	A + B + C + F + G
Producer surplus	C + D	B + C + D + E
Government spending	0	−(B + C + E + F + G + H)
Total surplus	A + B + C + D	A + B + C + D − H
Deadweight loss	0	−H

The cost to society, in deadweight loss, is the area labeled "H."

Day 47

At the lower world price, domestic consumers would increase the quantity demanded, but domestic suppliers would reduce quantity supplied. The difference between Q_1 and Q_2 is supplied by foreign producers.

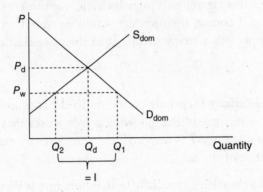

Day 48

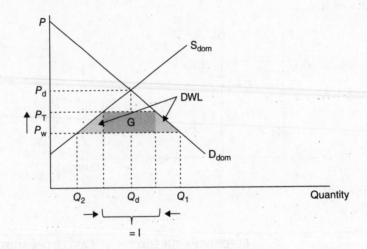

Day 49

Typical losers of import tariffs include domestic buyers of the product and foreign suppliers and their employees.

Typical winners of import tariffs include domestic workers and suppliers of the product.

The domestic government also collects tax revenue.

Day 50

Since Max knows that more than seven pieces of chocolate will make him sick, his total utility curve begins to fall after a quantity of seven. Marginal utility falls with more chocolate consumed and becomes negative beyond seven pieces.

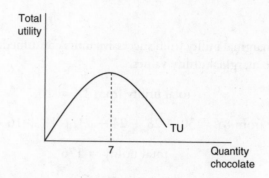

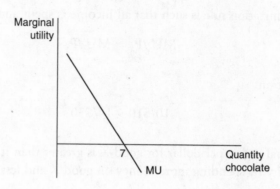

Day 51

When we consume something that brings us some amount of happiness, we say that the product provides utility. However, when consumption of a good or service actually makes us unhappy, or even ill, we call it disutility.

Suppose the person that you interview says they really dislike pickles and would never eat a pickle, even if it was free. Since the person claims to never get any utility from pickles, the total utility curve actually falls below zero as more pickles are consumed.

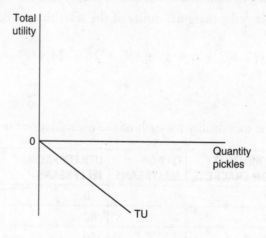

Day 52

a. The table shows marginal utility from successive units consumed. To get total utility, simply add up the marginal utility values.

$$\text{total utility from } 1X = 10$$

$$\text{total utility from } 8Y = 30 + 28 + 24 + 21 + 18 + 16 + 15 + 14 = 166$$

$$\text{total utility} = 176$$

The utility maximization rule is such that all income is spent and

$$MU_x/P_x = MU_y/P_y$$

At this combination:

$$10/\$10 > 14/\$30$$

Since the marginal utility per dollar for good X is greater than it is for good Y, she can increase utility by spending more money on good X and less on good Y.

b. To find the utility maximizing combination, we need to find combinations that spend all of Mary's income and satisfy:

$$MU_x/P_x = MU_y/P_y$$

$$\text{Or } MU_x/\$10 = MU_y/\$30$$

In other words, the marginal utility of good Y must be three times the marginal utility of good X. The combination of 4X and 7Y satisfy both necessary conditions. Total spending on this combination is exactly $250, and the marginal utility of the fourth unit of X is $\frac{1}{3}$ the marginal utility of the seventh unit of good Y.

$$\text{Total utility} = (10 + 7 + 6 + 5) + (30 + 28 + 24 + 21 + 18 + 16 + 15) = 180$$

Day 53

a. Simply add up the total utility for each of the combinations in the table.

QTY OF CRACKERS	TOTAL UTILITY FROM CRACKERS	QTY OF JELLYBEANS	UTILITY FROM JELLYBEANS	
0	0	0	0	
2	70	1	80	
4	130	2	150	
6	180	3	210	
8	220	4	260	
10	250	5	300	

# CRACKERS	# JELLYBEANS	TOTAL UTILITY
0	5	300
2	4	330
4	3	340
6	2	330
8	1	300
10	0	250

Theo maximizes his utility with 4 crackers and 3 jellybeans.

b. Marginal utility is the change in total utility divided by the change in consumption.

QTY OF CRACKERS	UTILITY FROM CRACKERS	MU_C	MU_C/P_C	QTY OF JELLYBEANS	UTILITY FROM JELLYBEANS	MU_B	MU_B/P_B
0	0			0	0		
2	70	35	7	1	80	80	8
4	130	30	6	2	150	70	7
6	180	25	5	3	210	60	6
8	220	20	4	4	260	50	5
10	250	15	3	5	300	40	4

Remember the utility max rule is such that all income is spent and:

$$MU_x/P_x = MU_y/P_y$$

The marginal utility per dollar spent is equal in four different combinations, but the only combination where Theo spends his income exactly is 4 crackers and 3 jellybeans. Again, the total utility is 340.

Day 54

Accounting profit begins with total revenue and subtracts only the explicit cost of operating the business. Economic profit also subtracts the opportunity costs of running the shop. Accounting profit shows a profit of $80,000, but when you consider the opportunity costs of running the shop, the economic profit is actually –$10,000. You are better off taking the accountant job and renting the shop.

Day 55

The key to distinguishing a variable cost from a fixed cost is asking whether it increases as more miles are driven (variable) or if it stays the same, even if zero miles are driven (fixed). Here is a sample list.

Variable costs: gasoline, oil, wear and tear on things like tires, belts, and windshield wiper blades

Fixed costs: insurance, licensing, interest payments (if you're repaying a car loan)

Day 56

Once again, the key to distinguishing a variable cost from a fixed cost is asking whether it increases as more nights are spent at the residence (variable) or if it stays the same, even if you were out of town for the entire month (fixed). Here is a sample list.

Variable costs: groceries, electricity, natural gas, water, and other utilities

Fixed costs: cable or satellite TV, Internet service, property taxes, insurance, rent or mortgage payments (if you're repaying a home mortgage)

Day 57

a. It is important to know how marginal product and average product are derived from total product.

$$MP_L = \Delta TP_L/\Delta L$$

$$AP_L = TP_L/L$$

# OF CARPENTERS	TOTAL PRODUCT (# OF CABINETS PER MONTH)	MARGINAL PRODUCT	AVERAGE PRODUCT
0	0	X	X
1	8	8	8
2	18	10	5
3	26	8	8.67
4	32	6	8
5	36	4	7.2
6	38	2	6.33
7	36	−2	5.14

b. If we can ignore the cost of hiring carpenters, then we would want to maximize total number of cabinets made in a month and hire 6.

Day 58

The key to this phenomenon in production is the fact that this is taking place in the short run. In the short run, the quantity of capital (machinery or the size of the production area) is fixed, so adding more labor to this fixed capital creates a problem: ultimately there is not enough capital or space for these additional employees. The total production may continue to rise, but the *marginal* production of the next unit of labor eventually falls.

Day 59

The key to determining what the MP_L curve looks like is to know the relationship between TP_L and MP_L.

Recall that $MP_L = \Delta TP_L/\Delta L$.

Since our graphs plot TP_L on the vertical (y) axis and L on the horizontal (x), the previous equation for MP_L is also the slope of the TP_L curve ($\Delta y / \Delta x$).

Graph A

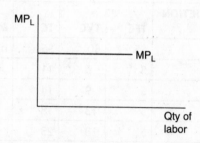

Graph A, an upward-sloping straight line, tells us that the MP_L is a constant value, never rising and never falling. The next worker contributes exactly the same additional output as each of the workers that were employed before.

Graph B

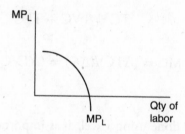

Graph B, with a TP_L that rises and eventually falls, implies that workers hired early have a higher MP_L than those who are hired later. In fact, beyond the point where the TP_L actually falls, the MP_L becomes negative.

Graph C

Graph C, a TP_L curve that keeps rising at a faster and faster rate, tells us that the MP_L of the next worker is even greater than the MP_L of the workers that were hired before.

The graph that makes the most economic sense is B. The MP_L should fall in the short run as additional workers find fewer units of capital to work with, or less work space in which to work.

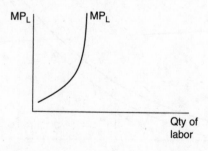

Day 60

In the short run, there are fixed costs (TFC) that must be paid, even when output is zero. The variable costs (TVC) are zero when output is zero, but increase as output increases.

PRODUCTION (Q)	TFC	TVC	TC	MC
0	$5	$0	$5	n/a
1	5	6	11	6
2	5	9	14	3
3	5	13	18	4
4	5	18	23	5
5	5	25	30	7
6	5	34	39	9
7	5	45	50	11
8	5	58	63	13

The key formulas are:

$$TC = TVC + TFC$$

and

$$MC = (\Delta TC)/(\Delta Q) = (\Delta TVC)/(\Delta Q)$$

Day 61

The following graphs were done using Excel. It is important to see the relationships between these curves.

- The TFC curve is a horizontal line because it doesn't change with output.
- The TC curve lies $5 above the TVC curve because of the $5 of TFC.
- The MC curve is the slope of both TC and TVC curves. At higher levels of output, the TC and TVC get steeper.
- At the lowest levels of output, MC falls, but soon begins to rise and continues rising.

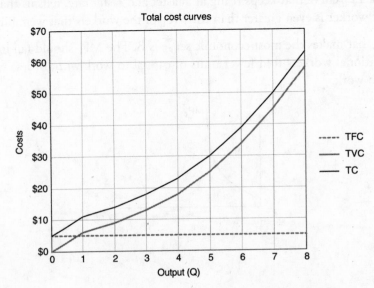

(Continued)

Answers

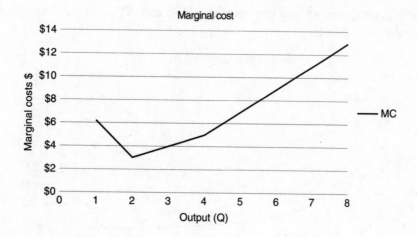

Day 62

The important formulas that you need to use are:

$$AFC = TFC/Q$$
$$AVC = TVC/Q$$
$$ATC = TC/Q$$

PRODUCTION (Q)	TFC	TVC	TC	MC	AFC	AVC	ATC
0	$5	$0	$5		XX	XX	XX
1	5	6	11	$6	$5.00	$6.00	$11.00
2	5	9	14	$3	$2.50	$4.50	$7.00
3	5	13	18	$4	$1.67	$4.33	$6.00
4	5	18	23	$5	$1.25	$4.50	$5.75
5	5	25	30	$7	$1.00	$5.00	$6.00
6	5	34	39	$9	$0.83	$5.67	$6.50
7	5	45	50	$11	$0.71	$6.43	$7.14
8	5	58	63	$13	$0.63	$7.25	$7.88

Day 63

The following graphs were done using Excel. It is important to see the relationships between these curves.

- The AFC curve continues to decline as output rises.
- The AVC and ATC curves are approximately U-shaped.
- The ATC curve lies above the AVC curve by an amount equal to AFC.

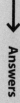

- The MC curve rises up and intersects the AVC and ATC curves at approximately their minimum points.

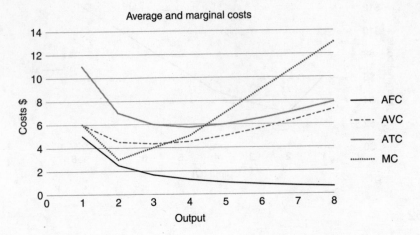

Day 64

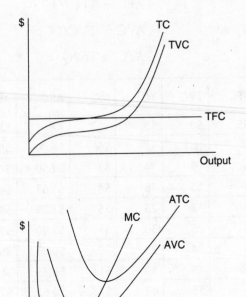

Day 65

- Many small independent buyers and sellers
- Firms produce a standardized (identical) product
- No barriers to entry or exit
- Firms are price takers

Day 66

At a price of $230, just multiply by quantity of output to complete the TR column. The profit/loss column is total revenue minus total cost at each quantity.

Compute the level of profit each producer would earn.

OUTPUT (Q)	TOTAL REVENUE = $P \times Q$	PROFIT (+) OR LOSS (−) = TR − TC
0	$ -	$(500.00)
1	$230.00	$(420.00)
2	$460.00	$(240.00)
3	$690.00	$(70.00)
4	$920.00	$80.00
5	$1,150.00	$200.00
6	$1,380.00	$290.00
7	$1,610.00	$340.00
8	$1,840.00	$340.00
9	$2,070.00	$280.00
10	$2,300.00	$150.00

When $P = \$230$, the profit-maximizing output is $Q = 8$.

Redo the total revenue and profit table for a price of $180 and you get the following:

OUTPUT (Q)	TOTAL REVENUE = $P \times Q$	PROFIT (+) OR LOSS (−) = TR − TC
0	$ -	$(500.00)
1	$180.00	$(470.00)
2	$360.00	$(340.00)
3	$540.00	$(220.00)
4	$720.00	$(120.00)
5	$900.00	$(50.00)
6	$1,080.00	$(10.00)
7	$1,260.00	$(10.00)
8	$1,440.00	$(60.00)
9	$1,620.00	$(170.00)
10	$1,800.00	$(350.00)

When $P = \$180$, the firm should produce $Q = 7$ to maximize profits or minimize losses.

Day 67

To use the profit-maximization rule, we must find the level of output where MR = MC. In perfect competition, $P = \text{MR} = \text{MC}$.

We know that the price is $290, so that is equal to MR. Marginal cost (MC) is calculated by looking at the table. A column for MC has been added to the following table.

When the price is \$290, MR = MC at a quantity of 9 bushels. Profit is:

$$\Pi = \$290 \times 9 - \$1{,}790 = \$820$$

What happens when the price falls to \$80? At first glance, the profit-maximization rule says that the farmer should produce $Q = 4$ because that is where MC = \$80. However, if we calculate profit:

$$\Pi = \$80 \times 4 - \$840 = -\$520$$

Losses of \$520 are even worse than what we would lose if we shut down and produced nothing. In that event, we would lose only our fixed costs of \$500. In other words, this price is too low to produce any amount of output. Our total revenue of \$320 does not pay for our total variable costs of \$340 at $Q = 4$. So we are wise to shut down.

OUTPUT (Q)	TFC	TVC	TC	MC
0	\$500	\$0	\$500	XX
1	\$500	\$150	\$650	\$150
2	\$500	\$200	\$700	\$50
3	\$500	\$260	\$760	\$60
4	\$500	\$340	\$840	\$80
5	\$500	\$450	\$950	\$110
6	\$500	\$590	\$1,090	\$140
7	\$500	\$770	\$1,270	\$180
8	\$500	\$1,000	\$1,500	\$230
9	\$500	\$1,290	\$1,790	\$290
10	\$500	\$1,650	\$2,150	\$360

Day 68

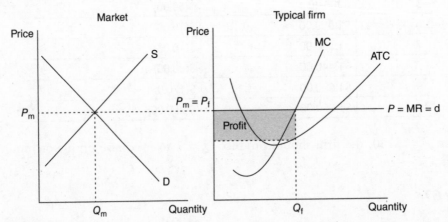

Make sure that you extend the market price over to the graph of the typical firm, because they are price takers. Also be sure to find Q_f at the point where the P = MR = MC curves intersect. The rectangle of profit should also be labeled.

Day 69

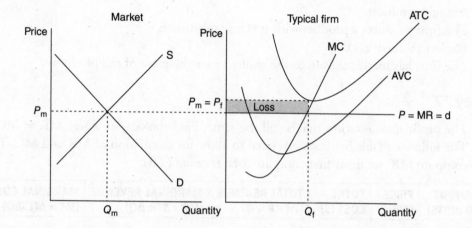

It is important to include the AVC curve and draw the price between ATC and AVC curves. This placement identifies the firm in a loss-minimization situation and not a shutdown situation.

Day 70

a. In the long run, new firms will begin to enter this market. With more suppliers, the market supply curve shifts outward, lowering the market price. With lower and lower prices, the positive economic profits decrease and firms begin to produce fewer units of output. Ultimately, the profits are reduced to zero as the market price is equal to average total cost.

b. In the long run, some existing firms will begin to exit this market. With fewer suppliers, the market supply curve shifts inward, increasing the market price. With rising prices, the negative economic profits increase (become less negative) and firms begin to produce more units of output. Ultimately, the profits are reduced to zero as the market price is equal to average total cost.

c. No matter whether positive or negative profits are happening in the short run, the long-run equilibrium graphs always look like this.

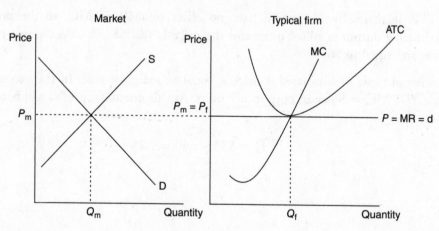

Day 71

- A single producer
- The firm produces a product with no close substitutes
- Barriers to entry exist
- The firm has market power, or the ability to set the price of the product

Day 72

a. The profit-maximization rule is still the same: Find the output where MR = MC. The following table has been extended to allow for calculation of MR and MC. To compute MR, we must first compute total revenue (TR).

OUTPUT (Q UNITS)	PRICE ($P)	TOTAL COST ($)	TOTAL REVENUE (TR = $P \times Q$)	MARGINAL REVENUE (MR = $\Delta TR/\Delta Q$)	MARGINAL COST (MC = $\Delta TC/\Delta Q$)
0	12	5	$0		
1	11	10	$11	$11	$5
2	10	15	$20	$9	$5
3	9	20	$27	$7	$5
4	8	25	$32	$5	$5
5	7	30	$35	$3	$5
6	6	35	$36	$1	$5
7	5	40	$35	−$1	$5
8	4	45	$32	−$3	$5
9	3	50	$27	−$5	$5
10	2	55	$20	−$7	$5
11	1	60	$11	−$9	$5
12	0	65	$0	−$11	$5

At $Q = 4$, MR = MC = $5. The monopolist would charge $8 to sell those 4 units. Profit is equal to total revenue minus total cost:

$$\Pi = \$32 - \$25 = \$7$$

b. If TFC increases by $1, it will have no effect on MR or MC, so the profit-maximizing output is still 4 units and the price is still $8. However, profit is $1 lower and equal to $6.

c. Deadweight loss is eliminated if price is equal to marginal cost. In the preceding table, $P = MC = \$5$ at an output of 7 units. At this outcome, profits will become losses.

$$\Pi = \$35 - \$40 = -\$5$$

Day 73

When you're drawing a monopoly, remember that the marginal revenue curve is downward sloping and lies below the demand curve. Find Q_m at the intersection of MR = MC, and then go up to the demand curve to find P_m. The area of profit is a rectangle with a height equal to $(P_m - ATC)$ and length of Q_m. It is also helpful to show the MC curve intersecting ATC at the minimum of the ATC curve.

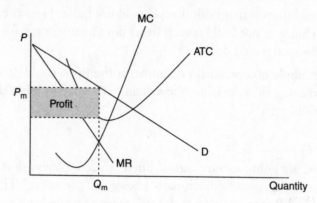

Day 74

- Relatively large number of firms
- Differentiated products
- Easy entry and exit
- Some ability to set the price

Day 75

a. In the long run, new firms will enter this market. The demand for existing firms will shift to the left, decreasing price, output, and profit. Entry of new firms will stop when all firms are breaking even.

b. In the long run, some existing firms will exit this market. The demand for remaining firms will shift to the right, increasing price, output, and profit. Exit of firms will stop when all firms are breaking even.

c. The difficult part of drawing this graph is drawing the demand curve tangent to the ATC curve and having that point of tangency directly above the intersection of MR = MC. I suggest drawing the ATC curve last.

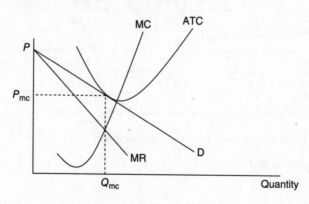

Day 76

a. Hamm has a dominant strategy of "don't build." If Rye is going to build, Hamm earns more profit if they don't build (6 > 5), and if Rye is not going to build, Hamm earns more profit if they don't build (4 > 3). Rye also has a strategy of "don't build." If Hamm is going to build, Rye should not build (7 > 5), and if Hamm is not going to build, Rye earns more profit if they don't build (2 > 1).

b. The Nash equilibrium is that both firms should not build: Hamm earns 4 and Rye earns 2. The choice to not build is each firm's dominant strategy (or best response) to anything the rival would do.

c. Yes, it is an example of a prisoner's dilemma. If the firms could cooperate (or collude) before making their decision, they could both agree to build the factory, and both firms would earn 5.

Day 77

Of course, results are going to vary across different game players, but one successful strategy in a repeated prisoner's dilemma is known as "tit-for-tat." This strategy was developed by Anatol Rapoport and has the advantage of being both simple and effective. The player (you) would begin the game by cooperating, and then in each successive round you adopt the strategy of your rival from the previous round. So if today your rival cheated (played their dominant strategy) and you cooperated, tomorrow you will also cheat as a way of punishing their selfish behavior. If your rival goes back to their cooperative ways, so will you, and both players will earn higher profits. Go back to the games and see if this strategy is successful for you.

Day 78

a. This means she sells her product in a perfectly competitive output market and hires labor in a perfectly competitive input market.

b. The completed graph follows. You must first find the marginal product of labor (MP_L) and then multiply by the constant price of a pizza.

QUANTITY OF LABOR (WORKERS)	QUANTITY OF PIZZA	$MRP_L = P \times MP_L$
0	0	
1	9	$2 \times 9 = $18
2	15	$12
3	20	$10
4	24	$8
5	27	$6
6	29	$4
7	30	$2

c. Set $W = MRP_L = 8 and we find this intersection at $L = 4$.

The graph is shown as follows.

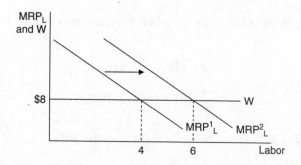

d. This doubles the MRP_L, shifting the demand for labor outward, and now she will hire $L = 6$. Adjust the graph accordingly.

Day 79

a. Diesel fuel and semitruck drivers are complementary inputs, so the falling price of fuel should increase the demand for drivers, increasing both wages and employment.

b. More stringent requirements would decrease the supply of teachers, increasing wages but decreasing employment.

c. Rising interest rates usually decrease the demand for capital because firms often borrow to purchase such equipment. Weaker demand for capital equipment should decrease the price of capital and the quantity of capital employed.

d. The rising sea level would inundate existing beachfront property, reducing the supply of it. The reduced supply would increase the price and reduce the quantity of it exchanged in the market.

Day 80

Obviously results are going to vary, but the idea is that you now know there is a good resource out there to provide you with some occupational background and projections.

Day 81

a. The MRP is the price of output ($0.50) multiplied by the MP of each resource.

QTY OF LABOR EMPLOYED	MARGINAL PRODUCT OF LABOR	MRP OF LABOR	QUANTITY OF CAPITAL EMPLOYED	MARGINAL PRODUCT OF CAPITAL	MRP OF CAPITAL
1	20	$10	1	20	$10
2	16	$8	2	18	$9
3	12	$6	3	16	$8
4	10	$5	4	12	$6
5	8	$4	5	8	$4
6	4	$2	6	6	$3
7	2	$1	7	4	$2
8	1	$0.50	8	2	$1

b. The least-cost combination is found when you have produced 144 units of output and:

$$MP_L/w = MP_K/r, \text{ or}$$

$$MP_L/\$1 = MP_K/\$2$$

This means that the MP_K must be twice as large as the MP_L.

At $L = 6$ and $K = 5$, we have:

$4/\$1 = 8/\$2$ and output adds up to 144 units $= (20 + 16 + 12 + 10 + 8 + 4) + (20 + 18 + 16 + 12 + 8)$

c. The profit-maximizing hiring rule is to hire a resource up to the point where the MRP is equal to the resource price.

For labor: $MRP_L = w = \$1$ at $L = 7$

For capital: $MRP_K = r = \$2$ at $K = 7$

d. Total output $= (20 + 16 + 12 + 10 + 8 + 4 + 2) + (20 + 18 + 16 + 12 + 8 + 6 + 4)$

$$= 156$$

Profit $= TR - TC = (\$0.50 \times 156) - (\$1 \times 7) - (\$2 \times 7) = \$57$

Day 82

a. Private good because it is both excludable and rival. It is excludable because sellers of milk will exclude you from having the milk if you refuse to pay. It is rivalrous because once you buy that gallon of milk, another person cannot buy the same gallon.

b. Public good because it is nonexcludable and nonrival. It is nonexcludable because it would be impossible to turn the light on only for the motorists who stop and pay for it, but keep the lamp unlit for those who refuse to pay. It is nonrival because my consumption of the illumination does not reduce your ability to consume the same thing. In other words, when I drive under the light I don't reduce the available units of the light for anyone who drives past it later.

c. Private good. The attorney will not provide me with her advice if I refuse to pay (excludable), and if I'm consuming an hour of the attorney's time, it is one hour that another person cannot consume (rival).

d. Trick question! This is called a "common resource" because it is nonexcludable but also rival. Fish or shellfish are considered nonexcludable because anyone can basically attempt to harvest them. However, they are rival because once I harvest a lobster, you cannot harvest the same lobster. These common resources are often overharvested and create a problem called the "tragedy of the commons."

Day 83

After playing the game, you probably saw that there was a profit incentive to catch more fish than the other boats. Economists think that this happens to resources like fish in the ocean because there are no private property rights to the fish. If a person had a fishing pond on their own property, they wouldn't harvest all of the fish in one summer; they would want *their private fish* to multiply so that there were more fish next summer. However, in the open ocean, there are no property rights to the fish; they are common resources. If a person has a boat and their livelihood relies on income from the fish that are caught, they are going to catch as many as possible. Tragically, this spells extinction for the fish and also for the fishing industry.

Day 84

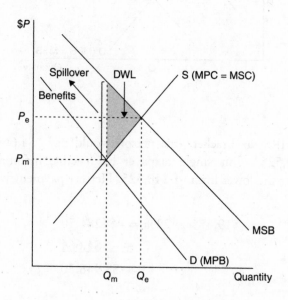

Day 85

Fernando is correct. Payton's apple orchard is surely benefiting from the positive externality that Quinton's bees provide. Fernando would call the pollination services that the bees provide the apple trees a spillover benefit. Payton receives this benefit but doesn't pay for it. When a positive externality exists in a market, that market will underproduce the product; it fails to produce the quantity where MSB = MSC, and deadweight loss exists. One way to remedy this underproduction is to subsidize either the consumption or the production of the good (bee hives in this case) that is providing these spillover benefits. If Payton were to send Quinton some cash (the subsidy), he could install more beehives. This would benefit his honey production, but it would also benefit Payton's apple production. The subsidy would move the market outcome closer to the socially efficient outcome and eliminate some or all of the deadweight loss.

Day 86

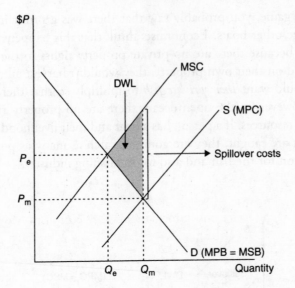

Day 87

According to the IRS tax bracket, this person would pay "$4,664 + 22% of the amount over $40,525." Our single taxpayer has taxable income of $60,000, so she is $19,475 over the lower limit of $40,525. Her tax payment would therefore be calculated as:

$$\$19,475 \times 22\% = \$4284.50$$
$$\underline{+ \quad \$4,664}$$
$$= \$8,948.50$$

Day 88

Of course, the results of this little environmental treasure hunt are going to differ. The point is that you have become a little more familiar and informed about the quality of your local environment.

Day 89

Since both consumers plan to spend $100 on clothing, each consumer would pay $7 in tax (7% of $100). As a fraction of weekly income, those $7 in sales tax are:

Eric: ($7/$1,000) × 100 = 0.70%

Melanie: ($7/$2,000) × 100 = 0.35%

So even though each person spends $7 in sales tax on $100 of clothing, those $7 are a larger share of Eric's income, making a sales tax a regressive tax.

Day 90

The historic distribution of income in the United States shows a clear trend toward a greater share of total income being earned by the top quintile and top 5%, and a decreased share by the lower quintiles. For example:

YEAR	LOWEST FIFTH	SECOND FIFTH	THIRD FIFTH	FOURTH FIFTH	HIGHEST FIFTH	TOP 5%
2015	3.1	8.2	14.3	23.2	51.1	22.1
1995	3.7	9.1	15.2	23.3	48.7	21.0
1985	3.9	9.8	16.2	24.4	45.6	17.6
1975	4.3	10.4	17.0	24.7	43.6	16.5

There are likely several explanations for this trend, and economists will disagree over which is the most important, but the income tax system has become less progressive over this time period. For example, the highest personal income tax bracket for a single person was taxed at 70% in 1967, and in 2021 that tax rate was 37%. Another possible explanation is that the economy has changed from a manufacturing and farming economy to a high-tech service and information-based economy. More and more jobs in the new economy require advanced degrees, and since education is positively correlated with income, those that receive more education are going to leave those that do not further and further behind.

Among the most highly developed nations, the United States has one of the highest Gini coefficients (.489), or one of the least equal income distributions. Our largest trading partner and closest neighbor, Canada, has a Gini closer to .333. When nations are ranked by the 2019 Human Development Index, the United States ranks seventeenth (HDI = 0.926), a strong showing.

5 Minutes to a 5

90 AP Macroeconomics Activities and Questions in

5 Minutes a Day

Check off each activity as it is completed.

1. ❑	24. ❑	47. ❑	70. ❑
2. ❑	25. ❑	48. ❑	71. ❑
3. ❑	26. ❑	49. ❑	72. ❑
4. ❑	27. ❑	50. ❑	73. ❑
5. ❑	28. ❑	51. ❑	74. ❑
6. ❑	29. ❑	52. ❑	75. ❑
7. ❑	30. ❑	53. ❑	76. ❑
8. ❑	31. ❑	54. ❑	77. ❑
9. ❑	32. ❑	55. ❑	78. ❑
10. ❑	33. ❑	56. ❑	79. ❑
11. ❑	34. ❑	57. ❑	80. ❑
12. ❑	35. ❑	58. ❑	81. ❑
13. ❑	36. ❑	59. ❑	82. ❑
14. ❑	37. ❑	60. ❑	83. ❑
15. ❑	38. ❑	61. ❑	84. ❑
16. ❑	39. ❑	62. ❑	85. ❑
17. ❑	40. ❑	63. ❑	86. ❑
18. ❑	41. ❑	64. ❑	87. ❑
19. ❑	42. ❑	65. ❑	88. ❑
20. ❑	43. ❑	66. ❑	89. ❑
21. ❑	44. ❑	67. ❑	90. ❑
22. ❑	45. ❑	68. ❑	
23. ❑	46. ❑	69. ❑	

CHAPTER 5 – USING THE FOUR ECONOMIC RESOURCES IN WRITING A RESEARCH PAPER

Suppose you are assigned a 10-page research paper on the Great Depression. List the four economic resources that you would use to complete the research assignment. Be as specific as possible.

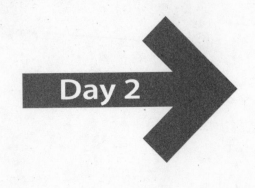

THE OPPORTUNITY COST OF GOING ON A DATE

You're going to go on a date with a significant other. What is the opportunity cost of this activity?

You will need to do a little research on all of the costs involved. First, determine what you plan to do on the date. For example, if you are going to go see a movie, you should search the cinema's website to investigate ticket prices. If you plan to go out to dinner, check out the restaurant's menu to estimate your share of the final bill, including tax and tip.

1. Figure out what you plan to do on your date.

2. Do you need to buy a ticket, food and drink, or anything else?

3. Will you require transportation? If you are using a car, estimate the amount of gasoline you will require and the local price of that gasoline.

4. Determine how much time, including the transportation time, you will need for the date. What is the value of your time as measured by an hourly wage you could receive if you had worked instead?

5. Use all of this information to determine the total opportunity cost of going on the date.

HOW MANY TACOS WILL YOU EAT?

Imagine a day when you've skipped lunch, and you're very hungry for dinner. You know a taco truck that sells tacos at $1 each. In this hypothetical situation, how many tacos do you think you would purchase and eat?

Now, with this number in mind, draw a graph of marginal benefit and marginal cost curves that shows your decision to stop buying tacos.

YOUR PRODUCTION POSSIBILITIES

Suppose that each day you have 16 waking hours to divide between studying (measured in pages read) and socializing (measured in text messages sent).

a. Assuming constant opportunity costs, draw your production possibility curve (PPC) with pages read on the *x*-axis and text messaging on the *y*-axis.

b. Now suppose your wireless Internet speed is cut in half, reducing the speed at which text messages are received and sent. Adjust your PPC from part (a).

c. How has the opportunity cost of studying changed? Can you explain *why* it has changed?

COMPARATIVE ADVANTAGE AROUND THE HOUSE

Let's say that there are two tasks that need to be performed around the house: folding clean towels in the laundry and washing dirty plates in the sink. The information below summarizes how many towels could be folded and how many plates could be washed by two kids in the household.

Hourly Output for Eli: 16 towels and 0 plates, or 0 towels and 8 plates

Hourly Output for Theodore: 6 towels and 0 plates, or 0 towels and 6 plates

a. Does either kid have an absolute advantage in these two tasks? How do you know?

b. If Eli and Theodore each split their time equally between folding towels and washing plates, what is their combined output in 1 hour?

c. If Eli and Theodore specialized their tasks based on comparative advantage, what is their combined output in 1 hour?

ALLOCATIVE EFFICIENCY, PRODUCTIVE EFFICIENCY, AND EQUITY

Suppose you were going to order a delivered pizza for yourself and three friends. When the pizza arrives, you will also determine how many slices (there are 16 in total) each person receives.

1. How would the pizza be baked if the pizza makers were productively efficient in the restaurant kitchen? Hint: it might be easier to think of a situation where the pizza was produced inefficiently.

2. How might the 16 slices be distributed if your goal was an equitable distribution?

3. Suppose your goal was an allocatively efficient distribution of the 16 slices. How might you change your equitable distribution from part 2 to reflect this new goal?

GROWTH

Imagine an economy that produces only two items: automobiles (representing the manufacturing sector) and wheat (representing the agricultural sector). For the sake of simplicity, we will assume that there are constant opportunity costs along the production possibility curve (PPC). Our initial PPC has been drawn as follows.

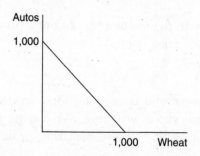

a. Adjust the PPC to reflect new technology that increases maximum automobile production by 25% but has no impact on wheat production. How does this affect the opportunity cost of wheat?

b. Adjust the PPC to reflect new seeds that produce drought-resistant wheat that increases maximum wheat production by 50% but has no impact on automobile production. How does this affect the opportunity cost of automobiles?

c. Adjust the PPC to reflect new technology that increases maximum automobile production by 50% and also increases maximum wheat production by 50%. How does this affect the opportunity cost of wheat?

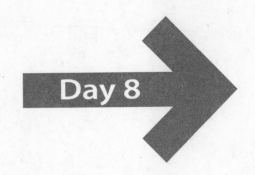

Day 8

ARE FREE THINGS REALLY FREE?

We often find ourselves enjoying some "free" leisure time by watching a TV show, texting with friends, or just reading. We do these things because they are enjoyable, but are they really free? Economists know that nothing is truly free, because there is always a second activity that was sacrificed to pursue the first activity.

In this exercise, we will try to figure out a way to put a price on both the enjoyment of an activity and the cost of pursuing it.

Measuring Benefit

Your task is to find someone who is enjoying some leisure. Maybe you can locate a family member or friend who is watching TV; playing a video game; texting or chatting on their phone; or reading a book, magazine, or newspaper.

Suppose you find someone watching a TV show. Your economic brain tells you that this person is choosing to watch TV because they believe the benefit exceeds the cost. How can we measure the benefit?

Measuring Cost

Let's return to our person watching TV. Ask them, "If our cable/satellite connection suddenly stopped, what would you do instead?" Make sure that the person provides you with their *next best* choice for the use of this time. How can we measure the cost of skipping that second-best activity?

HAVE YOU EXPERIENCED MORE PRODUCTIVITY?

The production possibilities curve can increase (shift to the right) if the resources become more productive. The same is true for an individual. Watch this short video from the Bureau of Labor Statistics, "What Is Productivity?":

http://www.bls.gov/lpc/

When you're done with the video, think about tasks that you now perform more quickly or better than when you first started doing those things. Are there things that you have learned to do around the house, or at school, that have made you more productive over time?

CHAPTER 6 – DEMAND DETERMINANTS (CURVE SHIFTERS)

Even though you are studying for a macroeconomics exam, it is critical that you have a solid grasp of the factors that shift demand curves to the left or to the right.

For each of the following, describe how the demand for coffee will be affected. Be sure to determine which, if any, of the demand shifters is at work.

a. The American Medical Association reports that drinking coffee will lower your risk of cancer, increase your IQ, and improve your love life.

b. The price of coffee increases.

c. The state of the economy is rapidly improving, and coffee is a normal good.

d. The price of energy drinks, another caffeinated beverage, is rising.

e. The price of coffee-making machines is increasing.

SUPPLY DETERMINANTS (SUPPLY SHIFTERS)

It is also very important that you have a solid grasp of the determinants of supply.

For each of the following, describe how the supply of oak tables will be affected. Be sure to determine which, if any, of the supply shifters is at work.

a. Producers have developed a faster way of constructing the oak tables.

b. The price of oak lumber has decreased.

c. A boom in the market for maple tables has increased the price that consumers are willing to pay for maple tables.

d. New manufacturers of oak tables have recently begun production and sale of oak tables.

e. The price of oak tables has fallen.

SHORTAGES AND SURPLUSES

The table below shows the quantity of Cheezbows that are demanded (Q_d) and supplied (Q_s) at several prices.

PRICE	Q_d	Q_s	
$10	15	30	
$9	18	28	
$8	21	26	
$7	24	24	
$6	27	22	
$5	30	20	
$4	33	18	
$3	36	16	
$2	39	14	
$1	42	12	

At each price, determine whether there exists a shortage or a surplus of Cheezbows, and calculate the size of the shortage or surplus.

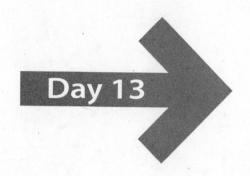

CHANGES TO MARKET EQUILIBRIUM 1

Suppose the competitive market for oranges is in equilibrium. Given the following scenarios, you must (1) identify the specific shifter that is happening, (2) state which direction a curve is shifting, and (3) predict changes to the equilibrium price and quantity of oranges.

Note: A diagram is not required to answer these questions, but might be useful to you.

a. All else equal, the cost of labor used in picking oranges has increased.

b. All else equal, the *New York Times* reports that eating oranges increases your life span.

c. All else equal, the price of pears has decreased.

d. All else equal, combine the effects of parts (a) and (b).

CHANGES TO MARKET EQUILIBRIUM 2

Suppose the competitive market for peanut butter is in equilibrium. Given the following scenarios, predict changes to the equilibrium price and quantity of peanut butter. Be sure to determine which of the market shifters is at work. A diagram is not required, but might be useful to you.

a. All else equal, the government places a per-unit tax on each jar of peanut butter produced.

b. All else equal, the price of strawberry jelly has decreased.

c. All else equal, the wholesale price of raw peanuts has decreased

d. All else equal, combine the events from parts (b) and (c).

CHANGES TO MARKET EQUILIBRIUM 3

Suppose the competitive market for coffee is in equilibrium. Given the following scenarios, predict changes to the equilibrium price and quantity of coffee. Be sure to determine which of the market shifters is at work. A diagram is not required, but might be useful to you.

a. All else equal, better farming methods have increased the harvest of coffee beans.

b. All else equal, the price of coffee-making machines has increased.

c. All else equal, the price of coffee is expected to rise next month.

d. All else equal, combine the events from parts (a) and (b).

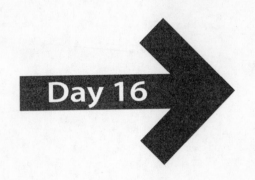

CHAPTER 7—GDP: WHAT IS INCLUDED, AND WHAT IS NOT? PART 1

It is 2020 in Theodoria, a nation that calculates Gross Domestic Product in ways identical to those used in the United States. Which of the following transactions would be part of the official calculations of Theodoria's GDP in 2020? Can you explain your reasoning?

a. Max purchases a pound of carrots grown on a Theodorian farm.

b. Eli buys a used couch at a yard sale.

c. Melanie pays Eliza, one of her students, cash for walking her dog.

d. Dodgerburger, a Theodorian fast-food franchise, opens several new restaurants across the nation.

GDP: WHAT IS INCLUDED, AND WHAT IS NOT? PART 2

It is 2020 in Theodoria, a nation that calculates Gross Domestic Product in ways identical to those used in the United States. Which of the following transactions would be part of the official calculations of Theodoria's GDP in 2020? Can you explain your reasoning?

a. The government-run Theodorian postal service buys new delivery trucks that are domestically produced.

b. Eric's Construction Company buys boxes of nails that will be used in building new homes.

c. Foxy buys gluten-free bread and buns that are produced in the neighboring nation of Maxyland.

d. Eli agrees to help Sissy with her geometry homework, if Sissy helps him study his French flash cards.

Day 18

CHAPTER 7 – LOCATING GROSS DOMESTIC PRODUCT DATA

Today you will need to do a little bit of searching on the Internet to find answers to the following:

- Can you find the government agency that calculates the GDP in the United States?
- Can you find annual data for real (also called "chained dollar") GDP for the five most recent years? Hint: Look for a downloadable Excel spreadsheet.
- Can you calculate the percentage change in real GDP between the most recent year available and the year prior to that year?

Day 19

VALUING PRODUCTION IN A SIMPLE ECONOMY

Suppose a very simple pizza-based economy produces only three items: pizza, breadsticks, and sodas. The following table shows the quantity of each item produced in the last two years and the prices that prevailed for those items. Complete the table by computing the value of the production of each item and the GDP in each year.

2014	QUANTITY	PRICE	VALUE OF PRODUCTION
Pizzas	200	$10	
Breadsticks	150	$2	
Sodas	400	$1	
Totals		N/A	
2015	**QUANTITY**	**PRICE**	**VALUE OF PRODUCTION**
Pizzas	300	$10	
Breadsticks	150	$2	
Sodas	300	$1	
Totals		N/A	

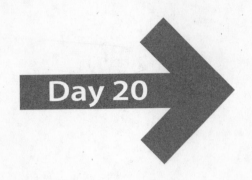

Day 20

A SIMPLE CIRCULAR FLOW DIAGRAM

The following is a very simple version of the circular flow diagram. In this economy there is no role for the government and there is no connection to foreign countries. Draw arrows that reflect the flow of resources (or factors of production), goods/services, and the payments for those factors and for those goods/services. Make sure your arrows are correctly labeled. Hint: There should be four arrows connecting the households and the firms.

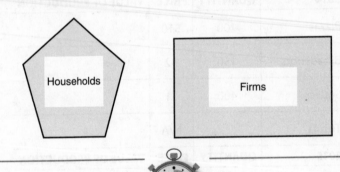

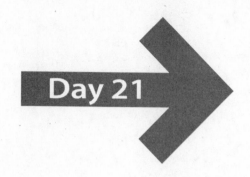
THE COMPONENTS OF GDP

If one were to compute GDP by adding up the four sectors of spending, you would have the familiar:

$$GDP = C + I + G + (X - M)$$

Your job is to go back to the government agency that collects GDP data and find each of these spending components for the most recent quarter. Hint: Look for a recent news release and links to a "Full Release and Tables" PDF file.

Make note of how large each of the four sectors is as a percentage of the total.

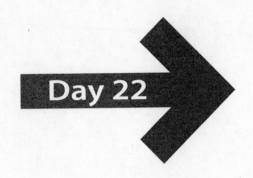

CREATING A HYPOTHETICAL PRICE INDEX

The most commonly used price index in the United States is the Consumer Price Index (CPI), but we can create a price index for anything. All we need are a few prices over a few time periods and a decision on what time period is going to be our base year. The price index in the current year is computed by:

$$100 \times \text{(Price in current year)/(Price in the base year)}$$

The following table provides some hypothetical prices for a hypothetical product, a Whizzling. Use this as practice in creating a price index, the WPI. Use 2012 as your base year and complete the table.

YEAR	PRICE	WPI
2011	$5	
2012	$10	
2013	$6	
2014	$8	
2015	$10	
2016	$12	

FIND THE CONSUMER PRICE INDEX

Today you will need to do a little bit more searching on the Internet to find answers to the following:

- Can you find the government agency that calculates the rate of inflation in the United States?
- Can you find monthly data for the Consumer Price Index (CPI-U) for a few recent years? Hint: Look for databases.
- Can you calculate the percentage change in the CPI-U between the most recent month available and the previous month? This is the monthly inflation rate.
- Can you find monthly data for the inflation rate for a few recent years? This is also available in a downloadable form.

DEFLATING NOMINAL VALUES TO REAL VALUES

If we want to track the monetary value of anything, including a nation's output over time, we need to fix the prices that we use to a base year and then measure nominal dollars in a given year by using the prices that existed in that base year. This process of adjusting nominal values into inflation-adjusted, or real, values is called "deflation."

To adjust a nominal value into a real value, we make the following computation:

Real value in a year = 100 × (Nominal value in that year)/(Price index in that year)

The following table shows a person's nominal salary over a period of a few years and the average monthly CPI that existed in those years. Looking at the nominal salaries, we see that this person appears to be earning more money in 2016 than in 2012. Use the CPI to adjust those nominal salary values into real values. The current base year for the CPI is 1984. Once this table is completed, we will be able to determine if this person's salary has *really* risen once inflation has been accounted for.

YEAR	NOMINAL SALARY	CPI (1984 = 100)	REAL SALARY
2011	$50,000	129.453	
2012	$52,500	131.976	
2013	$53,000	133.592	
2014	$55,000	135.524	
2015	$58,000	135.362	

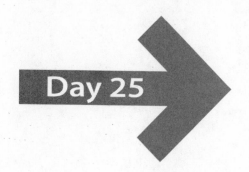

Day 25

WHO DATES THE BUSINESS CYCLE

You have learned that there is something called a business cycle that shows the expansion and contraction of economic activity over time. Do some more searching on the Internet to discover the organization that determines when expansions and recessions in the United States start and stop. Then find a list of recessions in the history of the U.S. economy. Look at the length of the most recent recession, and compare it to the average length of a recession in the years since 1945. What does this tell you about the most recent recession?

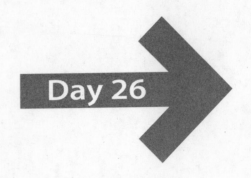

PERSONAL STORIES FROM THE GREAT RECESSION

The Great Recession of 2007–2009 was long in its duration and painful in its consequences. If you are in high school now, you might not recall many details about that time in U.S. history. Your task is to find someone who does have clear memories of that time. Ask a few people if they have any stories about the impact of the recession on their lives, on the lives of people that they know, or on the company in which they were employed at the time. Take a little time to learn about this Great Recession from the stories and anecdotes that these people have to share.

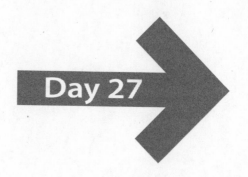

Day 27

INFLATION RATES OVER TIME

The Federal Reserve Bank of St. Louis has an excellent source of data called "FRED." Go to their website at:

https://fred.stlouisfed.org/

Search for "inflation, consumer prices for the United States." You should find at least one graph that shows inflation rates in the United States over a period of a few decades.

- What is the worst period of inflation in this period of time, and when did it occur?
- Looking at your graph, does it appear that inflation rates have become more erratic or more stable as the graph gets closer to the present day?
- Vertical bars in the graph show periods of recession. What usually happens to inflation rates during recessions? Why do you think that happens?

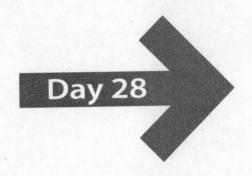

Day 28

CALCULATING UNEMPLOYMENT RATES

A country has the following labor statistics for the civilian population:

Population under 16 years old .... 2.5 million

Population over 16 years old who are working part time .... 4 million

Population over 16 years old who are working full time .... 14 million

Those without jobs and who are actively seeking jobs .... 2.5 million

Those without jobs and not actively seeking jobs .... 1.5 million

a. Calculate the size of the civilian labor force and the unemployment rate.

b. Suppose that one million of those who were without jobs but seeking work become "discouraged" and drop out of the labor force. Recalculate the unemployment rate. Why does this happen?

EMPLOYED, UNEMPLOYED, OR OUT OF THE LABOR FORCE?

Read the following document that the Bureau of Labor Statistics provides.

https://www.bls.gov/cps/cps_htgm.pdf

Once you think you have a good grasp of how the government classifies people as either employed, unemployed, or out of the labor force, see if you can correctly classify the following six people.

1. Theo is a 14-year-old student who mows lawns in the neighborhood on the weekends at $7 per hour.

2. Eli is a 23-year-old graduate student working on his Ph.D. in economics. He was offered a job six months ago, but decided he would rather focus on his courses and declined the offer.

3. Melanie is a 33-year-old college professor who has an annual salary of about $60,000.

4. Max is a 20-year-old college student who waits tables for 16 hours on the weekend and usually earns about $400 in tips.

5. Tommy used to work on the dock, but the union has been on strike, and he feels down on his luck. He doesn't know when the strike will end, so he's trying to find a job playing his six-string guitar, but so far he has not found any work.

6. Gina used to work in the diner all day, but she was recently fired. Since then, she has applied for several job openings and is waiting to hear whether she got the job or not. Until then, she dreams of running away.

UNEMPLOYMENT RATES OVER TIME

Once again it's time to consult the FRED to look at unemployment rates in the past. Search for something like "Civilian Unemployment Rate" and find a good graph over time.

- In the graph that you find, what is the highest unemployment rate, and in what year did it occur?
- Does the unemployment rate appear to be more erratic or more stable as the graph gets closer to the present day?
- Looking at the vertical gray bars that identify recessions, what happens to the unemployment rate during recessions? Why do you suppose that happens?

Day 31

THE DIFFERENT UNEMPLOYMENT RATES

The official unemployment rate reported by the U.S. Bureau of Labor Statistics (BLS) is referred to as "U-3" but there are other, more broadly defined, measures of unemployment and underemployment. Find the most recent Current Population Survey (CPS) report. This is the monthly report that summarizes the state of the labor market. Begin your search here:

https://www.bls.gov/cps/

When you find the most recent CPS report, go to the bottom for additional tables of data. Look for Table A-15 "Alternative Measures of Unemployment." Acquaint yourself with the measures of U-4, U-5, and U-6. Get a sense of what is meant by a "marginally attached worker" and a "discouraged worker." What do you think it means to be "employed part time for economic reasons," and why might it be important to track the number of people who fall into this category? You might dig around the BLS website and try to find definitions of these important labor force categories.

CHAPTER 8 – CONSUMPTION AND SAVINGS SCHEDULES

We have seen that consumption spending in the United States amounts to nearly 70% of GDP, so it is very important to have a grasp of how changes to consumption can greatly impact the economy. For now we will assume that there are no taxes or transfers in the economy, so household disposable income (DI) is equal to consumption spending (C) plus saving (S).

Suppose that Pam is a typical consumer. For every additional $1,000 of disposable income, Pam will consume $900 of it and save $100. If she had no income at all, she would still consume $100 by drawing down her accumulated savings by the same amount.

Complete the following table so that we have a complete schedule of her consumption and savings at several levels of disposable income.

DISPOSABLE INCOME (DI)	CONSUMPTION (C)	SAVINGS (S)
$0	$100	–$100
$1,000		
$2,000		
$3,000		
$4,000		
$5,000		
$6,000		

DERIVING A CONSUMPTION FUNCTION

We have already completed the consumption and saving schedules for Pam, our typical consumer. We will now introduce Pam's grandmother, Gram. Let's try to create an equation for Pam's consumption function, and then we'll do the same for Gram.

PAM			GRAM		
DISPOSABLE INCOME (DI)	**CONSUMPTION (C)**	**SAVING (S)**	**DISPOSABLE INCOME (DI)**	**CONSUMPTION (C)**	**SAVING (S)**
$0	$100	−$100	$0	$100	−$100
$1,000	$1,000	$0	$1,000	$700	$300
$2,000	$1,900	$100	$2,000	$1,300	$700
$3,000	$2,800	$200	$3,000	$1,900	$1,100
$4,000	$3,700	$300	$4,000	$2,500	$1,500
$5,000	$4,600	$400	$5,000	$3,100	$1,900
$6,000	$5,500	$500	$6,000	$3,700	$2,300

These functions are straight lines, and the equation of a line is typically described as: $y = mx + b$.

For the consumption function, we plot consumption on the vertical axis and disposable income on the horizontal axis.

With this information, derive the consumption equations for Pam and Gram.

DERIVING A SAVINGS FUNCTION

Once again here are the consumption and savings schedules for our consumers, Pam and Gram.

PAM			GRAM		
DISPOSABLE INCOME (DI)	**CONSUMPTION (C)**	**SAVING (S)**	**DISPOSABLE INCOME (DI)**	**CONSUMPTION (C)**	**SAVING (S)**
$0	$100	−$100	$0	$100	−$100
$1,000	$1,000	$0	$1,000	$700	$300
$2,000	$1,900	$100	$2,000	$1,300	$700
$3,000	$2,800	$200	$3,000	$1,900	$1,100
$4,000	$3,700	$300	$4,000	$2,500	$1,500
$5,000	$4,600	$400	$5,000	$3,100	$1,900
$6,000	$5,500	$500	$6,000	$3,700	$2,300

Use the same techniques for building a consumption function to build the savings functions.

For the savings function, we plot savings on the vertical axis and disposable income on the horizontal axis.

THE ROLE OF INVESTMENT

In the overall economy, consumption spending amounts to nearly 70% of all spending. While investment spending is a much smaller percentage of the total, it can be much more volatile and critical to shaping the business cycle.

Return to the FRED website for the St. Louis Federal Reserve:

https://fred.stlouisfed.org/

Search for "real gross private domestic investment," and see what you can find. Once you find a good graph of this important component of spending, try to identify any long-term trends. Now look more closely at the vertical gray bars that identify recessions. Do you notice anything about changes in investment around those recessions? What about the *timing* of change in investment?

THE MARKET FOR LOANABLE FUNDS 1

In a correctly labeled graph of the loanable funds market, show how a general feeling of business optimism would affect the market and the equilibrium real interest rate.

THE MARKET FOR LOANABLE FUNDS 2

In a correctly labeled graph of the American loanable funds market, show how the market would change if foreign households and firms decided to put their money in American banks, rather than their own domestic banks. Show how this will affect the equilibrium real interest rate.

THE SPENDING MULTIPLIER

We will assume that people spend 90% of all income and save the rest. Complete the following table. To get you started, the first two rounds have been completed. In round one, Person A takes $1,000 out from under her mattress and spends it at person B's store. In round 2, person B has spent $900 at person C's business. After 12 rounds have been completed, add up the total spending generated by the initial $1,000.

TRANSACTION	SPENDING	SAVING
A to B	$1,000	N/A
B to C	$900	$100
C to D		
D to E		
E to F		
F to G		
G to H		
H to I		
I to J		
J to K		
K to L		
L to M		
Totals =		

A TABLE FULL OF SPENDING MULTIPLIERS

The size of the simple spending multiplier (*M*) is directly related to the marginal propensity to consume (*MPC*) and inversely related to the marginal propensity to save (*MPS*).

$$M = \frac{1}{(1 - MPC)} = \frac{1}{MPS}$$

Complete the table below to see how this works.

MPC	MPS	M
1.00	0.00	
0.90	0.10	
0.80	0.20	
0.75	0.25	
0.67	0.33	
0.60	0.40	
0.50	0.50	
0.40	0.60	
0.33	0.67	
0.20	0.80	
0.10	0.90	
0.00	1.00	

SOME MULTIPLIER SCENARIOS

For each of the following four scenarios, use the spending multiplier (M) to estimate the eventual impact on GDP in the economy.

- A nation with an $MPC = 0.80$ experiences an increase in autonomous investment spending of $10 billion.
- A nation with an $MPC = 0.75$ experiences a decrease in autonomous net exports of $6.5 billion.
- A nation with an $MPC = 0.50$ experiences an increase in autonomous government spending of $15 billion.
- A nation with an $MPC = 0.90$ experiences a decrease in autonomous consumption spending of $5 billion.

THE TAX MULTIPLIER

Suppose the government has sent person A $1,000 in tax rebates. We assume that people spend 90% of all income and save the rest. Complete the following table. To get you started, the first two rounds have been completed. In round 1, person A takes her $1,000 tax rebate and spends $900 at person B's store. In round 2, person B has spent $810 at person C's business. After 12 rounds have been completed, add up the total spending generated by the initial $1,000 tax rebate.

TRANSACTION	SPENDING	SAVING
A to B	$900	$100
B to C	$810	$90
C to D		
D to E		
E to F		
F to G		
G to H		
H to I		
I to J		
J to K		
K to L		
L to M		
Totals =		

5 Minutes to a 5

A TABLE FULL OF TAX MULTIPLIERS

The size of the tax multiplier (T_m) is directly related to the marginal propensity to consume (MPC) and inversely related to the marginal propensity to save (MPS). There are a couple of different ways to compute the tax multiplier, but it will always be smaller than the spending multiplier (M).

$$T_m = (MPC) \times \frac{1}{(1 - MPC)} = \frac{MPC}{MPS} = MPC \times M$$

Complete the table below to see how this works.

MPC	MPS	M	T_M
1	0	∞	
0.90	0.10	10	
0.80	0.20	5	
0.75	0.25	4	
0.67	0.33	3	
0.60	0.40	2.5	
0.50	0.50	2	
0.40	0.60	1.67	
0.33	0.67	1.5	
0.20	0.80	1.25	
0.10	0.90	1.11	
0	1	1	

SOME TAX MULTIPLIER SCENARIOS

For each of the following four scenarios, use the tax multiplier (T_m) to estimate the eventual impact on GDP in the economy.

- A nation with an $MPC = 0.80$ experiences an increase in transfer payments of $10 billion.
- A nation with an $MPC = 0.75$ experiences a decrease in taxes of $6.5 billion.
- A nation with an $MPC = 0.50$ experiences an increase in taxes of $15 billion.
- A nation with an $MPC = 0.90$ experiences a decrease in transfer payments of $5 billion.

BALANCED BUDGET MULTIPLIER

The nation of Theodorea has a marginal propensity to consume of 0.75. The government wishes to spend $3 billion on some new infrastructure, but legislators insist that taxes be increased by $3 billion to pay for the projects.

a. Use the spending multiplier to compute how much GDP will change due to the increased government spending.

b. Use the tax multiplier to compute how much GDP will change due to the increased taxes.

c. Based on your results, what is the eventual impact of this balanced-budget project on the Theodorean economy?

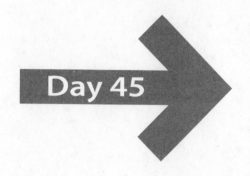

CHAPTER 9 – THE AD CURVE

Without looking at your text or class notes, can you explain why the AD curve is downward sloping from these three effects?

- Foreign sector substitution effect
- Interest rate effect
- Wealth effect

CHANGES IN THE AD CURVE

For each of the following, determine how the AD curve will increase or decrease. What component(s) of AD is changing?

a. Households are pessimistic about the state of the economy and their immediate job security.

b. Interest rates are at historically low levels.

c. The government has passed legislation that increases military spending.

d. Large economies in Asia are experiencing recessions.

Day 47

MORE CHANGES IN THE AD CURVE

Once again, for each of the following, determine how the AD curve will increase or decrease. What component(s) of AD is changing?

a. Firms are becoming more optimistic about the profitability of expansion projects.

b. The stock market is growing and households have experienced increased wealth.

c. The government has decided to increase taxes on household income.

d. Products made in the domestic economy are becoming more popular for foreign consumers.

THE SHAPE OF THE SHORT-RUN AS CURVE

The SRAS is usually drawn with an upward slope. Without looking at your textbook or notes, can you explain why?

SHIFTS IN THE SRAS CURVE

For each of the following, determine how the SRAS curve will increase or decrease.

a. A new tax system is legislated that offers tax rebates on new research and development.

b. The economy is experiencing widespread increases in input prices.

c. Unnecessary and redundant business regulation is removed.

d. A nation is hit with a crippling drought and water shortages that require enormous sacrifice.

DRAWING A RECESSIONARY GAP

Use a graph of the AD/AS model to show a recessionary gap. In your graph, make sure that you distinguish between the SRAS and LRAS curves. Label current price level as PL_r, current output as GDP_r and full-employment output as GDP_f.

DRAWING AN INFLATIONARY GAP

Use a graph of the AD/AS model to show an inflationary gap. In your graph, make sure that you distinguish between the SRAS and LRAS curves. Label current price level as PL_i, current output as GDP_i, and full-employment output as GDP_f.

PREDICTING CHANGES IN REAL GDP AND THE PRICE LEVEL

Assume the economy is operating at full employment. In each of the following, predict the impact on AD or SRAS and how the event will likely change the price level and real GDP.

a. Firms are less optimistic about future profitability.

b. Foreign consumers are experiencing higher household incomes.

c. Household wealth is increasing due to a strong real estate market.

d. Input prices are steadily rising.

e. The government has created tax incentives designed to increase productivity.

5 Minutes to a 5

HISTORICAL DIFFERENCES BETWEEN REAL GDP AND POTENTIAL GDP

Find the following graph at the FRED website:

https://fred.stlouisfed.org/series/GDPPOT

This graph shows the real potential GDP in the United States since the late 1940s. We want to compare potential real GDP to actual real GDP. At the top right of the window, select "Edit Graph" and then select "Add Line." Now type something like "real GDP," and you should get several options. Make sure you choose actual dollars, not the percentage change in real GDP. Once you have found it, select "Add Data Series" and now your graph should have two lines on it.

Try zooming in on a recession from U.S. economic history (vertical gray bars). What do you notice about your graph during those times? Are there times when actual real GDP was above potential? Are there times when real GDP was below potential but the economy was not in a recession?

DRAWING THE PHILLIPS CURVE

Suppose that the full employment in the economy occurs at 5% unemployment and 2.5% inflation. This is also called the NAIRU, or "non-accelerating inflation rate of unemployment." In a correctly labeled graph, draw the long-run and short-run Phillips curves that reflect this information.

Now suppose that the actual unemployment rate rises to 6% and the inflation rate falls to 2%. Show this in the graph as point *U*. In the AD/AS model, what would explain a movement to point U?

BILL PHILLIPS' MONIAC

Originally built in 1949 by New Zealand economist Dr. Bill Phillips, the MONIAC (Monetary National Income Analogue Computer) is one of the coolest models of the macroeconomy you will ever see. Powered by water, this device shows the circulation of money through the economy and how policy changes (like monetary policy) can affect all aspects of the economy. Take a look at some of the Reserve Bank of New Zealand's explanatory video, then investigate the virtual MONIAC, and you'll be impressed by the ingenuity of this device and you'll have another insight into the complexity of the circular flow model in the real world.

https://www.youtube.com/watch?v=gkNaZJmii28

https://www.rbnz.govt.nz/research-and-publications/videos/making-money-flow-the-moniac

CHAPTER 10 – FISCAL POLICY PRESCRIPTION

You are the lead economist for the president, and you know that the economy is currently in the situation depicted by the following graph. What are the fiscal policy options that you might prescribe to the president? How would these policies alter the graph? Are there any downsides to your policies?

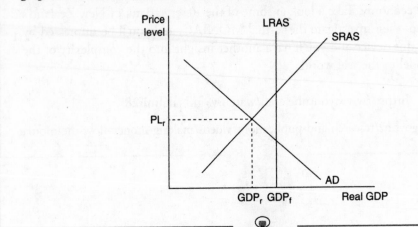

MORE FISCAL POLICY PRESCRIPTIONS

You are the lead economist for the president, and you know that the economy is currently in the situation depicted by the following graph. What are the fiscal policy options that you might prescribe to the president? How would these policies alter the graph? Are there any downsides to your policies?

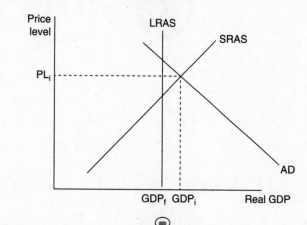

WHAT IS CROWDING OUT?

One criticism of expansionary fiscal policy is that it can lead to "crowding out." Without looking at your textbook or notes, can you explain what this means?

CROWDING OUT IN THE LOANABLE FUNDS MARKET

Suppose the government has a balanced budget when the economy enters a recession. To combat the recession with fiscal policy, the government cuts taxes and increases spending. The resulting deficit requires the government to borrow by issuing Treasury bonds.

In a correctly labeled graph, show the following:

- Initial equilibrium interest rate r_1 and quantity of loanable funds F_1
- The impact that borrowing has on the market (we can assume that borrowing is included in the demand side of the market)
- The new equilibrium interest rate r_2 and quantity of loanable funds F_2
- The new quantity of private investment PF_1 and the quantity of government borrowing B

NATIONAL DEBT AS A SHARE OF THE ECONOMY

The U.S. national debt has grown quite a bit since the 1940s, but then again so has the size of the overall economy. One of the better measures of how much debt the nation has accumulated is to measure it as a percentage of the GDP in that year. Go back to the St. Louis FRED and search for such a graph. Make note of any trends that you see.

https://fred.stlouisfed.org/series/FYFSGDA188S

Day 61

MORE CROWDING OUT

Another type of crowding out due to government borrowing centers on net exports.
Without looking at your textbook or notes, can you explain this "net export effect"?

A HANDS-OFF CLASSICAL APPROACH TO RECESSIONS

The following graph shows a short-run equilibrium with a recessionary gap. Rather than use fiscal policy to try to return the economy to full employment GDP, describe the "Classical" adjustment to long-run equilibrium. Adjust the graph accordingly.

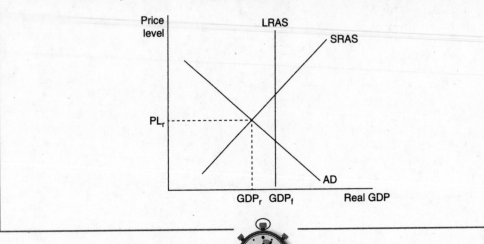

A HANDS-OFF CLASSICAL APPROACH TO INFLATION

The following graph shows a short-run equilibrium with an inflationary gap. Rather than use fiscal policy to try to return the economy to full employment GDP, describe the "Classical" adjustment to long-run equilibrium. Adjust the graph accordingly.

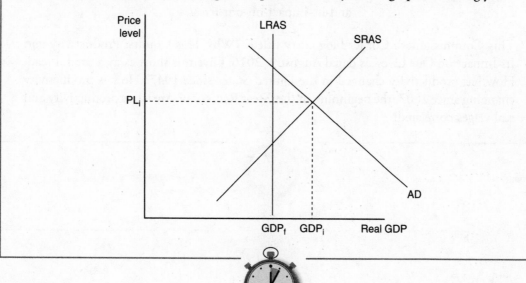

MORE GROWTH AND PRODUCTIVITY

Economic growth can be represented by an outward shift in a nation's production possibility curve. In an earlier activity you watched a video about productivity from the BLS website. Head back to the BLS website and access this archived blog entry:

https://blogs.bls.gov/blog/2016/08/09/why-this-counts-productivity-
and-its-impact-on-our-lives/

This Commissioner's Corner blog entry titled, "Why This Counts: Productivity and Its Impact on Our Lives" is dated August 9, 2016. Give this short essay a careful read. How has productivity changed in the United States since 1947? How is productivity changing since 2007, the beginning of the Great Recession? Are labor productivity and real wages correlated?

CHANGES IN HUMAN CAPITAL

An important factor in greater labor productivity is higher levels of education. The percentage of a nation that has completed a certain level of education is called educational attainment, and this data is collected by the Census Bureau. The following report describes how educational attainment has changed in the United States over time, and how it differs for men and women and whites and non-whites:

https://www.census.gov/library/publications/2016/demo/p20-578.html

After reading the document, describe how educational attainment has changed since the 1940s. Can you summarize differences between men and women, and between whites and non-whites?

SHOWING ECONOMIC GROWTH IN THE AD/AS MODEL

We have seen that economic growth can be shown as an outward shift of the PPC, but how is economic growth shown in the AD/AS model? The following is a graph that shows the economy in long-run equilibrium. Adjust the graph to show long-run growth, perhaps due to policies that encourage productivity gains of all kinds.

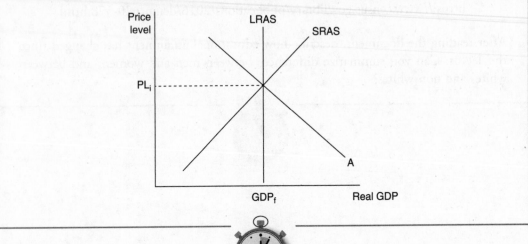

5 Minutes to a 5

WHAT WE CAN LEARN FROM BABYSITTING CO-OPS AND POW CAMPS

Watch this video in which economist Tim Harford describes two situations that fostered a different type of money and how each system slipped into a recession. He also compares the two recessions and how the "government" in each case could, or could not, act to fix the recessions.

https://www.youtube.com/watch?v=AOljR_tKlBk

Do you see the active role of government stimulus in the babysitting co-op story? How does it relate to the fiscal policy tools that you have learned?

What does Dr. Harford mean when he describes the POW camp as being hit by a recessionary "shock"? How is this different from the babysitting co-op recession?

CHAPTER 11 – STOCKS VS. BONDS

A firm can use stocks and/or bonds as ways of raising money. These are both forms of financial assets for those that possess them. Without looking at your textbook or your notes, can you describe the difference between a stock and a bond?

Day 69

HISTORY OF MONEY

The paper currency and coins (a.k.a. fiat money) that you might have nearby is the result of thousands of years of experimentation with different forms of money. Here are links to a couple of amusing short videos about the history of money. Once you have watched them, can you explain why we use money rather than barter to acquire the goods and services we desire? And how does our current fiat money satisfy the three functions of money better than eggs would?

https://www.youtube.com/watch?v=ADaY6THQp3Y

https://www.youtube.com/watch?v=AjTwcQYgISA

SOME TIME VALUE OF MONEY CALCULATIONS

Let's get out the calculators and work on some problems.

a. You are borrowing $50 from a friend and promise to repay her in 1 year. If you agree to a 4% interest rate, how much will you return to your friend 1 year from today?

b. Your grandpa agrees to send you $100 in a year. If the interest rate you can receive in a bank is 5%, what is the present value of Grandpa's promised gift?

c. You have won a raffle that promises to pay you $5,000 in two years or you can take $4,500 now. Banks are paying 10% interest rates today. Which of these two offers should you accept?

THE MONEY SUPPLY

How much money is out there in circulation? The measure $M1$ is the basis for counting up all of the money circulating. Return to the St. Louis FRED website and search for "$M1$ Money Stock." Do you see any trends in $M1$? What might explain any trends?

https://fred.stlouisfed.org/

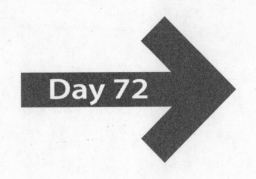

MULTIPLE DEPOSIT MONEY CREATION

The system of fractional reserve banking has been around for a long time and allows for new deposits to multiply and expand the money supply. It is also fundamental to the success of any monetary policy. Let's see how this works with a simple example. Assume that the bank is required to keep 10% of all checking deposits in reserve and lends out the rest. Borrowers immediately deposit all of their borrowed cash into their own checking accounts.

Keep track of all new checking deposits in the following table. We begin with person A taking $1,000 from his sock drawer and depositing it into the First Bank of Madville (FBM). The FBM holds $100 of his deposit in reserve and lends $900 to person B, who deposits the money into her checking account. These first two rounds are done for you. The arrow shows you the connection between a new loan and a new checking deposit. Stop with the deposit in round 7.

ROUND	DEPOSIT	CASH IN RESERVE	A LOAN IS MADE
1	$1,000 from person A	$100	$900 to person B
2	$900 from person B	$90	$810 to person C
3			
4			
5			
6			
7			
	Total = $		Total = $

THE MONEY DEMAND CURVE

Without looking at your textbook or your class notes, can you explain why the demand for money is drawn downward sloping?

THE RELATIONSHIP BETWEEN BOND PRICES AND INTEREST RATES

Remember a bond is like an IOU, or a promise that the issuer makes to repay the purchaser, plus interest. There is an inverse relationship between the price of a bond and the interest rate bondholders receive at maturity. Let's try to figure out how this works.

Suppose you buy a Treasury bond for $900 and you are promised repayment of $1,000 when it matures. What is the interest rate on this bond?

Now suppose that the demand for bonds rises and the same bond is now selling for a price of $950, with the same repayment of $1,000 upon maturity. What is the interest rate now?

Why would the demand for bonds increase in the first place? Can you speculate a couple of reasons why this might happen?

A SHIFT IN MONEY DEMAND

In a correctly labeled graph of the money market, show the current equilibrium nominal interest rate. Suppose the economy gets some momentum and nominal GDP is rising this year. Adjust your graph to reflect this change. How does this affect the nominal interest rate?

THE MONEY MULTIPLIER

Historically, the Federal Reserve set the reserve requirement (*rr*) for banks in the United States. This is the minimum fraction of checking deposits that must be kept on reserve in the bank. We have seen how a deposit can create even more new money within the fractional banking system. This money multiplier effect is critically dependent on the reserve requirement:

$$M = 1/rr$$

Complete the table with several different values of *rr*.

RESERVE REQUIREMENT (RR)	MONEY MULTIPLIER
0.01	
0.05	
0.10	
0.20	
0.25	
0.50	

5 Minutes to a 5

THE TRADITIONAL TOOLS OF THE FED

Without looking at your textbook or class notes, can you list the three traditional tools of the Federal Reserve in conducting monetary policy? How would each be changed if the Fed wanted to increase the money supply?

MONETARY POLICY 1

Economic indicators have told you, an economist at the central bank, that real GDP has significantly slipped below potential GDP and that the unemployment rate has been rising for several months in a row. If you were to propose an OMO to the chair, what would it be? In a graph of the money market, show how your proposal would affect interest rates. In an AD/AS graph of the economy, show how your proposal should affect the economy.

Day 79

MONETARY POLICY 2

Economic indicators have told you, an economist at the central bank, that real GDP has significantly increased above potential GDP and that the unemployment rate has fallen below the NAIRU. While this might appear to be good news, the inflation rate has steadily been increasing to unacceptable levels. If you were to propose an OMO to the Chair, what would it be? In a graph of the money market, show how your proposal would affect interest rates. In an AD/AS graph of the economy, show how your proposal should affect the economy.

MONETARY POLICY IN THE GREAT RECESSION

You have learned that the Fed should expand the money supply and lower interest rates to stimulate the economy in a recession. But what happens when a *really big* recession hits? The following link is to an essay that describes the Fed's reaction to the Great Recession of 2007–2009. One of the difficulties that the Fed faced is what is known as a "liquidity trap." Do a little background reading, maybe from your textbook, on what is meant by a liquidity trap. Try to find mention of this problem in the Fed's essay. When faced with the liquidity trap, what other measures did the Fed pursue during this very challenging time for the U.S. economy?

https://www.federalreservehistory.org/essays/great-recession-of-200709

A good video describing the financial aspects of the Great Recession can be found here:

https://www.youtube.com/watch?v=dI6HNi5I8d4

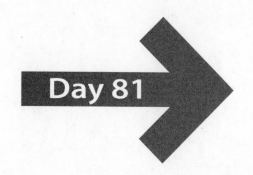

KEYNES VS. HAYEK

The macroeconomic debate surrounding fiscal and monetary policy is whether or not each is actually useful, and if not, whether it should be abandoned. The proactive approach, where the government has a strong hand in steering the economy, has come to be called the Keynesian approach after John Maynard Keynes. The Keynesians believe that a stagnant economy needs to be boosted by government spending or lower interest rates from Fed action. They think that the economy will take too long to self-correct, thus creating a lot of long-term pain.

The alternative to an active government role is no role at all; let the economy come to long-run equilibrium without interference. This belief is strongly cemented in the philosophy of F. A. Hayek, a strong champion of how unfettered markets can cure economic downturns and that expansionary monetary policy (and the low interest rates that accompany it) will only lead to inflation.

For an entertaining take on these competing philosophies, watch this video and see if you can find some logical points in each of the arguments:

https://www.youtube.com/watch?v=d0nERTFo-Sk

https://www.youtube.com/watch?v=GTQnarzmTOc

CHAPTER 12 – COMPARATIVE ADVANTAGE AND TRADE

These two countries are producing textiles and wheat using equal amounts of resources. Use the following table to answer the following questions.

	COUNTRY A		COUNTRY B	
Bushels of wheat	15	0	10	0
Units of textiles	0	60	0	60

a. Which nation has comparative advantage in wheat production, and which nation has comparative advantage in textile production? Show your work.

b. If trade is done based on comparative advantage and specialization, create a specific trade agreement that would allow both nations to consume beyond their production possibility curves.

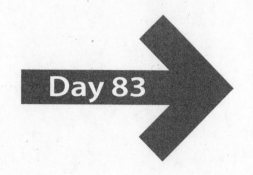

DEMAND FOR THE U.S. DOLLAR

For each of the following scenarios, determine if the European demand for the dollar would increase or decrease, and explain your reasoning.

a. Interest rates in the United States are lower than in Europe.

b. Products made in the United States are more popular among European consumers.

c. European nations are experiencing a significant recession.

d. The price level in the United States is very stable, while European price levels are rapidly rising.

CONNECTING MONETARY POLICY TO FOREIGN EXCHANGE

Suppose the U.S. economy is experiencing a recession.

a. How will the Fed use an open market operation to combat the recession, and how will this action affect interest rates in the U.S. economy?

b. How will the Fed's action affect the value of the U.S. dollar and net exports in the United States? Explain.

A HOTEL ROOM ABROAD

Search the Internet for a hotel room in the European Union (EU), and find the price of a room in euros. Hint: You might have to go directly to the hotel's website (rather than Travelocity) to get the prices in euros. Now go to a website like the one that follows, and find the exchange rate between the U.S. dollar and the euro. Find how many dollars it costs to buy one euro. Now use this exchange rate to determine how many dollars it would cost you to book that hotel room. Use the same currency exchange website to determine the exchange rate a year ago; then use it to compute the price of that room one year ago. If you were to take a vacation to Europe now, would it be more or less expensive than it was a year ago?

http://www.xe.com/

Day 86

GRAPHING THE CURRENCY MARKET

Create a correctly labeled graph of the market for the euro, priced in U.S. dollars. If interest rates in the European Union were higher than they were in the United States, how would the market for the euro be affected? Add this to your graph and show whether the euro would appreciate or depreciate against the dollar.

THE OTHER SIDE OF THE PREVIOUS MARKET

In the previous exercise, we were looking at what happened to the market for the euro, but something was also happening in the market for the U.S. dollar. Can you draw the changes in the market for the dollar? The dollar is priced in euros.

Day 88

THE BENEFITS OF INTERNATIONAL TRADE

Watch the following video that describes how international trade has benefited the U.S. economy in many quantitative ways.

https://www.youtube.com/watch?v=uuYuYax04Vk

There is a lot of data presented here. See if you can extract some of the important conclusions about how more trade is associated with a stronger U.S. economy.

THE U.S. BALANCE OF PAYMENTS

Go to the Bureau of Economic Analysis at the following website, and find the most current news release of the "International Transactions."

https://www.bea.gov/

One important part of the balance of payments is the current account. The current account describes the flow of exports and imports of goods and services, and income payments to and from the United States. The current account is where we find whether a nation had a trade surplus (exports exceed imports) or a trade deficit (imports exceed exports). Take a look at the news release; there should also be summary tables near the end. Did the United States have a trade surplus or a deficit? How big was it?

ANOTHER GAINS FROM TRADE EXERCISE

Take a look at the following PPCs for two nations, Theodoria and Elijastan. Based on only these two graphs, determine how these two nations could specialize and gain from trade. You will need to determine which nation exports steel and which nation exports food. Finally, find acceptable terms of trade that would benefit both nations.

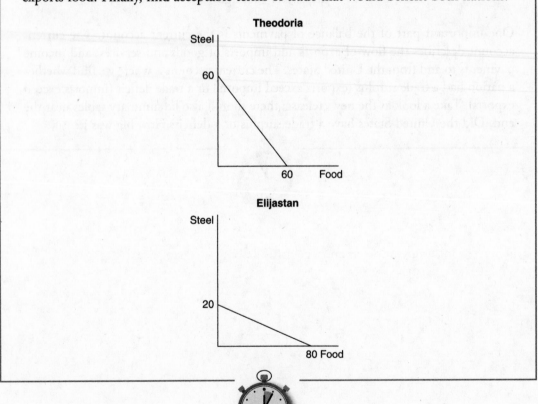

Answers

Day 1

1. Labor: Your efforts in doing the research and typing the paper

2. Capital: The library or Internet site in which you found research; the computer on which you typed the paper

3. Natural resources: The electricity used to operate the computer and printer; the paper on which you printed the research paper

4. Entrepreneurial ability: Your know-how and creativity in bringing all of the other resources together to create a high-quality final product

Day 2

Note: The following numbers are hypothetical but give you an idea of how to compute *your actual* opportunity cost.

1. I selected a movie and a pizza, and I would offer to pay for the entire date. The local price of a movie ticket is $10 and a pizza for two people is $15.

2. I will buy two drinks during the movie, and this will cost about another $6.

3. The nearest cinema is 6 miles away, the pizza place is another 1 mile away, and my date lives ½ mile from my house, so I would drive 15 total miles. My car gets about 30 miles per gallon, so I would use ½ gallon of gas. Local prices are about $2.50 per gallon so my driving costs are about $1.25.

4. The movie lasts 122 minutes, eating a pizza takes another 60 minutes, and the drive is estimated to be 15 minutes each way, for a total of 212 minutes, or 3.53 hours. If I could make a wage of $10 per hour, I could have earned $35.33 (ignoring taxes) during the movie.

5. Total opportunity cost of this movie = ($10 × 2) + $15 + $6 + $1.25 + $35.33 = $77.58.

Day 3

Since each taco costs $1, the marginal cost curve should be drawn horizontal at $1. The marginal benefit curve is drawn downward sloping because the next taco provides less additional benefit. After all, your hunger is partially satisfied with each taco, so the next taco isn't quite as great as the one that came before.

So if your hypothetical number of tacos was 5, the graph should look something like this:

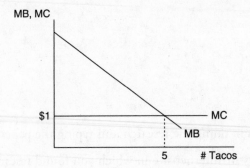

Day 4

a. A PPC with constant opportunity costs should be drawn as a straight line.

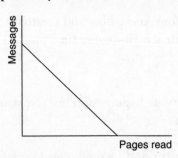

b. Since the Internet speed is cut in half, the PPC should move inward along the *y*-axis but not along the *x*-axis.

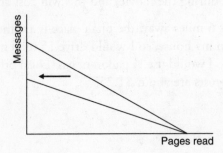

c. The opportunity cost of studying has now decreased. Remember that the opportunity cost of an activity, studying in this case, is what you have given up to engage in that activity. Now that your Internet speed has been cut in half, every hour spent studying comes at a smaller sacrifice in the number of messages you could have been sending and reading.

Day 5

a. Yes. Eli has an absolute advantage in both tasks because he can outproduce Theodore in both folding towels and washing plates.

b. If Eli splits his time equally, he can fold 8 towels and wash 4 plates.

If Theodore does the same, he can fold 3 towels and wash 3 plates.

Total output: 11 towels + 7 plates = 18.

c. A person is said to have a comparative advantage in a task if they can perform that task at a lower opportunity cost.

For every plate that Eli washes, he gives up 2 towels folded, so that is his opportunity cost of washing plates. On the other hand, for every towel that he folds, he gives up washing half of a plate.

For every plate that Theodore washes, he gives up 1 towel folded. And for every towel he folds, he gives up 1 washed plate.

So we can see that Theodore has a lower opportunity cost of washing plates (1 towel) when compared to Eli's opportunity cost of washing plates (2 towels). Theodore has a comparative advantage in washing plates. On the other hand, Eli has the comparative advantage in folding towels because he gives up ½ washed plate while Theodore gives up 1 washed plate.

If they specialize based on comparative advantage, Eli should spend all of his time folding towels, and Theodore should spend all of his time washing plates.

Total output with specialization: 16 towels + 6 plates = 22.

Day 6

1. Productive efficiency is achieved when you produce the maximum amount of output for a given level of technology and resources. If the pizza makers were inefficient in the kitchen, they might use the correct quantity of ingredients, but only a smaller pizza with eight slices. Another way of being productively inefficient would be to produce a perfectly sized (and tasty) pizza, but waste some of the ingredients in the process (like dropping a handful of cheese on the floor or spilling some sauce).

2. Most people, if equity was the goal, would give each person four slices. Of course this outcome depends on how you define "equitable." Rather than this egalitarian outcome, another might define equitable by giving the most slices to the person with the highest GPA or other arbitrary measure of merit. This is similar to saying that the highest wages should be paid to those who are most productive.

3. Allocative efficiency would be achieved if the slices were distributed to maximize the happiness of the four people eating them. One way to do this would be to give the most slices to the person who most desired them (or was the hungriest) and the fewest slices to the person who had the least desire for pizza. Alternatively, you could give each person four slices and then allow them to trade slices among themselves. When there are no more trades to be made, it's likely you have found an efficient allocation.

Day 7

a.

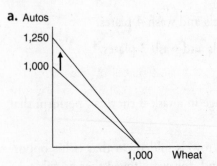

A 25% increase in maximum automobile production moves the vertical intercept up to 1,250 autos. Remember that the slope of the PPC gives us the opportunity cost of wheat. Prior to the technology, 1 unit of wheat costs 1 automobile, but now 1 unit of wheat costs 1.25 automobiles. Because automobile-producing technology has improved, devoting resources to wheat costs society more automobiles that could have been produced.

b.

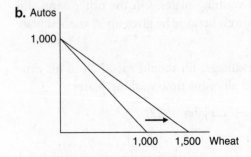

A 50% increase in maximum wheat production moves the horizontal intercept out to 1,500 units of wheat. Remember that the inverse of the slope of the PPC gives us the opportunity costs of automobiles. Prior to the drought-resistant seeds, 1 automobile costs 1 unit of wheat, but now 1 automobile costs 1.5 units of wheat. Because of the improved wheat production, devoting resources to automobiles costs society more units of wheat that could have been produced.

c.

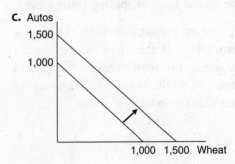

Better technology has improved production of both goods by the same degree. The new opportunity cost of wheat is still 1 auto, and the opportunity cost of 1 auto is still 1 unit of wheat.

Day 8

To measure the benefit of an activity that has no price tag, economists can try to create a hypothetical auction.

Ask this person, "How much money would I need to pay you to stop watching TV and forgo the enjoyment (utility) you are receiving from it? Would you take $1, $5, $10?" Keep increasing the bid until this person accepts a hypothetical compensation to give up doing something they enjoy: watching TV. Once you reach this number, you know how much economic value (money) this person places on watching TV. After all, if the person would accept $20 to turn off the TV, watching the TV must be worth $20 to them.

We can do a similar exercise to try to measure the opportunity cost of not doing a second-best use of our time. You have asked a person to tell you what they would be doing if the TV signal suddenly ended and they could not watch TV during this time. Of course, this person could give you any of dozens of possible activities, but suppose the person tells you that they would be playing a game on their smartphone. Now ask this person, "If you were playing a game on your smartphone, how much money would I need to pay you to stop?" Begin the auction at $1 and gradually raise the hypothetical price until the person accepts a value that would compensate for turning off the game.

If the person would need to be paid $10 to turn off the game, this is the value the person places on playing the game. Because the person is watching TV at the moment, and not playing the game, then missing the game means the person is sacrificing $10 of potential enjoyment. This is the opportunity cost of watching TV.

If your friends or family members are acting like economists predict, the dollar value they give you for the benefit of watching TV should exceed the dollar value they give you for giving up the second-best activity. If they do not, it opens the door for an interesting conversation about why they would choose to watch TV if the costs exceed the benefit.

Day 9

In the video, Beth sees an increase in her productivity when she learns how to make better birdhouses more quickly. Her productivity is measured as an increase in her output for the same number of inputs. We can also see productivity if she makes the same number of birdhouses with fewer inputs.

If you can think of a task around the house or at school that you can complete now more quickly than when you first attempted it, then you have increased your productivity.

Day 10

a. This is an increase in tastes and preferences, so demand for coffee shifts to the right.

b. This will not cause a shift in the demand for coffee; it will cause the quantity of coffee to increase downward along the demand curve.

c. This is an increase in income; because coffee is a normal good, demand shifts to the right.

d. This is an increase in the price of a substitute good, so demand for coffee shifts to the right.

e. This is an increase in the price of a complementary good, so the demand for coffee shifts to the left.

Day 11

a. Faster-production technology will increase the supply (shift it to the right) of oak tables.

b. Oak lumber is a critical input, so a lower price of the lumber will shift the supply of oak tables to the right.

c. Tables made of maple are production substitutes for tables made of oak. If the price of maple tables is rising, producers will decrease the supply of oak tables (shift to the left).

d. As more producers of oak tables enter the market, the supply of oak tables will shift to the right.

e. Tricky one! This is not a shift in the supply of oak tables; it is a movement downward along the supply curve. A lower price decreases the quantity of tables supplied, but does not shift the curve.

Day 12

A surplus exists when quantity supplied exceeds quantity demanded, and these are seen at all prices above \$7. The size of the surplus is equal to Q_s minus Q_d.

A shortage exists when quantity demanded exceeds quantity supplied, and these are seen at all prices below \$7. The size of the shortage is equal to Q_d minus Q_s.

The only price where there is neither a shortage nor a surplus is \$7, and this is the market equilibrium price.

PRICE	Q_d	Q_s	SHORTAGE OR SURPLUS
$10	15	30	Surplus = 15
$9	18	28	Surplus = 10
$8	21	26	Surplus = 5
$7	24	24	Equilibrium, $Q_d = Q_s$
$6	27	22	Shortage = 5
$5	30	20	Shortage = 10
$4	33	18	Shortage = 15
$3	36	16	Shortage = 20
$2	39	14	Shortage = 25
$1	42	12	Shortage = 30

Day 13

a. The price of a key input is rising, so this would shift the supply of oranges to the left, causing a decrease in the quantity and increase in price.

b. A health benefit (longer life span) would increase tastes and preferences for oranges, causing an increase in the demand and eventual increase in both price and quantity.

c. The price of a substitute good is decreasing, so demand for oranges will decrease, causing a decrease in both price and quantity.

d. When we combine a decrease in the supply with an increase in the demand for oranges, the price will certainly rise, but the change in market quantity will depend on which shift is larger. If the supply shift is larger, quantity will fall. If the demand shift is larger, quantity will rise.

Day 14

a. A tax on the production of peanut butter will act like a higher input cost and decrease the supply. A decrease in the supply will increase the price of peanut butter and decrease equilibrium quantity.

b. Strawberry jelly is likely a complementary product, so a lower price will increase the demand for peanut butter, increasing both the price and quantity in the market.

c. A lower price of raw peanuts is a lower input price for making peanut butter. The supply of peanut butter will increase, causing a lower market price and higher market quantity.

d. When we combine an increase in demand with an increase in supply, we know for certain that equilibrium quantity will increase. However, the change in the equilibrium price is uncertain and depends on which shift is larger. If the demand shift is larger, the price will increase. If the supply shift is larger, the price will decrease.

Day 15

a. If better farming technology increases the harvest of coffee beans, the price of this key ingredient will decrease, thus shifting the supply of coffee to the right. When the supply of coffee shifts to the right, the market price will fall and the market quantity will rise.

b. A coffee-making machine is a complementary product to the coffee itself. When the price of these complementary goods is rising, the demand for coffee begins to fall. A decrease in the demand for coffee will cause the price and quantity in the market to also fall.

c. When consumers expect prices to rise in the future, they will increase current demand for coffee. The increase in demand will increase the price and quantity of coffee in the market.

d. When an increase in supply is combined with a decrease in demand, we know for sure that the price of coffee will fall, but the change in market quantity is ambiguous. If the increase in supply is larger than the decrease in demand, the market quantity will rise. However, if the decrease in demand is larger than the increase in supply, the market quantity will fall.

Day 16

a. Included. Because these carrots were grown within the nation's borders, Max's purchase of carrots would be counted as consumer spending in official GDP calculations.

b. Excluded. The purchase of the used couch is not counted, even if the couch was originally produced in Theodoria. The value of the new couch would have been included in GDP in the year in which it was produced.

c. Excluded. Although Melanie has purchased dog walking services from Eliza, this sort of informal cash transaction would not be included in GDP calculations. On the other hand, if Melanie had hired a professional dog walking service to do the job, it would have been included.

d. Included. When a company like Dodgerburger opens new restaurants, it would be officially counted as investment spending in GDP calculations.

Day 17

a. Included. The purchase of new, domestically produced delivery trucks would be counted as government spending in Theodorian GDP.

b. Excluded. The value of the boxes of nails will *eventually* be included in GDP when the new houses are produced. The nails are referred to as "intermediary goods" used to produce the final good of the house.

c. Excluded. The bread and buns are treated as imported goods because, although they were purchased by a domestic consumer, they were produced in another nation. Gross Domestic Product calculates the value of goods and services produced within the nation's borders.

d. Excluded. Barter style transactions, while productive to both parties, are not a part of official GDP calculations. If Eli has hired a professional tutoring service for help studying French, it would be included.

Day 18

- The Bureau of Economic Analysis, an office within the Department of Commerce, produces the GDP numbers in the United States. Website: http://www.bea.gov/
- Under the heading of "U.S. National Accounts," you should be able to find downloadable data for real GDP. Website: https://www.bea.gov/national/index.htm#gdp The following table shows annual real GDP from 2011 to 2015. Notice that the dollars are presented in billions of 2009 dollars. That means that the base year being used is 2009, so the output in each of these years was valued using prices that existed in 2009.

YEAR	REAL GDP (BILLIONS OF 2009 DOLLARS)
2011	$15,020.6
2012	$15,354.6
2013	$15,612.2
2014	$15,982.3
2015	$16,397.2

The percentage change between the two most recent years in this table is calculated by:

%Δreal GDP = 100 × (2015 real GDP − 2014 real GDP)/(2014 real GDP)

= 100 × ($16,397.2 − $15,982.3)/($15,982,3) = 2.60%

Day 19

To compute the value of production, multiply the quantity produced by the price. Then sum up the quantity column and the value of production column.

2014	QUANTITY	PRICE	VALUE OF PRODUCTION
Pizzas	200	$10	$2,000
Breadsticks	150	$2	$300
Sodas	400	$1	$400
Totals	Total = 750	N/A	Total = $2,700
2015	**QUANTITY**	**PRICE**	**VALUE OF PRODUCTION**
Pizzas	300	$10	$3,000
Breadsticks	150	$2	$300
Sodas	300	$1	$300
Totals	Total = 750	N/A	Total = $3,600

Notice that the total number of products sold is the same in each year (750), but the value of production has risen. This has happened because the *mix* of the products has changed and now the economy is producing more pizzas, the most valuable product, and fewer sodas, the least valuable product.

Day 20

Households and firms are connected in two ways:

- Households supply factors of production (e.g., labor) in exchange for payments (e.g., wages).
- Firms supply goods and services to households in exchange for expenditures.

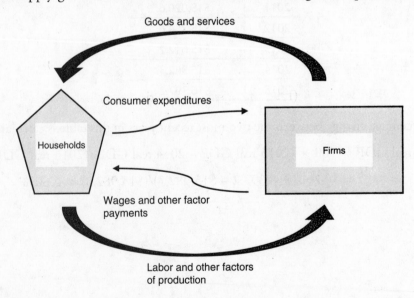

Day 21

At this writing, the most recent quarterly release was the third quarter of 2021. You will find these released reports here:

http://www.bea.gov/national/index.htm#gdp

Here is the link to the full release and tables from November 2016:

https://www.bea.gov/news/2021/gross-domestic-product-third-estimate-gdp-industry-and-corporate-profits-revised-3rd

Table 3 of this report has the relevant information.

In the column for the third quarter of 2021, GDP (in billions of seasonally adjusted dollars) is broken down into the components. If you add the four components, the total is likely going to be slightly different due to rounding.

Third Quarter 2021

$$GDP = \$23,202.3$$
$$C = \$15,964.9 \text{ (68.8\% of the total)}$$
$$I = \$4099.6 \text{ (17.7\%)}$$
$$G = \$4084.9 \text{ (17.6\%)}$$
$$X - M = -\$947 \text{ (–4.1\%)}$$

While your numbers will be different than these, you will probably find that consumption spending is nearly 70% of all spending in the economy.

Day 22

Using the following formula for the WPI, the table should look like this.

$$WPI = 100 \times \text{(Price in current year)/(Price in the base year)}$$

A price index is always equal to 100 in the base year.

YEAR	PRICE	WPI
2011	$ 5	= 100 × ($5/$10) = 50
2012	$10	= 100
2013	$ 6	= 60
2014	$ 8	= 80
2015	$10	= 100
2016	$12	= 120

Day 23

- The Bureau of Labor Statistics (BLS) computes and reports the CPI every month. The BLS website is found here: https://www.bls.gov/
- Near the top of the page you will find a drop-down menu for "Subjects" and you should see "Consumer Price Index." There are several ways to find recent values of the CPI. One way is to explore the section of "CPI Databases." Look for the option of "All Urban Consumers" and "Top Picks" here: https://www.bls.gov/cpi/data.htm
Check the top box that says "U.S. City Average, All items," and then select the button for "Retrieve data." You should now see about ten years of monthly data for the CPI that uses the period of 1982–1984 as the base year.
- To calculate the monthly inflation rate between two consecutive months (October to November 2016 as an example), we do this:

$$\text{Monthly inflation} = 100 \times (\text{CPI November} - \text{CPI October})/(\text{CPI October})$$

$$= 100 \times (241.353 - 241.729)/241.729 = -0.16\%$$

You might see along the right-hand side of the main page some little subheadings for inflation and the CPI. These should be accompanied by a little icon that looks like a graph. Look for something that says "CPI-U, U.S. City Average, All Items," as this is the broadest measurement of inflation. You might find a page similar to this:

https://data.bls.gov/timeseries/CUUR0000SA0?output_view=pct_12mths

Day 24

To deflate nominal salaries into real salaries, we use this formula:

$$\text{Real salary in a year} = 100 \times (\text{Nominal salary in that year})/(\text{CPI in that year})$$

YEAR	NOMINAL SALARY	CPI (1984 = 100)	REAL SALARY
2011	$50,000	129.453	=100 × ($50,000)/(129.453) = $38,624
2012	$52,500	131.976	$39,780
2013	$53,000	133.592	$39,673
2014	$55,000	135.524	$40,583
2015	$58,000	135.362	$42,848

We can now see that this person's salary, after adjusting for inflation, did gradually rise from 2011 to 2015, but actually took a small decrease between 2012 and 2013.

Day 25

The National Bureau of Economic Research (NBER) is a professional organization of economists that does empirical research across many fields in economics. One aspect of the NBER is the Business Cycle Dating Committee. This is the group of economists that determines when recessions begin and end. Here is the website:

http://www.nber.org/cycles/cyclesmain.html

The "Great Recession" began in December 2007 (the peak of the cycle) and ended in June 2009 (the trough of the cycle). This duration of 18 months is much longer than the average of 11.1 months in the business cycles since 1945, which tells us that the "Great Recession" was noteworthy for how long it lasted.

Day 26

Clearly there are no correct answers for this exercise. If you speak with enough people, you might hear stories that involve:

- A lost job
- Wages and/or benefits either declined, or pay raises that were canceled
- A lost home due to foreclosure
- A nearby business that closed
- Personal savings that were exhausted
- A vacation or other large purchase that was given up

Day 27

With a little bit of searching on the FRED, you probably found a graph like this one:

https://fred.stlouisfed.org/series/FPCPITOTLZGUSA

- The highest rate of inflation in this graph was 13.5% in 1980.
- The ups and downs of the inflation graph appear to be more stable as we get into the 1990s and 2000s. You can see this in fewer dramatic spikes and valleys in the graph. Yes, there are ups and downs in the last 15 years, but they aren't as high or as low.
- The inflation rate almost always declines in the recessionary period. You can really see this in the most recent Great Recession. In fact the inflation rate in 2009 was actually negative 0.36% in 2009. The logical explanation is that recessions are associated with less spending throughout the economy. When there is less spending on goods and services, there is little pressure on prices to rise; in fact they usually fall.

Day 28

a. Nobody below the age of 16 is considered part of the labor force. The labor force consists of all those above the age of 16 who are employed (working at least one hour a week) plus those who are unemployed (without work but seeking a job). If a person does not have a job and has chosen to not seek a job, they are out of the labor force.

$$\text{Employed } (E) = 4 + 14 = 18 \text{ million}$$

$$\text{Unemployed } (U) = 2.5 \text{ million}$$

$$\text{Labor Force } (E + U) = 18 + 2.5 = 20.5 \text{ million}$$

The unemployment rate (UR) is the ratio of the number of unemployed (U) divided by the labor force (LF).

$$UR = 100 \times (U/LF) = 100 \times (2.5/20.5) = 12.2\%$$

b. When one million of the unemployed stop looking for work, the ranks of the unemployed *and* the total labor force is one million people smaller. The new unemployment rate is:

$$UR = 100 \times (U/LF) = 100 \times (1.5/19.5) = 7.7\%$$

The unemployment rate has significantly fallen because the "discouraged" workers are no longer counted among the unemployed; they are considered out of the labor force.

Day 29

1. Theo is younger than 16, so he is not counted as a member of the labor force, even though he is actually working as a lawn mower in the neighborhood.

2. Eli does not have a job right now, but he is not in the labor force because he is not actively seeking a job.

3. Melanie is employed and is working full-time.

4. Max is employed and is working part-time.

5. Tommy is considered employed. He has a job but has not been working due to a labor dispute. Although he is not working and is actively searching for work as a guitar player, his status as employed (although on strike) supersedes what would normally qualify him as unemployed.

6. Gina is considered unemployed. She has lost her job and is actively seeking a new job. We can only presume that she is living on a prayer.

Day 30

You probably found a graph similar to this one:

https://fred.stlouisfed.org/series/UNRATE

- The highest unemployment rate was 14.8% in April 2020.
- It might be a little difficult to see, but the unemployment rate has become slightly more stable since the early 1980s. Before about 1980 there were wider increases and decreases, and after 1980 there were fewer and they were not rising as high or dropping as low. The exception, of course, is the COVID-19 recession when unemployment rates increased steeply and then rapidly decreased in a short period of time.
- In all of the recessionary periods, unemployment was rising. The explanation is simple and relates to the circular flow diagram. When it feels like the economy is weakening, people reduce their spending. When households spend less on goods and services, firms employ fewer factors of production, and this reduces household income. And when household income falls, households spend less, and the downward cycle continues.

Day 31

Below is unemployment information from the November 2016 report. A portion of the table of unemployment measures is replicated as follows.

MEASURE	NOV. 2016
U-3 Total unemployed, as a percent of the civilian labor force (official unemployment rate)	4.6
U-4 Total unemployed, plus discouraged workers, as a percent of the civilian labor force, plus discouraged workers	5.0
U-5 Total unemployed, plus discouraged workers, plus all other persons marginally attached to the labor force, as a percent of the civilian labor force, plus all persons marginally attached to the labor force	5.8
U-6 Total unemployed, plus all persons marginally attached to the labor force, plus total employed part time for economic reasons, as a percent of the civilian labor force, plus all persons marginally attached to the labor force	9.3

If you have done a little digging and read the fine print in the footnotes of Table A-15, you might have discovered the following:

Marginally attached: This refers to a person who is currently not working and was not searching for work last month, but indicates that they would like to work and had searched for work at some point in the last year.

The official rate of U-3 would not include these people, because they were not currently looking for work. However, they are interested in working and have searched for work in the last year, so they have not completely given up and permanently left the labor force.

Discouraged worker: This is a subset of the marginally attached people. They have not been searching for work because they don't believe there is anything available to them. They might feel like they don't have sufficient skills, or that they are too young/old for any work, or that they are discriminated against for any number of reasons.

We can see in November 2016 that the inclusion of discouraged workers would increase the unemployment rate from the official 4.6% to 5% (U-4).

If we included all of the marginally attached workers, the unemployment rate would rise again to 5.8% (U-5).

Working part-time for economic reasons: This definition describes people working 1–34 hours per week (part time) but would rather be working more than 35 hours a week (full time). They are working part time because they cannot find a full-time position or their employer has cut back their hours due to weak demand for the firm's products. Since these people are not unemployed, we might think of them as underemployed.

In November 2016 if this final group of the underemployed is added, the unemployment rate rises to 9.3%.

In any month that you choose, you will find the same pattern of an increasing rate of unemployment as we move from U-3 to U-6. This is simply a result of how the BLS for many decades has decided to draw the line on what constitutes an unemployed person. If you have been searching for work in the last month, you're unemployed; if not, you're out of the labor force.

Day 32

Since Pam consumes $900 for every additional $1,000 of disposable income, the column of C rises by $900 each time. In a similar way, the column for S rises by $100 every time DI increases by $1000.

DISPOSABLE INCOME (DI)	CONSUMPTION (C)	SAVINGS (S)
$0	$100	−$100
$1,000	$1,000	0
$2,000	$1,900	$100
$3,000	$2,800	$200
$4,000	$3,700	$300
$5,000	$4,600	$400
$6,000	$5,500	$500

Day 33

Once again, the equation of a line is $y = mx + b$.

In the consumption equation, the vertical intercept (b) is the value of consumption when disposable income is zero. This is called autonomous consumption. The slope (m) is the change in consumption divided by the change in disposable income. This is called the marginal propensity to consume (MPC).

We can see from the tables that both Pam's and Gram's autonomous consumptions are $100.

Pam's consumption rises by $900 when her disposable income rises by $1,000, so her MPC is 0.90.

On the other hand, Gram's consumption rises by only $600 when her disposable income rises by $1,000, so her MPC is 0.60.

This gives us enough information to construct the consumption equations.

$$\text{Pam: } C = 100 + (0.90 \times DI)$$
$$\text{Gram: } C = 100 + (0.60 \times DI)$$

Day 34

In the savings equation, the vertical intercept (b) is the value of savings when disposable income is zero. This is called autonomous savings. The slope (m) is the change in savings divided by the change in disposable income. This is called the marginal propensity to save (MPS).

We can see from the tables that both Pam's and Gram's autonomous savings are –$100.

Pam's savings rises by $100 when her disposable income rises by $1,000, so her MPS is 0.10.

On the other hand, Gram's savings rises by $400 when her disposable income rises by $1,000, so her MPS is 0.40.

This gives us enough information to construct the savings equations.

$$\text{Pam: } S = -100 + (0.10 \times DI)$$
$$\text{Gram: } S = -100 + (0.40 \times DI)$$

Day 35

You might have found a graph like this one:

https://fred.stlouisfed.org/series/GPDIC1

Even after holding prices constant (2009 dollars), it is clear that investment spending has dramatically increased since the 1950s. A closer look at the actual numbers shows that real investment spending in 2021 is more than 15 times greater than it was in 1947.

It is also clear that investment spending drops during economic recessions. This isn't surprising, because recessions are associated with less spending across the board. However, if you take a look at *when* investment spending begins to decline, it is usually at least two quarters before the recession officially begins. Because of this, economists use changes in investment spending as an important "economic indicator" of a potential change in the business cycle.

Day 36

The market for loanable funds has a downward sloping demand and an upward sloping supply curve. The real interest rate is on the vertical axis. Hint: Make sure that you label your vertical axis as the real rate (or $r\%$).

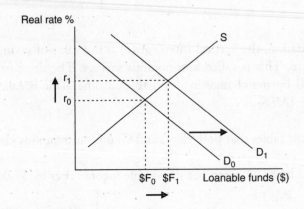

Increased business optimism would likely mean more capital investment and an increase in the demand for loanable funds. A shift to the right would increase the equilibrium interest rate and the quantity of funds borrowed and lent.

Day 37

Once again, you should draw the market for loanable funds with a downward-sloping demand and an upward-sloping supply curve. The real interest rate is on the vertical axis.

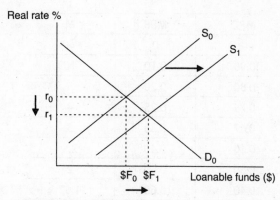

When households and firms show increased saving in American banks, the supply of loanable funds shifts to the right. A supply shift to the right would decrease the equilibrium interest rate and increase the quantity of funds borrowed and lent.

Day 38

After 10 more rounds of spending the initial $1,000 has generated a total of $7,175.70. In other words, it has multiplied by more than seven times the initial amount of spending. This is the spending multiplier at work.

TRANSACTION	SPENDING	SAVING
A to B	$1,000	N/A
B to C	$900	$100
C to D	$810	$90
D to E	$729	$81
E to F	$656.10	$72.90
F to G	$590.49	$65.61
G to H	$531.44	$59.05
H to I	$478.30	$53.14
I to J	$430.47	$47.83
J to K	$387.42	$43.05
K to L	$348.68	$38.74
L to M	$313.81	$34.87
Totals =	**$7,175.70**	**$686.19**

Day 39

Technically you cannot compute M when the *MPC* is one and the *MPS* is zero, but if you imagine dividing by something very close to zero, we would get a spending multiplier that is very, very big.

MPC	MPS	M
1	0	∞
0.90	0.10	10
0.80	0.20	5
0.75	0.25	4
0.67	0.33	3
0.60	0.40	2.5
0.50	0.50	2
0.40	0.60	1.67
0.33	0.67	1.5
0.20	0.80	1.25
0.10	0.90	1.11
0	1	1

The table makes it clear that if the *MPC* is quite high (or *MPS* quite low), an injection of spending from any sector will eventually multiply to a much greater amount.

Day 40

For each scenario, you must first compute the spending multiplier and then determine whether GDP would increase or decrease by a magnitude equal to that of the multiplier.

• A nation with an $MPC = 0.80$ experiences an increase in autonomous investment spending of $10 billion.

$M = 1/0.20 = 5$. If I increases by $10 billion, this should eventually cause an increase of $50 billion in GDP.

• A nation with an $MPC = 0.75$ experiences a decrease in autonomous net exports of $6.5 billion.

$M = 1/0.25 = 4$. If $(X–M)$ decreases by $6.5 billion, this should eventually cause a decrease of $26 billion in GDP.

• A nation with an $MPC = 0.50$ experiences an increase in autonomous government spending of $15 billion.

$M = 1/0.5 = 2$. If G increases by $15 billion, this should eventually cause an increase of $30 billion in GDP.

• A nation with an $MPC = 0.90$ experiences a decrease in autonomous consumption spending of $5 billion.

$M = 1/0.9 = 10$. If C decreases by $5 billion, this should eventually cause a decrease of $50 billion in GDP.

Day 41

After 12 rounds of spending, the $1,000 tax rebate created $6,458.13 of new spending. The tax rebate generated more than six times the amount of money circulating in the economy than the initial rebate. This is the tax multiplier at work.

TRANSACTION	SPENDING	SAVING
A to B	$900.00	$100.00
B to C	$810.00	$90.00
C to D	$729.00	$81.00
D to E	$656.10	$72.90
E to F	$590.49	$65.61
F to G	$531.44	$59.05
G to H	$478.30	$53.14
H to I	$430.47	$47.83
I to J	$387.42	$43.05
J to K	$348.68	$38.74
K to L	$313.81	$34.87
L to M	$282.43	$31.38
Totals =	**$6,458.13**	**$717.57**

Day 42

Again, we see that the tax multiplier falls as the MPC falls. The T_m is always smaller than the spending multiplier because a change in autonomous spending (G) immediately impacts the circular flow of spending, while a change in taxes (or transfer payments) must first go through a consumer's consumption function, and in that function a fraction will be saved, not spent.

MPC	MPS	M	T_m
1	0	∞	∞
0.90	0.10	10	9.00
0.80	0.20	5	4.00
0.75	0.25	4	3.00
0.67	0.33	3	2.00
0.60	0.40	2.5	1.50
0.50	0.50	2	1.00
0.40	0.60	1.67	0.67
0.33	0.67	1.5	0.50
0.20	0.80	1.25	0.25
0.10	0.90	1.11	0.11
0	1	1	0.00

Notice that if the MPC is quite small in an economy, a change in taxes or transfers will have a negligible multiplied impact on GDP.

Day 43

For each scenario, you must first compute the tax multiplier and then determine the eventual impact of the tax or transfer change on GDP.

- A nation with an $MPC = 0.80$ experiences an increase in transfer payments of $10 billion.

$T_m = 0.8/0.2 = 4$, so an increase in transfer payments of $10 billion will multiply to a $40 billion increase in GDP.

- A nation with an $MPC = 0.75$ experiences a decrease in taxes of $6.5 billion.

$T_m = 0.75/0.25 = 3$, so a decrease in taxes of $6.5 billion will multiply to a $19.5 billion increase in GDP.

- A nation with an $MPC = 0.50$ experiences an increase in taxes of $15 billion.

$T_m = 0.5/0.5 = 1$, so an increase in taxes of $15 billion will multiply to a $15 billion decrease in GDP.

- A nation with an $MPC = 0.90$ experiences a decrease in transfer payments of $5 billion.

$T_m = 0.9/0.1 = 9$, so a decrease in transfer payments of $5 billion will multiply to a $45 billion decrease in GDP.

Day 44

a. The spending multiplier $M = 1/0.25 = 4$, so an increase in $G = $3 billion will multiply to a $12 billion *increase* in GDP.

b. The tax multiplier $T_m = 0.75/0.25 = 3$, so an increase in taxes of $3 billion will multiply to a $9 billion *decrease* in GDP.

c. Net impact of this balanced-budget project = $12 billion – $9 billion = $3 billion.

Day 45

- *Foreign sector substitution effect*

  If the aggregate price level in the United States is falling relative to that of other nations, consumers in other nations will wish to purchase more goods from the United States. At the same time, American consumers would wish fewer products from foreign nations. As a result, net exports would rise and GDP increases downward along the AD curve.

- *Interest rate effect*

  If the aggregate price level is falling in the United States, there will need to be less borrowing to afford big-ticket items. This puts downward pressure on interest rates and with lower interest rates current spending increases. This creates a downward movement along the AD curve.

- *Wealth effect*

    If the aggregate price level falls in the United States, the purchasing power of accumulated wealth will rise, and current spending rises. This also creates a downward movement along the AD curve.

Day 46

a. Pessimistic households will decrease consumption (*C*) and decrease AD (shift to the left).

b. Low interest rates will increase investment (*I*) and also consumption (*C*) and increase AD (shift to the right).

c. More military spending is an increase in government spending (*G*) and increases AD.

d. Recessions in Asia make it more difficult to export to those nations, so net exports (*X − M*) decreases and decreases AD.

Day 47

a. When firms are more optimistic about profitability, investment rises (*I*) and AD increases.

b. More household wealth increases consumption (*C*) and increases AD.

c. Higher income taxes decreases consumption (*C*) and decreases AD.

d. Stronger foreign preference of domestic products increases net exports (*X − M*) and increases AD.

Day 48

The reason the SRAS is believed to be upward sloping is that input prices are thought to rise more slowly than the aggregate price level. So when the price level rises, firms can increase output, and with input prices lagging behind, firms are more profitable in the short run.

Day 49

a. Policies like tax rebates for research and development allow companies to increase production and increases SRAS. Note: This kind of policy can also increase the long-run AS (LRAS) curve over a longer time period.

b. Widespread increases in input (or factor) prices causes the SRAS to shift to the left.

c. The elimination of redundant business regulation should increase the SRAS.

d. An environmental disaster, like a drought, would decrease the SRAS. Note: If a short-term lack of water turns into a permanent situation, the LRAS might also shift to the left.

Answers

Day 50

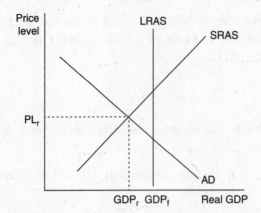

A recessionary gap means that current GDP falls below full-employment (or potential) GDP so you want to draw your intersection of AD and SRAS to the left of the vertical LRAS line.

Day 51

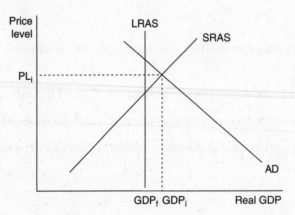

An inflationary gap means that current GDP lies above full-employment (or potential) GDP so you want to draw your intersection of AD and SRAS to the right of the vertical LRAS line.

Day 52

a. Firms with less optimistic expectations will decrease investment spending, and AD decreases. The price level and real GDP will both fall.

b. When foreign consumers have more income, they will buy more domestic-made products, increasing next exports. The increase in AD will increase both price level and real GDP.

c. More household wealth causes consumption spending to rise, increasing AD. The increased AD causes both the price level and real GDP to increase.

d. Input prices that are rising will cause the SRAS to decrease, causing the price level to rise and real GDP to fall.

e. Policies designed to increase productivity should increase the SRAS, causing the price level to fall and real GDP to rise.

Day 53

If you were successful in combining both data series in one graph, it probably looks a little like this.

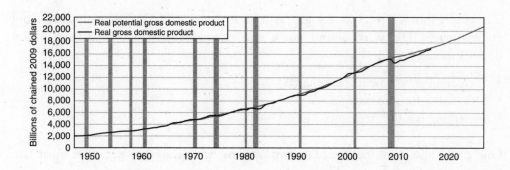

When you zoom in on recessionary periods, the real GDP dips significantly below potential GDP. This is a classic recessionary gap that we see in the AD/AS model as a decrease in AD. There are some periods where actual real GDP exceeds the potential GDP, the most recent being the quarters between 2005 and 2007, right before the Great Recession. If you look back, there are several instances where a period like this (actual exceeding potential) ended with a recession. There are many years when the economy is not officially in a recession, yet real GDP is below potential GDP. This illustrates the difference between simply producing below potential and *really* producing below potential. The recovery that began in the middle of 2009 caused the economy to emerge from the Great Recession, but wasn't until 2019 that real GDP caught up to potential GDP.

Day 54

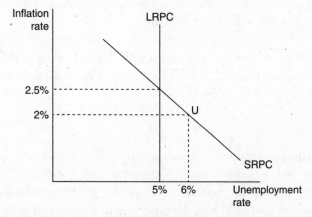

The LRPC is always drawn as a vertical line at the NAIRU, and the SRPC is downward sloping to reflect the trade-off between lower unemployment rates and higher inflation rates.

In the AD/AS model, this is explained by a decrease in the AD curve. Such a shift would decrease real GDP, increasing the unemployment rate, and decreasing the price level, reducing inflation.

Day 55

There are no answers for this activity. ☺

Day 56

The graph shows a recessionary gap as indicated by real GDP currently below full employment GDP. With output down and unemployment up, your fiscal policy options should include:

- Increasing government spending (G)
- Decreasing income taxes
- Increasing transfer payments

One could also combine these last two options by stating that net taxes must fall: Net taxes = (Tax revenue – Transfer payments).

If these policies are to be effective, they must shift the AD curve to the right, increasing real GDP and decreasing the unemployment rate. There are two potential downsides: a higher price level and a larger budget deficit.

Day 57

The graph shows an inflationary gap as indicated by real GDP currently above full employment GDP. While output is quite high, so is inflation, so your fiscal policy options should include:

- Decreasing government spending (*G*)
- Increasing income taxes
- Decreasing transfer payments

Again, you could also combine these last two options by stating that net taxes must rise: Net taxes = (Tax revenue – Transfer payments).

If these policies are to be effective, they must shift the AD curve to the left, decreasing real GDP and decreasing the price level. There is one clear downside in that unemployment will rise.

Day 58

When the government engages in expansionary fiscal policy, the usual plan is to increase spending and decrease taxes; this creates a budget deficit. The typical way of paying for the deficit is to borrow money from the public and financial institutions in the form of issuing bonds. When the government borrows a lot of money, there is pressure on interest rates to rise. Higher interest rates reduce private investment that would have, if interest rates had remained lower, otherwise been done. In other words, the government borrowing "crowds out" private investment.

Day 59

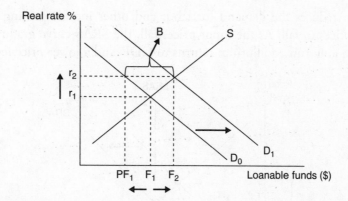

Real rate %

B S

r_2
r_1

D_0 D_1

PF_1 F_1 F_2 Loanable funds ($)

The borrowing increases the demand curve to D_1 and this increases equilibrium interest rates. However, the quantity of private borrowing/investment falls from F_1 (no deficit) to PF_1 (deficit spending). The difference between the private borrowing/investing and the total is the amount of government borrowing (B). The decrease from F_1 to PF_1 is the crowding out of private investment.

Day 60

Searching around the FRED, you might have found a graph that looks like this.

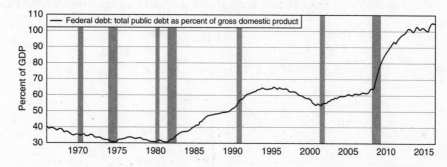

This graph clearly shows that the national debt, as a percentage of the GDP, has been rising since about 1980. Although this graph doesn't go back as far as World War II, this ratio was about 120% in 1946 as the government spending was ramped up to support the military. More recently, we can see there was a steady increase in the 1980s, then a modest decline in the late 1990s, a slow increase in the early 2000s, and then a precipitous increase during and after the Great Recession.

Day 61

More government borrowing increases interest rates in the United States. When foreign citizens and firms see that they can earn higher interest in the United States, they deposit more of their currency in American banks. This increases the demand for the U.S. dollar, which increases the value of the dollar in currency markets. Finally, a more expensive dollar makes American-made goods more expensive to foreign consumers, so exports fall. It also makes foreign goods less expensive for American consumers, so imports rise. The combination of these effects is a decrease in (or a crowding out of) net exports.

Day 62

The recession reduces the demand for labor and other inputs, putting pressure on those input prices to fall. As the input prices fall, the SRAS curve gradually shifts to the right. The long-run equilibrium returns to GDP_f and a lower price level PL_f.

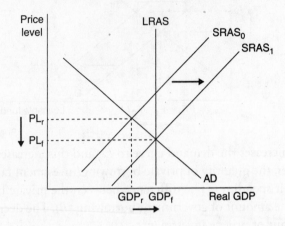

Day 63

The inflationary gap increases the demand for labor and other inputs, putting pressure on those input prices to rise. As the input prices rise, the SRAS curve gradually shifts to the left. The long-run equilibrium returns to GDP_f and a higher price level PL_f.

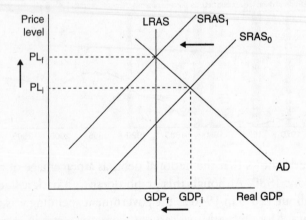

Day 64

Productivity has certainly risen since 1947. According to the blog post, "Compared to 1947, we now produce 330 percent more goods and services per hour of work. On average, thanks to advances in technology, education, management, and so on, you can do in 15 minutes what your grandparents or great grandparents needed more than an hour to do in 1947."

Since 2007, productivity has risen only 1% each year, which is much lower than the long-term average of 2.2% each year.

The graph that compares productivity to real hourly wages shows almost a perfect match before about 1970. Since then, the productivity line has risen at a faster rate than the real hourly wage line, creating a widening gap.

Day 65

According to data presented in the Census report (and Figure 1 in the report), in 1940 only about 25% of people above the age of 25 had completed high school, but by 2015 that had increased to 88%. In 1940 about 5% of people had a bachelor's degree or more, but in 2015 that number was up to 33%. Clearly the American workforce has more educational attainment today than it did after World War II.

Table 1 in the report provides data that shows that a greater percentage of women have completed a high school degree or more (88.8% to 88%), and a greater percentage of women have completed a bachelor's degree or higher (32.7% to 32.3%).

There are also some differences in educational attainment across the races. For example, Asians have the highest percentage of having a bachelor's degree or higher (53.9%), while Hispanics had the lowest rate (15.5%).

Day 66

Long-run growth is shown as a rightward shift of the LRAS curve. When the economy comes to a new long-run equilibrium, the new level of full employment GDP will be higher. The new price level could be higher or lower, or the same, depending on the magnitude of the AD and SRAS shifts that will eventually accompany the LRAS shift.

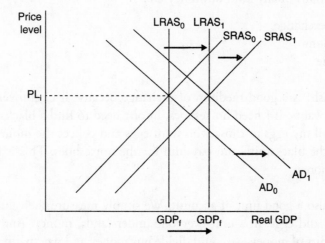

Day 67

When the babysitting co-op was floundering and members were not spending often enough, the committee running it pumped more money (tokens) into the system. This is akin to a tax cut or rebate in our study of fiscal policy. When the members had more tokens in their accounts, they spent them and the co-op flourished.

Dr. Harford describes the "shock" as an unexpected hit to the economic system from something outside the system. Unlike the early struggles of the babysitting co-op, the POW camp's economy was running smoothly, with sophisticated features like a futures market for bread and coffee exports to Germans on the outside of the fence. The external shock was that the Red Cross shipments were prevented from delivering the goods. This caused the economy to collapse. In the babysitting co-op, there was no external shock, the economy just needed a stimulus to accelerate the rate of spending.

Day 68

A share of stock represents a claim on the ownership of a firm. A firm issues shares of stock to raise money (equity financing), but in exchange relinquishes a small degree of control over management and profits of the firm.

A bond is a certificate of indebtedness (an IOU). A firm issues a bond to raise money (debt financing), but in exchange commits the firm to repaying the principle of the bond, plus interest.

Day 69

The big difficulty with the barter system is the "double coincidence of wants." If I am an egg farmer, and I want to go shopping, I must find other merchants who want my eggs in exchange for the goods they produce. This is a pretty inefficient way to conduct commerce.

The three functions of any kind of money are:

- Medium of exchange
- Unit of account
- Store of value

Fiat money (cash) is a good medium of exchange because it circumvents the double coincidence of wants. If I need horseshoes, I don't need to find a blacksmith who also wants eggs. I sell my eggs to those who want eggs and collect the money. Then I take the money to the blacksmith and pay him for the horseshoes. This is far superior to using eggs as money.

Fiat money is also a good unit of account. We simply measure the value of all things, like horseshoes and eggs, in a unit everyone understands, money. And if there was a price of 0.50 units of money, we could divide our money and pay that price. If we tried to use eggs as our money, all things would be measured in how many eggs it would cost to purchase them. Since not all people want eggs, and since 0.50 eggs aren't going to work very well, this isn't going to be a good pricing system.

Fiat money is a good store of value as it can last a long time. Eggs will go bad in a few days, making them worthless as money. Fiat money does lose value if inflation is rampant, so it is important for the central bank to maintain the value of the money.

Answers ↑

Day 70

To solve these problems, we must use the present value formula:

$$PV = \frac{FV}{(1+r)^t}$$

where FV is some dollar amount received or paid t years into the future, and r is the interest rate (or discount rate). Or we can solve the equation for future value and we have:

$$FV = PV(1 + r)^t$$

a. The present value of your loan is $50, the interest rate is 4%, and you agree to repay the loan in one year.

$$FV = PV/(1 + r)^t = 50(1.04) = \$52$$

b. The future value of the gift is $100, the interest rate is 5%, and you have to wait one year to receive it.

$$PV = \frac{FV}{(1+r)^t} = \frac{\$100}{10.5} = \$95.24$$

c. There are two ways to make this comparison. The first is to compute the present value of $5,000 received in two years.

$$PV = \frac{FV}{(1+r)^t} = \frac{5,000}{(1.10)^2} = \$4,132.23$$

Since the present value of these winnings is less than $4,500, you should take the $4,500 now.

The second way to make the comparison is to compute the future value of $4,500 today, if you put it in the bank for two years.

$$FV = PV(1 + r)^t = 4,500(1.10)^2 = \$5,445$$

Since this future value is greater than the winnings of $5,000, you should still take the $4,500 now and put it in the bank for two years.

Day 71

You probably found a graph that looks like this.

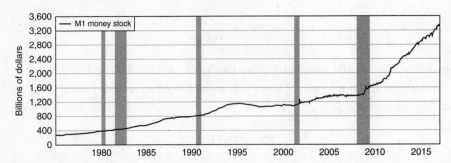

The stock of *M*1 has risen slowly since the 1980s, was fairly constant in the late 1990s and early 2000s, and then increased more rapidly since the Great Recession. Of course, the reason for the rapid increase was to combat, along with the government's aggressive fiscal policy, this very deep recession and the slow recovery from it.

Day 72

The completed table is below.

ROUND	DEPOSIT	CASH IN RESERVE	A LOAN IS MADE
1	$1,000 from person A	$100	$900 to person B
2	$900 from person B	$90	$810 to person C
3	$810 from person C	$81	$729 to person D
4	$729 from person D	$72.90	$656.10 to person E
5	$656.10 from person E	$65.61	$590.49 to person F
6	$590.49 from person F	$59.05	$531.44 to person G
7	$531.44 from person G		
	Total = $5,217.03		Total = $4,217.03

The table shows how money is created by simply holding a fraction in reserve (10%) and lending the rest to new borrowing customers. If we subtract the initial $1,000 deposit (because it was already in circulation), the loans and deposits from persons B through G amount to $4,217.03 that did not previously exist. Think of this as *new money* circulating in the economy.

Day 73

The money market graph has the nominal interest rate on the vertical axis, and the quantity of money demanded rises as the nominal interest rate falls. The reason is that money is another type of financial asset. When it is held (demanded) in your pocket, it is very useful for making transactions, but it doesn't earn any interest as an asset. As the interest rate rises, you could earn more interest income, so you will put that money back into another financial asset, like the purchase of a Treasury bond, and demand less of it in your pocket. The nominal interest rate is simply the opportunity cost of holding money in your pocket, and as we already know, when opportunity cost of something rises, we demand less of it.

Day 74

In the first case, you will earn $100 when the bond matures ($1,000 − $900), and since you paid $900 for the bond, you have earned an interest rate of 11.1% ($100/$900). In the second case, you will earn $50 when the bond matures ($1,000 − $950), so the interest rate is now 5.26% ($50/$950). As you can see from this quick example, when the price of a bond rises, the effective interest rate is going to fall.

The demand for bonds can rise for many different reasons. One reason might be that the rate of return on other financial assets is not very high. For example, if the stock market is slumping, people might put more money into bonds, thus increasing the demand for bonds and their prices. Another reason for an increase in demand for bonds is uncertainty. The U.S. Treasury bond is deemed one of the safest, if not *the* safest, financial assets available. Relative to other parts of the world, the U.S. government is stable and always repays the bonds that have been issued. So if financial markets in Europe or Asia are in turmoil, or if there is widespread geopolitical unrest, investors might return to U.S. Treasury bonds, increasing their demand. Another reason for higher demand for bonds is that there is a surplus of money in the money market. With a surplus of money in circulation, households and firms are going to look for a place to put this money, and the market for U.S. Treasury bonds is one such place.

Day 75

Be sure to draw your money supply curve as vertical and money demand as downward sloping. Also be sure to label the vertical axis as the nominal interest rate (or "nir").

The initial equilibrium in the money market is at an interest rate of i_1. A stronger economy and increased nominal GDP will increase the demand for money, as people are making more transactions. The shift to the right of MD creates a shortage of money at the original interest rate. With not enough money in circulation, people will sell their bonds and this increases the supply of bonds, decreasing the price, and increasing interest rates.

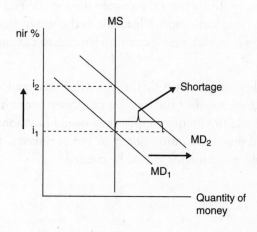

Day 76

Use the formula for the money multiplier:

$$M = 1/rr$$

The completed table follows.

RESERVE REQUIREMENT (rr)	MONEY MULTIPLIER
0.01	100
0.05	20
0.10	10
0.20	5
0.25	4
0.50	2

If (a big IF) the reserve requirement was 0.01, banks would need to hold only 1% of deposits in reserve and could lend out the remaining 99%. This could dramatically increase the multiplication of any deposits but would also put the bank at risk. What if many depositors showed up and wanted to withdraw all of their money (aka, a bank run) on the same day? With only 1% of all deposits being held, this could wipe out the bank. To lessen this risk, the Fed has chosen an $rr = 10\%$ and allows banks that find their reserves to be insufficient on any given day to borrow from either other banks or the Fed itself.

Day 77

1. Change the reserve requirement. If the Fed wanted to increase the money supply, they could decrease the reserve requirement, allowing banks to lend a larger percentage of all deposits and increasing the money multiplier.

2. Change the discount rate. The discount rate is the rate the Fed charges banks that wish to borrow money. To increase the money supply, the Fed could lower the discount rate, making these loans more affordable to the banks. Banks borrow from the Fed, increasing excess reserves, and increasing lending to customers, thus increasing the supply of money.

3. Execute open market operations (OMOs). The Fed buys and sells Treasury securities in the open market to affect the amount of money banks have in reserve. If the Fed wanted to increase the money supply, they would buy bonds from large banks. These banks would now have more money in excess reserves, they would start the lending process, and more money would be created.

Day 78

To fight a recessionary gap, you should propose an OMO whereupon you are buying securities from banks. These purchases will inject money into the banks and the money multiplier effect will increase the money supply.

The graph should show the vertical money supply curve shifting to the right, decreasing the nominal interest rate.

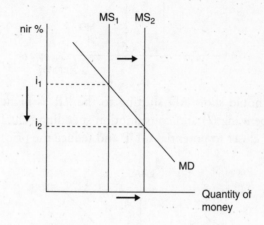

The AD/AS graph should show AD shifting to the right as lower interest rates will boost investment spending (I) and consumption spending (C). This increase in AD should get real GDP closer to potential GDP and reduce the unemployment rate.

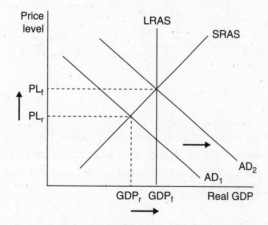

Day 79

To fight an inflationary gap, you should propose an OMO whereupon you are selling securities to banks. These sales will withdraw money from the banks, and the money multiplier effect will decrease the money supply.

The graph should show the vertical money supply curve shifting to the left, increasing the nominal interest rate.

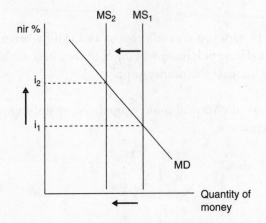

The AD/AS graph should show AD shifting to the left as higher interest rates will reduce investment spending (*I*) and consumption spending (C). This decrease in AD should get real GDP closer to potential GDP and reduce the price level and inflation.

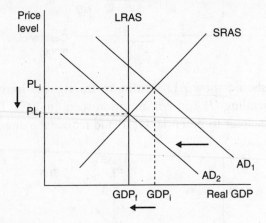

Day 80

A liquidity trap occurs when interest rates are pushed down to zero. Unlike other economic variables (like net exports), interest rates cannot be negative values. So if the money supply is increased to the point where interest rates hit zero, there is no further benefit to expansionary monetary policy.

In the essay from the Fed, when the author refers to the "effective lower bound" of interest rates, he is describing the liquidity trap. With the economy continuing to languish, the Fed was forced to look for nontraditional methods of sparking the economy.

The first thing that is discussed in the article is the Fed's use of key language in their reports to the banking industry and general public. The Fed wanted to reassure banks that the nearly zero percent interest rates were going to last for a while. They hoped that this would allow banks to begin lending again and plan for a more certain future.

The Fed also began to purchase certain financial assets from banks and financial institutions. Part of the reason that banks were not lending was because they were saddled with billions of dollars of nearly worthless mortgages and a popular investment called "mortgage-backed securities." The thinking was that if the Fed took those nearly worthless investments out of the banks, it would free them to return to normal business.

Of course we know now that recovery from the Great Recession, despite the combined efforts of fiscal and monetary policy, was quite slow.

Day 81

There really are no solutions to this activity, but it does provide food for thought and some hard-to-answer questions. Is a weak economy like a dead car battery that just needs a spark of spending? Should the government bail out firms that are failing? What would we do with the people who are unemployed if we waited for the economy to self-correct?

Many economists agree that there are valid points to be made by both sides of this philosophical divide. And all economists agree that the real world is much more complex than the theoretical models presented in textbooks. However, these models, imperfect as they are, provide us with a baseline for understanding how the economy works and how policies *might* have effective impacts on it.

Day 82

a. To find comparative advantage, we must compute the opportunity cost of producing each commodity.

Nation A:

Producing $1W$ costs $4T$

Producing $1T$ costs $1/4W$

Nation B:

Producing $1W$ costs $6T$

Producing $1T$ costs $1/6W$

Nation A produces wheat at a lower cost than can nation B, so nation A has comparative advantage in W. Nation B produces textiles at a lower cost than can nation A, so nation B has comparative advantage in T.

b. Nation B is going to specialize in T, but they want some W. If they produced their own W, it would cost $6T$, so they need a lower price for W from a trading partner. Maybe they try to get $1W$ for a price of $5T$.

Would nation A go for this?

They are specializing in W. If they gave up $1W$ on their own, they would gain $4T$, but nation B is offering them $5T$.

So both nations would agree to a deal that involves $1W$ exchanging for $5T$, or $1T$ exchanging for $0.20W$.

Day 83

a. Low interest rates will deter savers from depositing money in American banks, and they will keep their money in European banks where the return is higher. This will decrease the demand for the dollar.

b. If American products are more popular, demand for those products rises and the demand for the dollar rises with it.

c. A recession in Europe decreases the demand for imported goods from the United States, so demand for the dollar falls.

d. If European prices are rising and prices in the United States are not, American products are going to be more affordable and demand for the dollar will rise.

Day 84

a. The Fed should increase the money supply, probably with an open market purchase of bonds from large banks. An increase in the money supply will cause interest rates to fall, boosting AD and lessening the recessionary gap.

b. Lower interest rates make foreign saving in U.S. financial institutions less attractive, so the demand for the dollar will decrease, causing the value of the dollar to fall. Another way to say this is that the dollar is depreciating (or weakening) against other currencies. If the dollar is less expensive to foreigners, it makes American-made products less expensive to foreign consumers, so the United States will export more products. At the same time, a weaker dollar means that Americans find foreign goods to be more expensive, so imports in the U.S. economy fall. With exports rising and imports falling, net exports $(X - M)$ increase.

Day 85

A few years ago I found a Hilton Doubletree hotel in Madrid, Spain, that had a room in April 2017 priced at 209 euros. At that time, $1 could get you 1.05415 euros, or 1 euro could get you $0.94863, so to pay for the room in euros I would need:

$$209 \text{ euros} \times (0.94863 \text{ \$/euro}) = \$198.26$$

One year earlier, the exchange rate was 1 euro equal to $0.94829, so the room a year ago would have cost:

$$209 \text{ euros} \times (0.94829 \text{ \$/euro}) = \$198.19$$

Since this hotel room is basically the same price (in U.S. dollars), I will assume that my European vacation in 2017 would cost about the same as it would have cost in 2016.

Day 86

The tricky part of drawing currency markets is getting the vertical axis labeled correctly. We are drawing the market for the euro (€), so the vertical axis needs to be labeled as the price of a euro. Since we are going to price it in U.S. dollars, we should label the vertical axis as "dollars per euro" or the "dollar price of a euro" or simply "$/€."

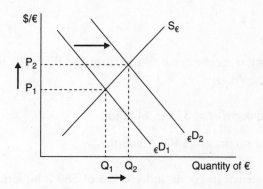

Higher interest rates in Europe will attract savers from the United States, and this increases the demand for the euro, causing the euro to appreciate in value. It would now cost more dollars to acquire more euros or products made in the European Union.

Day 87

We are drawing the market for the U.S. dollar, and so the vertical axis needs to be labeled as the price of a dollar. Since we are going to price it in euros, we should label the vertical axis as "euros per dollar" or the "euro price of a dollar" or simply "€/$."

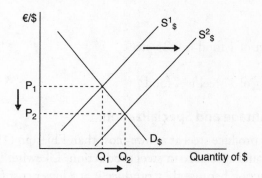

Higher interest rates in Europe will attract savers from the United States, and this increases the demand for the euro, causing the euro to appreciate in value. At the same time, the supply of dollars is increasing. Think of it this way: If Americans are demanding more euros, they must offer more dollars in exchange. The graph shows that the price of a dollar is falling; the dollar is depreciating. It would now cost fewer euros to acquire more dollars or products made in the United States.

Day 88

There are several trends that support the assertion that trade benefits the U.S. economy. For example, the very first chart shows that U.S. exports have risen sharply over the same period of time that U.S. real GDP has risen gradually. Trade in the U.S. economy is now about 30% of total GDP. The video also describes how the "made in America" slogan is no longer true, as firms often import raw materials to produce a final product. The video also discusses the fact that trade does reduce employment in some sectors and some regions of the country, but that trade creates other jobs. In fact, labor-saving technology (like robotics) is the primary cause of lost manufacturing job losses, not trade.

Day 89

At this writing, the most recent news release from the BEA was for November 2021. From the report, we see that:

Exports of goods and services = $224.26 billion.

Imports of goods and services = $304.4 billion.

So there was a trade deficit in goods and services of $80.2 billion.

Day 90

We need to determine opportunity costs to figure out which nation has comparative advantage in steel and food.

Theodoria:

The opportunity cost of 1 food is 1 steel.

The opportunity cost of 1 steel is 1 food.

Elijastan:

The opportunity cost of 1 food is 0.25 steel.

The opportunity cost of 1 steel is 4 food.

Comparative Advantage and Specialization:

Since Theodoria can produce steel at a lower cost than Elijastan (1 food compared to 4 food), Theodoria should specialize in steel production. Likewise, Elijastan should specialize in food production because they produce it at a lower cost (0.25 steel compared to 1 steel) than Theodoria.

Terms of Trade:

One possibility that would benefit both nations is if they exchanged 1 steel for 2 food. To see how this would work, suppose Elijastan sent 40 food to Theodoria in exchange for 20 steel.

Would Elijastan find this acceptable? Without trade, if Elijastan wanted 20 steel they would need to sacrifice 80 food. With trade, they need to give up only 40 food. So definitely Elijastan is happy with this arrangement.

Would Theodoria benefit from this trade? Without trade, if Theodoria wanted 40 food they would need to sacrifice 40 steel. With trade, they have to give up only 20 steel. Theodoria is also pleased with this arrangement.

Appendixes

Further Reading
Websites
Glossary
Important Formulas and Conditions

Dodge, Eric, and Melanie Fox. *Economics Demystified.* New York: McGraw-Hill, 2012.

Krugman, Paul, and Robin Wells. *Microeconomics,* 6th ed. New York: Worth Publishers, 2020.

Mankiw, N. Gregory. *Principles of Economics,* 9th ed. Boston, MA: Cengage Publishing, 2021.

McConnell, Campbell L., Stanley L. Brue, and Sean Flynn. *Microeconomics,* 22nd ed. New York: McGraw-Hill/Irwin, 2020.

WEBSITES

Here is a list of websites that you might find useful in your preparation for the AP Microeconomics exam.

https://apstudent.collegeboard.org/home

https://www.economy.com/economicview/

https://www.economist.com/economics-a-to-z

www.councilforeconed.org

https://online.reffonomics.com/

absolute advantage The ability to produce more of a good with the same quantity of resources, or the same quantity of goods with fewer resources than all other producers.

absolute (or money) prices The price of a good measured in units of currency.

accounting profit The difference between total revenue and total explicit cost.

all else equal The assumption that all other variables are held constant so that we can predict how a change in one variable affects a second. Also known as the "ceteris paribus" assumption.

allocative efficiency Production of the combination of goods and services that provides the most net benefit to society. This is achieved when the MSB = MSC of the next unit.

average fixed cost (AFC) Total fixed cost divided by output.

average product of labor (AP$_L$) Total product divided by the labor employed.

average tax rate The proportion of total income paid to taxes.

average total cost (ATC) Total cost divided by output.

average variable cost (AVC) Total variable cost divided by output.

capitalist market system (capitalism) An economic system based on the fundamentals of private property, freedom, self-interest, and prices.

cartel Firms that agree to maximize their joint profits rather than compete.

circular flow of economic activity (or circular of goods and services) A model that shows how households and firms circulate resources, goods, and incomes through the economy. This basic model is expanded to include the government and the foreign sector.

collusive oligopoly Models where firms agree to work together to mutually improve their situation.

comparative advantage The ability to produce a good at lower opportunity cost than all other producers.

complementary goods Two goods that provide more utility when consumed together than when consumed separately.

constant returns to scale The horizontal range of long-run average total cost where LRAC is constant over a variety of plant sizes.

constant returns to scale in production The long-run outcome when output exactly doubles from a doubling of all inputs.

constrained utility maximization Given prices and income, a consumer stops consuming a good when the price paid for the next unit is equal to the marginal utility received.

consumer surplus The difference between a buyer's willingness to pay and the price actually paid.

cross-price elasticity of demand A measure of how sensitive the consumption of good X is to a change in the price of good Y.

deadweight loss The lost net benefit to society caused by a movement from the competitive market equilibrium.

decreasing returns to scale in production The long-run outcome when output less than doubles from a doubling of all inputs.

demand curve Shows the quantity of a good demanded at all prices.

demand for labor Shows the quantity of labor demanded at all wages. Labor demand for a firm hiring in a competitive labor market is MRP$_L$.

demand schedule A table showing quantity demanded for a good at all prices.

derived demand Demand for a resource arising from the demand for the goods produced by the resource.

determinants of demand The external factors that shift demand to the left or right.

determinants of supply The external factors that influence supply. When these variables change, the entire supply curve shifts to the left or right.

diseconomies of scale The upward part of the long-run average total cost curve where LRAC rises as plant size rises.

disequilibrium Any price where the quantity demanded does not equal the quantity supplied.

domestic price The equilibrium price of a good in a nation without trade.

dominant strategy A strategy that is always the best strategy to pursue, regardless of what a rival is doing.

economic costs The sum of explicit and implicit costs of production.

economic growth The increase in an economy's PPF over time.

economic profit The difference between total revenue and total economic cost.

economics The study of how society allocates scarce resources.

economies of scale The downward part of the long-run average total cost curve where LRAC falls as plant size rises.

egalitarianism The philosophy that all citizens should receive an equal share of the economic resources.

elasticity Measures the sensitivity, or responsiveness, of a choice to a change in an external factor.

elasticity along the demand curve At the midpoint of a linear demand curve, $E_d = 1$. Above the midpoint demand is elastic, and below the midpoint demand is inelastic.

excess capacity The difference between the long-run output in monopolistic competition and the output at minimum average total cost.

excess demand The difference between quantity demanded and quantity supplied. A shortage.

excess supply The difference between quantity supplied and quantity demanded. A surplus.

excise tax A per-unit tax on a specific good or service.

explicit costs Direct, purchased, out-of-pocket costs, paid to resource suppliers outside the firm. Also referred to as accounting costs.

exports Goods and services produced domestically but sold abroad.

factors of production Inputs or resources that go into the production function to produce goods and services.

firm An organization that employs factors of production to produce a good or service that it hopes to profitably sell.

fixed inputs Production inputs that cannot be changed in the short run.

four-firm concentration ratio The sum of the market share of the four largest firms in an industry.

free rider An individual who receives the benefit of a good without incurring any cost for the good.

free-rider problem The lack of private funding for, or production of, a public good due to the presence of free riders.

game theory An approach for modeling the strategic interactions of firms in oligopoly markets.

Gini ratio A measure of income inequality. As the Gini ratio gets closer to zero, the more equally the income is distributed. As the Gini ratio gets closer to one, the more unequally the income is distributed.

human capital The amount of knowledge and skills that labor can apply to the work that they do.

implicit costs Indirect, nonpurchased, or opportunity costs of resources provided by the entrepreneur.

imports Goods produced abroad but consumed domestically.

incidence of tax The division of a tax between consumers and producers.

income effect Due to a higher price, the change in quantity demanded that results from a change in the consumer's purchasing power (or real income).

income elasticity A measure of how sensitive consumption of a good is to a change in consumers' income.

increasing returns to scale in production The long-run outcome when output more than doubles from a doubling of all inputs.

inferior goods A good for which demand decreases with an increase in consumer income.

law of demand All else equal, when the price of a good rises, the quantity demanded of that good falls.

law of diminishing marginal returns As successive units of a variable input are added to a fixed input, beyond some point the marginal product declines.

law of diminishing marginal utility In a given time period, as consumption of an item increases, the marginal (additional) utility from that item falls.

law of increasing costs As more of a good is produced, the greater is its opportunity (or marginal) cost.

law of increasing marginal cost As a producer produces more of a good, the marginal cost rises. This is very similar to the idea of increasing opportunity costs.

law of supply All else equal, when the price of a good rises, the quantity supplied of that good rises.

least-cost rule The combination of labor and capital that minimizes total costs for a given production rate is where $MP_L/P_L = MP_K/P_K$.

long run A period of time long enough for the firm to alter all production inputs, including capital and the plant size.

Lorenz curve A graphical device that shows how a nation's income is distributed across the nation's households.

luxury A good for which the proportional increase in consumption exceeds the proportional increase in income.

marginal The next unit, or increment of, an action.

marginal analysis Making decisions based on weighing the marginal benefits and costs of that action. The rational decision maker chooses an action if $MB \geq MC$.

marginal benefit (MB) The additional benefit received from the consumption of the next unit of a good or service.

marginal cost (MC) The additional cost of producing one more unit of output.

marginal productivity theory The theory that a citizen's share of economic resources is proportional to the marginal revenue product of their labor.

marginal product of labor (MP_L) The change in total product resulting from a change in the labor input.

marginal resource cost (MRC) The change in a firm's total cost from the hiring of an additional unit of an input. Some authors refer to this as marginal factor cost (MFC) or the marginal cost of labor MC_L.

marginal revenue product of labor (MRP) The change in a firm's total revenue from the hiring of an additional unit of labor. If the output market is competitive, some authors call this the value of the marginal product (VMP) of labor.

marginal social benefit The additional benefit that society receives from the consumption of the next unit of a good or service.

marginal social cost The additional cost that society incurs from the production of the next unit of a good or service.

marginal tax rate The rate paid on the last dollar earned, calculated by taking the ratio of the change in taxes divided by the change in income.

marginal utility The change in an individual's total utility from the consumption of an additional unit of a good or service.

market A group of buyers and sellers involved in the exchange of a good or service.

market economy An economic system in which resources are allocated through the decentralized decisions of firms and consumers.

market equilibrium Exists at the only price where the quantity supplied equals the quantity demanded. Or, it is the only quantity where the price consumers are willing to pay is exactly the price producers are willing to accept.

market failure A market outcome for which the quantity produced is not allocatively efficient ($MSB \neq MSC$) and either too many or too few units are produced.

market power The ability to set a price above the perfectly competitive level.

monopolistic competition A market structure characterized by a few small firms producing a differentiated product with easy entry into the market.

monopoly A market structure in which one firm is the sole producer of a good with no close substitutes in a market with entry barriers.

monopsony A factor market in which there is a sole firm that has market power, i.e., a wage setter.

Nash equilibrium The outcome of a game for which each player's strategy maximizes their payoff, given the strategies used by the rival players.

natural monopoly The case where economies of scale are so extensive that it is less costly for one firm to supply the entire range of demand than for multiple firms to share the market.

necessity A good for which the proportional increase in consumption is less than the proportional increase in income.

negative externality The existence of spillover costs upon third parties from the production or consumption of a good.

noncollusive oligopoly Models of industries in which firms are competitive rivals seeking to gain at the expense of their rivals.

nonrenewable resources Natural resources that cannot replenish themselves.

normal goods A good for which demand increases with an increase in consumer income.

normal profit The opportunity cost of the entrepreneur's talents. Another way of saying the firm is earning zero economic profit.

oligopoly A very diverse market structure characterized by a small number of interdependent large firms, producing either a standardized or differentiated product in a market with a barrier to entry.

opportunity cost The value of the sacrifice made to pursue a course of action.

perfect price discrimination The type of price discrimination in which each consumer pays exactly their maximum willingness to pay.

perfectly elastic $E_d = \infty$. In this special case, the demand curve is horizontal, meaning consumers have an instantaneous and infinite response to a change in price.

perfectly inelastic $E_d = 0$. In this special case, the demand curve is vertical and there is absolutely no response to a change in price.

positive externality The existence of spillover benefits upon third parties from the production or consumption of a good.

price ceiling A legal maximum price above which the product cannot be sold.

price discrimination The sale of the same product to different groups of consumers at different prices.

price elasticity of demand (E_d) Measures the sensitivity of consumers' quantity demanded for good X when the price of good X changes.

price elasticity of supply (E_s) Measures the sensitivity of producers' quantity supplied for good X when the price of good X changes.

price floor A legal minimum price below which the product cannot be sold.

prisoner's dilemma A game where the two rivals achieve a less desirable outcome because they are unable to coordinate their strategies.

private goods Goods that are both rival and excludable.

producer surplus The difference between the price received and the marginal cost of producing the good.

production function The mechanism for combining production resources, with existing technology, into finished goods and services.

production possibilities The different quantities of goods that an economy can produce with a given amount of scarce resources.

production possibility curve (or frontier) A graphical device that shows the combination of two goods that a nation can efficiently produce with available resources and technology.

productive efficiency Production of maximum output for a given level of technology and resources. On the cost side, a given quantity of output is being produced at the lowest possible cost.

productivity The quantity of output that can be produced per worker in a given amount of time.

profit maximizing resource employment The firm hires a resource up to the point where MRP = MRC.

progressive tax A tax where the proportion of income paid in taxes rises as income rises.

proportional tax A tax where the proportion of income paid in taxes is constant no matter the level of income.

protective tariff An excise tax levied on an imported good that is produced in the domestic market so that it may be protected from foreign competition.

public goods Goods that are both nonrival and nonexcludable.

quintiles When you rank household income from lowest to highest, each quintile represents 20 percent of all households.

quota A maximum amount of a good that can be imported into the domestic market.

regressive tax A tax where the proportion of income paid in taxes decreases as income rises.

relative prices The price of one unit of good X measured not in currency, but in the number of units of good Y that must be sacrificed to acquire good X.

renewable resources Natural resources that can replenish themselves if they are not overharvested.

resources Also called factors of production, these are commonly grouped into the four categories of labor, physical capital, land or natural resources, and entrepreneurial ability.

revenue tariff An excise tax levied on goods that are not produced in the domestic market.

scarcity The imbalance between limited productive resources and unlimited human wants.

shortage A situation in which, at the going market price, the quantity demanded exceeds the quantity supplied.

short run A period of time too short to change the size of the plant, but many other, more variable resources can be adjusted to meet demand.

specialization Production of goods, or performance of tasks, based on comparative advantage.

spillover benefits Additional benefits to society, not captured by the market demand curve from the production of a good.

spillover costs Additional costs to society, not captured by the market supply curve from the production of a good.

subsidy A government transfer, either to consumers or producers, on the consumption or production of a good.

substitute goods Two goods are consumer substitutes if they provide essentially the same utility to the consumer.

substitution effect The change in quantity demanded resulting from a change in the price of one good relative to the price of other goods.

supply curve Shows the quantity of a good supplied at all prices.

supply schedule A table showing quantity supplied for a good at various prices.

surplus A situation in which, at the going market price, the quantity supplied exceeds the quantity demanded.

tax bracket A range of income on which a given marginal tax rate is applied.

technology A nation's knowledge of how to produce goods in the best possible way.

total cost (TC) The sum of total fixed and total variable costs at any level of output.

total fixed costs (TFC) Production costs that do not vary with the level of output.

total product of labor (TP$_L$) The total quantity of output produced for a given quantity of labor employed.

total revenue The price of a good multiplied by the quantity of that good sold.

total revenue test Total revenue rises with a price increase if demand is price inelastic and falls with a price increase if demand is price elastic.

total utility The total happiness received from consumption of a number of units of a good.

total variable costs (TVC) Production costs that change with the level of output.

total welfare The sum of consumer surplus and producer surplus. Some authors label this as total surplus.

trade-offs The reality of scarce resources implies that individuals, firms, and governments are constantly faced with difficult choices that involve benefits and costs.

unit elastic demand $E_d = 1$. The percentage change in price is equal to percentage change in quantity demanded.

utility Happiness, or benefit, or satisfaction, or enjoyment gained from consumption of goods and services.

utility maximizing rule The consumer chooses amounts of goods X and Y, with their limited income, so that the marginal utility per dollar spent is equal for both goods.

utils A hypothetical unit of measurement often used to quantify utility; aka "happy points."

variable inputs Production inputs that the firm can adjust in the short run to meet changes in demand for the firm's output.

world price The global equilibrium price of a good when nations engage in trade.

IMPORTANT FORMULAS AND CONDITIONS

Chapter 5

1. Optimal Decision Making: $MB = MC$

2. Opportunity Cost from a Production Possibility Curve (PPC):

   Good X: The slope of the PPC

   Good Y: The inverse of the slope of the PPC

Chapter 6

1. Market Equilibrium:

   $Q_d = Q_s$

2. Shortage:

   $Q_d - Q_s$

3. Surplus:

   $Q_s - Q_d$

4. Total Welfare:

   $=$ Consumer surplus $+$ Producer surplus

Chapter 7

1. Price Elasticity of Demand:

   $E_d = $ (%Δ in quantity demanded of good X)/ (%Δ in the price of good X)

2. Percentage Change:

   %$\Delta = 100 \times$ (New value – Old value)/ Old value

3. Total Revenue:

   $=$ Price $\times$ Quantity demanded

4. Income Elasticity:

   $E_I = $ (%Δ Q_d good X)/(%Δ income)

5. Cross-Price Elasticity:

   $E_{x,y} = $ (%Δ Q_d good X)/(%Δ price good Y)

6. Price Elasticity of Supply:

   $E_s = $ (%Δ in quantity supplied of good X)/ (%Δ in the price of good X)

7. Marginal Utility:

   $MU = \Delta TU/\Delta Q$

8. Utility Maximizing Rule:

   $MU_x/P_x = MU_y/P_y$ or $MU_x/MU_y = P_x/P_y$

9. Revenue from a Tariff:

   $=$ Per-Unit Tariff $\times$ Units Imported

Chapter 8

1. Accounting Profit:

   TR – Explicit costs

2. Economic Profit:

   TR – Explicit costs – Implicit costs

3. Marginal Product of Labor:

   $MP_L = \Delta$ in TP_L/Δ in L

4. Average Product of Labor:

   $AP_L = TP_L/L$

5. Total Costs:

   $TC = TVC + TFC$

6. Marginal Costs:

   $MC = \Delta TVC/\Delta Q$

7. Average Fixed Cost:

   $AFC = TFC/Q$

8. Average Variable Cost:

   $AVC = TVC/Q$

9. Average Total Cost:

   $ATC = TC/Q = AFC + AVC$

10. Marginal Cost and Marginal Product of Labor:

    $MC = w/MP_L$

11. Average Variable Cost and Average Product of Labor:

$$AVC = w/AP_L$$

Chapter 9

1. Profit Maximization Point:

$$MR = MC$$

2. Demand for Firm's Product (Perfectly Competitive Market):

$$P = MR = AR$$

3. Profit:

$$\pi = TR - TC = P \times q_e - TC = q_e \times (P - ATC)$$

4. Breakeven Point:

$$P = ATC$$

5. Shutdown Point:

$$P < AVC \text{ or } TR < TVC$$

6. Allocative Efficiency:

Produce output q where $P_c = MR = MC$

7. Excess Capacity in Monopolistic Competition:

$$Q_{atc} - Q_{mc}$$

8. Perfectly Competitive Long-Run Equilibrium:

$$P = MR = AR = MC = ATC$$

9. Monopoly Long-Run Equilibrium:

$$P_m > MR = MC$$

Chapter 10

1. Marginal Revenue Product:

$$= \frac{\text{Change in total revenue}}{\text{Change in resource quantity}}$$

$$= MR \times MP_L$$

a. Under perfectly competitive price-taking conditions:

$$MRP_c = MR \times MP_L = P \times MP_L$$

b. Under conditions of market power, $MR < P$:

$$MRP_m = MR \times MP_L < MRP_c$$

2. Marginal Resource Cost:

$$= \frac{\text{Change in total resource cost}}{\text{Change in resource quantity}}$$

$$= \text{Wage (in a competitive resource market)}$$

3. Least-Cost Hiring Rule:

$$MP_L/P_L = MP_K/P_K \text{ or equivalently,}$$

$$MP_L/MP_K = P_L/P_K$$

4. Profit Maximizing Resource Employment:

$$MRP = MRC$$

5. Monopsony Hiring Decision:

$$MFC = MRP > W$$

Chapter 11

1. Socially Optimal Output:

$$MSB = MSC$$

2. Marginal Tax Rate:

$$= (\Delta \text{ taxes due})/(\Delta \text{ taxable income})$$

3. Average Tax Rate:

$$= (\text{Total taxes due})/(\text{Total taxable income})$$

5 Steps to Teaching AP Microeconomics

TEACHER'S MANUAL

Amanda Stiglbauer

AP Microeconomics Teacher
Blythewood High School, Blythewood, SC

Thanks to Greg Jacobs, AP Physics teacher at Woodberry Forest School in Virginia, for developing the 5-step approach used in this teaching manual.

Introduction to the Teacher's Manual

Advancements in technology and networking continue to fuel the plethora of resources available to teachers for the AP Microeconomics class. As teachers become less reliant on instructor-centered lectures and textbooks, the learning experience of students has been enriched by online simulations, apps, video lectures and activities, etc. Even the College Board itself has aided this transformation of learning as we know it, as it provides so many useful materials related to the AP Microeconomics exam that the typical teacher—and student—can easily become overwhelmed by an excess of teaching materials and resources.

While you may find many of these resources useful in your class, this book has proven to be a vital resource to teachers of AP Microeconomics. The straightforward language explains exactly what students need to know for the AP Microeconomics exam and provides detailed review strategies for students as they prepare for the test.

This teacher's manual will guide you through the 5 steps of teaching AP Microeconomics. These 5 steps are:

1. Prepare a strategic plan for the course

2. Hold an interesting class every day

3. Evaluate your students' progress

4. Get students ready to take the AP exam

5. Become a better teacher every year

Throughout this section of the book, I'll discuss each of these steps, providing suggestions and ideas that have been successful in my classroom. I present them here because, over the years, I have found that they work. You may have developed a different course strategy, teaching activities, and evaluation techniques. That's fine! Different things work for different teachers, and our styles make us all unique. I hope you find in this teacher's manual something that will be useful to you.

STEP 1

Prepare a Strategic Plan for the Course

The Course and Exam Description (CED) from the College Board can be found at https://apcentral.collegeboard.org/pdf/ap-microeconomics-course-and-exam-description.pdf?course=ap-microeconomics. You can also find it by searching for "microeconomics CED." This important document outlines the suggested scope and sequence for the AP Microeconomics course. It is my suggestion to follow the recommended sequence and pacing for the first few years as you become acquainted with the course and its content. The College Board and master teachers have worked carefully to ensure the content progression is logical and builds upon previous skills. As you gain experience and feel more comfortable with the content, you may elect to rearrange some topics. For example, I typically teach Topic 2.9 International Trade and Public Policy during Unit 6 because I have found that Unit 2 is very long and drawn out and the content addressed in this topic provides a nice ending to the course.

As you consider the planning and pacing of your lessons, it is crucial to ascertain the number of class periods you will have to teach the necessary units of study. Do you teach the course as a semester class or are you allocated a full year? Below you will find suggested pacing for each of these options.

Semester Pacing Schedule

TOPICS	% OF EXAM	PACING	5 STEPS TO A 5
Unit 1: Basic Economic Concepts	12–15%	9–11 Class Periods	Chapter 5 pp. 51–66
Unit 2: Supply and Demand	20–25%	13–15 Class Periods	Chapters 6 & 7 pp. 67–113
Unit 3: Production, Cost, and Perfect Competition	22–25%	11–13 Class Periods	Chapters 8 & 9 pp. 114–154
Unit 4: Imperfect Competition	15–22%	8–10 Class Periods	Chapter 9 pp. 129–154
Unit 5: Factor Markets	10–13%	6–8 Class Periods	Chapter 10 pp. 155–168
Unit 6: Market Failure and the Role of Government	8–13%	9–11 Class Periods	Chapter 11 pp. 169–180

Year-Long Pacing Schedule

TOPICS	% OF EXAM	PACING	5 STEPS TO A 5
Unit 1: Basic Economic Concepts	12–15%	18–22 Class Periods	Chapter 5 pp. 51–66
Unit 2: Supply and Demand	20–25%	26–30 Class Periods	Chapters 6 & 7 pp. 67–113
Unit 3: Production, Cost, and Perfect Competition	22–25%	22–26 Class Periods	Chapters 8 & 9 pp. 114–154
Unit 4: Imperfect Competition	15–22%	16–20 Class Periods	Chapter 9 pp. 129–154
Unit 5: Factor Market	10–13%	12–16 Class Periods	Chapter 10 pp. 155–168
Unit 6: Market Failure and the Role of Government	8–13%	18–22 Class Periods	Chapter 11 pp. 169–180

STEP 2

Hold an Interesting Class Every Day

AP Microeconomics is a very relatable and practical class that encourages students to "think at the margin." This concept can and should be taught from the first day of class, as students evaluate the methods of rational decision-making many times each day.

Get to know your students and their interests early on and you will be able to capitalize on this knowledge to make valuable content connections. For example, do you have a class of athletes? Challenge them to consider the opportunity cost associated with choosing practice over studying for an economics exam!

No matter the age or interest, I have found that students thrive on a certain degree of predictability. This doesn't mean that your lessons are boring; rather, that they have a clearly distinguished purpose and a beginning, middle, and end. I have found this structure to be useful:

► **Get Started or Grapple.** This is the time to set the purpose for the day. Share a question of the day from AP Classroom to allow them the opportunity to practice mock exam questions, or engage them with a turn-and-talk about a big question like "What is the goal of businesses?" This 5–10 minutes allows students to set their focus for the day and gives you the opportunity to conduct any necessary housekeeping items like attendance or passing out papers. Reviewing the question of the day or eliciting responses from students is also a valuable formative assessment that allows you to push forward or reteach concepts if necessary.

► **Content Discovery.** Decide how you want students to access content for the course.

Many times, new teachers rely heavily on PowerPoints or slides that are dense with content. Know that is okay! As you grow more comfortable with the content, you may decide to omit some information and instead choose to include those topics in discussions. Whatever your method, presenting students with a learning target or goal for the day is beneficial to center the focus of the lesson.

I have chosen to vary the instructional segment of class from time to time in order to keep it interesting. Typically, content discovery includes back-and-forth discussion with my students on important concepts I have prepared on a slide show (PowerPoint, Google Slides, NearPod, Pear Deck). I have grown to really enjoy NearPod and PearDeck because of the ability of students to interact based on different comfort levels and the ability to imbed quick, fun, formative assessments.

In a 45-minute class period, content discovery should be limited to 20 minutes max, if at all possible. The success of AP Microeconomics students is highly dependent on their ability to apply the key concepts, formulas, and skills in different situations. Because of this, often the most important portion of any lesson is practice—whether it's guided practice, an activity, or simulation.

► **Guided Practice/Activity/Simulation.** The second portion of class should be devoted to practicing the new skills and concepts students have just learned. I am a big fan of partner or small group work, so I often use this time to have students practice free-response questions from AP Classroom together, or work through a short multiple-choice question set I created on AP Classroom. I have learned that students really thrive on competition, so we often set a goal and make our practice a competition for a small prize.

When it is possible, use a simulation to teach a concept; this is a very valuable learning tool! Many simulations exist for supply and demand and production functions. The hands-on learning and the race against the clock of simulations make these exemplary learning tools.

▶ **Debrief.** Never underestimate the importance of a good wrap up. Debriefing at the end of a lesson is helpful in reviewing the main concepts and determining whether students met the learning target or goal. Some of my favorite ways to wrap up a lesson are exit tickets, a quick game of Kahoot, or a parking lot. 3-2-1 exit tickets may require a bit more time than a traditional exit question, but they provide important reflections on the learning process. Students are asked to write 3 things that they learned, 2 things they found interesting or want to know more about, and 1 question they still have. As students get used to this reflection format, thoughtful completion can take 5 minutes or less!

Other Useful Activities

Other activities that I have found very useful in providing variety to the course are:

▶ **Individual whiteboards.** These are wonderful investments for this course! Whether you're asking students to graph various market structures, or asking "Jeopardy!" style questions, whiteboards can be a fun, quick way to check for understanding.

▶ **Graph relays.** While AP Microeconomics is far from a physical education class, we can infuse some fun for our kinesthetic (and competitive) learners. Here's how it works: Divide students into two groups on opposite sides of the room facing the whiteboard. Explain to students that they will be asked to work together to draw the graph you ask for with two important catches—they may not talk *and* each person must only add (or subtract) one thing to the graph. Set a timer for anywhere from 1–2 minutes and watch your students use their non-verbal communication and economics skills to collaboratively master graphs. Spice up the excitement by giving students 30-second and 10-second warnings. Graph relays are a great way to not only review important graphs at the beginning or end of class but also to build community among the students.

▶ **Current event articles.** The COVID-19 pandemic shifted our worlds in ways that made us cope with scarcity and choice in novel ways. This was the lightbulb that truly made all students in my class find economics in their everyday world. I encourage you to find a few news sources or daily podcasts that keep you up to speed with what's going on in the world and find ways to share this with your students. The passion and knowledge you transfer will ultimately find its way into class discussions led by students themselves!

Homework

To give or not to give? That is the buzzing question in many pedagogical circles today. While it is not necessary to load students down with hours (or even one hour!) of homework each night, it is important for students to practice content daily. My homework assignments can typically be completed in 30 minutes or less. These tasks often include a worksheet related to the topic, a free-response problem, a multiple-choice problem set I create using the question bank in AP Classroom, reading from 5 *Steps to a 5* or the textbook, or viewing a video from one of the resources I've listed at the end of this teacher's manual. Whatever your stance on homework, I have found that students do appreciate extra practice and well-thought-out assignments (not "busy work").

Test-Taking Strategies

As with any exam, we must prepare our students to be good test-takers. This involves devoting class time to test-taking strategies so that students can demonstrate their knowledge to the AP Readers who will grade their exams. Here are several tips I share with my students throughout the year.

▶ Respond clearly and concisely. The AP Microeconomics exam is quite different from many of the other AP exams your students may have taken in the past in that essay responses are not required and are even discouraged. Teach students from the very beginning of this course to state the answer, with an explanation if needed, and get out! *Discourage* paragraph responses and *encourage* bullet point-style answers. A written response in which a student provides conflicting or contradictory information will likely not receive credit.

▶ Stay on the same "railroad." Students often "hedge" their responses when they are unsure in hopes that one incorrect response followed by a correct response will earn points. For questions that require follow-up analysis, it is important that students stick with the reasoning in the first part of their response as they proceed through the question. Here's an example.

Part A: What happens to the price of noodles, an inferior good, if consumer income rises?

▶ Correct Answer: The price and quantity would decrease.

▶ Student Response: The price and quantity would increase. (Incorrect)

Part B: Given your response in Part A, what would happen to the price and quantity of rice, a substitute good?

▶ Correct Answer: The price and quantity of rice would decrease because the price of its substitute, noodles, decreased.

▶ Scoring note: This would be incorrect in terms of the student's response to Part A. Thus, in order to earn credit for this part of the question, the student would need to state that, given the response in Part A, the price and quantity for rice would rise since the price of its substitute has increased. Again, it is important for the student to follow the same line of reasoning.

▶ Pay close attention to the action verbs in the prompt and address these appropriately.

▶ *Identify/State* means to provide a specific answer, which might be a list or a label on a graph without any explanation or elaboration.

▶ *Explain* means to take the reader through all the steps and linkages in the line of economic reasoning. Graphs and symbols are often acceptable as part of the answer.

▶ *Show* means use a diagram or graph to illustrate your answer. Correct labeling of all elements, including axes of graphs, is necessary to receive full credit. It is also important to emphasize that students show the direction of any change and do not rely on internal labels.

▶ *Calculate* means to use mathematical formulas to generate a numerical solution. It is imperative that students show their work for each step of the process. In addition, make sure that students become comfortable with doing math without a calculator, as these devices are prohibited on the exam.

▶ Answer every question! Points are only earned on this exam, not taken away. It is in the student's best interest to guess if they are unsure.

Using This Book in Your Classroom

From the very beginning of the year, I include the relevant chapters from *5 Steps to a 5: AP Macroeconomics* in the unit plan that I share with students. Students who are not particularly motivated to read the textbook find this guide accessible and informative. Additionally, students who regularly read the assigned textbook report that it is a valuable resource that helps them to identify and remember the most important information. The book can be used hand-in-hand with your textbook as you go through the course.

5 Steps to a 5: AP Microeconomics Elite Edition

The Elite Edition of this book provides additional questions that can be used in your class. It contains 90 activities and questions that require five minutes a day. While they are primarily intended to be used by students studying for the test, you can use these as daily warm-ups in your course. To do this, you will need the table below that organizes these questions and activities by unit.

UNIT	QUESTIONS/ACTIVITIES IN THE ELITE EDITION
Unit 1: Basic Economic Concepts	Days 1–10
Unit 2: Supply and Demand	Days 11–53
Unit 3: Production, Cost, and Perfect Competition	Days 54–70
Unit 4: Imperfect Competition	Days 71–77
Unit 5: The Factor Market	Days 78–81
Unit 6: Market Failure and the Role of Government	Days 82–90

STEP 3

Evaluate Your Students' Progress

As mentioned previously, I frequently use questions from the AP Classroom for practice in the classroom or homework for each topic. I review the commonly missed questions in class and reteach concepts that are difficult for students. For quizzes and unit tests, I also highly recommend using multiple-choice and free-response questions from AP Classroom. While students find the wording and complexity of these questions challenging to begin with, they quickly learn and adjust to the style and rigor the College Board expects through regular practice.

Just as many areas in teaching, assessment can be a very personal decision. In many cases, the weighting of grades is determined by the school or district, while other teachers have more flexibility in this arena. At the school level, it is important to demonstrate consistency as students move vertically through AP courses of like subjects.

In my course, unit tests comprise 60% of the grade, while formative assessments and quizzes make up the remaining 40%. Because I teach this course as a 40-minute class, I elect to give a multiple choice test *and* a free response test on successive days for each unit to mirror the exam experience students will see in May. I typically reserve a class period after the tests to review with students and allow them to ask clarifying questions.

Test Corrections

I have offered the opportunity for students to complete test corrections. When I do extend this invitation, I either allow students to earn up to ½ of the points back for high-quality corrections, or alternatively, the corrections count as a classwork grade. While learning from mistakes is important, I also do not want students' grades to be inflated. I have provided an example below of my requirements for test corrections.

Checklist for Test Corrections

In order to earn the opportunity to do test corrections, you must print and complete the checklist below by ___(date)___ . You may earn up to half of the points back for these corrections, depending on your explanations and adherence to the instructions.

- ▶ Complete item analysis for every incorrect question using the form provided.

- ▶ Complete test correction for every incorrect question using the form provided. Do not give answers like a, b, c, d . . . That is trivial and does not help you master the content.

- ▶ Attach your original test.

- ▶ Complete tutoring session and have this form signed by teacher here: _____

Please staple all items together in the following order:

1. Completed checklist (this document)

2. Test item analysis and corrections form

3. Original test

Test Item Analysis and Corrections

Question #	Test Item Analysis	Test Corrections
	Why did you get this question wrong? Why was your answer incorrect? ▶ I got this question wrong because: ▶ This answer is incorrect because:	What is the correct answer? Why is this correct? ▶ The correct answer is: ▶ This is the correct answer because:

Note to Teacher: Continue this form for the entire page allowing plenty of space for student to provide the test corrections. Students may have to use more one page.

Peer FRQ Evaluation

Peer Free Response Question (FRQ) evaluation is also a very powerful tool. While this process often takes an entire class period, it helps students discover the intricacies of the rubric and how responses earn points on the exam.

First, I give students the FRQ to complete on their own. This is a timed assignment, another strategy to help students practice pacing for the exam. I typically give students 25 minutes for long FRQs and 15 minutes for short questions. After this time has elapsed, I collect students' responses. I then reveal the rubric for students to examine and redistribute papers to different students in class. We go through each part of

the question (a, b, c, etc.) and discuss what earns credit according to the rubric and what does not. I allow students to ask questions about "iffy" responses and talk to their table partners, just as AP readers often do. After we have analyzed each part of the question and students have had the opportunity to seek clarification on any ambiguities, the graders assign a score at the top of the paper and take the responses to their owners.

While this exercise is enlightening, it is important to note that its success is dependent on the community you have built in the classroom. Explain that this is an exercise used to help students be better test takers and not a "gotcha" or punitive assessment.

STEP 4

Get Students Ready to Take the AP Exam

Ideally, I like to have at least three weeks at the end of the course to review before the exam. After I have finished all content for the course, I administer a full-length AP Microeconomics exam. This practice exam is a celebration of learning. Students devote part of their Saturday to taking the mock exam, parents volunteer to provide lunch or snacks, and we conduct a post-exam debrief.

Within the week, I make sure that students have their results returned and a study plan in place. I use the document below to help students analyze their results and create a study plan for the weeks leading up to the exam.

Individual Item Analysis: AP Microeconomics Practice Exam

Directions: List the questions you answered incorrectly on the multiple-choice section of the practice exam. Then, make useful notes/comments to help you master the concept(s) before the AP Exam.

QUESTION #	UNIT AND TOPIC	CONTENT	COMMENTS/NOTES

Creating Your Study Plan

Directions: Complete the questions to assist you with creating a study plan.

1. What are your strongest areas?

2. Which unit is your area of weakness? BE SPECIFIC. (at least 2 bullet points with detail)

3. Which specific topics were the worst for you? (at least 4 bullet points with detail)

4. What is your second area of weakness (include the topic)? (at least 2 bullet points with detail)

5. What is your study strategy for the next 15 days as a result? BE SPECIFIC. Your strategy should include the resources you plan to use, time spent per day, and topics you should study.

Provide After-School, Lunch, or Virtual Study Sessions

If you choose to do so, outside-of-class study sessions prove to be extremely beneficial for students. I typically create a schedule for students that details the dates and topics I plan to review at each session. Due to extracurricular activities and other commitments, I offer a variety of after-school, lunch, and evening virtual sessions. I try to make these sessions both useful and fun, alternating between free-response and multiple-choice practice using gamification tools like Kahoot or Gimkit. I typically offer six targeted review sessions, one for each unit outlined in the AP Microeconomics Course and Exam Description, and offer incentives for students to participate. In the past, it has worked well to offer extra credit for students who attend a certain number of review sessions. I allow students to work in small groups during reviews and offer small prizes to groups who accumulate the most points or win the games.

Here's a sample of the schedule I have given my students in the past:

	UNIT 1 REVIEW SESSIONS	UNIT 2 REVIEW SESSIONS	UNIT 3 REVIEW SESSIONS	UNIT 4 REVIEW SESSIONS	UNIT 5 REVIEW SESSIONS	UNIT 6 REVIEW SESSIONS
Topics	Scarcity Comparative Advantage Marginal Analysis	Supply and Demand Elasticity Price Controls	Cost of Production and Perfect Competition	Imperfect Competition - Monopoly, Oligopoly, Monopolistic Competition	The Factor Market	Government Involvement
After School Sessions	Monday, April 22	Wednesday, April 24	Monday, April 29 Tuesday, April 30	Wednesday, May 1	Thursday, May 2	Tuesday, May 7
Lunch Sessions	Monday, April 22 Tuesday, April 23	Wednesday, April 24 Thursday, April 25	Monday, April 29 Tuesday, April 30	Wednesday, May 1 Thursday, May 2	Friday, May 3 Monday May 6	Tuesday, May 7 Wednesday, May 8

Encourage a Thorough Review of Important Graphs and Formulas

Once all content is completed for this course, students value a thorough review of the graphs and formulas that they need to remember. Rather than providing students with a "cheat sheet" of graphs on one document, I like to have them create their own graph booklets. As an AP Economics teacher, one important thing I have learned over the years is that nothing can replace students taking time to practice drawing correctly labeled graphs. The summative review assignment below is what I use to help students organize the important graphs into an easy-to-use booklet. These graphs are listed in the order in which content is taught (the order used in this book).

Summative Review Assignment
Important Graphs for AP Microeconomics

Instructions: In order to help you prepare for the AP Microeconomics exam, the final booklet we will create is one with important graphs. Your booklet must contain each of the items listed below, be extremely neat and organized, and be accurate. ALL GRAPHS SHOULD BE PROPERLY LABELED AND EASY TO READ. **Extra points will be awarded for those who go ABOVE and BEYOND!**

Graphs: NEATLY draw correctly labeled graphs of the following concepts. Be sure to include labels for each curve. For profit maximization, show the direction of any change and areas of profit/loss, if applicable.

- Marginal Benefit and Cost Curve

- Production Possibilities Frontier

  - What shifts it?

  - What causes a movement?

  - Points inside, outside, along the curve

- Supply and demand together

  - Shifters of supply

  - Shifters of demand

  - Movement along supply and demand curves

- Supply and demand together—price ceiling

  - Label impact on CS, PS, DWL

- Supply and demand together—price floor

  - Label impact on CS, PS, DWL

- Graphing tax incidence

  - Shift the supply curve—how do you do it?

  - When is tax incidence shared?

  - When is it entirely on the buyer? Entirely on the seller?

- Total product curve labeled with the following sections (increasing marginal returns, diminishing marginal returns, negative marginal returns)

  - What is happening to the MARGINAL PRODUCT in each of these phases?

- Marginal product and average product graph and then marginal cost and average cost graph. Then, explain the relationship between marginal product and marginal cost and the relationship between average product and average cost.

- ▶ Long Run Cost Curves—economies of scale, constant returns to scale, diseconomies of scale (and what does this mean?)

- ▶ Side-by-side graphs of perfectly competitive market and firm:

  - ▶ Breaking even/normal profit/long-run equilibrium

  - ▶ Earning a short-run profit

  - ▶ Earning a short-run loss

  - ▶ At the shutdown point

  - ▶ Where is the firm's short-run supply curve?

  - ▶ What changes on the graph to make long-run equilibrium occur?

- ▶ Monopoly

  - ▶ Three different graphs: Profit, loss, and natural monopoly

  - ▶ Welfare/efficiency analysis: Show profit, CS, PS, and DWL

- ▶ Monopolistic Competition—short-run and long-run

- ▶ Perfectly Competitive Factor Market—side-by-side graphs

- ▶ Monopsonistic Factor Market

  - ▶ Monopsony with minimum wage

- ▶ Positive externality (with DWL)

- ▶ Negative externality (with DWL)

- ▶ Lorenz Curve with analysis

5 Steps to a 5 as a Tool for Review

For many years, my students and I have relied on *5 Steps to a 5: AP Microeconomics* as a thorough and precise review book no matter what stage of the process. If you have multiple copies of this book, students can include it when creating their study plans.

Did taking the practice test show the student was lacking in understanding of a particular unit? The student can read or review the corresponding chapter(s) in the book. This book has clear explanatory material, questions to check student understanding, and answers and explanations for all the questions. I have even witnessed the least motivated students who struggled all year put the "pedal to the metal" in the last few weeks of this course and pass the exam. I can only attribute this success to the digestibility and preciseness of *5 Steps to a 5: AP Microeconomics*.

Did taking the practice test show that there were terms that the student didn't understand? Key terms are listed in each chapter's Rapid Review section along with their definitions. These terms can also be found in the glossary in the back of the book. The online Cross-Platform Edition of this book has electronic flashcards that students can use to check their understanding of the key terms. (See the back cover of this book for instructions for accessing the Cross-Platform Edition.)

Students can make taking another timed practice exam part of their study plan. Students can take one of the full-length practice exams found at the end of the book and score themselves; these tests have explanations for all the answers. Since taking the test eats up so much class time, a good option is to have the students do it at home timing themselves and use class time to check their answers and evaluate their progress. My students have found great benefit in taking at least one more practice exam in a timed setting.

Finally, draw students' attention to the "Important Formulas and Conditions" in the appendix of this book. Students should know these formulas!

STEP 5

Become a Better Teacher Every Year

For First-time AP Microeconomics Teachers

For the first-year AP teacher, you can do this! You are teaching this course for the first time with so many resources you might have trouble sifting through to find the diamonds. Just remember— slow and easy wins the race. Focus on learning the content unit by unit. Supplement this *5 Steps to a 5* book with a good, thorough college textbook of your choice.

Attending an AP Summer Institute (APSI) is a must! Not only will you receive invaluable instruction and resources during this training, but you will also hear great tips on pacing and textbook selection from professionals. Make connections with other teachers at this institute and share ideas. Ideally, you will form lasting relationships and collaborate to create your courses together. Don't be afraid to ask for help and resources from other experienced teachers.

Practice multiple-choice and free-response questions in AP Classroom and be sure you understand the correct answers before assigning these to students. Even as an economics major, I was often only a couple of days ahead of my students in content. Take heart in that it does get easier each and every year!

For All AP Microeconomics Teachers

A good AP teacher sets goals and tries to improve their practice each year. Spend some quiet time reflecting on what you did well and what you would like to change for the upcoming year. Did you lecture too much? Spend some time searching for activities or student-centered simulations to complement your lessons. Did you struggle with finishing the content in time for the exam? Reevaluate your scope and sequence and adjust the pacing of the course to better address your needs and the needs of your students.

While we would all love to achieve a 100% pass rate each year, understand that this goal is often not realistic. It can even wear you down. I have found that the years in which I do more work than the students are the years when my students have scored the lowest. It is imperative that students learn to become leaders of their own learning, not only so that they will be successful in this course and on the exam, but also because these skills will serve them well in college and in the workforce. Be driven, but do not take things too personally. Our students are all different and come with various backgrounds in math, test-taking skills, and AP exam experience. In truth, some of our brightest students are capable of passing the exam without us, while a "2" for some students shows tremendous growth throughout the year.

The Chief Reader's Report released after the conclusion of exam scoring each year is a vital resource to help you see the breakdown of scores and on which topics students scored well or poorly. You can also utilize AP Classroom to see the breakdown of your own students' scores and how well they did on multiple choice questions from each unit. This can often lead to adjustments in the way you teach certain topics or the amount of time spent on those concepts or skills.

It is also important to attend an APSI after you have taught the course for a few years. Teachers often report gaining tremendous insights into how to tweak their instructional strategies from experienced teachers and mentors from the College Board. Many subjects offer an advanced APSI for experienced teachers, which I highly recommend. These institutes focus on teaching strategies for some of the most misunderstood concepts of the course, and teachers often work collaboratively to create lessons geared toward these challenging topics.

Regardless of how you personally measure success, strive to grow each year. If there is anything that didn't work as well as you had hoped, there's always next year. The message is the same whether you are an AP novice or veteran: Your goal is to become a better teacher every year.

Additional Resources for Teachers

BOOKS FOR PARALLEL RECOMMENDED READING

Friedman, Thomas. *The World Is Flat*. Farrar, Straus, Giroux, 2005

Jevons, Marshall. *Murder at the Margin*. Princeton University Press, 1978

Levitt, Steven D., and Stephen J. Dubner. *Freakonomics*. Harper Trophy, 2006.

Roberts, Russell. *The Choice: A Fable of Free Trade and Protectionism*. Prentice Hall, 1994.

Roberts, Russell. *The Price of Everything: A Parable of Possibility and Prosperity*. Princeton University Press, 2008.

Wheelan, Charles J. *Naked Economics: Undressing the Dismal Science*. Norton, 2002.

WEBSITES

SITE AND DESCRIPTION	WEB ADDRESS
EconEdLink: Free lesson plans, videos, activities, and professional development webinars	www.econedlink.org
Foundation for Teaching Economics: Active learning lesson plans, activities, and simulations	www.fte.org
Marginal Revolution University: Lesson plans, assessments, and video lessons	www.mru.org
Federal Reserve Education (FRED): Lesson plans, tools, games, and webinars	www.federalreserveeducation.org

REVIEW VIDEOS AND YOUTUBE CHANNELS

SITE AND DESCRIPTION	WEB ADDRESS
AP Classroom (Daily Videos): Videos on every topic in the Course and Exam Description, created by experienced AP Microeconomics teachers	apclassroom.collegeboard.org
MR University: A comprehensive microeconomics course created by professors at George Mason University	https://mru.org/principles-economics-microeconomics
ReviewEcon Channel: A unit-by-unit and free response review channel created by AP Microeconomics reader Jacob Reed	https://www.youtube.com/c/ReviewEcon
ACDC Economics: Review videos on each topic from the AP Microeconomics Course and Exam. Description created by former AP Economics teacher Jacob Clifford	https://www.youtube.com/c/ACDCLeadership
Khan Academy: A comprehensive online course for microeconomics	https://www.khanacademy.org/economics-finance-domain/microeconomics
Reffonomics: Free, comprehensive microeconomics course created by long-time AP reader Steve Reff	https://online.reffonomics.com/courses/principles-of-microeconomics